THE POLITICAL IDEAS OF MARX AND ENGELS

[II]

Classical Marxism, 1850–1895

University of Pittsburgh Press

The Political Ideas of

MARX

and

ENGELS

Classical Marxism
1850–1895

RICHARD N. HUNT

Published by the University of Pittsburgh Press, Pittsburgh, Pa., 15260
Copyright © 1984, University of Pittsburgh Press
All rights reserved
Feffer and Simons, Inc., London
Manufactured in the United States of America

Library of Congress Cataloging in Publication Data

Hunt, Richard N.
    Classical Marxism, 1850–1895.

    (The Political ideas of Marx and Engels ; 2)
    Bibliography: p. 407
    Includes index.
    1. Marx, Karl, 1818–1883 — Political science.
2. Engels, Friedrich, 1820–1895 — Political science.
3. Communist state.   I. Title.   II. Hunt, Richard N.
Political ideas of Marx and Engels ; 2.
JC233.M299H85 vol. 2   320.5′315s   [320.5′315]   84-5218
ISBN 0-8229-3496-5

This publication has been supported by a grant from the National Endowment for the Humanities, a federal agency.

To my children,
Fabi, Chris, Jennie

Contents

Preface

"DEMOCRACY WITHOUT PROFESSIONALS" is not a phrase that Marx or Engels themselves ever used. I have introduced it here to designate what seems to me the crucial and distinguishing feature in their conception of the communist polity. They expected that leadership functions would not only be elective but would be rotated frequently among the general citizenry in such a way that no *professional* cadre of leaders would exist. All citizens would participate in public life on a part-time or short-time basis. The idea of such a participatory democracy, organized without any professional leaders at all, forms the central — though not exclusive — theme of the present volume. It is linked conceptually to Marx's theory of the parasite state, introduced in the first volume of this study, and to be developed at length in the early chapters below. Democracy without professionals is exactly what Marx and Engels perceived and admired in the Paris Commune, which will provide much of the material for our analysis in the central chapters of the book. It is likewise an idea that separates Marx and Engels from both the mainstream of twentieth-century Communist thinking and the mainstream of subsequent social democratic thinking. It is in fact an idea that has almost been forgotten, and where not forgotten, misunderstood, by all but a few. It deserves therefore a proper rehabilitation and reemphasis as the core of Marx and Engels' political ideas.

The chronological-biographical framework laid down in volume 1 will be continued here, though we will not need to use it as rigorously. Where volume 1 dealt with Marx and Engels' political ideas as they emerged and developed in the first half of their lives, up to 1850, this volume will focus on the second half of their lives, but will not exclude pre-1850 writings by any means. Where the first volume endeavored mainly to establish what Marx and Engels were *not* (viz. totalitarians, or "totalitarian democrats"), volume 2 will focus more on their *positive* political values and theories. If volume 1 stressed what separated Marx and Engels from the later doctrines of Leninism — and a few remaining tasks of de-Russification must be included below — the present volume will also here make clear what separates them from the later attitudes of social democracy.

[XI]

I feel obliged to add a word of explanation for the lamentably long gap between the appearance of the two halves of the book. The bulk of the manuscript for this volume was completed during a sabbatical in 1975–1976, after which I was drafted to serve a term as chairman of my department. Only after stepping down from that rewarding but onerous post was I able to complete the present work. Since 1974 an imposing body of literature has appeared on Marx and Engels' political ideas. I could certainly no longer complain, as I did in the preface to volume 1, of a lack of scholarly interest in the subject. The most comprehensive of these new works, and in some respects the most similar to my own, is Hal Draper's multi-volume study (see bibliography). But perhaps there is room for more than one extended study of so important and controversial a topic. Our interpretations, though similar in their general spirit, differ in some important ways. Draper does not, for example, recognize two separate theories of the state and does not emphasize deprofessionalization as the core of Marx and Engels' political goals. Readers of course will be able to form their own judgments from the evidence presented in both books. At the end of so many years of work on what was to be a "comprehensive" study, I am also more aware of its actual limitations. I have not dealt at all with Marx and Engels' views on international relations, for example, especially relationships between more advanced and less advanced countries, or the political aspects of ethnic minority conflicts, or women's rights issues — all topics of considerable current interest. But I am pleased to see that other writers are taking up such subjects and will fill out the gaps left in this book.

Since the publication of volume 1 there has also begun to appear the definitive English-language edition of Marx and Engels' writings — the *Collected Works*. Seventeen of an anticipated fifty volumes have appeared as of this writing, which include all of the masters' works up to 1860 (except for correspondence). In the present volume I have used this collection for all quotations from pre-1860 writings — although a price had to be paid in terms of consistency of translation. As the acute reader will notice, there are minor discrepancies of translation between passages quoted in volume 1 and then *requoted* in volume 2. I have adopted the new translations below for the obvious reason that the *Collected Works* will become the standard collection of reference for scholars all over the English-speaking world.

I would like to acknowledge the generous assistance of the John Simon Guggenheim Memorial Foundation in the completion of this volume. I would also like to repeat the thanks I offered in the preface to volume 1 to those colleagues and students who have read parts of the manuscript or listened to the exposition of my findings, and who served as a sounding board for the interpretations developed below. Jan Leja and Geri Toth provided much appreciated assistance in the preparation of the manuscript. I would like to thank the Director of the University of Pittsburgh Press and my old friend, Frederick A. Hetzel, for his saintly patience in waiting for volume 2 and for his quiet encouragement. Beyond words is my gratitude to my wife, Françoise, whose courage and esprit have supported me through the illness that has marred the otherwise happy completion of this book.

Richard N. Hunt

This preface was completed by my husband days before his untimely death. I extend my heartfelt thanks to Paul Le Blanc who spent many hours verifying the accuracy of the quotations in this work and undertook the arduous task of collating and checking the internal reference notes to the contents of this volume.

Françoise Hunt

Classical Marxism, 1850–1895

❧[1]❧

The Origins of the State

Marx and Engels' feverish political activity among the revolutionary exiles of London in 1849–1850 brought to a finale the concerns of volume 1. With the fading of prospects for a fresh revolution, the two men gradually lost interest in exile politics and settled in for an indefinite stay in their adoptive country, Marx with his growing family in London, Engels with his Irish lover, Mary Burns, in Manchester. Marx made an extremely meager living through journalism as he labored on his magnum opus, *Das Kapital*, the first volume of which was eventually published in 1867. Engels had better luck financially: he was able to resume his old role as his father's representative in the cotton-spinning firm of Ermen and Engels. Here he toiled unwillingly for the next twenty years, but accumulated enough money both to give constant and generous support to the Marx household and to retire himself in 1870 so that he could once again join forces with his partner in London.[1]

These two decades between the revolutions of 1848 and the Paris Commune of 1871 offered little opportunity for direct political involvement but much opportunity for study and reflection. As regards the political thought of Marx and Engels, it was the period that gave birth to the theories of Bonapartism and Oriental despotism. Since these two theories cannot be understood without reference to the dichotomy between the class state and the parasite state, introduced in volume 1, it seems an appropriate time at which to step back and examine both concepts more fully, in the first three chapters, by looking at the origins of the state and its subsequent evolution. The underlying aim will be to separate out, conceptually and historically, these two ideas that so frequently have been muddled indiscriminately together, both by Marx and Engels themselves and even more by their followers. If the prime emphasis here falls on the parasite state idea rather than the class state, it is not because of any inherently greater importance, but only because the former has received

[3]

so little attention and understanding that it deserves a lengthier analysis to redress the balance. Most of all, it will be crucially important to keep the two theories sharply separated in order to grasp, in later chapters, Marx and Engels' conception of the workers' state and of its ultimate disappearance in the classless society.

It will be remembered from volume 1 how the two theories of the state were born in the early 1840s, the one fathered by Marx, the other by Engels.[2] The latter, more familiar, theory had come empirically from Engels' experience in Britain, where he took part in the Chartists' struggles to gain control of a sovereign parliament that was already the object of contentious wrangling between the rising manufacturing interest and the declining landed interest, all of which had suggested an historical succession of class dominations, from aristocracy to bourgeoisie to proletariat, in which the state machinery served each class in turn as an instrument of organized coercion against the other(s). Marx's initial theory, by contrast, had grown out of his encounter with the bureaucratic and absolutist Prussian state which, he decided, did not really serve the general interest of society as Hegel had taught, but only its own selfish interest as a state, as a cadre of professional bureaucrats who regarded the state as their private property and drew their sustenance from civil society as a parasite from its host. Engels' state was a mere instrument; Marx's state was autonomous, its own master. Engels' theory gave prime importance to coercion, class coercion, as the essence of state power; Marx's theory stressed its caste egoism and estrangement from civil society. Thus Engels' theory conjures up images of guns and bayonets pointed at the workers, of proscribed newspapers and closed meeting halls, of prisons and penal colonies. Marx's theory, while not oblivious to coercion, conjures up other images, images of placehunting bureaucrats and ubiquitous tax collectors, of arrogant judges and bespangled generals, all concerned with the advancement of their own careers and the defense of their own collective interests against those of civil society.

The two theories had been merged and at least formally reconciled in Marx and Engels' first collaborative work, *The German Ideology* (1846), where the class state idea was invoked for the principal historical epochs (ancient, feudal, bourgeois, and anticipated proletarian), while the parasite state idea appeared only in early modern absolutism, a form of government that had lingered on in backward Germany. It is not clear at all whether this merger was a conscious fusion, openly discussed between the two men, or simply a happy accident. In their subsequent writings one sometimes senses that they were quite aware of using two different concepts, but more often one senses the contrary. In any event, their most famous writing, the *Communist Manifesto,* concerned itself *only* with the class state, as did their other political writings of 1848–1850. The idea of the parasite state seemed forgotten, and indeed has been forgotten until quite recently by virtually all students of Classical Marxism.

Marx and Engels themselves — especially the former — were drawn back to the idea of the parasite state during the 1850s, for it helped them explain the otherwise puzzling phenomena of Bonapartism and Oriental despotism. Louis Napoleon's dramatic coup d'état in December 1851 appeared prima facie as a victory *over* the French bourgeoisie, bringing its class rule to an end, and so Marx depicted it in what is perhaps the most acute of all his political writings, *The Eighteenth Brumaire of Louis Bonaparte,* published in 1852. He presented Napoleon's victory as the consequence of a temporary stalemate in the broader class struggle in which the proletariat was not yet ready to rule and the bourgeoisie no longer confident enough to rule in its own right. Under such circumstances it became possible for an otherwise ridiculous military adventurer to seize power and rule through executive force alone, promising each class to protect it from the rapacity of the other. Subsequently the two men were to find striking similarities in the regime Bismarck constructed for Germany, and Engels particularly became inclined to view Bonapartism as a probable if not inevitable stage in the development of every capitalist country. Scarcely a year after *The Eighteenth Brumaire,* Marx again drew upon the idea of the parasite state in an entirely different context. As European correspondent for the *New York Daily Tribune* Marx undertook to cover the English parliamentary debates on India in 1853 for his American readers. To prepare himself he characteristically plunged into an extensive study of traditional Indian society, and Asian societies more generally, where he was able to discover no class struggles properly so called but an essentially static society composed of undifferentiated, economically self-sufficient peasant communities that were organized and exploited by a remote state apparatus controlling both the means of production and the means of coercion. Oriental despotism came to represent for Marx and Engels an early sidetrack in human history, a path which once taken led nowhere at all, to no further social evolution, until at length it would be destroyed or transformed from the outside by European imperialism.

While the theory of Bonapartism was the first to be developed, and that of Oriental despotism inspired by it in all probability, it will make more sense here to survey the evolution of the state — as perceived by Marx and Engels — in *its* chronological development. To extend this logic one step further, we should begin with their conception of how the state arose in the first place out of primitive communism. Such an extension will carry us temporarily into post-1870 writings.

The Dual Emergence

From the time of their earliest collaboration in Brussels, Marx and Engels asserted the existence of an original stateless condition at the beginning of human social evolution, and the subject would occupy them increasingly toward the end of their lives. Surely it will illuminate our subsequent scrutiny of various *kinds* of states if we start off here by asking: How did they conceive primitive society to have been organized as a polity and why did they prefer not to call this organization a state? At what point and for what reasons did a state subsequently arise? What essential features distinguish this state from the social organization that preceded it? As we review Marx and Engels' several treatments of these questions, we can also be on the lookout for possible changes of opinion or emphasis, and possible differences between the two men.

Their earliest treatment in 1846 was collaborative. *The German Ideology* touched on primitive society only in the most cursory fashion, approaching the subject more by philosophical conjecture than empirically. Human history at large was presented as the gradual unfolding of the division of labor, thus presupposing an original condition in which labor was not permanently divided. When tribal groups initially lived simply "by hunting and fishing," while certain individuals might have been excused from certain activities for specific reasons (youth, infirmity, etc.), still basically the entire tribe took part in councils and religious ceremonies as a group, fashioned tools as a group, went on the hunt as a group, and so forth. Corresponding to this initial stage, they conjectured, there existed no private property but "*Stammeigentum*," tribal ownership of the means of production, notably of the tribal hunting lands. They also spoke of "*patriarchalische Stammhäupter*," or "patriarchal tribal chieftains" who presumably exercised public functions in some way — as yet undefined — that did not involve real state power.[3] Such a society, Marx and Engels continued, proceeds to develop and evolve

> through increased productivity, the increase of needs, and, what is fundamental to both of these, the increase of population. With these there develops the division of labor, which was originally noth-

ing but the division of labor in the sexual act, then the division of
labor which develops spontaneously or "naturally" by virtue of natural predisposition (e.g., physical strength), needs, accidents, etc.,
etc. Division of labor only becomes truly such from the moment
when a division of material and mental labor appears.

Out of this unfolding of the division of labor then emerge: (1) "the *distribution*, and indeed the *unequal* distribution, both quantitative and
qualitative, of labor and its products, hence property"; (2) distinct social
classes based on this unequal distribution of property; and (3) a new institution that can properly be called a state.[4] This third excrescence requires closer scrutiny.

"Further," Marx and Engels explained, "the division of labor also implies the contradiction between the interest of the separate individual or
the individual family and the common interest of all individuals who have
intercourse with one another." This "cleavage," as they alternatively
labeled it, presumably results when one distinct kind of labor devolves
permanently upon a given individual or group within society. Such a development inevitably gives that individual or group a special or vested
interest to watch over as against the rest of society, a special interest that
could not have existed when all individuals participated consecutively
in all tribal activities. They continued:

> Out of this very contradiction between the particular and the com-
> mon interests, the common interest assumes an independent form
> as the *state*, which is divorced from the real individual and collec-
> tive interests, and at the same time as an illusory community, al-
> ways based, however, on the real ties existing in every family con-
> glomeration and tribal conglomeration — such as flesh and blood,
> language, division of labor on a larger scale, and other interests —
> and especially, as we shall show later, on the classes, already im-
> plied by the division of labor, which in every such mass of men
> separate out, and one of which dominates all the others.[5]

In this monumental but still too brief sentence one can perceive elements
of both Marx's parasite state and Engels' class state, each growing out
of the emerging division of labor but for different reasons. The parasite
state arises dialectically with the arising of selfish individual interests.
As each individual increasingly devotes himself to a single occupation,
minding his own business in the literal sense, he leaves it to others to mind

the community interest, but some of these others discover that the community interest can become their own business, a selfish interest like any other, so that the original authentic community interest becomes an illusory one, "divorced from the real individual and collective interests," in actuality the private interest of the new rulers. In the original manuscript at this point there appears a marginal note in Marx's hand: "Just because individuals seek *only* their particular interest, which for them does not coincide with their common interest, the latter is asserted as an interest 'alien' to them, and 'independent' of them, as in its turn a particular and distinctive 'general' interest."[6] Asserting this fraudulent 'general' interest one would find the earliest ancestors of those haughty bureaucrats against whom Marx had railed in the *Rheinische Zeitung*.

Engels' class state emerges at the other end of the monumental sentence as an institution based on the emergence of social classes, "one of which dominates all the others." *The German Ideology* treated the city-states of classical antiquity as the first states to have evolved out of tribal society, and they became necessary because of the spreading practice of slaveholding. "The citizens hold power over their laboring slaves only in their community. . . . [The slave population] constitutes the communal private property of the active citizens who, in relation to their slaves, are compelled to remain in this spontaneously derived form of association." This association is no longer, as it was in tribal society, coextensive with the entire population, since the slaves are excluded; it has become a special coercive force to hold down the exploited class and thus meets Engels' primordial criterion for a state. Similarly, in medieval times, the "feudal organization was, just as much as the ancient communal property, an association against a subjected producing class." In general, "the state is the form in which the individuals of a ruling class assert their common interests."[7]

As the two men wrestled to fit both conceptions of the state within that single monumental sentence, the key words for Marx would have been "independent" and "divorced," which appear at the beginning; the key word for Engels, "dominates," at the end. What remains problematic in this famous passage is that both kinds of state appear to arise simultaneously, yet have different and seemingly incompatible characteristics: the emergent parasite state stands against civil society as a whole, including all its classes, while the emergent class state includes the entire possessing class of slaveowners that is very much a part of civil society. Logically, a state cannot be both independent, its own master, and simultaneously the mere instrument of a possessing class.

In the years immediately following *The German Ideology* Marx and Engels had little opportunity to discover or ponder such difficulties. They were more occupied with fighting the existing state than inquiring into its remote antecedents. Only during the long years of exile in Great Britain was their attention eventually drawn back to early human history. Thus the *Communist Manifesto* had blithely ignored primitive communism in its grand opening declaration, "The history of all hitherto existing society is the history of class struggles," an oversight that by 1888 nettled Engels sufficiently to write the following explanatory footnote for the new English edition then being prepared:

That is, all *written* history. In 1847, the pre-history of society, the social organization existing previous to recorded history, was all but unknown. Since then, Haxthausen discovered common ownership of land in Russia, Maurer proved it to be the social foundation from which all Teutonic races started in history, and by and by village communities were found to be, or to have been the primitive form of society everywhere from India to Ireland. The inner organization of this primitive Communistic society was laid bare, in its typical form, by Morgan's crowning discovery of the true nature of the *gens* and its relation to the *tribe*. With the dissolution of these primeval communities society begins to be differentiated into separate and finally antagonistic classes.[8]

These diverse writings helped to spur on Marx and Engels in their historical-anthropological interests from the communal villages of India to those of Germany and Russia, and finally via Lewis Henry Morgan to the North American Iroquois. The book Marx had intended to write on primitive society survives only as notes and excerpts taken before he died in 1883. We must therefore rely mainly on Engels, who addressed the pertinent questions twice, first in *Anti-Dühring* (1878) and then much more extensively when he elaborated upon Morgan's findings in *The Origin of the Family* (1884).

Herr Eugen Dühring's Revolution in Science, more commonly known as *Anti-Dühring*, was published by Engels after he had read the entire manuscript to Marx, so most authorities assume the latter either agreed with or, at least, had no strenuous objection to the views presented.[9] The book was a lengthy polemic against the writings of a now obscure German socialist intellectual. Eugen Dühring had asserted — among other things — the primacy of political relationships, specifically of force, over economic relationships throughout human history. As against this view Engels naturally wanted to insist on the primacy of socioeconomic relationships and so felt the need to explain the origin of political domination, of the state, in socioeconomic terms. "It arose in two ways," he declared; the two processes of state formation he then proceeded to sketch out are the same ones we found implicit in *The German Ideology*, but this time he sketched them with obvious consciousness of the dichotomy. In primitive communities, he wrote, "there prevailed a certain equality in the conditions of life, and for family heads a kind of equality of social position—at least an absence of social classes." Further:

> In each such community there were from the beginning certain common interests the safeguarding of which had to be handed over to individuals, though under the control of the community as a whole: adjudication of disputes; repression of trespasses on the part of individuals who went beyond their rights; control of water supplies, especially in hot countries; and finally, given the primitive simplicity of conditions, religious functions. Such delegations of office [*Beamtungen*] are found in the aboriginal communities of every period—in the oldest German marks and even today in India. They are naturally endowed with a certain measure of authority and are the beginnings of state power [*Staatsgewalt*].[10]

Notice that such "delegations of office" (recalling the "patriarchal tribal chieftains" of *The German Ideology*) do not yet constitute a state in Engels' perception; he evidently regarded these arrangements as necessary and legitimate, even where the possible "repression" (*Repression*) of individual trespasses might be involved.

The first process of state formation Engels described next as a consequence of expanding "productive forces" and "increasing density of population." What had been only "delegations of office" under community control now become more fixed "organs" supervising several communities and incorporating a further subdivision of labor. He continued:

> These organs which, if only because they represent the common interests of the whole group [of communities], hold a special position in relation to each individual community—in certain circumstances even one of opposition—soon make themselves still more independent, partly through an inheritance of offices which enters the scene

almost as a matter of course in a world where everything is so close to nature, and partly because they become increasingly indispensable owing to the growing number of conflicts with other groups. It is not necessary for us to examine here *how this independence of social functions vis-à-vis society could increase with time until it developed into domination over society; how he who was originally the servant, where conditions were favorable, changed himself gradually into the lord;* how this lord, depending on conditions, emerged as an Oriental despot or satrap, the dynast of a Greek tribe, chieftain of a Celtic clan, and so on; to what extent he subsequently had recourse to force in this transformation, and how finally the individual rulers united into a ruling class. Here we are only concerned with establishing the fact that the exercise of a social function was everywhere the basis of political rule. (Italics added)[11]

If delegated authority under community control does not by itself signify political domination for Engels, then hereditary offices and self-interested autonomy are what transforms public servants into oppressive masters and create the parasite state *par excellence*, recognizable first and foremost in the shape of Oriental despotism. Notice that private property is not mentioned at all.

The second, alternative process of state formation, Engels went on, can be found especially "in countries where the old common ownership of the land had already disintegrated or at least the former joint cultivation had given place to the separate cultivation of parcels of land by the respective families." More efficient production made it "possible" for these families to use outside workers, whose labor now created more value than it cost to feed them; "labor-power acquired a *value*." But since no significant internal reservoirs of untapped labor-power existed, it was only natural to use captives taken in war, who in earlier times, when their labor could produce no net gain, had simply been killed, or even eaten. Thus:

Slavery had been invented. It soon became the dominant form of production among all peoples who were developing beyond the old community, but in the end was also one of the chief causes of their decay. It was slavery that first made possible the division of labor between agriculture and industry on a larger scale, and thereby also Hellenism, the flowering of the ancient world.[12]

In this fashion there arose that primordial division of labor "between the masses discharging simple manual labor and the few privileged persons directing labor, conducting trade and public affairs, and, at a later stage, occupying themselves with art and science." Such a division self-evidently required a coercive apparatus separated from the masses, a state, with "the function of maintaining by force the conditions of existence and domination of the ruling class against the subject class."[13] Here one can see the class state emerging in pure form.

It is particularly interesting to observe how these passages from *Anti-Dühring* offer a possible solution to the problem left over from *The German Ideology*. The two kinds of state could indeed appear at roughly the same stage in human cultural evolution if they appear in different *places*. And a geographical separation is clearly what Engels had in mind, as he proceeded to explain why the introduction of slavery, however repulsive it might seem, nonetheless represented historical progress when compared to the alternative:

> Where the ancient communes have continued to exist, they have for thousands of years formed the basis of the cruelest form of state, Oriental despotism, from India to Russia. It was only where these communities dissolved that the peoples made progress of themselves, and their next economic advance consisted in the increase and development of production by means of slave labor. . . . In the historical conditions of the ancient world, and particularly of Greece, the advance to a society based on class antagonisms could be accomplished only in the form of slavery.[14]

Here Engels followed the schema one finds in Marx's writings on Oriental despotism (especially the *Grundrisse*), to be examined in the next section, where that form of state appears not as a universal stage in all human social evolution but as one possible path out of primitive communism, an alternative to the slave-based but more dynamic societies of Greece and Rome. By this reading, then, the parasite state arose in the East, the class state in the West. Yet Engels meant to say more than this, for among his examples of servants who turned themselves into lords, though the Oriental despot came first, one also finds the "dynast of a Greek tribe" and the "chieftain of a Celtic clan." As we will see in later writings, Engels — and Marx too — regarded a *tendency* toward parasitism to exist even in class states, a tendency that develops to its logical conclusion in the West only much later and by way of exception in the forms of absolutism and Bonapartism.

Gentile Democracy

By far the most extensive account of the emergence of the state is to be found in Engels' *The Origin of the Family, Private Property and the State*, published in 1884. This volume can be viewed as a joint work in the very limited sense that it was "the execution of a bequest," as Engels put it in the preface, a "meagre substitute" for the work Marx had intended to write at the time of his death the previous year. It did represent the fruit of the by then intense interest both men took in primitive social life and particularly of their enthusiasm for the findings of the American ethnologist, Lewis Henry Morgan, whose *Ancient Society* had appeared in 1877. Marx's extensive preparatory notes, which Engels studied before he undertook his own account, have recently been published in a painstakingly scholarly edition, and, while disappointingly thin as a source, they offer some basis for comparing what Engels actually wrote with what Marx might have written.[15]

Morgan's principal firsthand observations concern the Iroquois tribes of his native New York State. Here he perceived a social structure based on certain kinds of kinship bonds and organized without social classes, private property, or a state. Drawing evidence from other Amerindian cultures as well, Morgan generalized these conditions as a universal stage in the evolution of mankind and then scoured the earliest history of Greece and Rome pointing out the remnants of what seemed to be parallel conditions. Marx and Engels' enthusiasm for these views is understandable enough: here was independent expert testimony corroborating the existence of primitive communism, for what else was a society organized without social classes, private property, or a state? Engels even followed Morgan's general plan of organization, beginning with a description of Iroquois society and proceeding from there to Greece and Rome. As much as possible we must confine ourselves to the political dimension of Engels' subject — the absence of a state among the Iroquois, and the emergence of a state among the Greeks and Romans.

The basic unit of Iroquois society — the unit held to be common to all primitive peoples at a certain stage of development — was the *gens*, a clan or kinship group whose members were all related on the female side, all descendents of a common female ancestor, and who were not permitted to intermarry. Concerning social relations within the gens, Engels quoted Morgan approvingly:

> All the members of an Iroquois gens were personally free, and they were bound to defend each other's freedom; they were equal in privileges and in personal rights, the sachem and chiefs claiming no superiority; and they were a brotherhood bound together by the ties of kin. Liberty, equality, and fraternity, though never formulated, were cardinal principles of the gens.[16]

Each gens, Engels went on to explain, "has a council, the democratic assembly of all male and female adult gentiles, all with equal votes." This council elected the two principal leaders of the group, the sachem, or headman in peacetime, and the chief, who commanded military expeditions. "The gens deposes the sachem and war chief at will," Engels noted. "This also is done by the men and women jointly. After a sachem or chief had been deposed they became simple braves, private persons, like the other members." On the other hand, to replace a leader who had been deposed or who had died, the council "often" elected his brother or his sister's son, thus giving encouragement to the hereditary principle that would later destroy gentile democracy. Engels went on to emphasize that "the authority of a sachem within the gens was paternal and purely moral in character; he had no means of coercion." Judicial functions were performed by the entire council acting as a body. If a member was slain by a person from another gens, the council would seek redress from the gens council of the slayer, usually in the form of presents and expressions of regret, but if it were not satisfied in this way, it might appoint one or more "avengers" to pursue and kill the slayer. The latter's gens would then have no right to complain.[17]

Several gentes linked together by intermarriage constituted a tribe, although in some larger tribes an intermediate grouping, the phratry, also existed. The tribal council involved representative democracy, as against the direct democracy of the gens, since only the sachems and war chiefs of the individual gentes gathered there. Engels insisted, however, that they were "genuinely representative because they could be deposed at any time." Moreover, the tribal council "held its deliberations in public surrounded by the other members of the tribe, who had the right to join freely in the discussion and make their views heard." Among the Iroquois tribes one sometimes finds a head-chief, whose powers however are "*very slight.*" "He is one of the sachems, and in situations demanding swift action he has to take provisional measures until the council can assemble and make the definite decision." It is the council alone that could make permanent decisions on the basis of a unanimous vote; it had the right to depose individual sachems and war chiefs (even against the wishes of their gens); most importantly, it handled relations with other tribes, sending embassies, declaring war, and making peace. Wars were fought essentially by volunteers: a few prominent braves would begin a war dance, and "whoever joined in the dance announced thereby his participation in the expedition." Prisoners taken in war who were not slain immediately were adopted by one of the gentes and became full and equal members of the tribe.[18]

Such was the organization, Engels summed up, "of society which still has no *state*," for "the state presupposes a special public power separated from the body of the people," whereas the Iroquois managed their own affairs directly as a group:

> And a wonderful constitution it is, this gentile constitution, in all its childlike simplicity! No soldiers, no gendarmes or police, no nobles, kings, regents, prefects, or judges, no prisons, or lawsuits— and everything takes its orderly course. All quarrels and disputes are settled by the whole of the community affected, by the gens or the tribe, or by the gentes among themselves. . . . There is no need for even a trace of our complicated administrative apparatus with all its ramifications. . . . All are equal and free—the women included. There is no place yet for slaves. . . . And what men and women such a society breeds is proved by the admiration inspired in all white people who have come into contact with unspoiled Indians, the personal dignity, uprightness, strength of character, and courage of these barbarians. . . .
>
> That is what men and society were before the division into classes.[19]

This glowing pictures of gentile society, together with its assumed universality as a stage in human evolution, has left Engels exposed to a large volume of criticism, especially from twentieth-century anthropologists who dispute whether primitive societies have been universally democratic, granted equality to women, lacked class distinctions, and so forth.[20] In a more restrained moment Engels himself allowed that Morgan's generalizations only apply to primitive communism "in its typical form."[21] For our particular purposes, however, it matters little whether Engels saw primitive society through rose-colored glasses, whether his image of that society corresponded to reality, for it is precisely his image that matters to us. And his image of a thoroughly democratic polity at the beginning of mankind's evolution appears to have been shared by Marx, insofar as we can ascertain from his surviving notebooks. In his excerpts from Morgan, Marx showed the greatest interest in the chapters dealing with the political organization of gentile society, and then he used Morgan's findings as the standard by which to measure other writers. Upon finding an assertion in Henry Sumner Maine, for example, that tribal societies generally chose a new chief from the family of the old one "as representing the purest blood of the brotherhood," Marx scoffed at the English scholar's "unfamiliarity with the essence [*Wesen*] of the gens." Such an idea, he continued, is "nonsense if one is speaking of real primitive communities. See for example Red Indian *Iroquois*. Rather the other way around, [it is] because the election often continues traditionally in the same [gens], or in certain gentes, and then again in a certain family of the same gens, even though later under changed circumstances this might pass for 'representing the purest blood.'" Marx went on to insist that, contrary to Maine, the war chief is a different person from the civil leader, but is also "elected according to his individual capacities." In these and other comments Marx showed himself no less convinced than Engels that Iroquois political organization was basically and originally democratic and represented the "essence" of a universal — or at all events typical — stage in human evolution.[22]

Why did not Marx and Engels regard the fairly elaborate political organization of gentile society as constituting a real state? Certainly there existed instrumentalities for coercion, most obviously for external purposes when the braves gathered together to form a war party, but even domestically in the appointment of "avengers," for instance. One may observe that these coercive instrumentalities were not used by a possessing class to hold down an exploited class, and thus do not meet the criterion for a class state. But Engels himself stressed the parasite-state criterion when he declared that the Iroquois polity did not yet involve "a special public power separated from the body of the people." The process of institutionalization had not yet produced a permanent ruling cadre, the kings and nobles, prefects and judges, soldiers and gendarmes, who are the flesh and bone of a real state. For Marx and Engels a society possesses a state only when the division of labor has proceeded to the point that a special body of persons exists to exercise the means of coercion; once entrenched they will employ that coercion either in the interest of a possessing class or simply in their own interest. Thus, because Iroquois warriors and avengers did not enforce the will of a possessing class, but also because neither they nor the chiefs stood apart as a permanent cadre, there could be no question of an Iroquois state for Marx and Engels.

Some writers have claimed to see a difference between Marx and Engels in the latter's rhapsodic praise of gentile society; he almost sounded regretful that mankind ever left this blissful condition. Indeed, in another passage Engels went on to lament that these primordial communities were "broken by influences which from the very start appear as a degradation, a fall from the simple moral greatness of the old gentile society. The lowest interests — base greed, brutal appetites, sordid avarice, selfish robbery of the common wealth — inaugurate the new, civilized, class society." But Engels also dutifully set down that in gentile society no law was recognized beyond the limits of the tribe, war was waged with great cruelty, the undeveloped form of production gave rise to an attitude toward nature "of almost complete subjection to a strange incomprehensible power," and this in turn was reflected in "childish religious conceptions."[23] Ultimately he was no more in doubt than his partner on the need to pass beyond primitive communism, although his natural exuberance may well have produced a few rhapsodic strains that Marx would have denied himself. Even so, in the latter's notebook we find a poignant characterization of "the tearing of the individuality loose from the originally not despotic chains . . . , but rather satisfying and agreeable bonds of the group, of the primitive community — and therewith the one-sided elaboration of the individuality."[24]

Surely both men saw something admirable in primitive society, and precisely because, as Marx put it philosophically back in 1843, "the primitive state of things is a naive Flemish painting of the *true* state of things."[25] A classless, propertyless, stateless condition at the beginning of man's self-development foretold his ultimate destiny, and Engels could find no better words with which to conclude *Origin of the Family* than those of Morgan himself, predicting a future society which *"will be a revival, in higher form, of the liberty, equality and fraternity of the ancient gentes"* (Engels' italics).[26] Just as primitive people governed themselves without requiring any external coercive agency, so in the future communist society people would govern themselves but not with a state. We will see how closely, even in many details, Marx and Engels' conception of the future polity matched Iroquois practice — or in any event their image of Iroquois practice. For in the future as well there would be elective, nonprofessional, and removable leadership, direct democracy at the local level but representation at higher levels, equal rights of participation for all, and with moral constraint as the general rule instead of physical constraint.

The Dualism Reconciled

In the subsequent chapters of *The Origin of the Family*, Engels proceeded to account for the emergence of the state in what is by far the fullest description we have from either man. Beginning among the Athenians as "particularly typical," the "purest, classic form," Engels then went on to the Romans, the Celts, and Germans, and finished with a few allusions to the peoples of the ancient Middle East.[27] He had a difficult time wrestling such disparate material into a single intelligible pattern, which may help to account for the confusion notorious in the concluding chapter where we find a particularly muddled and seemingly unconscious intertangling of the two concepts of the state. It is a misfortune that this account has been the principal source for the subsequent Marxist tradition. Nonetheless, by untangling the two processes through which Engels saw the state emerging, and by turning for help to his other contemporaneous writings, we may be able to reconcile the dualism to a surprising extent.

To start with, everywhere Engels was at pains to show the state arising out of a prior gentile organization of society. Everywhere he associated its emergence with the development of private property, of a wealthy class of proprietors, of the monogamous patriarchal family. Private property emerged first in movable property, the seed of which had usually existed in gentile society. Tools and other instruments of production, herds of domestic animals, slaves taken as captives in war — all eventually fell under individual proprietorship, and then finally the land as well. With these changes there arose a possibility of differences in wealth that would have been inconceivable in gentile society, a possibility not only of amassing great wealth but also of losing one's means of livelihood through debt, of becoming propertyless, or worse, the ultimate degradation of being sold into slavery for debt. In Greece this expansion of the original slave system eventually produced, by Engels' estimation, four times as many slaves as citizens in Athens, and ten times as many in some other Greek city-states. The nascent social antagonisms of classical antiquity thus found the wealthier citizens pitted against the impoverished ones, and both pitted against the slave majority. Against this socioeconomic background Engels depicted the emergence of the state as a direct result of the wealthier citizens' need to hold down the poorer citizens, and of both to hold down the slaves.[28] As he set forth these familiar steps in the formation of the class state, however, he simultaneously sketched in what appears as a semiautonomous process of institutionalization in which we can recognize the key elements of the parasite state. He saw four processes working in combination here:

First, kinship gave way to domicile as the basis for political structures. Given the socioeconomic evolution outlined above, more and more gens members left the locality of their kin group, while more and more outsiders — including slaves — came in, making it more and more difficult to handle common concerns on the basis of gens, phratry, and tribe. In the successive constitutions of ancient city-states, Engels followed Morgan in pointing to the increasing substitution of simple domicile as the basis for organizing political participation, military levies, and taxation. Engels did not relate this change directly to class interests but seemed to perceive it as an inevitable practical consequence of the new geographical mobility of the individual, for which gentile institutions were "inadequate."[29] But the process of substitution perceptible in the recorded history of Greece and Rome helped him, as it had Morgan, make a case for the prior universal existence of a gentile social organization.

Second, election gave way to heredity as the basis for leadership. We have already noted Marx's comments on this process; Engels likewise began from the Iroquois deformation whereby "in the course of time, preference when filling vacancies was given to the nearest gentile relative — brother or sister's son — unless there were reasons for passing him over." From the same kind of practice arose, for example, the Roman patriciate. Originally the Roman senate was an elected tribal council composed of the chiefs of the three hundred Roman gentes:

> It was because they were the elders of the gens that they were called fathers, *patres*, and their body, the senate (council of the elders, from *senex*, old). Here again the custom of electing always from the same family in the gens brought into being the first hereditary nobility. These families called themselves "patricians" and claimed for themselves exclusive right of entry into the senate and tenure of all other offices.

In similar fashion a supreme military commander, "aiming at the position of tyrant," might eventually establish a hereditary claim as *basileus* or *rex*, thus creating kingship in the ancient world:

The customary election of their successors from the same families is gradually transformed, especially after the introduction of father right, into a right of hereditary succession, first tolerated, then claimed, finally usurped; the foundation of the hereditary monarchy and the hereditary nobility is laid.[30]

No doubt Engels saw an intimate relationship between this process and the concurrently growing inequalities of wealth: the families making these hereditary claims would tend to be the same as those accumulating large fortunes. Yet nowhere did he attempt to argue that people acquired hereditary privileges just because they became wealthy. The process through which hereditary rule arose seemed in his eyes to have a certain degree of autonomy, a momentum of its own, driven perhaps by the hunger for power, "aiming at the position of tyrant," and not merely by avarice.

In presenting all this as a universal process growing out of gentile democracy, Engels encountered a number of factual difficulties, at least one of which we should note in passing. The recorded history of Athens seemed to suggest the reverse development from kingship and hereditary nobility, through an oligarchy of wealth, to the fifth-century Periclean democracy of all citizens. Engels handled the first part of the problem predictably enough by positing gentile democracy before recorded history and conjecturing the growth of early hereditary rule in the usual manner, a rule which then in the course of time was broken by a rising merchant class, whose oligarchy was in turn upset by the revolt of the poorer citizens in a debtors' revolution during the time of Solon that harked back in some respects to gentile democracy and established equal rights of participation and office-holding for all citizens. This citizens' democracy, however, on a broader social canvas, constituted a citizens' oligarchy over the much larger slave population. In any event, hereditary rule reemerged later on in both Greece and Rome, marking their republican periods as but a temporary resistance to the more pervasive long-range trend.[31]

Third, the armed people gave way to a special armed force at the service of the new hereditary elite. Or as Engels put it himself: "The true 'people in arms,' organized for its self-defense in its gentes, phratries and tribes, was replaced by an armed 'public force' [*öffentlichen Gewalt*] in the service of these state authorities and therefore at their command for use also against the people." Here was the most crucial transformation of all for Engels, who all his life reiterated the idea that the "essential characteristic of the state is the existence of a public force differentiated from the mass of the people."[32] Such an *öffentliche Gewalt* includes, to be sure, "material appendages" such as "prisons and coercive institutions of all kinds," but at its core must be a body of armed men, ideally a professional police force. The police force as an institution, Engels generalized, "is as old as the state itself; for which reason the naive French of the 18th century did not speak of civilized peoples but of policed peoples (*nations policées*)."[33] Once again the "classic" Athenian example proved recalcitrant, for the only police force in sight was composed of slaves and was used to keep order among the citizens! "The state could not exist without police," Engels explained, but "the free Athenian considered police duty so degrading that he would rather be arrested by an armed slave than himself have any hand in such despicable work." Engels then got round the larger difficulty by arguing that the Athenian citizens' militia, while it obviously did not stand apart from the citizens as a public force, did form such a body vis-à-vis the underlying slave population. "The people's army of the Athenian democracy confronted the slaves as an aristocratic public force and kept them in check." The case was the same in Rome, where the militia not only held the slaves in check but the poorest class of freemen, the "so-called proletarians," as well.[34] In these ancient city-states generally, it is interesting to note that the state was not really a special force in the service of the possessing class; rather it was the possessing class itself serving as a special force. The well-to-do did their own fighting, including whatever was necessary for domestic repression.

If the military institutions of classical antiquity served direct class needs in this fashion, Engels also allowed that such institutions could acquire autonomous interests and a vitality of their own. We have already noted his observation that with the decline of gentile institutions it was the war chief rather than the peacetime leader who typically began asserting hereditary claims, "aiming at the position of tyrant." More dramatically, in the case of the Germanic tribes Engels related how entire military formations broke loose from their original social function and followed their own independent path. These were the "retinues," associations formed for private warlike purposes which developed into standing bodies:

> A military leader who had made himself a name gathered around him a band of young men eager for booty whom he pledged to personal loyalty, giving the same pledge to them. The leader provided their keep, gave them gifts, and organized them on a hierarchic basis: a bodyguard and a standing troop for smaller expeditions,

and a regular corps of officers for operations on a larger scale. . . . They could only be kept together by continual wars and plundering expeditions. Plunder became an end in itself. If the leader of the retinue found nothing to do in the neighborhood, he set out with his men to other peoples where there was war and the prospect of booty.

In this fashion Germanic retinues ravaged the entire Roman Empire, eventually settling down to dominate more systematically where they had only pillaged before, and becoming a main constituent part of the new landed aristocracy of medieval Europe.[35] To this extent at least we find Engels describing how an autonomous military force created a state and took over the means of production, making itself the possessing class — rather than the other way around.

Fourth, returning to the last of Engels' processes, unpaid public service gave way to taxation, required to maintain the new apparatus of coercion. Taxes were "completely unknown to gentile society," but became necessary once there were public officials and soldiers who did not engage in productive activity themselves.[36] Engels did not develop the subject further but taxation also calls to mind the parasite state inasmuch as officials and soldiers live from the productive activity of others.

Thus all four processes described lead toward the parasite state more obviously and directly than to the class state. Engels' own thoughts, in any event, seemed to move in that direction, for his next paragraph began: "In possession of the public power [*öffentlichen Gewalt*] and of the right of taxation, the officials stand there as organs of society, but now *above* society"; they are "bearers of a power that is estranging itself from society." A few paragraphs earlier he had also referred to the state as "this power, arisen out of society but placing itself above it and increasingly alienating itself from it." In such prose we recognize the features of the parasite state as they might have been pictured by the young Marx when he had Prussian absolutism in mind. And just as that state for Marx dominated all the classes of civil society, so any state described as alienated from and standing above society (not "apparently" but actually) would seem to be a state that dominates the wealthy as well as the poor.[37]

Engels seemed to sense that his formulations created such a difficulty, for in these same concluding paragraphs he managed to modify his own pronouncements quite into their opposite, transforming the independent parasite state into the familiar class state. Thus the "officials" mentioned above, in a reformulated phrasing, are "forced to *pose* as something outside and above" society; and the state becomes a power *"apparently standing above society"* (italics added).[38] At length the class state emerges clearly through the fog:

> As the state arose from the need to keep class antagonisms in check, but also arose in the thick of the fight between the classes, it is normally the state of the most powerful, economically dominant class, which by this means becomes also the politically dominant class and so acquires new means of holding down and exploiting the oppressed class.

So we are led from a state depicted as independent, to one that is only "apparently" independent, to one that is the mere instrument of the economically dominant class. With the word "normally," however, Engels offered a possible way out of these difficulties. After proceeding to list the familiar class states — ancient, feudal, modern bourgeois — he then added:

> Exceptional periods, however, occur when the warring classes are so nearly equal in forces that the state power, as apparent mediator, acquires for the moment a certain independence in relation to both. This applies to the absolute monarchy of the 17th and 18th centuries, which balanced the nobility and the bourgeoisie against one another, and to the Bonapartism of the First and particularly of the Second French Empire, which played off the proletariat against the bourgeoisie and the bourgeoisie against the proletariat.[39]

Here the parasite state appears temporally distinct from the class state, as an exception, just as it had in *The German Ideology*, with Bonapartism now given as an additional example. Engels did not mention Oriental despotism, the most obviously missing form of state, but he had previously declared he would exclude Asia from his treatment for reasons of space.[40]

A final text from a contemporaneous (1890) letter will help us round out and elucidate what Engels was trying to say. In it he described the unfolding division of labor first in the economic sphere, where production is always primary, but where trade eventually develops as a separate occupational specialization. "When the trade in products becomes independent of production itself, it follows a movement of its own." He used this idea as a parallel when he came to the origin of the state:

The thing is easiest to grasp from the point of view of the division of labor. Society gives rise to certain common functions which it cannot dispense with. The persons selected for these functions form a new branch of the division of labor *within society*. This gives them particular interests, distinct too from the interests of those who gave them their office; they make themselves independent of the latter and — the state is in being. And now the development is the same as it was with commodity trade and later with money trade; the new independent power, while having in the main to follow the movement of production, also, owing to its inward independence (the relative independence originally transferred to it and gradually further developed) reacts in its turn upon the conditions and course of production. It is the interaction of two unequal forces: on the one hand the economic movement, on the other the new political power, *which strives for as much independence as possible,* and which, having once been established, is also *endowed with a movement of its own.* On the whole, the economic movement gets its way. (Italics in penultimate sentence added)[41]

The four processes described in *The Origin of the Family* appear here as a *striving* of the state power "for as much independence as possible," even against those who control the "economic movement" of society; Engels' economic determinism was flexible enough to allow every state a certain "movement of its own." Under normal conditions this striving does not reach fulfillment and the independence of the state is only apparent — an illusion perhaps deliberately fostered by the possessing class — but under particular circumstances it may become real enough, as in absolutism.[42] In this letter almost at the end of his life Engels finally stated clearly that he conceived the parasitic tendencies as a striving to be found in all states but fulfilled only in certain exceptional types. By this understanding the two theories may be reconciled most satisfactorily.

How would Marx have dealt with all these questions if he had lived to write *The Origin of the Family* himself? As to the parasite state we have some rich descriptions to scrutinize in the next chapter, but as to the origins of state power, his surviving notebook comments are, alas, too meager to provide answers for any but the most general questions. Like his partner, Marx clearly regarded state power in the West as emerging in association with private property and class antagonisms. Thus he commented on the critical transition period among the Greeks: "Property difference within the same gens had transformed the unity of their interests into antagonism of its members; in addition, beside land and cattle, money capital had become of decisive importance with the development of slavery!" In a nearby comment he linked these changes to political leadership:

> The expression of Plutarch that "the humble and poor readily followed the summons of Theseus" and the judgement of Aristotle that Theseus "was inclined toward the people" appear, however, despite Morgan, to indicate that the chiefs of the gentes etc., through wealth etc. had already reached a conflict of interest with the common people of the gentes, which is unavoidably connected through private property in houses, lands, herds with the monogamous family.[43]

Marx made all the crucial linkages here that Engels was to make in tracing the emergence of the class state. Even less than his partner did he answer the seemingly important question whether it was the wealthy who made themselves rulers, or the rulers who made themselves wealthy.

Neither did Marx discuss here any striving for independence on the part of the state, although that idea had appeared clearly enough in *The Eighteenth Brumaire*, as we will see presently, in his depiction of a French state apparatus which historically "strove for power of its own [*nach Eigenmacht strebte*]."[44] Marx's only allusion in these notes to the possible independence of the state occurs in a rather different context. He was seconding Maine's criticism of Jeremy Bentham and John Austin, and pinpointed the basic error of those two "blockheadish British lawyers" as follows: "that political superiority, whatever its peculiar shape, and whatever the ensemble of its elements, is taken as something standing above society and founded upon itself." In contrast Marx advanced his own view "that the seeming supreme independent existence of the State is itself only seeming and that it is in all its forms an excrescence of society; just as its appearance itself arises only at a certain stage of social development, it disappears again as soon as society has reached a stage not yet attained."[45] At first glance this appears parallel to the "seeming" independence Engels ascribed to the class state. But in fact Marx spoke of the state "in all its forms" and asserted, not a specific dependence on the possessing class, but a general dependence on the stage of socioeconomic development. The Oriental despot, as we will see shortly, does not serve any dominant social class, but his kind of state depends very much on a specific Asian configuration of socioeconomic conditions.

Engels alluded to this second kind of general dependence as well, when he incorporated Marx's thought in his book: "The state is therefore by no means a power imposed on society from without; just as little is it 'the reality of the moral idea,' . . . as Hegel maintains. Rather, it is a product of society at a particular stage of development."[46]

In none of these notebook comments, then, did Marx express an obvious substantive difference with Engels, although one can well imagine his being annoyed at some of the confusions and inept formulations, as well as the occasional rhapsodizing, to be found in his partner's work. In the succession of their writings from *The German Ideology* to *The Origin of the Family*, the most observable change is that the treatment becomes less conjectural and philosophical, more empirical and detailed; but the underlying interpretation of the origin of state power seems to remain essentially the same. By separating out the two distinct concepts of the state implicit within this interpretation, one may at least offer a formulation of it that avoids the charge of being self-contradictory. In Marx and Engels' view, the state emerges in the form of a coercive public power, separated from the mass of society and thus capable of being used against it. Under certain conditions this public power serves a possessing class, in which case it only apparently stands above social conflicts, and its autonomous strivings exist only as a tendency (viz., the class states— ancient, feudal, and bourgeois). Under other conditions the state achieves genuine independence, in the sense of standing over and dominating society as a whole, in which case it is not the instrument of a possessing class (viz., the parasite states— Oriental, absolutist, Bonapartist). In all forms, however, the state is dependent on society in a second, more general sense: it remains an excrescence of its particular society, intimately bound up with a given stage of socioeconomic development; it cannot be understood when conceived as an independent abstraction apart from society, some eternal category of the philosopher's mind.

⟨[2]⟩

The Parasite State

IF ALL STATES REVEAL a tendency or striving to become independent, to be their own master, then under what circumstances do they succeed? In the course of their lives Marx and Engels described three distinct varieties of autonomous states, or parasite states, to use the label drawn from *The Eighteenth Brumaire*. By examining in succession Oriental despotism, European absolutism, and Bonapartism, we will be able to make out their common features, as well as the distinguishing features of each subtype. In addition to the general question posed above, several others seem worthy of examination: If not possession of the means of production, what gives a parasite state the power to dominate a whole society? If not as servant and instrument, how is such a state related to the possessing class (if any exists)? How is it related to the masses of the population? If there is no class rule in the more ordinary sense, should the state itself — its civil and military officials — be regarded as the ruling class? Is the independence of such a state real or only apparent?

It bears repeating that the stress placed here on the parasite state is not intended to give it an importance beyond that of the class state. Marx and Engels always treated parasite states as somehow exceptional and of marginal importance in the larger drama of mankind's self-realization. But the attention they did give them has been so thoroughly forgotten by most writers, or so thoroughly muddled together with the concept of the class state, that, for the sake of clarification and to redress the balance, a separate chapter seems appropriate. Such a treatment will also reveal in Marx and Engels' thought about the state a flexibility and sophistication, an appreciation of nuance, that subsequently disappeared in vulgar Marxism and that deserve to be reemphasized.

Oriental Despotism

As noted in the previous chapter, Marx first undertook serious study of Asian society in 1853, while reporting for the *New York Daily Tribune* on debates in the British Parliament concerning the renewal of the East India Company's charter. The letters Marx and Engels exchanged during this period reveal succinctly the emerging features of their concept of Asian society and its distinctive political form, Oriental despotism. Among the sources he consulted, Marx seemed most impressed with the travel description of François Bernier, and he quoted extensively from the seventeenth-century French physician's book in his letter to Engels of June 2, 1853, concluding: "Bernier correctly discovers the basic form of all phenomena in the East — he refers to Turkey, Persia, Hindostan — to be the *absence of private property* in land. This is the real key even to Oriental heaven."[1] To this Engels replied:

> The absence of property in land is indeed the key to the whole of the East. Herein lies its political and religious history. But how does it come about that the Orientals did not arrive at landed property, even in its feudal form? I think it is mainly due to the climate, taken in connection with the nature of the soil. . . . Artificial irrigation is here the first condition of agriculture and this is a matter either for the communes, the provinces or the central government. An Oriental government never had more than three departments: finance (plunder at home), war (plunder at home and abroad), and public works (provision for reproduction).[2]

Marx borrowed this adroit phrasing almost verbatim for his major article, "The British Rule in India," but, reflecting that Flanders and Italy also had produced large-scale irrigation systems, he added a second key element to explain Asia's distinctiveness:

> There have been in Asia, generally, from immemorial times, but three departments of Government; that of Finance, or the plunder of the interior; that of War, or the plunder of the exterior; and, finally, the department of Public Works. Climate and territorial conditions . . . constituted artificial irrigation by canals and waterworks the basis of Oriental agriculture. . . . This prime necessity of an economical and common use of water, which, in the Occident, drove private enterprise to voluntary association, as in Flan-

ders and Italy, necessitated, in the Orient where civilization was too low and the territorial extent too vast to call into life voluntary association, the interference of the centralizing power of Government. Hence an economical function devolved upon all Asiatic Governments, the function of providing public works.

This "low" level of civilization, he proceeded to explain, "has remained unaltered since its remotest antiquity," and was founded on a near subsistence village economy in which a "peculiar combination of hand-weaving, hand-spinning and hand-tilling agriculture" had made each unit self-sufficient for all practical purposes, with an extremely simple internal division of labor based typically on hereditary castes, and with scarcely any contact — or need for contact — with neighboring villages such as might produce a more sophisticated and dynamic economy. The only necessary relation with the outside world was with the government which provided the life-sustaining waters and took away the surplus product. Marx summed up:

> These two circumstances — the Hindoo, on the one hand, leaving, like all Oriental peoples, to the Central Government the care of the great public works, the prime condition of his agriculture and commerce, dispersed, on the other hand, over the surface of the country, and agglomerated in small centers by the domestic union of agricultural and manufacturing pursuits — these two circumstances had brought about, since the remotest times, a social system of particular features — the so-called *village system*, which gave to each of these small unions their independent organization and distinct life.[3]

It was precisely this primitive independence that gave the Indian community its phenomenal resilience, surviving all manner of conquests and civil wars, famines and pestilence, to provide ever again "the solid foundation of Oriental despotism." "Indian society has no history at all," Marx added in a later article. "What we call its history, is but the history of the successive intruders who founded their empires on the passive basis of that unresisting and unchanging society."[4] Among those conquerors only the last, the British, remained unsated by the usual forms of tribute; they insisted as well on transforming the villagers into customers. Cheap factory-produced textiles supplanted homespun goods, ruining village industries, impoverishing masses of people, and after so many millennia "thus produced the greatest, and, to speak the truth, the only *social* revolution ever heard of in Asia." Toward this revolutionizing process Marx made his own position totally unambiguous: however attractive in some respects these ancient communal villages might appear, their disappearance was an absolute precondition for social advance; however sordid the motives of the East India Company magnates might be — for essentially they were requesting Parliament to renew their "privilege of plundering India for the space of 20 years" — nonetheless they were acting as the unwitting instruments of history.[5] Thus Marx concluded his article:

> Now, sickening as it must be to human feeling to witness those myriads of industrious patriarchal and inoffensive social organizations disorganized and dissolved into their units, . . . we must not forget that these idyllic village-communities, inoffensive though they may appear, had always been the solid foundation of Oriental despotism, that they restrained the human mind within the smallest possible compass, making it the unresisting tool of superstition. . . . We must not forget that this undignified, stagnatory, and vegetative life, that this passive sort of existence evoked on the other part, in contradistinction, wild, aimless, unbounded forces of destruction and rendered murder itself a religious rite in Hindostan. We must not forget that these little communities were contaminated by distinctions of caste and by slavery, that they subjugated man to external circumstances instead of elevating man [to be] the sovereign of circumstances, that they transformed a self-developing social state into never changing natural destiny, and thus brought about a brutalizing worship of nature, exhibiting its degradation in the fact that man, the sovereign of nature, fell down on his knees in adoration of Kanuman, the monkey, and Sabbala, the cow.
>
> England, it is true, in causing a social revolution in Hindostan, was actuated only by the vilest interests, and was stupid in her manner of enforcing them. But that is not the question. The question is, can mankind fulfil its destiny without a fundamental revolution in the social state of Asia? If not, whatever may have been the crimes of England she was the unconscious tool of history in bringing about that revolution.[6]

From all this it becomes plain that Marx regarded the traditional "Asiatic mode of production" not as one of several steps on a universal ladder of social advance (suggested by his well-known 1859 listing of "the Asiatic, the ancient, the feudal and the modern bourgeois modes of production"), but rather as an early sidetrack in social evolution, a path once taken which stunts further growth, transforming "a self-developing social state into never changing natural destiny." Without any built-in motor for change, Asian societies seem fated to vegetate in this "stagnatory" sort of existence until at length they fall victim to the external forces of capitalist expansion. Nowhere did Marx, or Engels, suggest that any Asian society had evolved, or could evolve spontaneously, into a more advanced social form. Nowhere did they suggest that the slaveowning civilizations of Greece and Rome had evolved from a prior "Asiatic" stage.[7] Fresh evidence from the now famous *Grundrisse* of 1857–1858 confirms this view of Asian society beyond reasonable doubt. The *Grundrisse* was essentially Marx's first attempt to write *Capital*, a rough and difficult manuscript that was never published until 1939 and not fully appreciated or used as a source until the last decade or so. Here Marx alluded to an original condition of man in which he "appears as a *generic being, a tribal being, a herd animal*," organized in small separate tribal communities. From this original condition, however, communities might develop in different ways, depending on "various external, climatic, geographical, physical, etc., conditions as well as on their special natural make-up—their tribal character." Marx proceeded briefly to describe three possible paths of evolution: the Oriental, the ancient Greek and Roman, and the Germanic—all proceeding directly from the original tribal community rather than from each other in any temporal sequence. Further, the Germanic path appears to lead straight to feudalism without any prior slaveowning stage, all of which suggests a much more flexible and open-ended conception of historical development than Marx was traditionally thought to have espoused. In any event, among the three, Marx declared "the Asiatic form necessarily survives longest and most stubbornly," due to a "unity of agriculture and craft manufacture" in which "the circle of production is self-sustaining," and "the individual does not become independent of the community."[8]

Such a view surely does injustice to the variety and evolution of Asian societies, and just as surely must offend the ethnic sensibilities of Asian Marxists, who have tended to ignore the masters' writings on the Asiatic mode of production and Oriental despotism. This disregard, to be sure, was mightily encouraged in 1931 when Stalin had the entire theory of Oriental despotism banned as "Trotskyist" on the demonstrably false claim that Marx and Engels themselves had abandoned it. Stalin's motives were complicated, no doubt, but among them seemingly must have been the feeling that it was un-Marxist to acknowledge the concept of a state manifestly not controlled by a possessing class, a state which owned the means of production itself and exploited the masses directly. In such a concept, according to Karl Wittfogel, Stalin saw too many awkward similarities to his own despotic regime.[9] In any event, we must now turn to Marx and Engels' writings on this characteristic political excrescence of Asian society, and see how Oriental despotism fits into the broader idea of the parasite state.

Nothing Marx and Engels found in their sources on Asia suggested the dominance of a possessing class in the Western sense. One could find wealthy royal tax-gatherers but no authentic nobility such as in feudal Europe; one could find a vast village peasantry but no urban communities of citizen-slaveowners such as in classical antiquity. Indeed, one could find no cities at all in the European sense, as Marx noted in his initial letter to Engels. Bernier had explained the enormous size of Oriental armies by remarking that, in addition to actual fighting men, they included all manner of "porters, foragers, provisioners, merchants of all kinds and servitors whom these armies carry in their wake." Marx quoted further from Bernier's account, which called attention to "the particular condition and government of the country, namely that the *king is the one and only proprietor of all the land* in the kingdom, from which it follows as a necessary consequence that a whole *capital city* like Delhi or Agra lives almost entirely on the army and is therefore obliged to follow the king if he takes the field for any length of time. For these towns neither are nor can be anything like a Paris, *being virtually nothing but military camps.*"[10] A king who owns all the land, a capital city that is nothing but a military camp, a governing apparatus that periodically transforms itself into a horde of foraging locusts — here we find the makings of a parasite state par excellence.

Unlike the transitory parasite states of modern Europe, however, called forth by a temporary stalemate in the evolving class struggle, Oriental despotisms were age-old and rested upon an undifferentiated village society that had only barely emerged from primitive communism. Typically the village lands were still regarded as a communal possession, held in common from the crown. In this sense Engels could remark that "Oriental despotism was founded on common property" (thus constituting a major exception to the rule that the state emerges in concert with private property), which did not prevent him from asserting that it was also "the cruelest form of state."[11] For the system made the despot both sovereign and landlord, merging taxes and ground rents in an irresistible mechanism for extortion. As Marx explained in volume 3 of *Capital:*

> Should the direct producers not be confronted by a private landowner, but rather, as in Asia, under direct subordination to a state which stands over them as their landlord and simultaneously as sovereign, then rent and taxes coincide, or rather, there exists no tax which differs from this form of ground-rent. Under such circumstances, there need exist no stronger political or economic pressure than that common to all subjection to that state. The state is then the supreme lord. Sovereignty here consists in the ownership of land concentrated on a national scale.[12]

Earlier in the passage Marx described this link between the state and the villagers as a "tributary relationship." It is true he once also referred to "the general slavery of the Orient," but it seems likely he used the latter term in the same metaphoric sense as he used "wage-slavery," for in his more careful formulations he employed "tributary relationship," distinguishing it carefully from real chattel slavery as well as from serfdom. Thus he wrote in an earlier chapter:

> Under the slave relationship, serf relationship, tributary relationship (insofar as primitive communities are concerned), it is the slaveholder, the feudal lord, the tribute-collecting state that is the owner and hence the seller of the product.[13]

Here Oriental despotism appears as the "tribute-collecting state," owner of the (surplus) product, whose relationship to the exploited is functionally parallel to that of the slaveholders and feudal lords of the Western experience.

Communal possession of village land was only the most typical form and not a necessary condition of Oriental despotism, for both Marx and Engels came to recognize that common ownership no longer survived in China.[14] Even without it Oriental despotism rested solidly enough on the two prime supports Marx had singled out in his original article: state control of a centralized irrigation system, which he called "one of the material bases of the power of the State over the small disconnected producing mechanisms," combined with a civil society composed precisely of "small self-sufficient and disconnected villages." The former insured the revenues of the state, since it could cut off the life-sustaining water; the latter insured the ineffectiveness of any opposition, since the villages were too weak to resist singly, too isolated to join their forces. And their primitive self-sufficiency insured that they would not develop further from within, generating the social forces that might be capable of breaking the despotic power. Even outside conquerors were able to establish and maintain their rule easily "on the passive basis of that unresisting and unchanging society."[15] Marx summed it up in *Capital:*

> The simplicity of the organization for production in these self-sufficing communities that constantly reproduce themselves in the same form, and when accidently destroyed, spring up again on the same spot and with the same name — this simplicity supplies the key to the secret of the unchangeableness of Asiatic societies, and unchangeableness in such striking contrast with the constant dissolution and refounding of Asiatic States, and the never-ceasing changes of dynasty. The structure of the economic elements of society remains untouched by the storm-clouds of the political sky.[16]

Karl Wittfogel has chided Marx severely for failing to acknowledge that under Oriental despotism the bureaucracy (both civil and military) constituted the ruling class. While Marx never wrote those exact words, it is difficult to imagine he would have disagreed with the substantive point involved. Certainly he never thought a despotic power could consist of just one person. As he said of Prussia in 1849, "the *existence* of the state power is embodied precisely in its *officials*, the army, the administration and the courts. Apart from this, its physical embodiment, it is but a shadow, an idea, a name."[17] In *Theories of Surplus Value*, he described all three precapitalist forms of exploitation — slavery, serfdom, and the tributary relationship (here labeled "political dependency relationship") — as being based on "the forcible rule of one section [*Teil*] of society over another."[18] Whether the dominant "section" of Oriental society, its civil and military officialdom, should be called a class, as Wittfogel would prefer, or a "caste" as Marx once called the astronomer-priests who directed agriculture in ancient Egypt, or a "Celestial bureaucracy" as he once described the mandarin elite of traditional China, it remained at all events an exploitative minority which pumped surplus value out of the mass of direct producers by means of its effective control over the means of production.[19] As we will see later in connection with modern bureaucracies, neither Marx nor Engels seemed very concerned about how to label state officials as a group.

Another question Marx and Engels never addressed specifically was how Oriental despotism emerged as a state in the first place, especially since it emerged in the absence of private property. But if we combine what we have seen in *Anti-Dühring* with some very interesting remarks in the *Grundrisse*, a fairly clear picture nonetheless takes shape. In *Anti-Dühring*, it will be remembered, Engels' first model of state formation was not expressly linked to the emergence of private property but involved a process of institutionalization through which delegations of office gradually became hereditary and elected public servants transformed themselves into haughty masters. He cited the "Oriental despot" first among his examples and added that "finally the individual rulers united into a ruling class." Here, incidentally, he employed the phrase "ruling class" in a very broad sense to be sure, but one evidently intended to include local Oriental potentates who had banded together as a group.[20] At several points in the *Grundrisse* Marx offered reflections on what separated the Oriental path of development from the Western. "Ancient classical history," he observed, "is the history of cities, but cities based on land-ownership and agriculture; Asian history is a kind of undifferentiated unity of town and country (the large city, properly speaking, must be regarded merely as a princely camp, superimposed on the real economic structure)." Early Western development he asserted to be "the product of a more dynamic [*bewegten*] historical life," and its organization in city-states he linked primarily to military endeavors:

> War is therefore the great all-embracing task, the great communal labor, and it is required either for the occupation of the objective conditions for living existence or for the protection and perpetuation of such occupation. The community, consisting of kinship groups, is therefore in the first instance organized on military lines, as a warlike, military force. . . . Concentration of settlement in the city is the foundation of this warlike organization. The nature of tribal structure leads to the differentiation of kinship groups into higher and lower, and this social differentiation is developed further by the mixing of conquering and conquered tribes, etc.

He went on to speak of the emergence of unequally distributed private property in land and slaves, both of which presumably led—though he did not say so here in so many words—to the development of instrumentalities for internal coercion, the class state of the citizen-slaveowners of Greece and Rome.[21]

By contrast, the original Asian tribal communities appear, at least by negative inference, to have been less "dynamic," to have failed to organize themselves adequately for self-defense by concentrating their settlements in the form of sizeable city-states. Thus their village level of existence not only stunted the possibilities of economic development but also left them militarily helpless. Add to this the climatic factor necessitating large-scale irrigation and we have once again the basic ingredients leading to Oriental despotism: "irrigation systems (very important among the Asian peoples), means of communication, etc., will then appear as the work of the higher unity — the despotic government which is poised above the lesser communities." Marx ventured no further to explain how the "higher unity" organized itself in the first place, but he did offer the following reflections:

> The despot here appears as the father of all the numerous lesser communities, thus realising the common unity of all. It therefore follows that the surplus product . . . belongs to this highest unity. Oriental despotism therefore appears to lead to a legal absence of property. In fact, however, its foundation is tribal or common property, in most cases created through a combination of manufacture and agriculture within the small community which thus becomes entirely self-sustaining and contains within itself all conditions of production and surplus production.
>
> Part of its surplus labor belongs to the higher community, which ultimately appears as a *person*. This surplus labor is rendered both as tribute and as common labor for the glory of the unity, in part that of the despot, in part that of the imagined tribal entity of the god.[22]

In speaking of a "higher unity," Marx seems here to have reverted to the Hegelian terminology of his youth in order to suggest an institution whose content and function changed over time. If it "ultimately" appears as a person, a despot, Marx must have conceived it to have had a prior existence in another form, perhaps as a tribal council or a delegation of office such as Engels postulated in *Anti-Dühring*. Such public servants might then have made their positions hereditary and coalesced together to form the ruling hierarchy of Asian societies. But of course Marx did not say all this directly and indeed seemed generally indifferent to the institutional details of Oriental despotism.

This seeming indifference has itself excited a measure of scholarly interest, as we have already noted in Wittfogel's complaint. "Obviously the concept of Oriental despotism contained elements that paralyzed his search for the truth," Wittfogel declares, building up to his main point, which is that "Marx could scarcely help recognizing some disturbing similarities between Oriental despotism" and the "total managerial and dictatorial state" he himself wanted to see established.[23] Wittfogel judges Marx's intentions, of course, with the hindsight of Soviet and Chinese experience. But Marx never imagined, as we will see later, that the future socialist state and economy would be run by a hierarchy of professional bureaucrats and managers, and so had no reason whatsoever to perceive any "disturbing similarities" with Oriental despotism. In fact, the only feature of Asian society that genuinely excited Marx and Engels was the communal possession of land, which helped confirm their theories of primitive society and of the transitory career of private property as an institution. Here was massive living proof that private property was not ubiquitous throughout human civilization, as Victorian respectability supposed. Otherwise, they found traditional Asian society profoundly boring. For them, history was the unfolding of man's dormant powers, his emerging mastery over the brute forces of nature, over his own institutions and destiny. That is why, in their somewhat limited and Eurocentric perspective, traditional Asia had no history. Its sleepy village culture contained no internal dynamo for change as in the West, and its bureaucratic potentates were equally boring, whether one considered them a ruling class or not.

European Absolutism

A surprisingly large literature has been written about Marx and Engels' theory of Oriental despotism, all based necessarily on the handful of pertinent texts we examined in the last section. Scarcely anything has been written about their views on European absolutism, even though the original sources are considerably more plentiful.[24] To be sure, the two men never saw fit to address the topic systematically; they never claimed to have a "theory" of absolutism. But then, they never claimed to have a theory of Oriental despotism either, or of Bonapartism for that matter — it was later writers who elevated the masters' remarks to the status of theories. In any event, because of the belated survival of absolutism during their own lifetimes in Prussia, Austria, and Russia, their comments on it extend well beyond their historical writings. By putting these scattered remarks together, one can reconstruct Marx and Engels' views on the subject and, if one likes, dignify such a reconstruction as the "Marxist theory of absolutism."

Marx's initial concept of the state, it will be recalled, rested empirically on his experience with Prussian absolutism, and in this sense absolutism was the model for the parasite state in all its forms. It was in fact the only form of the parasite state recognized in *The German Ideology*, where Marx and Engels joined their two theories of the state together. Declaring the fully developed modern state to be "nothing more than the form of organization which the bourgeois are compelled to adopt, both for internal and external purposes, for the mutual guarantee of their property and interests," the two men immediately added the following qualification: "The independence of the state is only found nowadays in those countries where the estates have not yet completely developed into classes, where the estates, done away with in more advanced countries, still play a part and there exists a mixture, where consequently no section of the population can achieve dominance over the others. This is the case particularly in Germany." Somewhat later they developed the idea further: "During the epoch of absolute monarchy, . . . the special sphere which, owing to division of labor, was responsible for the administration of public interests acquired an abnormal independence, which became still greater in the bureaucracy of modern times. Thus, the state built itself up into an apparently independent force, and this position, which in other countries was only transitory — a transition stage — it has maintained in Germany until the present day." To reconcile the simple "independence" of the state in the first passage with its "apparently independent" character in the second is a task we will confront later; it is reminiscent of the dichotomy examined in the foregoing chapter.[25]

By 1847 both men had developed these ideas into their mature form by linking the phenomenon specifically to a temporarily stalemated class struggle between nobility and bourgeoisie. As Marx expressed it, "*absolute monarchy* appears in those transitional periods when the old feudal estates are in decline and the medieval estate of burghers is evolving into the modern bourgeois class, without one of the contending parties having as yet finally disposed of the other." Engels' version added some details with reference to Prussia in particular:

> The nobility had lost too much of its former strength, wealth and influence, to dominate the king as formerly it had done. The middle classes were not yet strong enough to overcome the dead weight of

the nobility, which cramped their commercial and industrial progress. Thus the king, representing the central power of the state, and
supported by the numerous class of government officers, civil and
military, besides having the army at his disposal, was enabled to
keep down the middle classes by the nobility, and the nobility by
the middle classes, by flattering now the interests of the one, and
then those of the other; and balancing, as much as possible, the influence of both.[26]

Many years later Engels came back to the subject more systematically
as he attempted a general history of Reformation Germany. We may pass
over his long discussion of the reasons for the rise of the middle class and
the decline of the nobility. With respect to the latter he pointed to the
perpetually accumulating tangle of incompatible claims and obligations
among European feudal lords generally, in a society where each lord was
likely to possess his own private cavalry:

> How could conflicts be avoided? Hence that century-long alterna-
> tion of the vassals' attraction to the royal center, which alone could
> protect them against external foes and against each other, and of
> their repulsion from that center, into which that attraction in-
> evitably and perpetually changed; hence that continuous struggle
> between royalty and vassals, whose tedious uproar drowned out
> everything else.

During the same period the rising middle class also, and somewhat more
consistently, turned to the central power for help in advancing their
own interests:

> It is plain that in this general chaos royal power was the progres-
> sive element. It represented order in confusion, and the budding
> nation as opposed to dismemberment into rebellious vassal states.
> All the revolutionary elements taking shape under the feudalistic
> surface gravitated just as much towards royalty as the latter gravi-
> tated towards them. The alliance of royalty and burgherdom dates
> back to the tenth century. Often interrupted by conflicts, because
> nothing pursued its course consistently in the Middle Ages, it was
> each time more firmly and vigorously renewed, until it helped roy-
> alty to its final victory [over the nobility], and royalty, by way of
> thanks, subjugated and plundered its ally.

Engels left no doubt here that royal absolutism, rather than either of the contending classes, won the decisive victory in this three-way contest.

Warming to his subject, Engels went on to speak of concurrent military developments that also abetted the consolidation of royal power. During the middle ages the nobility was not only the possessing class, but also as knights constituted the warrior class, enjoying an effective "monopoly on the bearing of arms." One reason for the relative weakness of medieval kings was the unavailability of any military force other than the knightly cavalry formed by calling up their vassals and their vassals' vassals, and so forth. Not surprisingly such monarchs found it difficult to combat the perpetual contumacy of the nobility

> with an army that was itself feudal, in which the soldiers were bound more closely to their immediate liegelords than to the royal army command. It was a vicious circle in which no headway could be made. From the beginning of the fourteenth century onward the kings strove to emancipate themselves from this feudal army, to create their own army. From this time on we find in the royal armies an increasing portion of enlisted or hired troops.

It was the monarchs' good fortune to find such footsoldiers for hire among the burghers and free peasants who, especially in Flanders and Switzerland, had taken up pikes, halberds, and eventually muskets, and themselves begun to challenge the noble monopoly over the means of violence. By the later fifteenth century the tide of warfare had turned: "In the triumphs of the Swiss over the Austrians, and particularly over the Burgundians, armored cavalry — whether mounted or dismounted — succumbed finally to footsoldiers, the feudal army to the budding modern army, the knight to the burgher and free peasant." By hiring such footsoldiers as a mercenary force, later by recruiting them for long-term service in a standing army, the monarchs of early modern Europe were able to break the independence of the nobility and secure to themselves a monopoly over the means of violence.[27] That monopoly, Engels seemed to be saying, sufficed to insure their dominance over all the classes of civil society, granted of course the temporary equilibrium between nobility and bourgeoisie as the primordial condition.

If one augments the repressive power of the new armies with the organizing power of the new bureaucracies, the formula for European absolutism would be complete. Marx alluded to this latter aspect when he wrote: "The seignorial privileges of the landowners and towns became

transformed into so many attributes of the state power, the feudal dignitaries into paid officials and the motley pattern of conflicting medieval
plenary powers the regulated plan of a state authority whose work is
divided and centralized as in a factory."[28] Thus the administrative and
judicial functions of the old nobility were usurped along with their military functions. All this did not mean, to be sure, that the absolute monarchs could afford totally to ignore aristocratic interests thereafter, any
more than they could be totally indifferent to bourgeois interests. In
a letter to Kautsky, Engels explained how he perceived the three-way
relationship:

> Absolute monarchy came into existence as a naturally evolved com-
> promise between nobility and bourgeoisie and . . . it therefore
> had to protect certain interests of both sides and distribute favors to
> them. In this process the nobility — politically put in retirement —
> got as its share the plundering of the peasantry and of the state trea-
> sury and indirect political influence through the court, the army,
> the church and the higher administrative authorities, while the
> bourgeoisie received protection through tariffs, monopolies and a
> *relatively* orderly administration of public affairs and justice.[29]

Engels recognized that the property rights enforced by absolute monarchy
guaranteed the nobility in its continued "plundering of the peasantry."
He recognized an "indirect political influence" the nobility was able to
exert through the holding of high state offices. Nonetheless, he did not
present absolutism, here or elsewhere, as the "indirect" or "disguised" class
rule of the nobility. To receive "favors" after having been "politically put
in retirement" — these are scarcely the attributes of a ruling class. In a
similar vein with respect to Russian absolutism Marx posed a sharp rhetorical question as he described an assembly of notables to be called in
1858 to discuss the fate of serfdom: "What if the nobles should insist upon
their own political emancipation as a condition preliminary to any concession to be made to the Czar with respect to the emancipation of their
serfs?"[30] Surely no authentic ruling class needs to insist on its own political emancipation.

The eventual downfall of absolutism in Western Europe was to come
when the further development of the bourgeoisie eventually destroyed
the class equilibrium upon which it rested. As Engels put it, "From the
moment when the bourgeoisie, still politically powerless, began to grow
dangerous owing to its increasing economic power, the Crown resumed

its alliance with the nobility, and by so doing called forth the bourgeois revolution, first in England and then in France." In 1847 Marx was clearly expecting the same outcome in Prussia:

> The absolute monarchy in Prussia, as earlier in England and France, will not let itself be amicably changed into a bourgeois monarchy. It will not abdicate amicably. The princes' hands are tied both by their personal prejudices and by a whole bureaucracy of officials, soldiers and clerics — integral parts of absolute monarchy who are far from willing to exchange their ruling position for a subservient one in respect of the bourgeoisie. Then the feudal estates also hold back; for them it is a question of life or death, in other words, of property or expropriation. It is clear that the absolute monarch . . . sees his true interest on the side of these estates.[31]

Like his partner Marx presented absolute monarchy as an autonomous force with vested institutional interests of its own to defend. Even in its final alliance with the nobility it acted as an independent power and not as the mere instrument of aristocratic interests.

While the unresolved conflict between nobility and bourgeoisie was the fundamental condition giving rise to absolutism, Marx and Engels also made allowance for variations according to local circumstances. In the Austrian Empire, for example, ethnic antagonisms greatly complicated the interplay of social forces but allowed a master juggler like Metternich to ride atop the confusion, playing off ethnic groups as well as classes, one against another. Engels wrote in 1849:

> In this state of affairs, Metternich achieved his master stroke. With the exception of the most powerful feudal barons, he deprived the nobility of all influence on state administration. He sapped the strength of the bourgeoisie by winning to his side the most powerful financial barons — he had to do this, the state of the finances made it compulsory for him. Supported in this way by the top feudal and financial aristocracy, as well as by the bureaucracy and the army, he far more than all his rivals attained the ideal of an absolute monarchy. He kept the burghers and the peasantry of each nation under control by means of the aristocracy of that nation and the peasantry of every other nation, and he kept the aristocracy of each nation under control by its fear of that nation's burghers and peasantry. The different class interests, the national features of narrowminded-

ness, and local prejudices, despite their complexity, were completely held in check by their mutual conteraction and allowed the old scoundrel Metternich the utmost freedom to manoeuvre.

In a later article Engels similarly characterized Metternich's government as having "full independence of action."[32]

In an 1854 series of articles on "Revolutionary Spain," Marx drew some very interesting parallels between its absolutist period and Oriental despotism. Spanish absolutism began typically enough under the Hapsburg, Charles I, who crushed all resistance in 1521: "It was, above all, the bitter antagonism between the classes of the nobles and the citizens of the towns which Charles employed for the degradation of both." But Marx saw a paradox which helped to explain Spain's early economic decline: "In the very country where of all the feudal states absolute monarchy first arose in its most unmitigated form, centralization has never succeeded in taking root." Without a uniform system of law, of money, of weights and measures, and so forth, a modern bourgeois economy could not really take off. "While the aristocracy sunk into degradation without losing their worst privilege, the towns lost their medieval power without gaining modern importance." Marx then continued:

> While the absolute monarchy found in Spain material in its very nature repulsive to centralization, it did all in its power to prevent the growth of common interests arising out of a national division of labor and the multiplicity of internal exchanges—the very basis on which alone a uniform system of administration and the rule of general laws can be created. Thus the absolute monarchy in Spain, bearing but a superficial resemblance to the absolute monarchies of Europe in general, is rather to be ranged in a class with Asiatic forms of government. Spain, like Turkey, remained an agglomeration of mismanaged republics with a nominal sovereign at their head. . . . Despotic as was the government it did not prevent the provinces from subsisting with different laws and customs, different coins, military banners of different colors, and with their respective systems of taxation.

Intense localism, then, may help to sustain absolutism in Europe, even as a parallel symbiosis of localism and despotism forms the central pillar of the Oriental political system.[33]

This symbiosis was even more evident in Russian absolutism, where the link to Oriental despotism was much more direct. For in that "semi-Asiatic" country, absolute monarchy emerged, not out of a stalemated conflict between nobles and bourgeois, but much earlier, out of primitive isolated village communities holding their land in common — just as in Asia. Engels explained in an 1875 article:

> Such a complete isolation of the individual communities from one another, which creates throughout the country similar, but the very opposite of common, interests, is the natural basis for *oriental despotism*, and from India to Russia this form of society, wherever it prevailed, has always produced it and always found its complement in it. Not only the Russian state in general, but even its specific form, tsarist despotism, instead of hanging in the air, is the necessary and logical product of Russian social conditions.[34]

If Russia was semi-Asiatic, it was also semi-European in its development beyond the communal village organization of society to produce a landowning boyar aristocracy and, for a time in the middle ages, also a flourishing commercial economy in Kiev and other cities. The traditions of despotism survived, however, partly in the regimes of the native princes, partly in the overlordship of Russia's numerous conquerors, especially in the cruel domination of the Tatars, which lasted for more than two centuries until the dawn of modern times. The communal villages likewise survived as the natural basis of such despotism.

Modern Russian absolutism, constructed in Muscovy largely by Ivan the Terrible in the sixteenth century, resembled only in part the state-building practices of the contemporaneous West European monarchs, for in Russia a dynamic commercial economy and a vital middle class no longer existed. The modernizing efforts of Russian rulers appeared, not so much as concessions or favors to an assertive bourgeoisie, but more as self-interested attempts by the crown to hold its own in an international struggle with more advanced powers. "Russia finds itself in a modern historical environment," Marx observed in 1881, "it is contemporaneous with a superior civilization."[35] To be a match for the more advanced powers of the West, if only in the military sphere, the czars were repeatedly obliged to modernize their state. In the sixteenth century Ivan the Terrible established trade with England and even requested military experts from Queen Elizabeth. In the eighteenth century Peter the Great embarked on a far more serious "Westernization" which obliged him, as Marx commented, "to *civilize* Russia":

In grasping upon the Baltic provinces, he seized at once the tools necessary for this process. They afforded him not only the diplomatists and the generals, the brains with which to execute his system of political and military action on the west, they yielded him, at the same time, a crop of bureaucrats, schoolmasters, and drill-sergeants, who were to drill Russians into that varnish of civilization that adapts them to the technical appliances of the Western peoples, without imbuing them with their ideas.[36]

By the mid-nineteenth century Russia experienced the most far-reaching state-sponsored modernization of all, evoked by her collapse in the Crimean War. That war proved, as Engels put it, "that Russia needed railroads and heavy industry, if only for purely military considerations. *Consequently the government set about breeding a Russian capitalist class*" (italics added).[37] He expanded upon this remarkable idea in a later article, beginning again from the purely military need for a "strategic network of railways":

> But railroads mean capitalistic industry and a revolutionizing of the primitive system of agriculture. On the one hand the agricultural products of even the remotest regions came into direct communication with the world market; on the other hand an extended railway system cannot be built and maintained without domestic industry which produces rails, locomotives, cars, etc. But one branch of large-scale industry cannot be introduced without taking into the bargain the entire system. . . . The expansion of existing banks and the founding of new ones was bound up with the railroads and factories. The setting free of the peasants from bonded serfdom created mobility, in expectation of what soon followed naturally: the setting free of a great part of these peasants from ownership of land. Thus in a short time all foundations of the capitalistic mode of production were laid in Russia.[38]

Far from owing its position to a stalemated class struggle, czarist absolutism prospered well enough (nourished by its roots in the isolated communal villages of the Russian countryside) without any bourgeoisie around, until at length it created such a class, incidentally as it were, while pursuing its own institutional needs in the international sphere. There is perhaps no more striking example than this of the autonomous power and freedom from class control which Marx and Engels ascribed to the parasite state. Classes that establish states to serve their needs are familiar enough in the Marxist tradition; states that create classes are rather more remarkable, and ought to give pause to those who interpret Marx and Engels' ideas as a unilateral economic determinism in which class interests are the only motive forces.

If under absolutism the state ruled in its own name, then did Marx and Engels regard its officials as the real ruling class? The question does not have an easy answer. On the one hand, they certainly did not believe absolutist government to be the work of the monarch alone. As noted in relation to Oriental despotism, Marx had declared in 1849, "the *existence* of state power is embodied precisely in its *officials*, the army, the administration and the courts. Apart from this, its physical embodiment, it is but a shadow, an idea, a name." The formula for Prussian state power in particular he summed up in the troika, "the Crown by the grace of God, the bullying bureaucracy, the independent army." Engels similarly spoke of the Prussian king as "representing the central power of the state, and supported by a numerous class of government officers, civil and military, besides having an army at his disposal."[39] In fact both men seem to have judged that, under normal circumstances, officialdom controlled the monarch rather than vice versa. We have already scrutinized Marx's 1847 assertion that "the princes' hands are tied" not only by personal prejudices but "by a whole bureaucracy of officials, soldiers and clerics — integral parts of absolute monarchy." He would later describe how Frederick William IV's sentimental efforts to recreate medieval institutions in Prussia ran aground on the intractable needs of the bureaucratic state: "the romantic King himself, was, after all, like all his predecessors, but the visible hand of a common-place bureaucratic Government which he tried in vain to embellish with the fine sentiments of by-gone ages."[40]

If Marx and Engels were unambiguous in asserting the *rule* of officialdom during the absolutist period, on the other hand they were not consistent in designating it as a *class*. Engels certainly did so on occasion, as in his "numerous class of government officials," just cited, or when he referred more deliberately to "the formation of a separate class of administrative government officials, in whose hands the chief power is concentrated, and which stands in opposition against all other classes."[41] More frequently, however, the two men referred to state officials as a "caste," on one occasion specifically contrasting the two terms: Prussia's rural *Landräte*, Marx declared in 1858, are hybrid notables, half bureaucrat and half landed aristocrat, but generally "their interests are more strictly bound up with the class and party interests of the landed aristocracy than with the caste interests of the Bureaucracy."[42] Since the time of the Enlightenment the word "caste" had been used as a term of abuse in conjunction with the institutions of the old regime based generally on the hereditary principle. In that same loose and pejorative sense Marx and Engels must have chosen the word, for they surely understood that the absolutist bureaucracy was not a literal caste. Indeed, they showed a pervasive indifference to terminological precision in this matter, sometimes also labeling officials as an "estate" (*Stand*), or even a "race of their own." Draper has argued — with an impressive number of examples — that the masters used all these terms interchangeably and thus with no serious intent to differentiate "class" from "caste," and so forth.[43]

It seems unlikely therefore that Marx and Engels would have objected to the "ruling class" characterization, except perhaps to point out that, unlike other classes, the bureaucracy was not an integral part of civil society, and that European bureaucracies, unlike their Oriental counterparts, could not be said to own or control the means of production. Because property was in the hands of powerful social classes — the nobility and the bourgeoisie — rather than in the hands of the state as such, European absolutism was bound to be weaker and more ephemeral than Oriental despotism. It ruled through its military and administrative power alone, but only so long as it could play off one class against the other during their temporary equilibrium. Thus the system depended on an intricate configuration of social forces and, as Engels insisted, was not just "hanging in the air." Even as czarist despotism was "the necessary and logical product of Russian social conditions" without being the instrument of any possessing class, so — to return finally to the dangling contradiction of *The German Ideology* — all absolutist states were only "apparently independent" of the society that produced them, while showing genuine "independence" from class control in a situation where "no section of the population can achieve dominance over the others."

Bonapartism

Of the three forms of the parasite state, Bonapartism was the one to receive the most systematic attention from Marx and Engels, particularly in the former's masterful *The Eighteenth Brumaire of Louis Bonaparte* (1852). Their conception of Bonapartism will serve nicely to round out our understanding of the differences they perceived among parasite states, and, more importantly, between parasite states and class states. The theory of Bonapartism is also regarded by many present-day writers as offering useful insights into the political trends of the twentieth century.[44]

To start with, it must be recognized that the theory of Bonapartism applied to the second Napoleon rather than the first. Admittedly, Engels included the uncle to create the neat symmetry we encountered in *The Origin of the Family*, where absolutism was tied to a balance between nobility and bourgeoisie, and the Bonapartism of *both* Napoleons to a parallel balance between bourgeoisie and proletariat.[45] In no other writing do we find the uncle linked to such a balance, or to the proletariat at all. In fact he seems generally slighted as a subject when one considers the lifelong interest both men exhibited in the history of the French Revolution. The most sustained comment Marx ever managed—one paragraph—appeared in *The Holy Family* (1845), where the Kreuznach dichotomy between the state and civil society still provided the theoretical frame:

> Napoleon, of course, already discerned the essence of the *modern state;* he understood that it is based on the unhampered development of bourgeois [civil] society, on the free movement of private interest, etc. He decided to recognize and protect this basis. He was no terrorist with his head in the clouds. Yet at the same time he still regarded the *state* as an *end in itself* and civil life only as a treasurer and his *subordinate* which must have no *will of its own.* . . . [He showed no] consideration for its essential *material* interests, trade and industry, whenever they conflicted with his political interests.[46]

Here we recognize the parasite state easily enough, autonomous and self-interested, but not resting on any equilibrium of class forces—the proletariat is nowhere mentioned. More surprisingly perhaps, in Engels' early writings Napoleon also figured as an independent power, mainly as the modernizing conqueror who deserved thanks for "flushing out the great Augean stable" of medieval institutions in Germany, thereby laying the basis for the emergence of the bourgeoisie. Indeed, in one 1847 article Engels went so far as to proclaim that "the creator of the German bourgeoisie was Napoleon"—the second case we have encountered where Engels ascribed to a despot the creation of an entire social class.[47] As with Marx there was no mention of any class equilibrium or of the proletariat at all, which would seem reasonable enough on empirical grounds since neither Germany nor France at the beginning of the nineteenth century possessed a modern proletariat large enough to contend for power, but which also would seem to leave the First Empire hanging just a bit in midair. Even after the theory of Bonapartism was elaborated in 1852 to explain the rule of Napoleon III, the first Napoleon was not automatically subsumed under it, at least until *The Origin of the Family*. In *The Eighteenth Brumaire*, Marx alluded in passing to the uncle's accomplishments: he "created inside France the conditions under which free competition could first be developed"; "beyond the French borders he everywhere swept the feudal institutions away"; and he "perfected" the "state machinery" he had inherited from absolutism and the first revolution. Still, Marx continued, under all these regimes "bureaucracy was only the means of preparing the class rule of the bourgeoisie" which came to fruition after 1815, while under Napoleon III bureaucracy was to become an end in itself.[48] On a broader historical canvas, Marx generalized in *The Civil War in France* (1871) that "Imperialism [here used to refer specifically to the two Napoleonic empires] is, at the same time, the most prostitute and the ultimate form of the State power which nascent middle-class society had commenced to elaborate as a means of its own emancipation from feudalism [Napoleon I] and which full-grown bourgeois society had finally transformed into a means for the enslavement of labor by capital [Napoleon III]."[49] In general the first Napoleon seems to have posed somewhat of a theoretical puzzle for Marx and Engels. He appears repeatedly in their writings neither as an instrument of class rule nor as the holder of a balance between contending classes, but rather in an almost metaphysical fashion as history's means of preparing for the class rule of the bourgeoisie.

Thus Marx's theory of Bonapartism endeavored to explain the second rather than the first Napoleon, and received its classic exposition in *The Eighteenth Brumaire*, which Marx began to write in December 1851, immediately following Louis Napoleon's coup d'état, and finished the following March. Many authorities on Marx, convinced that every state must represent some social class, have tried to interpret Marx's essay to mean that the French bourgeoisie still managed to rule indirectly under Napoleon, or alternatively that his rule marked the ascendency of the peasantry.[50] By choosing quotations carefully, a case can be made for either of these views, although with the same technique an even stronger case can be made for the ascendency of the lumpen proletariat. To be sure, Marx insisted strongly that the Bonapartist state was "not suspended in mid air." It was *related* to all these classes, and to the proletariat as well, but it was not related to any of them as servant to master. Insofar as Napoleon spoke for any group beyond himself, it was that "appalling parasitic body," the army and the bureaucracy, the state apparatus it-self, whose interests had now separated themselves from those of all the classes that made up civil society.

Let us examine more closely the exact relation Marx presented between Napoleon and the various groups and institutions mentioned, beginning with the most controversial and complex — the bourgeoisie. Surveying the brief history of the Second Republic, and summarizing from his own *Class Struggles in France*, Marx explained again how the hopeful demo-cratic forms of the February Revolution had been transformed step-by-step into the repressive martial-law republic controlled after May 1849 by a monarchist Legislative Assembly. In 1850 this government, speak-ing for the united factions of the bourgeoisie, or the Party of Order, as Marx characterized it, abandoned even the principle of universal suf-frage, reverting to a restricted franchise and thus naked class oligarchy. Insofar as Louis Napoleon Bonaparte, elected president of this republic in December 1848, respected his constitutional role, he himself served the class oligarchy. But of course, he did not respect that role very long, and the body of *The Eighteenth Brumaire* is the history of his ensuing conflicts with the assembly and his eventual triumph *over* the class oli-garchy of the bourgeoisie. In Marx's analysis the key issues of this con-flict were precisely the control of the state bureaucracy and of the armed forces.

The bourgeoisie lost round one in November 1849, when Napoleon dis-missed the Barrot ministry and successfully asserted the right to choose new ministers himself. As Marx explained the significance of this "deci-sive turning point," he also struck the leitmotif of the whole essay — the growing independence of the state machine from class control, the emer-gence of its *self*-interest:

> The Party of Order lost, never to reconquer it, an indispensable post for the maintenance of the parliamentary regime, the lever of execu-tive power. It is immediately obvious that in a country like France, where the executive power commands an army of officials number-ing more than half a million individuals and therefore constantly maintains an immense mass of interests and livelihoods in the most absolute dependence; where the state enmeshes, controls, regulates, superintends and tutors civil society from its most comprehensive manifestations of life down to its most insignificant stirrings, from its most general modes of being to the private existence of individu-als; where through the most extraordinary centralization this para-

sitic body acquires an ubiquity, an omniscience, a capacity for accelerated mobility and an elasticity which finds a counterpart only
in the helpless dependence, in the loose shapelessness of the actual
body politic — it is obvious that in such a country the National Assembly forfeits all real influence when it loses command of the ministerial posts.

The alternative for the bourgeoisie, as Marx saw it, would have been to
simplify and reduce this apparatus, and "let civil society and public opinion create organs of their own, independent of the governmental power."
But the early history of the Second Republic had convinced the bourgeoisie that too much freedom was dangerous: "its *political interests* compelled it to increase daily the repressive measures and therefore the resources and personnel of the state power." Hence the ironic result, that
"the French bourgeoisie was compelled by its class position to annihilate,
on the one hand, the vital conditions of all parliamentary power, and
therefore, likewise, of its own, and to render irresistible, on the other
hand, the executive power hostile to it."[51] Here and elsewhere in the
essay, the executive power triumphs, *nota bene,* as a force "hostile" to
the bourgeoisie, even though the bourgeoisie has contributed heavily to
the triumph.
    Early in 1851 the bourgeoisie lost round two, when it lost control over
an army that looked more and more to Napoleon to speak for its interests. Significantly, Marx presented this entire development as the victorious emergence of the army's institutional self-interest. Called upon
repeatedly to rescue the bourgeoisie from its class enemies, the army was
bound to become convinced of its own indispensability:

> Were not barrack and bivouac, sabre and musket, moustache and
> uniform finally bound to hit upon the idea of rather saving society
> once and for all by proclaiming their own regime as the highest
> and freeing civil society completely from the trouble of governing
> itself? . . . Should not the military at last one day play state of siege
> in their own interest and for their own benefit, and at the same time
> besiege the bourgeois purses?[52]

The decisive event in this case was Napoleon's peremptory dismissal in
January 1851 of the leading general sympathetic to the Party of Order,
Nicholas Changarnier. By meekly accepting this deed "and so surrender-
ing the army irrevocably to the President, the Party of Order declares

that the bourgeoisie has forfeited its vocation to rule." The assembly now remained "without the ministry, without the army, without the people, without public opinion, after its Electoral Law of May 31 no longer the representative of the sovereign nation, *sans* eyes, *sans* ears, *sans* teeth, *sans* everything."[53] Consonant with this theme, the subsequent coup d'état of Napoleon against the bourgeois assembly in December 1851 was repeatedly orchestrated with martial images, as the "shamelessly simple domination of the sabre," the *"république cosaque,"* in which "all classes, equally impotent and equally mute, fall on their knees before the rifle butt." Or again, Napoleon was "raised up as a leader by a drunken soldiery, which he has bought with liquor and sausages, and which he must continually ply with more sausage." Or finally, the republic had now replaced the old inscription, *"Liberté, Egalité, Fraternité* by the unambiguous words: Infantry, Cavalry, Artillery!"[54] It grows difficult to resist the conclusion that for Marx, Napoleon's coup represented the victory of the army and the state apparatus in general *over* the bourgeoisie.

If further proofs are demanded, however, one need only consult two other writings to find evidence that clinches the argument. In *Class Struggles in France* Marx had pointedly insisted that the martial-law dictatorship of General Cavaignac during the bloody June Days, however much it relied on the army, remained but an instrument of class rule: "Cavaignac was not the dictatorship of the sabre over bourgeois society; he was the dictatorship of the bourgeoisie by the sabre."[55] Bearing this assertion in mind, one may contrast Marx's sharpest characterization of the Napoleonic state, written in 1858 after the French dictator had metamorphosed himself into an hereditary emperor and consolidated the repressive apparatus of his regime. The article was significantly titled, "The Rule of the Pretorians":

> If in all the bygone epochs the ruling class, the ascendency of which corresponded to a specific development of French society, rested its *ultima ratio* against its adversaries upon the army, it was nevertheless a specific social interest that predominated. Under the second Empire the interest of the army itself is to predominate. The army is no longer to maintain the rule of one part of the people over another part of the people. The army is to maintain its own rule, personated by its own dynasty, over the French people in general.

It is to represent the *state* in antagonism to the *society*. Here Marx returns again to the ideas of Kreuznach in opposing the state to (civil)

society in general, rather than in opposing class to class. Here is the parasite state in pure form which dominates the possessing class as well as
masses of French society. Marx went on to suggest in this and other articles that if the army grew dissatisfied with Napoleon it would probably
turn him out.[56]

To be sure, Marx did not conceive the political defeat of the bourgeoisie to mark the end of the bourgeois era in a broader sense. *The Eighteenth Brumaire* included a number of distinctions and refinements, beginning with a differentiation between "the spokesmen and scribes of the
bourgeoisie, its platform and its press, in short, the ideologists of the bourgeoisie and the bourgeoisie itself." The latter, Marx went on to argue,
abandoned the former in the struggle against executive authority, quietly
permitting most of the "ideologists" to be arrested when Napoleon closed
down the assembly in his coup of December 1851. By this time, for the
bourgeoisie standing outside public life, "its *political power*, only troubled
and upset it, as it was a disturbance of private business":

> The bourgeoisie confesses that its own interests dictate that it should
> be delivered from the danger of its *own rule;* . . . that, in order
> to preserve its social power intact, its political power must be broken;
> that the individual bourgeois can continue to exploit the other classes
> and to enjoy undisturbed property, family, religion and order only
> on condition that their class be condemned along with the other
> classes to similar political nullity; that, in order to save its purse,
> it must forfeit the crown, and the sword that is to safeguard it must
> at the same time be hung over its head as a sword of Damocles.[57]

Marx's distinction between social power and political power is crucial
for understanding his meaning. Napoleon still enforced a code of laws
that protected bourgeois property rights and the command power of capital over labor within the factory. The cynical words Marx put into the
mouths of the French capitalists express the thought nicely: "'The crimes
are his,' was their general chuckle, 'but the fruits are ours. Louis Napoleon reigns in the Tuileries; while we reign even more securely and des-
potically on our domains, in our factories, on the Bourse, and in our
counting-houses.'"[58] Because they still reigned on their own domains, that
is, retained their social power, Marx might on occasion still refer to them
as the "ruling class," as in the drafts of his *Civil War in France* when
he characterized the Bonapartist state as "a force superior to the ruling
and ruled classes," as "humbling under its sway even the interests of the

ruling classes." By preserving the social power of the bourgeoisie, such a state remained very much "a means for the enslavement of labor by capital."[59] Engels expressed the same thought when he wrote: "In France, the bourgeoisie, which for two years only, 1849–50, had held power as a class under the republican regime, was able to continue its social existence only by transferring its power to Louis Bonaparte and the army."[60]

A last refinement appears in *The Eighteenth Brumaire*'s treatment of Napoleon's own motives and needs. "Bonaparte would like to appear as the patriarchal benefactor of all classes." In addition to the favors he would dispense to the workers and peasants, Marx declared, "Bonaparte feels it to be his mission to safeguard 'bourgeois order.' . . . He looks on himself, therefore, as the representative of the middle class and issues decrees in this sense. Nevertheless, he is somebody solely due to the fact that he has broken the political power of the middle class and daily breaks it anew."[61] Like the absolute monarchs of the previous epoch, Napoleon found it prudent to distribute favors to the bourgeoisie, but like them he did so not as their spokesman or puppet but in his own interests. While his interests and theirs might generally overlap, they were by no means identical: in an 1856 article Marx toyed with the idea that "Louis Bonaparte, the Imperial Socialist, will try to seize upon French industry by converting the debentures of the Crédit Mobilier into State obligations."[62] By 1858 he reached the conclusion that the French bourgeoisie, indeed the upper classes everywhere in Europe, had turned against their onetime hero: "They knew him long since as a villain; but they deemed him a serviceable, pliant, obedient, grateful villain; and they now see and rue their mistake. He has been using *them* all the time that they supposed they were using him."[63] The enigma for the bourgeoisie was how to make the emperor serviceable and pliant once again, now that he controlled all the instrumentalities of coercion and they remained "*sans* eyes, *sans* ears, *sans* teeth, *sans* everything." Only a popular revolution could eventually overthrow his despotic rule.

The relation of Napoleon to the other social classes can be treated more briefly. Immediately following the oft-quoted remark that Bonapartist "state power is not suspended in mid air," Marx asserted: "Bonaparte represents a class, and the most numerous class of French society at that, the *small-holding peasantry.*" But he proceeded to make clear that Napoleon represented the peasants only in the sense that they gave him their votes in the *hope* he would look after their interests. The isolated, almost self-sufficient nature of French peasant life precluded any political mobilization sufficient to enforce that hope in real life. "The identity of their interests," Marx observed, "begets no community, no national bond and no political organization among them":

> They are consequently incapable of enforcing their class interests in their own name, whether through a parliament or through a convention. They cannot represent themselves, they must be represented. Their representative must at the same time appear as their master, as an authority over them, as an unlimited governmental power that protects them against the other classes and sends them rain and sunshine from above. The political influence of the small-holding peasants, therefore, finds its final expression in the executive power subordinating society to itself.[64]

Here Marx left off his teasing to make his serious point: the French peasantry cannot rule as a class; their votes have simply helped to create the independent power that rules over them. "By its very nature," he added, "small-holding property forms a suitable basis for an all-powerful and innumerable bureaucracy," a thought that must have lingered in his mind as he took up the study of Asian societies a few months later.[65]

Marx could not resist one final tease. Just as he made Napoleon represent the peasantry, as well as being the representative of the middle class, so finally we learn that, "above all, Bonaparte looks on himself as the chief of the Society of December 10, as the representative of the lumpenproletariat." This society had been formed in 1849 to promote the political fortunes of Napoleon, "10,000 rogues who are to play the part of the people, as Nick Bottom that of the lion." Elaborating on its social composition, Marx outdid himself in scorn:

> Alongside decayed *roués* with dubious means of subsistence and of dubious origin, alongside ruined and adventurous offshoots of the bourgeoisie, were vagabonds, discharged soldiers, discharged jailbirds, escaped galley slaves, rogues, mountebanks, *lazzaroni*, pickpockets, tricksters, gamblers, *maquereaus*, brothel keepers, porters, *literati*, organ-grinders, rag-pickers, knife grinders, tinkers, beggars — in short, the whole indefinite, disintegrated mass, thrown hither and thither, which the French term *la bohème*.[66]

Whenever Napoleon spoke in public or traveled, elements of this society always turned up "to improvise a public for him, stage public enthusiasm, roar *vive l'Empereur*, insult and beat up republicans, of course under the protection of the police." Incipient political party as well as incipient *Sturmabteilung*, the Society of December 10 provided Napoleon with his most loyal support. As *"chief of the lumpenproletariat,"* he "recognizes in this scum, offal, refuse of all classes the only class upon which he can base himself unconditionally." Even more pointedly Marx declared: "The French bourgeoisie balked at the rule of the working proletariat; it has brought the lumpenproletariat to power [*zur Herrschaft gebracht*], with the chief of the Society of December 10 at the head."[67] Curiously perhaps, no writer has yet cited these lines as proof that France was ruled by the lumpen proletariat.

Even the main body of the working class found itself coquetted by Napoleon. His first major act after the December coup was to restore universal suffrage (albeit in a harmless form, as we will see presently). Proclaiming his sympathy for "socialist" ideas he launched various palliative schemes, such as a public subscription for the building of *"cités ouvrières,"* or workers' settlements. For Marx this social program amounted to "dissolution of the actual workers' associations, but promises of miracles of association in the future." In a manipulative way the French dictator sought to "represent" every group in the nation: "Bonaparte would like to appear as the patriarchal benefactor of all classes. But he cannot give to one class without taking from another." "Driven by the contradictory demands of his situation," he must spring "constant surprises," thus "keeping the public gaze fixed on himself."[68] Thus the Napoleonic state was manifestly not "suspended in mid air"; its success was intimately related to the condition of all social classes — to the panic and political withdrawal of the bourgeoisie, to the backwardness and gullibility of the peasantry, to the rascally opportunism of the lumpen proletariat, and to the temporary exhaustion of the as yet immature proletariat. But at the same time none of these classes actually ruled or was capable of ruling. Bonapartism marked the ultimate success of the striving for independence of a self-interested state apparatus, and thus the temporary end of political class rule. Marx summed it all up most succinctly when he wrote: "It was the only form of government possible at a time when the bourgeoisie had already lost, and the working class had not yet acquired, the faculty of ruling the nation."[69]

It was Engels rather than Marx who first extended the concept of Bonapartism to Germany. The informal division of labor worked out between them usually left German affairs in the hands of the younger man. From the beginning Engels also showed more interest than his partner in the manipulative features of Bonapartism, especially in the cynical use of universal suffrage to gain "democratic" legitimacy for the regime without exposing it to the hazards of genuine popular control. In Engels' letters to Marx during December 1851 we find a running commentary exposing Napoleon's fraud in the first of these elections. "What can come of the ridiculous elections?" Engels asked. "No press, no meetings, martial law in abundance, and on the top of it all the order to provide a deputy in fourteen days." With two-thirds of the country under martial law, he suggested, the authorities would invent pretexts to close down the polling places in hostile districts; ballot boxes would be stuffed; then the predictable "errors" in counting the ballots — all this would assure Napoleon an overwhelming victory.[70] In an 1865 polemic addressed to the nascent German workers' movement Engels was concerned to expose the idiosyncratic views of its leader, Ferdinand Lassalle, in particular his indifference to political rights and parliamentary government, oddly combined with a limitless faith in universal suffrage. Pointing to the Bonapartist regime across the Rhine, and analyzing its socio-political structure very much as Marx had done, Engels added: "With regard to universal and direct suffrage, one need only go to France to be convinced of the harmless elections it is possible to hold on this basis in a country with a large and stupid rural population, a well organized bureaucracy and a tightly controlled press, in a country where there are absolutely no political meetings and where associations are satisfactorily suppressed by the police." Under such conditions, he concluded, "it is almost impossible to vote for an opposition candidate," and universal suffrage becomes "not a weapon for the proletariat but a *trap*."[71] One cannot help wondering what choice comments Engels would offer on the way universal suffrage is used in present-day Communist countries.

In an event, in April 1866 when the hitherto ultra-reactionary Prussian statesman, Otto von Bismarck, proposed universal suffrage as the basis for reorganizing German political life, Engels immediately caught the strong scent of Bonapartism coming from Berlin. He commented to Marx:

> So Bismarck has made his universal suffrage coup, even though without his Lassalle. It looks as if the German bourgeois will agree to it after some token resistance, for after all Bonapartism is the real religion of the modern bourgeoisie. It is becoming clearer and clearer to me that the bourgeoisie has not the stuff in it for ruling directly itself, and that therefore where no oligarchy, as here in England, can take over for good pay the management of state and society in

the interest of the bourgeoisie, a Bonapartist semi-dictatorship is the normal form. It carries out the great material interests of the bourgeoisie, even against the bourgeoisie itself, allowing it no share of the real power.[72]

Ill at the time, Marx did not respond to Engels' suggestion that Bonapartism was the wave of the future, but in 1871, after the Franco-Prussian War had made it possible for Bismarck to crown his imitation with the proclamation of the German Empire, Marx announced testily that Bonapartism "has in fact, on the European continent at least, become the only possible stateform in which the appropriating class can continue to sway it over the producing class."[73]

The following year Engels summed up the chief characteristics of Bismarck's imitation in a remarkably trenchant passage that deserves full quotation:

In Prussia . . . there exists side by side with a landowning aristocracy, which is still powerful, a comparatively young and extremely cowardly bourgeoisie, which up to the present has not won either direct political domination, as in France, or more or less indirect domination as in England. Side by side with these two classes, however, there exists a rapidly increasing proletariat which is intellectually highly developed and which is becoming more and more organized every day. We therefore find here, alongside of the basic condition of the old absolute monarchy — an equilibrium between the landed aristocracy and the bourgeoisie — the basic condition of modern Bonapartism — an equilibrium between the bourgeoisie and the proletariat. But both in the old absolute monarchy and in the modern Bonapartist monarchy the real governmental authority lies in the hands of a special caste of army officers and state officials. In Prussia this caste is replenished partly from its own ranks, partly from the lesser primogenitary aristocracy. . . . The independence of this caste, which appears to occupy a position outside and, so to speak, above society, gives the state the semblance of independence in relation to society.

The state form which has developed with the necessary consistency in Prussia (and, following the Prussian example, in the new Reich constitution of Germany) out of these contradictory social conditions is pseudo-constitutionalism, a form which is at once both the present-day form of the dissolution of the old absolute monarchy and the form of existence of the Bonapartist monarchy.[74]

Here Engels described Bismarck's parasite state in exactly the same terms Marx had used for Napoleon's, as one in which "real governmental authority" is denied to any social class and rests instead in the hands of a "special caste" of military and civil officials. Such a state does not really stand "above" society in any Hegelian sense, since its existence depends on a particular and temporary equilibrium of class forces, but it does stand above the classes themselves, dominating all of civil society as an independent power ruling in its own interest. The peculiarity of the German case, as Engels pinpointed masterfully, lay in the direct transition from the absolutist parasite state to the Bonapartist one, without any intervening period of political rule by a social class. Consequently the Bismarckian state contained elements of both — a legitimate monarch rather than an adventurer turned emperor, but a similar "pseudo-constitutionalism" with its manipulative use of universal suffrage. In a later writing Engels pointed to the features of the Reich constitution that he had in mind in using the word "pseudo":

> The Reich Chancellor and his ministers were nominated by the King of Prussia independently of any parliamentary majority. The independence of the Army from Parliament . . . was retained in relation to the Reichstag. But the members of the Reichstag could console themselves for this by the uplifting thought that they had been elected by universal suffrage.

Marx employed similar language when he described the Bonapartist state in Germany, his pithiest characterization occurring within a single sentence — "a bureaucratically carpentered and police-guarded military despotism, embellished with parliamentary forms, alloyed with a feudal admixture, and at the same time already influenced by the bourgeoisie."[75]

If Engels' attention was drawn especially to the manipulative features of the Bonapartist state, Marx's instincts drew him back again and again to what he conceived as its core — the military and bureaucratic apparatus. We could find no better way to round out his conception of Bonapartism than to turn to the justly famous passage in *The Eighteenth Brumaire*, where in densely packed prose Marx described the historical emergence and eventual triumph of the state apparatus in France:

> This executive power with its enormous bureaucratic and military organization, with its extensive and artificial state machinery, with a host of officials numbering half a million, besides an army of another half million, this appalling parasitic body, which enmeshes

the body of French society like a net and chokes all its pores, sprang up in the days of the absolute monarchy, with the decay of the feudal system, which it helped to hasten. The seignorial privileges of the landowners and towns became transformed into so many attributes of the state power, the feudal dignitaries into paid officials and the motley pattern of conflicting medieval plenary powers into the regulated plan of a state authority whose work is divided and centralized as in a factory. The first French Revolution, with its task of breaking all separate local, territorial, urban and provincial powers in order to create the civil unity of the nation, was bound to develop what the absolute monarchy had begun: the centralization, but at the same time the extent, the attributes and the agents of governmental power. Napoleon perfected this state machinery. The Legitimatist monarchy and the July monarchy added nothing but a greater division of labor, growing in the same measure as the division of labor within bourgeois society created new groups of interests, and, therefore, new material for state administration. Every *common* interest was straightway severed from society, counterposed to it as a higher, *general* interest, snatched from the activity of society's members themselves and made an object of government activity, whether it was a bridge, a schoolhouse and the communal property of a village community, or the railways, the national wealth and the national university of France. Finally, in its struggle against the revolution, the parliamentary republic found itself compelled to strengthen, along with the repressive measures, the resources and centralization of governmental power. All revolutions perfected this machine instead of breaking it. The parties that contended in turn for domination regarded the possession of this huge state edifice as the principal spoils of the victor.

But under the absolute monarchy, during the first revolution, under Napoleon, bureaucracy was only the means of preparing the class rule of the bourgeoisie. Under the Restoration, under Louis Philippe, under the parliamentary republic, it was the instrument of the ruling class, however much it strove for power of its own.

Only under the second Bonaparte does the state seem to have made itself completely independent. As against civil society, the state machine has consolidated its position so thoroughly that the chief of the Society of December 10 suffices for its head.[76]

Interestingly, Marx seemed to find at least some historically progressive function and justification for the swelling state machinery prior to the Second Empire. First it prepared the way for bourgeois rule; then it served that class rule as a direct instrument. But it continually "strove for power on its own," and when that striving met with ultimate success under Louis Napoleon, the bureaucratic state ceased to serve any historical purpose at all for Marx. Pursuing its own interests alone it became purely parasitic, a drag on further social development. Marx's imagery in referring to "this appalling parasitic body" grew unremittingly negative and hostile—a net enmeshing the body of French society, a ubiquitous parasite feeding on the vitals of France, a deadening incubus, a boa constrictor entoiling the social body, and so forth.[77] All of Marx's animus toward the parasite state came to a focus in his dramatic assertion: "All revolutions perfected this machine instead of breaking it." The coming proletarian revolution, he went on to prophesy, would bring about "the demolition of the state machine," such that the entire edifice "will fall to the ground."[78]

The intensity of his language reveals a passionate hatred of bureaucracy that pervades Marx's political writings from the time of the *Rheinische Zeitung* to his final days. It is a sad irony that such a man should come to be identified nowadays on both sides of the East-West divide with the idea of bureaucratically administered state socialism. If the truth were known, today's strict laissez-faire conservatives might find a certain kindred spirit in a man who laments that every common social endeavor, from a schoolhouse to a bridge to a university, must become an object of governmental activity; who deplores the "helpless dependence" of a body politic where the state "enmeshes, controls, regulates, superintends and tutors" everything; or who elsewhere can quote Edmund Burke in full sympathy on the "littleness," the "close and abject spirit" of bureaucracy; who can denounce his native Prussia contemptuously as a land where "you can neither live nor die, nor marry, nor write letters, nor think, nor print, nor take to business, nor teach, nor be taught, nor get up a meeting, nor build a manufactory, nor emigrate, nor do any thing without *'obrigkeitliche Erlaubniss'*—permission on the part of the authorities."[79] How Marx reconciled his hatred of bureaucracy with his socialism, how he imagined a highly developed and socially owned economy could be administered without bureaucrats, is a question that will be addressed at considerable length later in this volume.

The experience of Bonapartism even seemed to give Marx second thoughts about the value of centralization. Having grown up in Restoration Germany where the need for central institutions was so apparent, Marx consistently equated centralizing processes with historical advancement until Napoleon's triumph made him begin to rethink and modify his views. Already in *The Eighteenth Brumaire* he announced: "The centralization of the state that modern society requires arises only on the ruins of the military-bureaucratic government machinery which was forged in opposition to feudalism." He added that "bureaucracy is only the low and brutal form of a centralization that is still afflicted with its opposite, with feudalism" — a discrimination that will be of use when we examine the whole question of centralism versus decentralism in chapter 5.[80]

Most frequently, as we have witnessed, Marx and Engels used the word "caste" in referring to the Bonapartist officialdom. Their writings include no discussion of terminological alternatives and it seems clear that, as in the case of absolutism, they chose the word for its pejorative connotation rather than with any intent to be technically precise.[81] As between the military and civil officials, Marx obviously believed the former to occupy a more powerful position since he spoke of the "rule of the Pretorians" and even speculated that the generals might get rid of the emperor if their interests diverged. The military officials after all held the monopoly on the means of violence that, given the temporary equilibrium of class forces, insured the parasite state's dominance over civil society.

Dominance over civil society at large was the central and distinguishing characteristic of the parasite state in all its varieties. It is clear Marx never forgot how he thought about the state in 1843. Like the absolutist regime he had in mind at that time, the Oriental and Bonapartist states were composed of a "caste" of professional soldiers and bureaucrats, supposedly serving the general interests of society but in fact estranged from it as its alienated social power and serving their own interests through a state apparatus they regarded as their own private property. The mature Marx would add that in all its varieties the parasite state rested on a predominantly agricultural society in which the mass of the population was formed by isolated, ignorant, and nearly self-sufficient peasants who could be bullied, duped, and milked by the powerful and remote state apparatus. In the case of Oriental despotism, the state and the peasantry were the sole elements in the social equation; European absolutism and Bonapartism involved more complex and dynamic societies with other social classes and a class conflict temporarily in stalemate. Absolutism arose out of the equilibrium of nobility and bourgeoisie, Bonapartism out of a parallel equilibrium between bourgeoisie and proletariat. Both these latter forms, because they rested on dynamic societies, were but passing phenomena, while Oriental despotism remained stable and unchanging through the ages.

The parasite states as a group stood clearly apart from the class states, where the coercive machinery served as mere instrument for the overt political rule of a possessing class. Oriental despotism required no possessing class at all, unless one wanted to define it as the state bureaucracy which in some sense collectively "owned" the means of production. In the Occident, where class rule was the norm, the parasite states appeared during exceptional periods as "a force superior to the ruling and ruled classes" alike. Even then, however, the possessing classes retained their property rights, their "social power," which placed the labor of the exploited classes, and most of the surplus product, at their command. Inasmuch as the parasite state recognized and enforced these property rights, it remained an engine of class oppression even though not controlled by the possessing class. This was the sense of Engels' assertion in *The Origin of the Family* that the state "in all *typical* periods is exclusively the state of the ruling class, and in *all* cases remains essentially a machine for keeping down the oppressed, exploited class" (emphasis added).[82] The two categories of states were also "seemingly" independent of society in two different senses: parasite states because they were shaped by the particular society that gave them birth; class states for this same broad reason but *also* more specifically because they served as coercive instruments for one part of society against another.

A final reflection may be in order which is implicit in Marx and Engels' thinking, though they did not say it themselves. A state apparatus can "strive" for independence from the possessing class only where it is distinct from that class, where it is composed of professional soldiers and bureaucrats whose primary interests derive from career rather than property. Prior to modern times in the West, the business of running the state was likely to be a part-time activity for the possessing class itself. Typically at least ancient slaveowner citizens and medieval nobles did their own fighting and their own administering. Under these circumstances a divergence of interest between the possessing class and the warrior class would have been quite impossible — they were one and the same body of men. It was the further subdivision of labor in modern times, in particular the professionalization of governmental functions, that opened up the possibility of such a divergence. Unlike previous possessing classes, the bourgeoisie was not disposed by tradition or inclination to do its own fighting; maximizing profits normally meant leaving such tasks to others.[83] The career officials who began to perform governmental functions on a full-time professional basis now formed a new branch in society's general division of labor and thus acquired particular "caste" interests of their own, overlapping with but distinct from the interests of the possessing classes. The parasite state in the West has been largely a product of the bourgeois epoch broadly defined.

⊰[3]⊱

The Bourgeois Class State

THIS CHAPTER WILL BE DEVOTED entirely to bourgeois forms of the class state. Marx and Engels' views on ancient and medieval class states could doubtless be reconstructed, as we have done in the case of absolutism, but the two men showed little interest in these long expended political forms, and their opinions in turn have provoked little controversy. The opposite would have to be said about their concept of bourgeois class rule, which seems destined to be debated endlessly.[1] Perhaps the reason for the disparity lies in the fact that the states of classical antiquity and feudal Europe never pretended to give their lower classes — slaves or serfs — equal political rights. Class privilege and class rule were embedded in the law itself, quite nakedly and without disguise. But when Marx and Engels argue that modern political forms incorporate a new class oligarchy, the case seems more difficult. Has not legal equality put an end to class privilege? Has not democracy made class rule a thing of the past?

Throughout the Cold War the system of "free enterprise" has inevitably been linked by its defenders with "democracy," and just as inevitably have its Communist opponents linked "capitalism" with "bourgeois democracy." It is a gross error, albeit a very common one on both sides of the ideological divide, to read back this linkage into the ideas of Marx and Engels, to suppose that they also associated parliamentary democracy with the rule of the bourgeoisie. It is true that they sometimes spoke of the democratic republic as the "highest" or "last"political form of bourgeois society, and as the most "consistent" according to the principles of liberty, equality, and fraternity, but they by no means regarded it as the most typical form or the form preferred by the bourgeoisie as a whole. For them the garden variety of bourgeois rule was an oligarchy of property owners under a constitutional monarchy. The demand for a democratic republic they might associate with the most radical *segment* of the

[64]

bourgeoisie, more often with the petty bourgeoisie, but it figured as a demand in which the proletariat was vitally interested as well. No doubt they believed it *possible* for the bourgeoisie to rule in a democratic republic, but only so long as the victims of capitalism did not yet form a conscious majority, and such rule was therefore inherently unstable and transitory, at least in Europe. "Bourgeois democracy" is not a term one encounters frequently in their writings, twentieth-century assumptions to the contrary, and for the simple reason that they found it a rare bird. Only in America did the two men recognize such democracy as more than a passing phenomenon, and to explain this exception it is highly interesting to find them once again invoking the idea of the parasite state.

Let us start off, however, in the Old World. At the time Marx and Engels set down the familiar *Manifesto* assertion that "the executive of the modern State is but a committee for managing the common affairs of the whole bourgeoisie," they could not have been thinking of democratic governments, for even the most advanced European states were still oligarchies of wealth in which the mass of the population could neither vote nor hold office. Equality before the law did not extend to the rights of active citizenship. Very likely the regime they had in mind was the current July Monarchy in France, where only the richest two hundred thousand citizens (approximately 3 percent of the adult male population) were entitled to vote and hold office. The contemporaneous Belgian constitution was copied almost verbatim from the French, while in Britain the only notable differences in this regard were a somewhat broader franchise (after 1832 approximately 12 percent of the adult male population could vote) and a firmer parliamentary control over the executive.[2] Engels' draft of the *Manifesto*, as we saw in volume 1, spelled out bourgeois rule very clearly in these terms:

Having become the first class in society, the bourgeoisie proclaimed itself also the first class in the political sphere. It did this by establishing the representative system, which rests upon civil equality before the law, the legal recognition of free competition, and which in European countries was introduced in the form of constitutional monarchy. Under these constitutional monarchies those only are electors who possess a certain amount of capital, that is to say, the bourgeois; these bourgeois electors elect the deputies, and these bourgeois deputies, by means of the right to refuse taxes, elect a bourgeois government.[3]

Four decades later, in *The Origin of the Family*, Engels still referred to the "political recognition of property distinctions" as the typical, if not essential, accoutrement of class rule:

> In most of the historical states, the rights of citizens are . . . apportioned according to their wealth, thus directly expressing the fact that the state is an organization of the possessing class for its protection against the non-possessing class. It was so already in the Athenian and Roman classification according to property. It was so in the medieval feudal state, in which the alignment of political power was in conformity with the amount of land owned. It is seen in the electoral qualifications of the modern representative states.[4]

Thus Marx and Engels were not nearly as concerned as their twentieth-century followers to "unmask" bourgeois class rule hiding behind democratic forms; in their day class rule generally wore no such mask. Too often nowadays we have forgotten that nineteenth-century parliamentary governments where the franchise was restricted by law were oligarchies of wealth, as naked and undisguised as the oligarchy of citizen-slaveowners in the classical polis or the oligarchy of titled aristocrats in medieval Europe.

It may also be recalled from volume 1 that in 1848 Marx and Engels expected the German bourgeoisie to create precisely such an oligarchy of wealth; it was *against* such class rule that they advanced the demand for a "unitary and indivisible republic" based on universal suffrage in their *Demands of the Communist Party in Germany*. The democratic republic was conceived by them not as a vehicle of bourgeois rule but, on the contrary, as a means by which the alliance of the majority classes — workers, peasants, petty bourgeois — could struggle against bourgeois rule. Initially the two men had the same hopes for the February Republic established in France. In more advanced Britain they expected the winning of democracy, in the form of the People's Charter, to produce forthwith the rule of the proletariat.[5] Everywhere in these early years they conceived democracy as a weapon against bourgeois rule and, as we will see, developments in the second half of the century did not really change their views profoundly.

Let us now look at how they portrayed bourgeois class rule in the only three large countries where they found it to exist during their lifetimes — Great Britain, France, the United States. At the same time we can deepen our understanding of their attitude toward democratic forms per se, which they conceived to undermine more often than sustain the rule of the bourgeoisie.

Great Britain

When they addressed human history as a whole, Marx and Engels were capable of setting forth sweeping and categorical assertions about the class character of the state. The *Communist Manifesto*, as just quoted, found the modern state "but a committee," and elsewhere declared that "political power, properly so called, is merely the organized power of one class for oppressing another." *Anti-Dühring* defined the state historically as "an organization of the particular class, which was *pro tempore* the exploiting class." *The Origin of the Family* reduced the state to "a machine for holding down the oppressed, exploited class."[6] Since these writings also have been traditionally the most easily accessible and widely read, they have given a widespread impression of simplistic and doctrinaire minds at work. If one proceeds more systematically, however, by assembling Marx and Engels' diverse comments on *particular* states, a very different impression emerges, as we have already seen in the previous chapter. Not only did they find some states to be free from class control, but even among those that were not they perceived many variations and subtle mixtures. Nowhere can this be observed better than in the case of Great Britain.

For Marx and Engels the modern bourgeois oligarchy in Great Britain developed, to be sure, out of the seventeenth-century revolutions, but not in a cut-and-dried overthrow of aristocratic rule. Rather they depicted 1688 as a compromise between a bourgeoisie, grown wealthy from trade and banking, and a segment of the high aristocracy that was involved in commercial agriculture and that had partly embraced bourgeois values. "The great puzzle of the conservative character of the English revolution," Marx observed, "is in fact explained by the lasting alliance of the bourgeoisie with the great landowners, an alliance which fundamentally distinguishes the English from the French revolution, the latter having destroyed large landed property by dividing it up into smallholdings."[7] Engels offered elaboration on the background of this distinctive alliance:

Fortunately for England, the old feudal barons had killed one another during the Wars of the Roses. Their successors, though mostly scions of the old families, had been so much out of the direct line of descent that they constituted quite a new body, with habit and tendencies far more bourgeois than feudal. They fully understood the value of money, and at once began to increase their rents by turning hundreds of small farmers out and replacing them by sheep. Henry VIII, while squandering the Church lands, created fresh bourgeois landlords by wholesale; the innumerable confiscations of estates, regranted to absolute or relative upstarts, and continued during the whole of the seventeenth century, had the same result. Consequently, ever since Henry VII, . . . there had always been a section of the great landowners willing, from economical or political reasons, to cooperate with the leading men of the financial and industrial bourgeoisie.

From the time of the Glorious Revolution, then, "the bourgeoisie was a humble, but still a recognized component of the ruling classes of England."[8] A "humble" component of an alliance in which the senior partners were commercially oriented aristocrats — this view fits, if not perfectly, at least far more comfortably with modern scholarship than the simple stereotype of bourgeois revolution so often associated with Marx's name.

Throughout the next century the bourgeoisie gradually improved the terms of this partnership until by the 1830s, their numbers and wealth phenomenally multiplied by the industrial revolution, they finally became the senior partners themselves by means of the Great Reform Act of 1832, and proceeded to drive the point home with the repeal in 1846 of the Corn Laws which protected British grain producers from foreign competition. The Tory party opposed these historic changes, while the Whigs embraced them. As Marx perceived it, writing in the 1850s, "the Tories represent the squireocracy, they are the Junker party, if you will."[9] They profess to admire the English Constitution as the eighth wonder of the world, and present themselves as

enthusiasts for the throne, the High Church, the privileges and liberties of the British subject. The fatal year, 1846, with its repeal of the Corn Laws, and the shout of distress which this repeal forced from the Tories, proved that they were enthusiasts for nothing but the rent of land, and at the same time disclosed the secret of their attachment to the political and religious institutions of Old England. These institutions are the very best institutions, with the help of which the *large landed property* — the landed interest — has hitherto ruled England, and even now seeks to maintain its rule.

The Tory party recruits its voting support "from the farmers, who either have not yet lost the habit of following their landlords as their natural superiors, or who are economically dependent upon them."[10]

By contrast the Whigs speak for that segment of the aristocracy that has allied itself with the bourgeoisie, though its role in the alliance Marx found utterly transformed by the 1850s:

> The Whigs, as well as the Tories, form a fraction of the large landed property of Great Britain. Nay, the oldest, richest and most arrogant portion of English landed property is the very nucleus of the Whig party.
>
> What, then, distinguishes them from the Tories? The Whigs are the *aristocratic representatives* of the bourgeoisie, of the industrial and commercial middle class. Under the condition that the Bourgeoisie should abandon to them, to an oligarchy of aristocratic families, the monopoly of government and the exclusive possession of office, they make to the middle class, and assist it in conquering, all those concessions, which in the course of social and political development have shown themselves to have become *unavoidable* and *undelayable*. . . . [We] find no other distinctive mark of Whigdom but the maintenance of their family oligarchy. The interests and principles which they represent besides, from time to time, do not belong to the Whigs; they are forced upon them by the development of the industrial and commercial class, the Bourgeoisie. After 1688 we find them united with the Bankocracy, just then rising into importance, as we find them in 1846, united with the Millocracy.[11]

The millocracy clearly now figured as the senior partner in this class alliance, as Marx confirmed in another article where he referred to the Whig oligarchy as "the governing caste, which in England is by no means the same as the ruling class." Engels struck a similar note as late as 1892 when he observed that "in England, the bourgeoisie never held undivided sway. Even the victory of 1832 left the landed aristocracy in almost exclusive possession of all the leading Government offices." He explained this survival in interesting psychological terms: "The English bourgeoisie are, up to the present day, so deeply penetrated by a sense of their social inferiority that they keep up, at their own expense and that of the nation, an ornamental caste of drones to represent the nation worthily at all State functions."[12] Although both Marx and Engels' characterizations suggest elements of the parasite state, neither man depicted the

Whig aristocrats after 1832 as possessing any longer much will of their own; they served principally as "representatives" of another class, as "drones" to ornament the rule of the bourgeoisie.

In virtually all their articles of the 1850s Marx and Engels stressed the undemocratic character of British politics, pointing repeatedly to the open ballot, intimidation and bribery that accounted for so much of the surviving aristocratic influence in the House of Commons, and pointing especially to the property qualifications for voters which insured a "voteless majority," the "voteless mass" that stood outside the electoral system even after the 1832 reforms.[13] For years the two men clung to the vain hope for a Chartist revival which would press once more for full democratization. In 1852 Marx wrote of universal suffrage, as Engels had done so often before, as the very touchstone of proletarian victory in Britain:

> Universal Suffrage is the equivalent for political power for the working class of England, where the proletariat forms the large majority of the population, where, in a long, though underground civil war, it has gained a clear consciousness of its position as a class, and where even the rural districts know no longer any peasants, but only landlords, industrial capitalists (farmers) and hired laborers. The carrying of Universal Suffrage in England would, therefore, be a far more socialistic measure than anything which has been honored with that name on the Continent.
>
> Its inevitable result, here, is *the political supremacy of the working class.*[14]

During the middle third of the nineteenth century, the heyday of bourgeois rule in Britain, Marx and Engels never described the government there as a "bourgeois democracy." On the contrary they stressed its oligarchic character and conceived of democracy as the way to overturn it.

Renewed suffrage agitation in the 1860s produced the Reform Act of 1867, a milestone in Britain's democratization. While still withholding universal suffrage, the act did extend the franchise to a full third of the adult male population, and in such a way as to include more than half of the urban working class. Ironically, it was the Tories who sponsored this measure, though not out of democratic enthusiasm; seeing that some extension was unavoidable, they hoped that by enfranchising the urban proletariat — class enemy of *their* class enemy — they could garner a harvest of grateful ballots. Initially this dangerous game worked, but the Whigs — or Liberals, as they now called themselves — learned quickly and soon outdid their rivals in the competition for plebeian votes, much to the disappointment of Marx and Engels. Yet at a deeper level the reform of 1867 introduced a permanent element of instability into the bourgeois political order in Britain, for henceforth its security rested on the demagogic ability of the two major parties to keep working-class voters within the fold. Henceforth that order could continue only because, as Marx put it in 1880, "the English working class know not how to wield their power and use their liberties, both of which they possess legally."[15]

Correspondingly, for Marx and Engels, the prime need of the British proletariat, now more than ever before, was a party of its own. In an 1881 appeal entitled, "A Working-Man's Party," Engels spelled out his hopes in a way that neatly reveals his assumptions concerning the British political system:

> There never was a more widespread feeling in England than now, that the old parties are doomed, that the old shibboleths have become meaningless. . . . Thinking men of all classes begin to see that a new line must be struck out, and that this line can only be in the direction of democracy. But in England, where the industrial and agricultural working-class forms the immense majority of the people, democracy means the dominion of the working-class, neither more nor less. Let, then, that working-class prepare itself for the task in store for it, — the ruling of this great empire; let them understand the responsibilities which inevitably will fall to their share. And the best way to do this is to use the power already in their hands, the actual majority they possess in every large town in the kingdom, to send to Parliament men of their own order. With the present household suffrage, forty or fifty working-men might easily be sent to St. Stephen's, where such an infusion of entirely new blood is very much wanted indeed.

With such a voting bloc in Parliament, Engels went on to say, the working class could determine the outcome of most reform legislation, including further democratization that would in turn strengthen their representation there. "The workpeople of England," he concluded, "have but to will, and they are the masters to carry every reform, social and political, which their situation requires."[16] Neither Engels nor his partner ever regarded the British worker's right to vote as mere "dupery," as they contemptuously labeled the French worker's right to vote under Louis Napoleon, for in Britain the franchise was linked with the freedom to organize and with a sovereign parliament. To the extent that the bourgeoisie allowed the country to be democratized, it undermined its own rule; "bourgeois democracy" was a formula for self-destruction. As we will see, this was really Marx and Engels' position everywhere on the matter of "bourgeois democracy." And it opened the door for the first time to the possibility of a legal and peaceful achievement of communism, which will be the subject of chapter 10.

All this is not to say Marx and Engels were oblivious to the legal restrictions and informal practices that kept "bourgeois democracy" less than fully democratic, and that tended to keep working-class voting strength from reaching its full potential. On the contrary, they called attention to such matters frequently; even in the last months of his life, for example, Engels complained to an American correspondent about the situation in Britain:

> So-called "democracy" here is very much restricted by *indirect* barriers. A periodical costs a terrible amount of money, a parliamentary candidature ditto, living the life of an M. P. – ditto, if only on account of the enormous correspondence entailed. A checking up of the miserably kept electoral register likewise costs a lot and so far only the two official parties can afford the expense. Anyone, therefore, who does not sign up with either of these parties has little chance of getting on the election list of candidates. In all these respects people here are a long way behind the Continent, and are beginning to notice this. Furthermore, we have no second ballots here and a relative majority or, as you Americans say, plurality, suffices. At the same time everything is arranged for *only two* parties. A third party can at most turn the scales in favor of one of the other two until it equals them in strength.

The point is, however, that Engels manifestly did not regard these obstacles to be so severe as to close the legal avenue to power. He had by this time lived long enough to greet the formation of the Independent Labor party in Britain and take pride in its first electoral successes. His confidence shines forth in the concluding sentence of this letter: "Yet here, as in your country, once the workers know what they want, the state, the land, industry and everything else will be theirs."[17] Ironically, perhaps, neither Marx nor Engels seems to have worried about the possibility that in the end the British proletariat might, like the bourgeoisie before it, settle for a partnership, or that a parallel sense of "social inferiority" might induce it to accept much less than was its due.

France

If Britain moved toward democratic institutions in steady incremental steps, nonetheless by the end of Marx and Engels' lives some restrictions on voting rights lingered on, not to mention the monarchy and House of Lords. France, by contrast, moved toward democracy in spasms and had produced no fewer than three democratic republics by the end of the nineteenth century, all of which provides us with an unparalleled opportunity to explore what relationship Marx and Engels perceived between the democratic republic as a form and the rule of the bourgeoisie. What we will discover is, far from seeing the democratic republic as the preferred or typical form of bourgeois rule in France, the two men regarded it as something forced upon that class on each of three separate occasions by pressure from below. In the first two cases the bourgeoisie then eviscerated and scuttled the republic as soon as it could; in the last case it gradually learned to live with democratic institutions, but only after having eradicated the proletarian danger at the outset through the suppression of the Paris Commune. As soon as the workers' movement developed into a threatening power once again, odds would be ten to one (according to Engels) that the bourgeoisie would scuttle the Third Republic as well, or in any event try to do so. The democratic republic was the "highest" or "last" form of bourgeois rule, not because it was the one most preferred by the bourgeoisie, but because it was the one forced upon it when the strength of the masses reached a certain point. Thus it was the form under which bourgeois rule would come to an end and the rule of the proletariat begin.

To start with the First Republic, Marx and Engels always regarded the democratic Jacobin Constitution of 1793 as the work of the urban lower classes, the sans-culottes (among whom modern proletarians formed but a small element); it was the more moderate but highly oligarchic constitutions of 1791 and 1795 that sprang from the wealthy bourgeoisie. In effect, for them, the bourgeoisie lost control of the revolution in 1792 and regained it only after the thermidoric reaction of 1794 — which is not to say the Jacobins had any chance of going seriously beyond the bourgeois order of things. All that these plebeian democrats really accomplished, as Engels put it, was "to lead the bourgeois revolution to victory in spite of the bourgeoisie themselves."[18] Marx explained that in 1789,

> the bourgeoisie was the class that *really* headed the movement. The *proletariat* and the *non-bourgeois strata of the middle class* had either not yet any interests separate from those of the bourgeoisie or

they did not yet constitute independent classes or class sub-divisions. Therefore, where they opposed the bourgeoisie, as they did in France in 1793 and 1794, they fought only for the attainment of the aims of the bourgeoisie, even if not *in the manner* of the bourgeoisie. *All French terrorism* was nothing but a *plebian way* of dealing with the *enemies of the bourgeoisie*, absolutism, feudalism and philistinism.

In another writing Marx added that "material conditions" had not yet developed sufficiently to make possible the definitive overthrow of the bourgeoisie and thus the Jacobin Republic could be "only an episode in the service of the *bourgeoisie revolution* itself. . . . The terror in France could thus by its mighty hammer-blows only serve to spirit away, as it were, the ruins of feudalism from French soil. The timidly considerate bourgeoisie would not have accomplished this task in decades."[19] While thus it served the bourgeois cause unwittingly, the Jacobin Republic was nonetheless created by the lower classes at a point where they "opposed the bourgeoisie" and sought to create a political form that would serve "plebian" interests. As soon as bourgeois elements regained control in 1794 they scuttled the Jacobin Republic as quickly as possible, creating the so-called Directory whose electoral law was adapted from the original constitution of 1791 and prescribed property qualifications so high that only the richest twenty-five thousand Frenchmen were able to stand as candidates for the legislature. Oligarchy, not democracy, was the preferred form of the French revolutionary bourgeoisie. In broader terms, the plebian republic figured as a transition between absolute monarchy and the kind of constitutional monarchy through which the French bourgeoisie —by means of property qualifications—became accustomed to govern.[20]

With the Restoration of 1815, as Marx saw it, political power devolved upon *"big landed property"* under the restored Bourbon dynasty and under a new constitution that limited voting rights to the wealthiest one hundred thousand property owners. But landed property no longer implied feudal rule, since the pre-1789 legal system was not restored and since much of the land itself had fallen into the hands of bourgeois families. Thus "large landed property, despite its feudal coquetry and pride of race, has been rendered thoroughly bourgeois by the development of modern society." It now figured for Marx simply as the Legitimist faction of the bourgeoisie. This oligarchy was then overturned by the July Revolution of 1830 to make room for the reign of Louis Philippe, duke of Orleans, and the rule of the wealthiest *two* hundred thousand property owners, the plutocrats of "high finance, large-scale industry, large-scale trade, that is, *capital*, with its retinue of lawyers, professors and smooth-tongued orators," who henceforth became for Marx the Orleanist faction of the Party of Order.[21] Under Louis Philippe, in fact, Marx perceived the purest form of bourgeois rule: "the July monarchy was nothing but a joint-stock company for the exploitation of France's national wealth, the dividends of which were divided among ministers, Chambers, 240,000 voters and their adherents." In this monarchy the new aristocracy of finance "sat on the throne, it dictated laws in the Chambers, it distributed public offices, from cabinet portfolios to tobacco bureau posts."[22]

The extremely narrow franchise still excluded whole layers of the bourgeoisie itself, some of which now embraced republicanism (though not necessarily universal suffrage) in the period leading up to the 1848 revolution. Coalescing around the newspaper, *National*, this republican faction of the bourgeoisie appeared to Marx not to be "held together by great common interests and marked off by specific conditions of production. It was a clique of republican-minded bourgeois, writers, lawyers, officers and officials."[23] Also opposed to the July Monarchy were the petty-bourgeois or democratic republicans, heirs of the Jacobin tradition, grouped around the newspaper, *Réforme*. Finally there was the proletariat itself which played the key role in the February Revolution and especially in its most radical achievement — the proclamation of a republic based on universal suffrage. "The *Provisional Government* which emerged from the February barricades necessarily mirrored in its composition the different parties which shared in the victory" — that is, the republican faction of the bourgeoisie, the democratic-republican petty bourgeoisie, and the red republican proletariat whose representatives on the provisional government were Louis Blanc and Albert. By insisting upon a democratic republic the proletariat had won "the terrain for the fight for its revolutionary emancipation, but by no means this emancipation itself." With the achievement of universal suffrage, "instead of only a few factions of the bourgeoisie, all classes of French society were suddenly hurled into the orbit of political power."[24] Thus Marx by no means regarded the initial February Revolution or the democratic republic it created as the work of the bourgeoisie. Far more, it was the work of the proletariat and its petty-bourgeois allies, along with which one faction of the bourgeoisie played a modest role. The initial February Republic was not depicted as a fraud or a mask for bourgeois dictatorship, but as something which hurled all classes "into the orbit of political power," and as the "terrain" on which the proletariat could eventually emancipate itself.

The peasant majority of France revealed its conservative face in the National Assembly elections of May 1848, leaving the bourgeois republicans with the upper hand in this constituent body. The provisional government was now replaced by a new executive from which all socialist influence was excluded and which then proceeded to provoke the Parisian workers into the hopeless June insurrection. Even as Marx received news of their crushing defeat, however, he urged the readers of the *Neue Rheinische Zeitung* not to conclude that the struggle to create the democratic republic had been futile or meaningless. "The republic has bared the head of the monster [the class struggle] by knocking off the crown which shielded and concealed it." He went on to generalize: "the best form of state is that in which the social contradictions are not blurred, not arbitrarily — that is merely artificially, and therefore only seemingly — kept down. The best form of state is that in which these contradictions reach a stage of open struggle in the course of which they are resolved."[25] The best form of state, in a word, is still the democratic republic.

Once the new French rulers had settled with the proletarian threat they went on in short order to tear out all the vital organs of the February Republic. Martial law (the state of siege) was extended from Paris to other trouble spots, until eventually half the departments of France fell under its iron grip. Then the two monarchist factions of the bourgeoisie pushed aside the weak republican faction and passed a law in March 1849 permitting them to close down any and all political clubs. This was followed in May 1850 by a crippling press law that destroyed what little remained of the right to free speech. Marx railed repeatedly against these measures, against the gross hypocrisy of a bourgeoisie that took back in its repressive legislation virtually all the individual rights it had inscribed in its constitution. We will save further discussion of this question until chapter 6 where Marx and Engels' views on individual rights will be analyzed at length. Finally, when the institution of universal suffrage — the very heart of democracy — began to produce threatening results in the by-elections of March 1850, it too was excised without further ado. The right to vote was restricted in such a way as to exclude, according to Marx's (somewhat exaggerated) estimate, two-thirds of the former electorate, as the bourgeoisie reverted to its more familiar oligarchical mode of rule. Though elected to power democratically enough, the bourgeois government had thus eviscerated the February Republic within the space of twenty months, and the republican shell itself survived only because no monarchist alternative could be found. The two dominant factions of the bourgeoisie, Legitimist and Orleanist, could not

agree *which* dynasty to restore and so continued to tolerate the republican form that was preferred by only the weakest bourgeois faction. "Only
under this form," Marx declared, "could the two great divisions of the
French bourgeoisie unite, and thus put the rule of their class instead of
the regime of a privileged faction of it on the order of the day." In this
sense only, the eviscerated and oligarchic republic could be said to have
become the preferred form of government for the *united* bourgeoisie — it
was the form that divided them least.[26]

It was this mockery of a republic that Marx labeled variously as a
"bourgeois republic," a "tricolor republic," or a "parliamentary republic," but never as a democratic republic and never, *nota bene,* as a
"bourgeois democracy." Surely no ground remained for regarding it as
democratic. This was also the only republic Marx ever declared to be a
"dictatorship of the bourgeoisie." Contrary to widespread impressions,
Marx did not regard all class government as inherently dictatorial; he
distinguished between governments that ruled under some system of
laws and those which ruled extralegally or with contempt for the law.
On this basis he held all provisional governments created by revolution
necessarily to be dictatorships, regardless of form, as we saw in volume
1. In the case at hand, the bourgeois government itself had declared a
"commissioned dictatorship" to deal with the June insurgents by means
of the state of siege, that is, outside the framework of ordinary law, and
such states of siege, extended all around the country, became the characteristic feature of its rule. Marx really only threw back in its face what
this government had proclaimed itself to be.[27] Neither Marx nor Engels
ever called the American republic a dictatorship or any British government except the Palmerston cabinet of 1855–1858, of which Marx said:
"Palmerston's administration was not that of an ordinary cabinet. It was
a dictatorship." Here is a classic exception that proves the rule: "ordinary" British governments were not dictatorial but Palmerston's high-
handed personal rule, especially his "penal dissolution" of the House of
Commons in March 1857, earned him the label. Marx and Engels used
the same label often enough in regard to Louis Napoleon and Bismarck,
for parallel reasons, and also to describe the capitalist's rule *within* the
factory, as we will see presently, but they did not use it for all governments indiscriminately. One never hears, for example, of feudal dictatorship or Athenean dictatorship.[28]

At all events, the martial law republic soon degenerated even further
into the personal despotism of the new Napoleon. As we observed in chapter 2, Marx summed up this process by reference to the needs of a bour-

geoisie which "was compelled by its class position to annihilate, on the one hand, the vital conditions of all parliamentary power, and therefore, likewise, of its own, and to render irresistible, on the other hand, the executive power hostile to it." Once again, as in 1793, the democratic republic had proved to be but a passing phase. For Europe generally Marx now drew the notable conclusion that *"the republic* signifies *in general only the political form of the revolutionizing of bourgeois society* and not its *conservative form of life."*[29] It could not be a conservative life form precisely because of its democratic features, because within its political forms lay the following "fundamental contradiction":

> The classes whose social slavery the constitution is to perpetuate, proletariat, peasantry, petty bourgeoisie, it puts in possession of political power through universal suffrage. And from the class whose old social power it sanctions, the bourgeoisie, it withdraws the political guarantees of this power. It forces the political rule of the bourgeoisie into democratic conditions, which at every moment help the hostile classes to victory and jeopardize the very foundations of bourgeois society.[30]

Far from guaranteeing bourgeois rule, then, the democratic republic puts the masses "in possession of political power," *if* they know how to use it, of course. As they begin to learn, the bourgeoisie simultaneously learns how dangerous democratic forms really are. It senses what Odilon Barrot, one of the bourgeois leaders of the Second Republic, recognized in despair: "legality is the death of us!" Soon enough legality, or in any event democratic legality, disappears. The example of the Second French Republic thus seemed to confirm the lessons of the first and fixed the pattern within which Marx thereafter thought about the republican form of government in Europe.

The Third Republic, created after two decades of Bonapartist rule, seemed at first but a third confirmation of the same lessons, as it mindlessly repeated — or appeared to repeat — the history of its predecessors. As Napoleon's praetorian rule collapsed ignominiously on the battlefield of Sedan, it was the forces of the petty bourgeoisie and proletariat in radical Paris that once again proclaimed a democratic republic in September 1870. But once again the peasant masses elected a conservative majority to the National Assembly. Once again the bourgeois executive chosen by this assembly provoked the Paris radicals into a showdown in which the short-lived Paris Commune was suppressed with a bitter fury that even exceeded the butchery of 1848. Once again the National Assembly then failed to restore a monarchy only because the various factions of the bourgeoisie could not agree *which* dynasty to restore. Small wonder, then, that Marx did not take this Third Republic very seriously. It was bound to end up eventually like its predecessors, as he insisted in the First Draft of his *Civil War in France:* "the other Republic can be nothing but the *anonymous* terrorism of all monarchical fractions, of the combined legitimists, orleanists, and bonapartists to land in an Empire quelconque [of whatever sort] as its final goal, the *anonymous* terror of class rule which having done its dirty work will always burst into an Empire!" Such a republic, he added in the Second Draft (in his still unpolished English) can "only be an interreign."[31]

Marx did not, it would seem, live long enough to revise his first impressions of the Third Republic seriously. Thus from his writings about France, and from those of Engels prior to his partner's death, we may sum up their opinions about the relation between the democratic republic and the various social classes of European society. They might call it the most "consistent form of bourgeois rule," insofar as it represented the most consistent application of the principles of freedom and equality which had been worked out by the bourgeoisie in its struggle against feudalism and absolutism: "on its banner it must inscribe human rights in place of the old system of social position based on birth. . . . Therefore, for consistency's sake, it must demand universal and direct suffrage, freedom of the press, association and assembly."[32] Nonetheless, only the most consistent spokesmen of the bourgeoisie, notably among its scribes and orators, pressed these demands with any conviction. The bulk of the bourgeoisie preferred open class oligarchy — through property qualifications — under a constitutional monarchy. The call for a "pure" democratic republic was more frequently to be found among spokesmen of the petty bourgeoisie, who sensed that in less developed capitalist countries with lingering peasant majorities universal suffrage would give power to the "little people," people like themselves. Simultaneously, however, it was a demand in which the proletariat itself was vitally concerned, because the rapidly expanding numbers of the working class would soon make it the majority class in all industrialized countries. Everywhere a democratic republic could be expected to be established eventually, either by the pressure of the petty bourgeoisie and proletariat combined or, if late enough, by the pressure of the proletariat alone — but in either case over the resistance of the high bourgeoisie. In this sense Marx and Engels could speak of the democratic republic as the "highest" or "last" form of state in bourgeois society, not because it was the most preferred by the bourgeoisie, but because it would eventually be forced upon that class by pressure from below. At the end of his life Engels remembered: "for forty years Marx and I have repeated to satiety that for us the democratic republic is the only political form in which the struggle between the working class and the capitalist class can first take on a universal character and then be completed through the decisive victory of the proletariat."[33]

With these understandings we might turn briefly to Marx's last major political writing, the paradoxical *Critique of the Gotha Program* (1875), which has been quoted by some to prove Marx a friend of the democratic republic and by others to prove him an enemy of democracy. Marx first reproached the drafters of this German socialist program because their political demands did not go *beyond* the democratic demands put forth by their rivals, the petty-bourgeois pale democrats: "its political demands contain nothing beyond the old democratic litany familiar to all: universal suffrage, direct legislation, popular rights, a people's militia, etc. They are a mere echo of the bourgeois People's Party."[34] He meant that the workers' party ought to distinguish itself from the pale democrats even within the sphere of purely political demands; the Paris Commune had just demonstrated how much further the workers' republic could go, for example, in the democratization of executive power — a subject we will come to in chapter 5. Marx scorned the "old democratic litany," not because he rejected democratic institutions, but as usual in order to point out the inadequacy of nonsocialist democracy.

A hesitancy to deal with executive power flawed the political section of the draft program, as Marx saw it, from beginning to end. Of the various reforms demanded, he commented: "all those pretty little gewgaws rest on the recognition of the so-called sovereignty of the people and hence are appropriate only in a *democratic republic*." The program drafters had not demanded a republic or, indeed, any democratization of the vast executive powers wielded by Bismarck in the name of the hereditary emperor. Marx regretted that the party did not have the "courage" to call for a "democratic republic," but since that was legally impossible, he though it wiser not to demand "things which have meaning only in a democratic republic from a state which is nothing but a police-guarded military despotism." He concluded with a backhanded compliment to the pale democrats:

Even vulgar democracy, which sees the millennium in the democratic republic and has no suspicion that it is precisely in this last
form of state of bourgeois society that the class struggle has to be
fought out to a conclusion — even it towers mountains above this
kind of democratism which keeps within the limits of what is permitted by the police and not permitted by logic.[35]

The democratic republic, though not the final goal of the workers' movement, was nonetheless an important intermediate goal. In Germany particularly that republic was not likely to be established by the bourgeoisie;
it would be imposed upon that class by mass revolution and would mark
the beginning of the end of bourgeois society. Assuming the workers began
their rule in such a provisionally established democratic republic, Marx
could also call it a proletarian dictatorship, that is, a democratically organized but extralegal revolutionary government of the proletariat. This
is why the *Critique of the Gotha Program* could call for a democratic
republic and *"the revolutionary dictatorship of the proletariat"* practically in the same breath. Under the circumstances Marx envisaged, they
would be one and the same thing. Exactly the same assumptions applied
to Engels' otherwise enigmatic assertion in his critique of the Erfurt Program sixteen years later that the German workers "can only come to power
under the form of a democratic republic. That is, indeed, the specific
form of the dictatorship of the proletariat."[36]
     These interpretations may be put to a final test by examining what
Engels wrote about France in the period following Marx's death. The
Third Republic became a "bourgeois democracy" properly so called, and
one that did not prove transitory. For history was not destined to repeat
itself a third time: the assorted monarchists continued to stalemate one
another while the tenuously established democratic institutions of the
Third Republic gradually took root. Perhaps it was *because* the radicalism of Paris had been so thoroughly crushed in 1871 that the forces of
order seemed to find democracy less dangerous this time, such that universal suffrage and parliamentary government survived to become permanent institutions of the Third Republic. The traditional political freedoms likewise survived, albeit frequently impaired for radical workers
by the sporadic harassment of their organizations during the early decades. Already in 1877 we find Engels expressing in private correspondence
the hope that "finally the conflict over the *form of state*, grown pointless
in France, should cease and the republic should appear for what it is —
the classical form of bourgeois rule"; we even find Marx wishing that

this "bourgeois republic wins out or else the old game will begin all over again."[37] By 1884 Engels would lump the Third Republic together with the American republic as a relatively stable form of bourgeois rule, although its dangers for the ruling class had not been forgotten. He wrote to Eduard Bernstein:

> The consistent form of bourgeois rule is precisely the democratic republic, which has become too dangerous, however, because of the already attained development of the proletariat — but which as France and America demonstrate is still possible for simple bourgeois rule. . . . Liberal constitutional monarchy is an adequate form of bourgeois rule (1) in the beginning when the bourgeoisie has not yet settled things with the absolute monarchy, and (2) in the end when the proletariat makes the democratic republic too dangerous. And nevertheless the democratic republic still remains the *last* form of bourgeois rule — the one in which it goes to pieces.[38]

The second phase of constitutional monarchy seems to be a reference to Bonapartism (the Second Empire in France was formally a constitutional one, likewise the Bismarckian empire). This is confirmed in another contemporaneous letter to Bernstein:

> In the class struggle between the proletariat and bourgeoisie, Bonapartist monarchy . . . plays a role similar to that of the old absolutist monarchy in the struggle between feudalism and bourgeoisie. But just as this struggle could not be fought out under the old absolutist monarchy but only under the constitutional (England, France 1789–92 and 1815–30), so the one between bourgeoisie and proletariat only in the republic. If therefore favorable conditions and a revolutionary tradition have helped to overthrow Bonap[arte] and to [establish] the bourgeois republic, then the French have the advantage over us, stuck in a mishmash of semifeudalism and Bonapartism, of possessing already the form in which the struggle must be fought out, and which we must first *conquer* for ourselves. They are politically a whole stage ahead of us.[39]

Thus Bonapartism still appeared to the aging Engels to be the "normal" penultimate form — precociously superseded by the French for special reasons — before the final democratic republic in which bourgeois rule "goes to pieces." France had joined America as an exception.

But how did the French bourgeoisie manage to retain its power for so many years in spite of democratic institutions? Engels provided the most general answer to this question in another 1884 writing, his *Origin of the Family*. He began with the observation quoted earlier, that "in most historical states" rights had been apportioned according to wealth, most recently "in the electoral qualifications in modern parliamentary states." But such arrangements were not essential to bourgeois rule:

> The highest form of the state, the democratic republic, which in our modern social conditions becomes more and more an unavoidable necessity and is the form of state in which alone the last decisive battle between proletariat and bourgeoisie can be fought out — the democratic republic no longer officially recognizes differences of property. Wealth here employs its power indirectly, but all the more surely. It does this in two ways: by plain corruption of officials, of which America is the classic example; and by an alliance between the government and the stock exchange, which is effected all the more easily the higher the state debt mounts. . . . And lastly the possessing class rules directly by means of universal suffrage. As long as the oppressed class — in our case, therefore, the proletariat — is not yet ripe for its self-liberation, so long will it in its majority recognize the existing order of society as the only possible one and remain politically the tail of the capitalist class, its extreme left wing. But in the measure in which it matures toward its self-emancipation, in the same measure it constitutes itself as its own party and votes for its own representatives, not those of the capitalists. Universal suffrage is thus the gauge of the maturity of the working class.[40]

Whatever the influence of corruption (to be dealt with in the next section), whatever the influence creditors might exert over their debtors, clearly for Engels the democratic republic could serve bourgeois needs only so long as majorities could be won for capitalist parties, that is, only so long as the proletariat was "not yet ripe for its self-liberation." And Engels never doubted for a moment that the proletariat would soon attain its maturity: whatever harassments the workers' movement might have to endure, whatever subtler forms of opinion manipulation the bourgeoisie might devise to retain its moral sway over the masses, the self-education and organization of the proletariat would move relentlessly forward. Engels noted in 1892 that, although the French bourgeoisie had now managed to keep possession of the helm for twenty years, "they are already showing lively signs of decadence. A durable reign of the bourgeoisie has been possible only in countries like America, where feudalism was unknown, and society at the very beginning started from a bourgeois basis. And even in France and America, the successors of the bourgeoisie, the working people, are already knocking at the door."[41] In the long run neither petty legal obstacles nor opinion manipulation could hold back the maturation of the working people; bourgeois democracy still remained a formula for self-destruction.

Would the workers, then, simply inherit the Third Republic by voting themselves into power? The question of peaceful revolution will be treated in chapter 10 below. For now, suffice it to say that, for Engels, nothing in the *forms* of such government would prevent a peaceful and legal assumption of power, and in 1891 he expressly included France on a list of countries where the peaceful possibility existed. But it was no more than a *possibility*, since it hinged on the willingness of the old ruling class to step down after electoral defeat, and the traditions of the French upper classes did not offer much hope in this respect. Thus it was "ten to one," Engels wrote Paul Lafargue in 1892, "that universal suffrage, intelligently used by the workers, will drive the rulers to overthrow legality": but such a development would not thwart the workers' victory for it would put them "in the most favorable position to make the revolution." On the other hand there was the opposite chance, the one-to-ten chance that the same democratic republic which had served as a vehicle for bourgeois rule would then serve for proletarian rule. This is suggested in another letter to Lafargue in 1894:

> A republic, in relation to the proletariat, differs from a monarchy only in that it is the *ready-made* political form for the future rule of the proletariat. You [French] have the advantage of us [Germans] in that it is already in being; we, for our part, shall have to waste 24 hours creating it. But a republic, like any other form of government, is determined by what composes it; so long as it is the form of *bourgeois* rule, it is quite as hostile to us as any monarchy whatsoever (save in the *forms* of that hostility).[42]

Thus the *forms* of the Third Republic seemed to Engels "*ready-made*" for future proletarian rule. While Marx and Engels sometimes spoke of the need to "smash" the bureaucratic and military apparatus of the existing state, they never spoke of smashing democratic institutions of representation and self-government, even bourgeois ones. They never even suggested that representation in the workers' republic must be based on organizations like the Russian soviets, as opposed to the traditional geographic constituencies of the bourgeois parliamentary tradition. On the other hand, though the forms of the bourgeois republic might be ready-made, Marx and Engels did not at all imagine that the leadership of the labor movement would simply move into the ministerial posts and other high offices of state to govern as a professional cadre in the manner of their bourgeois predecessors. Their expectations in this regard will emerge more fully in chapter 5.

The United States

If we venture across the Atlantic now, the most striking political difference obviously would be the existence of a stable democratic republic throughout the lifetimes of Marx and Engels. If in fact they conceived "bourgeois democracy" to be a rare bird and not the characteristic form of rule in capitalist society, then the American republic would have to be treated as an exception, requiring some special explanation for its existence and stability. Sure enough, from the earliest writings to the last, we find constant allusions to, and explanations for, America's *political* exceptionalism. To start with, Marx and Engels did not regard the American republic as the creation of the *high* bourgeoisie. They rather spoke of "small and middle land ownership of the farmers" as being "the basis of the whole political constitution." Engels added that the United States was "founded by *petits bourgeois* and peasants who ran away from European feudalism."[43] We have already seen how a "pure" democratic republic for Marx and Engels was the most suitable political form to meet the needs of the petty — as opposed to the high — bourgeoisie, so it would not be surprising to find such a republic constructed by the farmers and artisans who established themselves in the New World.

This is not to say the two men overlooked extremes of wealth and poverty: in 1847 Marx found them to appear all the more "harshly" in the absence of formal political inequalities. Subsequent comments, particularly after the period of the Civil War, would give increasing stress to the process of social polarization, but until the 1880s both men regarded the class struggle in America as relatively undeveloped.[44] This figured prominently in Marx's first major explanation of American exceptionalism in *The Eighteenth Brumaire:*

The republic signifies *in general only the political form of the revolutionizing of bourgeois society* and not its *conservative form of life,* as, for example, in the United States of North America, where, though classes already exist, they have not yet become fixed, but continually change and interchange their component elements in constant flux, where the modern means of production, instead of coinciding with a stagnant surplus population, rather compensate for the relative deficiency of heads and hands, and where, finally, the feverish, youthful movement of material production, which has to make a new world its own, has left neither time nor opportunity for abolishing the old spirit world.[45]

Engels struck some of the same chords in a contemporaneous article picking apart the anarchist slogan, "abolition of the state":

In *bourgeois* countries the abolition of the state means that the power of the state is reduced to the level found in North America. There, the class contradictions are but incompletely developed; every clash between the classes is concealed by the outflow of the surplus proletarian population to the west; intervention by the power of the state, reduced to a minimum in the east, does not exist at all in the west.[46]

Because of these various special circumstances, the emerging American bourgeoisie required but little organized coercion to maintain its property and its social domination — the democratic republic served it well enough.

In later years Engels gave particular stress to the absence of a feudal past in his explanations of American exceptionalism. An 1886 letter to Florence Kelley Wischnewetzky greeted the emergence of open class struggle in the United States and commented on the relative tardiness of its appearance:

America after all is the ideal of all bourgeois: a country rich, vast, expanding, with purely bourgeois institutions unleavened by feudal remnants of monarchical traditions, and without a permanent and hereditary proletariat. Here every one could become, if not a capitalist, at all events an independent man, producing or trading, with his own means, for his own account. And because there were not, *as yet,* classes with opposing interests, our — and your — bourgeois thought that America stood *above* class antagonisms and struggles. That delusion has now broken down.[47]

In another letter he commented on "how firmly rooted are bourgeois prejudices even in the working class in such a young country, which has never known feudalism and has grown up on a bourgeois basis from the beginning." These elaborations help flesh out Engels' rather bareboned conclusion quoted earlier that "a durable reign of the bourgeoisie has been possible only in countries like America, where feudalism was unknown, and society at the very beginning started from a bourgeois basis."[48]

Engels seemed particularly impressed that bourgeois rule in the United States required so little coercive force against the lower classes, at least until late in the century. His 1850 reference to the minimum of "intervention by the power of the state" in the East and its complete absence in the West was a theme to which he returned in *The Origin of the Family.* Here he identified the existence of a "public force" (army, police, prisons, etc.) as the distinguishing essence of any state, but then felt compelled to add: "it may be very insignificant, practically negligible, in societies with still undeveloped class antagonisms and living in remote areas, as at times and in places in the United States of America."[49] But if the "public force" was "practically negligible" throughout most of the American experience, that meant that the state of Engels' original conception was "practically negligible," that the machinery of class domination remained peripheral in America until toward the end of the nineteenth century.

Not only was bourgeois rule in America distinguished by minimal coercion, but also by the absence of property qualifications for voting such as typified bourgeois rule in Europe. With the obvious and gross exception of chattel slavery, Marx and Engels found surprisingly little to criticize when they wrote about American political forms *as forms.* Indeed, one is struck by how often they held up the American republic as an example for backward Europe. From volume 1 the reader may recall how the young Marx pointed to America's press laws as guarantees of free speech in contrast to Prussia's ruthless censorship, or how Engels praised its independent judiciary and jury system in order to expose Prussia's backwardness.[50] During the American Civil War, Marx wrote tirelessly to mobilize European opinion for the Northern cause. He grandly declared the war to be a conflict between "the highest form of popular self-government till now realized" and "the most shameless form of man's enslaving recorded in the annals of history." He went out of his way to emphasize how the planter elite had used secession as an excuse "to overthrow the internal constitutions of the slave states, to subjugate completely the part of the white population that had still maintained some independence under the democratic Constitution and protection of the Union."[51] In sharp contrast to this "democratic Constitution," the Confederate constitution was a "usurpation," he wrote to Engels, for "nowhere did they let the people en masse vote" on its ratification. Thus secession not only confirmed the enslavement of the entire black population, but amounted to "the strengthening and the sharpening of the hold of the oligarchy of 300,000 Southern slavelords over five million whites."[52] The "slaveowners revolt" and the "oligarchy of 300,000 slaveholders," became the standard epithets with which Marx excoriated the Southern cause.

As late as 1875, in his *Critique of the Gotha Program*, Marx still held up the American political model as he objected to the draft demand for *"elementary education by the state"*:

Defining by a general law the expenditures on elementary schools, the qualifications of the teaching staff, the branches of instruction, etc., and, as is done in the United States, supervising the fulfillment of these legal specifications by state inspectors, is a very different thing from appointing the state as educator of the people! Government and church should rather be equally excluded from any influence on the school. Particularly, indeed, in the Prusso-German Empire . . . the state has need, on the contrary, of a very stern education by the people.[53]

In parallel fashion, when it was his turn to criticize the Erfurt Program in 1891, Engels wanted to see the demands include "complete self-administration on the American model of each local community." The American model had demonstrated, he noted approvingly, that such administration could be accomplished without a bureaucracy.[54] From 1843, then, until 1891 there is almost uniform praise for the political forms of American democracy. Significantly, each time Marx or Engels spoke of specific countries where the workers' revolution might come peacefully and legally, the United States was consistently included.

Perhaps all this praise must be taken with a grain of salt since it was aimed at a European audience. Could it be that Marx and Engels accentuated the American positive as a foil for the European negative? Suspicions are certainly aroused in the case of their Civil War writings when we find Marx publicly extolling the Union as "the highest form of popular self-government till now realized" in 1861, but privately complaining to Engels in 1862 about its sluggish war effort, "only to be expected from a *bourgeois* republic, where fraud [*Schwindel*] has long reigned supreme." Engels agreed wholeheartedly, finding it "mortifying that a lousy oligarchy with only half the number of inhabitants proves itself just as strong as the unwieldy, great, helpless democracy," from which he drew the lesson that "even in America the bourgeois republic exposes itself in thoroughgoing fashion, so that in future it can never again be preached on its own merits, but solely as a means and a form of transition to the social revolution."[55]

The theme of fraud and corruption sounded here would rise fortissimo as the leitmotif of all Marx and Engels' subsequent comments on American politics. In an 1879 interview Marx declared that American workers must form their own party because "they can no longer trust politicians. Rings and cliques have seized upon the Legislature, and politics has been made a trade."[56] Engels also referred to "the republic of capitalist businessmen, in which politics are a business deal like any other." In an 1892 letter he offered some elements of an explanation by pointing to the inevitable divergence of interests within each class in so vast a country:

> Wholly different groups and interests are represented in each of the two big parties, depending on the locality, and almost each particular section of the possessing class has its representatives in each of the two parties to a very large degree, though *today* big industry forms the core of the Republicans on the whole, just as the big landowners of the South form that of the Democrats. The apparent haphazardness of this jumbling together is what provides the splendid soil for the corruption and the plundering of the government that flourish there so beautifully.

Under such circumstances, when any great public issue such as the tariff arises, "the leadership soon passes out of the hands of the people directly interested into those of professional politicians, the wire-pullers of the traditional political parties, whose interest is, not a settlement of the question, but its being kept open forever."[57] Here one begins to make out the features of the parasite state once again. This time it is not haughty bureaucrats or praetorian generals but corrupt professional politicians who exercise alienated social power, professional politicians who have made politics a "trade," a "business deal like any other," whose interests have thus diverged from those of their electors, and who now appear as an alien force standing over society and exploiting it for their own gain.

In 1891, not long after a trip to the United States that may have confirmed his impressions, Engels set down an absolutely classic indictment of American politics, in which the power of the state appears solely and purely as parasite, not at all as class oppression:

> Society had created its own organs to look after its common interests, originally through simple division of labor. But these organs, at whose head was the state power, had in the course of time, in pursuance of their own special interests, transformed themselves from the servants of society into the masters of society. This can be seen, for example, not only in the hereditary monarchy, but equally so in the democratic republic. Nowhere do "politicians" form a more separate and powerful section of the nation than precisely in North America. There, each of the two major parties which alternately succeed each other in power is itself in turn controlled by people who make a business of politics, who speculate on seats in legislative assemblies of the Union as well as of the separate states, or who make a living by carrying on agitation for their party and on its victory are rewarded with positions. It is well known how the Americans have been trying for thirty years to shake off this yoke, which has become intolerable, and how in spite of it all they continue to sink ever deeper in this swamp of corruption. It is precisely in America that we see best how there takes place this process of the state power making itself independent in relation to society, whose mere instrument it was originally intended to be. Here there exists no dynasty, no nobility, no standing army, beyond the few men keeping watch on the Indians, no bureaucracy with permanent posts or the right to pensions. And nevertheless we find here two great gangs of political speculators, who alternately take possession of the state power and exploit it by the most corrupt means and for the most corrupt ends — and the nation is powerless against these two great cartels of politicians, who are ostensibly its servants, but in reality dominate and plunder it.[58]

No army and no bureaucracy but nonetheless "two great gangs of political speculators" who constitute a parasite on the body politic, and who plunder it not so much in the interest of the bourgeoisie as in their own direct interest. It is doubtful that Engels meant to imply a parasite state in the same degree as the Bonapartist one—America remained for him a "republic of capitalist businessmen," but one in which the *tendency* toward parasitism was highly developed. Wherever political leadership had become professionalized, whether elective or not, this "striving" for independence which we analyzed in the last two chapters ("the process of the state power making itself independent" as Engels called it here) was bound to assert itself with growing force.[59]

How very interesting it is to find that Engels' last major statement on America should employ the same conceptual dichotomy as Marx's first one in 1843—the antagonism between "state power" and "[civil] society"! Marx's initial view of America, presented in volume 1, did not call attention to corruption to be sure, but neither did it suggest class rule of any sort. Rather it depicted the democratic republic as "man's *species-life* in *opposition* to his material life. All the presuppositions of this egoistic life remain in *civil society outside* the state." Moreover the democratic state seemed incapable of overcoming the egoism of civil society: it always ended up by "recognizing, re-establishing, and necessarily allowing itself to be dominated by it."[60] From the notion of a democratic republic mired in the egoism of civil society and "dominated" by it, little imagination is required to foresee the extension of egoism into the level of political leadership. Public corruption was the all too predictable result of a society which glorified egoism in private life; politics was bound to become a business deal like any other.

Throughout their lives, then, Marx and Engels found it easier to explain the American state in terms of social parasitism than class despotism. Without highly developed institutions of repression, without legally entrenched political privileges for the capitalist class, it remained something of an anomaly among class states. Its political forms might even be admired *as forms*, so long as one remembered how they were continually undermined by the egoism of its civil society, by the values of a society resting on private property and a capitalist division of labor, including those values which sanctioned the domination of the capitalist over his workers within the factory.

Capitalist Rule Within the Factory

It would be a gross disservice to Marx and Engels to discuss the various forms of bourgeois rule without giving attention to the form they considered primordial, even though that form is not considered *political* in the conventional sense of the word. We noted in the foregoing chapter

Marx and Engels' distinction between the political power and the social power of the bourgeoisie, and how the former might even be given over to a Napoleon the better to safeguard the latter.[61] Whatever form of state might exist in bourgeois society — whether a classic oligarchy of property owners under a constitutional monarchy, or a Bonapartist despotism dominating the ruling and ruled classes alike, or a democratic republic under bourgeois leadership — under all these forms the "social power" of the bourgeoisie remained intact. That social power included first and foremost the command power of capital over labor in the workplace. And such command power was, as Marx and Engels perceived it, utterly political in the broader sense of the word — having to do with the authority and domination of man over man. "The relationship of domination," Marx wrote in the *Grundrisse,* involves the "appropriation of another's *will,*" and it was precisely the workman's will — not just his labor but his "labor-power" — that the capitalist purchased for a given period.[62] The workman who sold his "labor-power" was obliged to place himself under the command of the capitalist for perhaps twelve or fourteen hours a day, and to do so again and again throughout his working life. Whatever the form of state, this authority of the capitalist within the factory was bound to affect the worker's life most directly and most pervasively.

To view the relationship of the capitalist and worker as essentially political is one of the central and distinctive features of Marx and Engels' philosophy and finds expression in all their major writings. As early as the Paris manuscripts of 1844 Marx depicted this relationship as one of master to servant, or *Herr* to *Knecht,* thus involving *Herrschaft* (rule or domination) and *Knechtschaft* (bondage or servitude); "capital," he declared, "is thus the *governing power* [Regierungsgewalt] over labor and its products."[63] The same theme was taken up by Engels in his first book, *The Condition of the Working-Class in England,* with a wealth of empirical detail drawn from his Manchester experiences. Within the factory, Engels asserted, "the despotic will of the manufacturer reigns supreme. He issues his arbitrary edicts and modifies them as he sees fit." He explained further:

> The slavery which the middle classes have imposed on the workers can be seen most clearly in the factory system. There, in law and in fact, the operative loses all his rights. He must arrive at the factory by half-past five in the morning. He is fined if he arrives a few minutes late. If he is ten minutes late he is locked out until after breakfast and loses a quarter of a day's pay, although he has only

actually missed 2½ hours work out of twelve. He is forced to eat, drink and sleep to a fixed routine. He is allowed only the minimum time to satisfy the most urgent demands of nature.

The manufacturer's private tyranny cannot be challenged through public law. "However absurd his rules may be, the worker can get no redress from the Courts. The magistrate says to him: 'After all, you are your own master. You need not have entered into such a contract if you didn't wish to.'" On the other hand employers often managed to have the courts imprison workers for breach of contract, where deductions from wages and the threat of dismissal did not provide sufficient sanction to compel their obedience.[64]

By the time of the *Communist Manifesto* Marx and Engels had introduced a military metaphor to characterize the relationship in question:

> Modern industry has converted the little workshop of the patriarchal master into the great factory of the industrial capitalist. Masses of laborers, crowded into the factory, are organized like soldiers. As privates of the industrial army they are placed under the command of the perfect hierarchy of officers and sergeants. Not only are they slaves of the bourgeois class, and of the bourgeois State; they are daily and hourly enslaved by the machine, by the overlooker, and, above all, by the individual bourgeois manufacturer himself. The more openly this despotism proclaims gain to be its end and aim, the more petty, the more hateful and the more embittering it is.[65]

The military metaphor reappeared in *Capital*, where the command function of the capitalist within the factory was likened to that of a general on the field of battle. Alternatively, Marx asserted that the power to direct the labor of great masses of people, a power once used by "Asiatic and Egyptian kings, Etruscan theocrats, etc." to construct the pyramids and other gigantic structures of antiquity, this power "has in modern society been transferred to the capitalist." Marx's principal work abounds with references to the "despotism of capital," the "autocracy of capital," and most interestingly, the "dictatorship of capital." If by dictatorship he meant the exercise of power unrestrained by law, Marx could scarcely have found a better example than the power exercised by the nineteenth-century capitalist within the factory.[66]

Reviewing Engels' evidence from Manchester textile mills, Marx pointed in particular to the elaborate "factory codes" specifying exact punishments in the form of fines deducted from wages for all manner of discipline infractions involving work standards, punctuality, mealtime pauses, and so on. With heavy sarcasm Marx contrasted these political arrangements in the private entrepreneurial realm with those favored by the bourgeoisie in the public sphere:

> The factory code in which capital formulates, like a private legis-lator, and at his own good will, his autocracy over his workpeople, unaccompanied by that division of responsibility, in other matters so much approved of by the bourgeoisie, and unaccompanied by the still more approved representative system, this code is but the capitalistic caricature of that social regulation of the labor-process which becomes requisite in cooperation on a great scale. . . . The place of the slave-driver's lash is taken by the overlooker's book of penalties. All punishments naturally resolve themselves into fines and deductions from wages, and the law-giving talent of the fac-tory Lycurgus so arranges matters, that a violation of his laws is, if possible, more profitable to him than the keeping of them.

It was not unknown for a worker to finish the week owing his employer more in fines than he had earned in wages. And of course even the "slave-driver's lash" was common enough where child labor predominated. The much vaunted liberal political conceptions of the bourgeoisie clearly did not extend inside the factory gate. Once the workers entered this private kingdom, "they have then ceased to belong to themselves," they have be-come the wage-slaves of the private dictator.[67] The phrase "wage-slavery" was thus more than simple metaphor or propaganda for Marx and Eng-els; capitalism was understood as a disguised system of effective slavery.

The disguise it wore had to do with the "free contract" alluded to by Engels' smug magistrate. On the surface, Marx allowed sarcastically, the contract between capitalist and worker was indeed "a very Eden of the innate rights of man":

> There alone rule Freedom, Equality, Property and Bentham. Free-dom, because both buyer and seller of a commodity, say of labor-power, are constrained only by their own free will. They contract as free agents, and the agreement they come to, is but the form in which they give legal expression to their common will. Equality,

because each enters into relation with the other, as with a simple owner of commodities, and they exchange equivalent for equivalent. Property, because each disposes only of what is his own. And Bentham, because each looks only to himself.[68]

Unlike earlier systems involving forced labor, both the buyer and the seller of labor-power appear free and equal in the eyes of the law, each pursuing his own interests.

The deceptive character of the free contract is exposed when one understands its implicit presupposition — the existence of a class of propertyless people who have no other means of keeping themselves alive. And the existence of such a class as a major segment of society is not some eternally given condition of human existence:

> Nature does not produce on the one side owners of money or commodities, and on the other men possessing nothing but their own labor-power. This relation has no natural basis, neither is its social basis one that is common to all historical periods. It is clearly the result of a past historical development, the product of many economic revolutions, of the extinction of a whole series of older forms of social production.

Peasants had to be separated from their land by the emergence of large-scale capitalist agriculture, craftsmen separated from their tools and workshops by the emergence of the factory and its power-driven machinery, shopkeepers separated from their tiny stores by the emergence of large-scale distributive enterprises, and so forth. It took a long time to transform the broadly distributed property of traditional society into the modern capitalist forms which leave a substantial and ever growing portion of the population without the means to produce their own sustenance: "It takes centuries ere the 'free' laborer, thanks to the development of capitalistic production, agrees, *i.e.*, is compelled by social conditions, to sell the whole of his active life, his very capacity for work, for the price of the necessaries of life, his birthright for a mess of pottage."[69] Once separated from the property accorded him in traditional society, the uprooted person finds he can stay alive only by selling his single remaining possession — his labor-power — to the capitalist. It is neither a matter of free choice nor a bargain struck between equals, as Engels argued poignantly on the basis of his early Manchester experience:

The worker is helpless; left to himself he cannot survive a single day. The middle classes have secured a monopoly of all the necessities of life. What the worker needs he can secure only from the middle classes, whose monopoly is protected by the authority of the State. In law and in fact the worker is the slave of the middle classes, who hold the power of life and death over him. The middle classes offer food and shelter to the worker, but only in return for an 'equivalent,' i.e. for his labor. They even disguise the true state of affairs by making it appear that the worker is acting of his own free will, as a truly free agent and as a responsible adult, when he makes his bargain with the middle classes. A fine freedom indeed, when the worker has no choice but to accept the terms offered by the middle classes or go hungry and naked like the wild beasts. A fine 'equivalent,' when it is the bourgeoisie alone which decides the terms of the bargain.[70]

Marx refined this argument in his popular 1849 writing, *Wage Labor and Capital*, where he described the relationship between the two as "the slavery of the worker, the domination of the capitalist," but where he nonetheless distinguished the free labor system from chattel slavery and serfdom:

> The slave, together with his labor power, is sold once and for all to his owner. . . . The serf belongs to the land and turns over to the owner of the land the fruits thereof. The *free laborer*, on the other hand, sells himself and, indeed, sells himself piecemeal. . . . The worker belongs neither to an owner nor to the land, but eight, ten, twelve, fifteen hours of his daily life belong to him who buys them. The worker leaves the capitalist to whom he hires himself whenever he likes, and the capitalist discharges him whenever he thinks fit, as soon as he no longer gets any profit out of him, or not the anticipated profit. But the worker, whose sole source of livelihood is the sale of his labor power, cannot leave the *whole class of purchasers, that is, the capitalist class*, without renouncing his existence. *He belongs not to this or that capitalist but to the capitalist class.*[71]

Thus, unlike the chattel slave who belongs to a particular master, or the serf who belongs to a particular estate, the wage-laborer belongs to the capitalist class as a class, since he can only stay alive by placing himself again and again under the domination of one or another capitalist. His much touted freedom reduces itself to the hollow choice of which particular master to serve.

In the *Grundrisse* Marx offered some additional thoughts on why the free contract *appears* to be a matter of freedom and equality:

> Both sides confront each other as persons. *Formally,* their relation has the equality and freedom of exchange as such. As far as concerns the legal relation, the fact that this form is a mere *semblance,* and a *deceptive semblance,* appears as an *external* matter. What the free worker sells is always nothing more than a specific, particular measure of force-expenditure [*Kraftäusserung* — MN]; labor capacity as a totality is greater than every particular expenditure. He sells the particular expenditure of force to a particular capitalist, whom he confronts as an independent *individual.* It is clear that this is not his relation to the existence of capital as capital, i.e. to the capitalist class. Nevertheless, in this way everything touching on the individual, real person leaves him a wide field of choice, of arbitrary will, and hence of formal freedom.[72]

Formal freedom and equality characterize the relationship only when perceived as a contract between two individuals for a limited term, but when perceived on a broader canvas as a quasi-permanent relationship between the worker and the entire capitalist class, then freedom and equality "prove to be inequality and unfreedom." For in reality "it is not individuals who are set free by free competition; it is, rather, capital which is set free." He went on to draw the conclusion: "This kind of individual freedom is therefore at the same time the most complete suspension of all individual freedom, and the most complete subjugation of individuality under social conditions which assume the form of objective powers."[73]

The question of individual freedom under capitalism will be explored further in chapter 6. What we have learned here about Marx and Engels' view of free contract, however, suffices to show why they regarded capitalist society as a system of domination down to its very core, quite regardless of the diverse political forms under which it might appear. Thus the capitalist class typically preferred to exercise state power as an open oligarchy of property owners. Under pressure from below it might tolerate a democratic republic, especially where it was confident of maintaining majority support. Where the class struggle grew threatening it was likely to abandon state power to a Bonapartist-style dictator. So long as these states all protected the rights of private property, however, they all preserved the fundamental command power of the capitalist in the workplace and therewith the day-in-day-out private domination of the capitalist class over the life activity of the working class. In this respect all these states were equally mechanisms of class oppression, even the otherwise admirable democratic republic.

⊰[4]⊱

The Paris Commune:
Revolutionary Strategy

MARX AND ENGELS' mature years coincided with the golden age of European bourgeois culture from the 1850s to the 1890s. With the exception of Bismarck's brief wars, international violence remained slight and far from home. Internal social violence was also minimal in an epoch of generally rising living standards, all of which seemed to find its microcosmic reflection in the outward quiet and stability of Marx and Engels' own lives in London and Manchester. There was only one interruption in this idyll of Victorian placidity — the Paris Commune of 1871. That popular uprising and its bloody suppression engaged their passions as nothing had since the glorious spring of 1848, momentarily rekindling the revolutionary ardor and hopes of their youth. It was indisputably the most important new influence on Marx and Engels' mature political thought, and what they wrote on the Paris Commune has justifiably attracted a great deal of commentary, scholarly and otherwise. From the exegetic literature alone, however, one could scarcely help concluding that the masters' writings on the subject must be full of ambiguity if not contradiction, paradox if not outright duplicity. Postponing some of these riddles for examination in chapter 5, we will concern ourselves here with those relating to revolutionary strategy.

Did Marx and Engels basically applaud the Communards and their undertaking, regretting only that their actions were not bolder still? Or did they oppose the whole effort as reckless adventurism foredoomed to failure? Even at so fundamental a level, rival interpretations stand one hundred eighty degrees apart.[1] And each school can produce impressive quotations to document its case, so long as the opposing set of quotations is ignored. Only by taking all the pertinent texts into account and arranging them in chronological order can one be fair to the evidence, which shows that the two men changed their minds — twice — about the questions at issue. In the present chapter, then, we must reconstruct Marx and Engels' changing strategy assessments during these most dramatic revolutionary events of their mature lives, and at the same time review these complicated events themselves, which will figure so prominently in our subsequent concerns.

Pre-March Cautiousness

Despite industrialization the French working class remained very much a minority at the end of the Second Empire in 1870. Concentrated in Paris and a half dozen other urban centers, it was still surrounded by the enormous peasant mass that constituted the majority of the French population. Only by making allies of these peasants, it will be argued, only by reconstituting the alliance of the majority classes described as Strategy II in the preceding volume, did Marx and Engels conceive the French workers could come to power successfully. The lessons Marx had drawn from the bloody June Days of 1848 remained just as appropriate: "the French proletariat, at the moment of a revolution, possesses in Paris real power and influence which spur it on to an effort beyond its means," hence to premature actions and inevitable repressions. The workers could not successfully smash the bourgeois order until a process of revolutionary development had "aroused the mass of the nation, the peasants and petty bourgeois, standing between the proletariat and the bourgeoisie, against this order, against the rule of capital, and had forced them to attach themselves to the proletarians as their protagonists."[2] This process of development included first and foremost the economic pressures toward concentration of ownership which could be expected increasingly to drive the peasants into bankruptcy, separating them from their small plots of land. Because Napoleon was raised to power and partly sustained by peasant support, as Marx added in *The Eighteenth Brumaire*, his regime would not survive the ruination of the smallholding system: "the entire state edifice erected on this smallholding will fall to the ground and *the proletarian revolution will obtain that chorus without which its solo becomes a swan song in all peasant countries*." This need to forge an alliance of the majority classes, to avoid another "swan song" à la 1848, provides the key for understanding Marx and Engels' otherwise puzzling shifts of position on the Paris Commune.[3]

The actual ruination of the French peasants proceeded, if at all, much more slowly than Marx and Engels had anticipated, and the two men

searched relentlessly for other signs of change, some external event perhaps, that would—if not bring the workers to power—at least destroy
the Napoleonic tyranny they hated so fiercely. The very shakiness of his
regime had propelled the French emperor into a series of risky foreign
adventures, some of which were successful enough to add luster to his
name. So it was that in July 1870 he launched his last foreign adventure—
a war against Prussia. This war, which Bismarck had invited and provoked in the hope it would advance German unification, was initiated
by Napoleon in the hope it would thwart that process, and also bring
territorial conquests to the empire along its northeastern frontier. Predictably enough, Marx and Engels immediately proclaimed themselves
in favor of a Prussian victory. "The death knell of the Second Empire
has already been sounded," Marx announced grandly in the address he
drafted for the general council of the International Working Men's Association. Marx was now at the height of his influence as a leader of this
London-based federation of workers' associations which had branches in
most European countries and in the United States. Through it he and
Engels might hope to have some modest influence on working-class attitudes toward the war and on the actions of the French workers in particular, if Napoleon's regime indeed collapsed. Marx added a warning
that the German workers should not "allow the present war to lose its
strictly defensive character," allow it to become a war of conquest
against France.[4]

While the two nations were mustering their forces during August, Marx
and Engels had a chance to review the French domestic scene and speculate on what kind of government might succeed Napoleon's. Peasant backwardness, they seemed to agree, precluded any *immediate* prospects for
the class-alliance strategy: Marx noted in the *First Address* that when,
only two months earlier, the French workers had attempted to use Napoleon's latest plebescite as a vote of no confidence in the regime, "the balance was turned by the heavy ignorance of the rural districts," producing a large progovernment majority. Moreover, Napoleon had followed
up the plebescite with a wave of arrests that left the French branch of
the IWA disoriented and leaderless. The entire twenty-year period of
Bonapartist rule, Engels lamented to Marx on August 8, has "produced
enormous demoralization. One is hardly justified in reckoning on revolutionary heroism."[5] Under the circumstances, once Napoleon suffered
defeat, a return to ordinary bourgeois rule appeared inevitable, perhaps through an immediate restoration of the Orleans dynasty, but more
likely through an interim bourgeois republic. Engels again: "I believe the

Orleanists — without the army — are not strong enough to be able to risk an immediate restoration. Since they have the only dynasty still possible, perhaps they will themselves give preference to a republican interregnum," especially since such a republic could then be saddled with the responsibility for accepting the Prussian peace terms. There was at least a silver lining in that "the French workers, whatever sort of government may succeed this one, are certain to have a freer field than under Bonapartism."[6] By mid-August the military balance seemed so heavily tipped against France that Engels categorically ruled out the possibility of a Jacobin-style *levée en masse* spawned by some radical revolution in Paris; such a government could "only make itself ridiculous in a parody of the [original] Convention."[7] When Blanqui and his followers attempted to carry out precisely such a revolution on August 14, their unmitigated fiasco was treated by Marx and Engels with the disdain of total silence.

On September 2 the Prussian armies won their decisive victory at Sedan, capturing Napoleon himself and setting in motion a rapid train of events. Paris responded to the news with mass demonstrations and a bloodless revolution on September 4 in which, faithful to Engels' predictions, a republic was declared and a "Government of National Defense" was formed that included Orleanists in all the key positions. When the new leadership immediately sued for peace, Bismarck showed his own hand by demanding the French provinces of Alsace and Lorraine. The provisional government refused to sacrifice a centimeter of French soil and the war now began again, with the Prussian armies advancing menacingly toward Paris. These events raised the political temperature in the capital to boiling point, as Blanquists were joined by neo-Jacobins and even some figures in the IWA, all scheming to bring about a second revolution and a *levée en masse* to save the capital and the nation from the insolent invader. Parody or not, Parisian radicals seemed determined to repeat the glorious deeds of 1792–1793.

Marx and Engels, who had not always themselves been immune from that seductive vision, nonetheless now combatted it from every side. Marx prepared his *Second Address* on the war, issued by the general council on September 9, which denounced the Prussian claims on Alsace-Lorraine and called upon the French workers to "perform their duties as citizens," and which also exposed the provisional government as an Orleanist bridge to monarchical restoration but simultaneously cautioned the French workers *not* to overthrow that government:

Any attempt at upsetting the new Government in the present crisis, when the enemy is almost knocking at the doors of Paris, would be a desperate folly. The French workmen must perform their duties as citizens; but, at the same time, they must not allow themselves to be deluded by the national *souvenirs* of 1792, as the French peasants allowed themselves to be deluded by the national *souvenirs* of the First Empire. They have not to recapitulate the past, but to build up the future. Let them calmly and resolutely improve the opportunities of Republican liberty, for the work of their own class organization. It will gift them with fresh Herculean powers for the regeneration of France, and our common task — the emancipation of labor. Upon their energies and wisdom hinges the fate of the Republic.[8]

"Republican liberty" should be used, then, to build up the organized strength of the working class, but not to overthrow the provisional government.

Privately, Marx acted with even greater dispatch. Already on September 6 he had Auguste Serraillier, a leading French member of the general council, sent on an urgent mission to Paris to "arrange matters" with the French branch. "This is especially necessary," Marx explained to Engels, "because today the entire *French Branch* is getting ready to commit stupidities in the name of the *International.* 'They' want to overthrow the Provisional Government, [and] establish a *Commune de Paris.*"[9] After reading Serraillier's first report from Paris, Marx found his fears confirmed and alluded gloomily to a "new *June Insurrection,*" in other words another swan song, if the Prussians did not subdue the capital swiftly enough.[10] Thus in September 1870 Marx regarded the desire to establish a Paris Commune as a pure "stupidity"; there is no reason, as we will see, to suppose that he had a different view six months later.

Simultaneously, in Manchester, Engels discussed the situation with Eugène Dupont, another French member of the general council, and agreed that the French branch should "hold back until peace has been concluded" and "make use of the freedoms unavoidably given by the Republic toward the organization of the party in France." The latter then dispatched a letter to his comrades in France: "The rôle of the workers, or rather their duty, is to let the bourgeois vermin make peace with the Prussians (for the shame of doing so will adhere to them always), not to indulge in outbreaks which would only consolidate their power, but to take advantage of the liberty which circumstances will provide to organize all the forces of the working class."[11] Engels was convinced the war was over. In a letter to Marx on September 12 he put forward the cold military appraisal "that France's active power of resistance is broken where this war is concerned, and that with it the prospects of repelling the invasion by a revolution fall to the ground too!" Further:

> Bismarck will soon be in a position to make peace, either by taking Paris or because the European situation obliges him to put an end to the war. However the peace may turn out, it must be concluded before the workers can do anything at all. If they were victorious now — in the service of national defense — they . . . would be needlessly crushed by the German armies and thrown back another twenty years. They themselves can lose nothing by waiting. The possible changes of frontier are in any case only provisional and will be reversed again. To fight for the bourgeoisie against the Prussians would be madness.

After the peace, opportunities for the workers' movement would be "more favorable" than ever before, Engels added, although even then, as he had suggested in a letter of September 7, "they will still have as their first need time to organize."[12]

For once, however, Engels' military expertise served him ill: French resistance did not collapse. To be sure, the Prussians surrounded Paris on September 19 and began a siege that was to last four months. During this period the most radical — or at all events the most vigorous — member of the provisional government, Léon Gambetta, escaped the capital by balloon to set up headquarters at Tours, later Bordeaux, where he proceeded to raise fresh armies and send them repeatedly, though unsuccessfully, against the Prussian juggernaut. His vigor contrasted markedly with the defeatist mood of the remaining members of the provisional government in Paris, led by Louis Trochu, a conservative old Orleanist general. These latter seemed to prefer Bismarck's mercy to the risks that would attend calling forth the armed manhood of the capital to break the encirclement. In the view of Paris radicals, at least, Trochu's fears of a second revolution, more than real military exhaustion or starvation, led to the capitulation of the Paris government on January 28, 1871.

During this four-month period the vision of 1792–1793 electrified the entire French left, and Marx and Engels, proved wrong by events, seemed carried along by its force as well, at least in a certain way. They were still not tempted by simple *émeutisme* of course: they heaped unremitting scorn upon Mikhail Bakunin's momentary seizure of power in Lyons on September 28, in which the anarchist leader and his friends took over the city hall and solemnly abolished the state by decree . . . until soldiers showed up to arrest them about an hour later.[13] But the example of Lyons *before* Bakunin's arrival there clearly won Marx's favor. Following the battle of Sedan, he wrote Edward Beesly, "at first everything went well" at Lyons:

> Under the pressure of the "International" section, the Republic was proclaimed before Paris had taken that step. A revolutionary government was at once established — *La Commune* — composed partly of workmen belonging to the "International," partly of Radical middle class Republicans. . . . The Bonapartist and Clerical intriguers were intimidated. Energetic means were taken to arm the whole people. The middle class began if not really to sympathize with, at least to quietly undergo, the new order of things. The action of Lyons was at once felt at Marseilles and Toulouse, where the "International" sections are strong.[14]

Communes were established in these latter cities as well, essentially local coalition governments of workers joined with radical bourgeois and petty bourgeois republicans, bringing together at least the urban components of Marx's desired alliance of the majority classes. The three provincial communes did not attempt to overthrow Gambetta, but on the contrary gave vigorous support to his national defense efforts. Marx and Engels seemed to take the same stand themselves, as they tirelessly worked to organize demonstrations in London aimed at pressuring the British government to recognize the French republic and intervene to enforce a peace without annexations.[15] Marx also transmitted a piece of Prussian military intelligence to Gambetta by way of Paul Lafargue, his son-in-law, then staying in Bordeaux. Engels drew up his own plans for the defense of France, at one point being tempted to go there in person and offer his services to Gambetta.[16] None of these activities suggests a desire to see Gambetta overthrown.

What Marx and Engels seem to have hoped for — the evidence is very meager — was an opening to the left that would have squeezed out the likes of Trochu without overthrowing the provisional government in toto, and would have established at the national level a collaboration of workers and "Radical middle class Republicans" like Gambetta.[17] Thus not only did Marx extol Lyons, Marseilles, and Toulouse as examples, but among the several efforts at political change in Paris he showed enthusiasm only for the October 31 attempt through a mass demonstration to force Trochu and company "to abdicate their usurped power into the hands of a commune to be freely elected by Paris."[18] Such a development, had it not been repulsed, might have altered the course of history, Marx judged retrospectively:

> The victorious establishment at Paris of the Commune in the beginning of November 1870 (then already initiated in the great cities of the [country — HD] and sure to be imitated all over France) would not only have taken the defense out of the hands of traitors, . . . it would have altogether changed the character of the war. It would have become the war of republican France, hissing [hoisting] the flag of the social Revolution of the 19th century. . . . It would have electrified the producing masses in the old and the new world.[19]

A "freely elected" commune in November 1870 could scarcely have resulted in anything but a coalition of workers with radical bourgeois and petty bourgeois republicans, as in the provincial cities. But such an opening to the left would have created the best obtainable postwar situation: if Gambetta's principal partners stood on his right, the Republic would surely be only transitory; if they were on his left, the Republic would be secure and the alliance of the majority classes could take root, spreading to the countryside as well. In October, Marx expressed to Beesly the fear that "the middle class on the whole prefers Prussian conquest to the victory of a Republic with Socialist tendencies."[20] His most sanguine hope appears to have been for such a "Republic with Socialist tendencies," not for the proletarian revolution per se. In this specific form the vision of 1792–1793 temporarily reasserted itself.

The next phase began with the capitulation of Trochu in an armistice with the Prussians on January 28, 1871. After a week of wrangling with his Paris colleagues, Gambetta, who wanted to continue the war, resigned in disgust. Bismarck insisted that the peace terms be accepted by an elected National Assembly, which was duly chosen on the basis of universal suffrage on February 8. The issue put to the voters was peace or war, with the political right favoring acceptance of Bismarck's terms and the left favoring continuation of the war. The mass of the population, particularly in rural areas, expressed its desire for peace by electing conservative spokesmen. Thus when the new National Assembly first met on February 13 in Bordeaux, only one-third of the deputies counted themselves as republicans at all, while fully two-thirds were monarchists (albeit divided among the three possible dynastic houses — Bourbon, Orleans, Bonaparte). To form its executive, the assembly chose an old Orleanist, Adolphe

Thiers, who proceeded to hammer out the remaining peace terms with Bismarck. The National Assembly completed its mission by ratifying these terms on February 28.

Meanwhile the radical, pro-war masses of the capital smoldered with resentment at this series of "capitulations." And instead of soothing their siege-frayed nerves, the Thiers government seemed to aggravate tensions deliberately: by ending the moratorium on debts (in effect during the siege); by cutting the pay of National Guardsmen; and by suppressing one radical newspaper after another in Paris. After accepting the peace treaty, the National Assembly added immeasurably to these tensions by deciding not to disband but instead to continue governing the country . . . from Versailles. In this single stroke the monarchist majority usurped the right to govern France indefinitely and prudently "decapitalized" the turbulent city of Paris. The final blow followed swiftly: Thiers sought to arrest radical leaders and disarm the National Guard in Paris, to extract its fangs by quietly hauling away some two hundred cannon that had been purchased for it by public subscription during the siege. In the early morning hours of March 18, 1871, Thiers' soldiers were caught in the attempt, and during the popular furor that ensued several persons on both sides were killed, including two generals of the regular army. In this open defiance of Thiers' authority, in the bloodshed of March 18, was now born the Commune de Paris.

Surviving documents that would reveal Marx and Engels' views during this crucial period are virtually nonexistent. We know that, initially, they shared Gambetta's stand that the war should be continued. On February 4 Marx wrote his son-in-law that, if Bismarck's terms were hard enough, "even the bourgeoisie will finally understand that it has more to lose by capitulating than by fighting!" He continued: "If France holds out, uses the armistice to reorganize its armed forces, if it finally comprehends that to lead a revolutionary war, revolutionary measures and revolutionary energy are required, then it can still be saved."[21] But this last ember of hope for a repetition of 1792–1793 must have flickered out with the news of Gambetta's resignation and then the overwhelming popular mandate for peace. Marx learned of these developments in Lafargue's return letter, which stressed the pro-peace, conservative mood of the countryside and predicted an Orleanist restoration, much as Engels had done the previous September. In fact, Lafargue drew the same conclusions as had been drawn by Marx and Engels in September, expressing the hope that "the revolutionaries are intelligent enough not to compromise themselves and not to frighten away the republican party,"

and that they will make use of the freer conditions "to organize and prepare themselves."[22]

The minutes of the IWA general council during February and March
reveal interest in the immediate past rather than the immediate future,
as its members debated in several tedious sessions what role Great Britain should have played in the war. Marx did comment on February 14
that France was "paralyzed," both internationally and domestically, so
long as Prussia occupied a third of the country, and the two men offered
no advice whatever when Serraillier returned on February 28 to report
on his five-month stay in Paris, a report that also focused on the past and
emphasized the disorder and wrangling within the IWA sections there.
Indeed, Engels' very last comment on France before the uprising was a
passing remark on March 14 that "in France our sections were disorga-
nized."[23] These minutes certainly seem to confirm Marx and Engels' oft-
repeated assertion that the general council had nothing to do with the
creation of the Paris Commune, "did not lift a finger to produce it," as
Engels wrote in a private letter to Friedrich Sorge.[24]

There is no evidence, then, and no reason whatsoever, to suppose that
Marx and Engels desired an uprising in Paris while France lay "paralyzed."
The realities of power were again basically what they had been back in
September when the two men had assumed—wrongly—that the war was
over. The radical workers of Paris, only just released from four months
of siege, not to mention twenty years of Bonapartist oppression, had
scarcely time to organize themselves, much less win over a skeptical peasant following in the countryside which alone could give them the strength
to defy Thiers. And the Prussian armies remained in their positions en-
circling the capital, ready to smash any radical (and hence anti-Prussian)
rebellion, if the forces of Thiers should prove insufficient. The prospects
were anything but rosy and we may well imagine Marx and Engels, privately between themselves, repeating their judgments of September—"a
desperate folly . . . stupidities . . . madness."

"The Defensive is the Death of Every Armed Rising"

If we now turn to the period of the Paris Commune itself, March 18
to May 28, 1871, our fund of evidence becomes thankfully more plentiful. The *pièce de résistance*, of course, is Marx's classic *Civil War in
France*, written in late May as the International's public vindication of
the Communards just then being slaughtered by the thousands. We also

have two earlier drafts of this document (the first one being much longer and therefore especially valuable as a supplement), together with Marx's excerpt notebooks where he gathered newspaper reports on the events in France. Marx and Engels' remarks in the weekly meetings of the IWA general council are preserved in its minutes and include the earliest indication of support for the Communards, only three days after the rising, on March 21.[25] Last but not least, we have some highly provocative correspondence.

Among the surviving letters two are particularly controversial, in that they seem to reveal a Marx carried away by the passions of the moment, advocating a Blanquist strategy of minority revolution and minority dictatorship over France. Following the violence of March 18, predictably enough, Blanquist leaders in Paris proposed that they themselves form a collective dictatorship of the insurrection. They called for an immediate march on Versailles to disperse the democratically elected National Assembly, after which the Paris dictators would govern the entire country in the name of the social revolution.[26] In actuality, the initial violence and subsequent withdrawal of Thiers' forces to Versailles left de facto authority in the hands of the Paris National Guard leaders, its central committee, who were reluctant to assume responsibility for a march on Versailles; rather they scheduled citywide elections for March 22 and turned over their authority to the communal assembly thus chosen. On April 6, Marx commented on these developments in a pessimistic letter to Wilhelm Liebknecht:

It seems the Parisians are succumbing. It is their own fault, but a fault which in fact was due to their too great *honnêteté* [decency, good nature—HD]. The Central Committee [of the National Guard—HD] and later the Commune gave that mischievous gnome Thiers time to concentrate hostile forces, (1) because they foolishly did not want to start the *civil war* — as if Thiers had not already started it by his attempt at the forcible disarming of Paris, as if the National Assembly, summoned only to decide the question of war or peace with the Prussians, had not immediately declared war on the *Republic!* (2) In order not to be saddled with the appearance of usurping power, they lost precious moments (the point was, to advance immediately on Versailles after the defeat — Place Vendôme — of the reaction in Paris) through the election of the Commune, whose organization etc. cost yet more time.[27]

A week later he repeated the same points to his friend, Ludwig Kugelmann, also betraying the extent of his own emotional engagement:

> What elasticity, what historical initiative, what a capacity for sacrifice in these Parisians! After six months of starvation and ruin, . . . they rise, beneath Prussian bayonets, as if there had never been a war between France and Germany and the enemy were not still at the gates of Paris! History has no similar example of similar greatness! . . . The present rising in Paris — even if it is crushed by the wolves, swine and vile curs of the old society — is the most glorious deed of our party since the June insurrection in Paris.[28]

This spontaneous private tribute should be required reading for those who think Marx never sympathized with the Communards at all but only used their sacrifice to manufacture a legend.

Do not these letters, to return to the main issue, reveal an essentially Blanquist program for dispersing the democratically elected government at Versailles and establishing the dictatorship of Paris, or more exactly, of the central committee of the Paris National Guard, over the entire nation? Was Marx not suffering, in the words of Bertram Wolfe, an "apparent relapse, after two decades of comparative realism, into the romantic-utopian mood of 1848, when a little handful of communists could hope to . . . take the heavens by storm"?[29] Closer analysis of the evidence suggests rather an adaptation to the given circumstances of our familiar Strategy II — revolutionary rule by the alliance of the majority classes.

Let us begin with the National Assembly. Although it professed to be horrified at the "illegal" actions of Paris, the assembly's own rule did not and could not rest on legality, since it was called into being by an entirely extralegal body, the provisional Government of National Defense, acting at the behest of a foreign conqueror. The reporter for the *London Daily News* set straight the legality issue in words that Marx copied down — gleefully, no doubt — in his notebook: "Let them not talk nonsense about the shamefulness of illegality in a country where every party except one, the high and dry Legitimists, who are in a desperate minority, have planted their standards in illegality, and through illegality have risen to power."[30] If not from legality, at least the National Assembly could claim legitimacy from its election by universal suffrage; it represented the will of the nation democratically expressed. But the will of the nation had been solicited solely on the question of war and peace, not on the question of France's future government. Organized in great haste, when the country had not known a free election in twenty years and one-third of its territory lay under Prussian occupation, the election call was received in many localities only on the eve of the event. At most the voting could be regarded as a plebescite on war and peace, and the assembly it created, as Marx insisted, "had but a single aim, clearly set down by the [armistice] agreement," whose precise stipulation he transcribed verbatim: "to decide if the war should be continued, or else sue for peace; and, in the latter case, to establish the conditions for such a peace and assure the evacuation of French territory as promptly as possible."[31] Even Thiers himself, for reasons of his own, had initially denied on several occasions that the assembly had any constituent function, that it had any right to determine France's future form of government.[32] Once the peace terms were ratified on February 28, then, the National Assembly properly should have dissolved itself, perhaps with a call to the nation to elect another body whose express mission would be the drafting of a constitution. But it chose instead to govern indefinitely (until 1876 as it turned out!), and Marx could scarcely disagree with the editorial sentiments he copied from the liberal *Daily News*: "From the moment, when it had ratified the *terms of peace*, the continuance of its own powers became an *unconstitutional usurpation.*" This was likewise the official position of the Paris Commune on the matter.[33]

As for Adolphe Thiers, he had been given the title "Chief of the Executive Power" (*chef du pouvoir exécutif*) by an assembly whose competence was restricted to the issue of war and peace. He proceeded to form a responsible cabinet, as a prime minister might do. Did he also have the right to command the armies and the entire executive apparatus of the country, as if he were a duly chosen chief of state? Marx clearly thought not: "M. Thiers commenced his regime by an usurpation. By the National Assembly he was appointed chief of the ministry of the Assembly; he appointed himself chief of the executive of France."[34] In any event, Thiers' rightful authority seemingly should have lapsed with that of the assembly on February 28.

Were not Marx and the Communards in any case simply splitting hairs? Would not a second National Assembly, duly elected to draw up a constitution, have had the same political coloration as the original one? There is considerable reason to suppose it would not, that the political center of gravity in 1871 lay somewhere *between* the Paris Commune and the monarchist assembly. The only contemporaneous indicators of public opinion on a nationwide basis were the municipal council elections held under Thiers' rule on April 30 while the Paris Commune was still maintaining its precarious existence. Of 700,000 councilors chosen in the 35,000 municipalities of France, only 7,800, or 1 percent, were monarchists of any stripe — compared with their two-thirds majority at Versailles.[35] The subsequent electoral history of the Third Republic fortifies this impression: by-elections in July 1871 to fill vacancies in the National Assembly returned only a dozen monarchists and nearly a hundred republicans; and when this assembly finally dissolved itself in 1876 the Chamber of Deputies that replaced it had a clear republican majority.[36] The overwhelming vote for peace in February 1871, then, had not been a simple vote for restoration, a state of affairs which must have been appreciated at Versailles if one notes, as Marx was bound to, the zeal with which the Versaillese hermetically sealed off communication between Paris and the rest of France, immediately passed legislation which strangled self-government in all towns of more than 20,000 inhabitants, adopted a new law restricting freedom of the press, and enacted what Marx characterized as a "new-fangled, Draconic code of deportation" for political offenses.[37] The National Assembly did not behave like a government confident of its own popular support, or one under which democracy would long survive.

If Versailles' patent to govern was more than dubious, was it not at least better than any that could be claimed for the central committee of the Paris National Guard, which Marx chastised in his April letters for not having marched to disperse the National Assembly? Did not Marx climb aboard the Blanquist bandwagon by urging the postponement of communal elections, which inevitably would have left the central committee in possession of dictatorial power? One must recognize, first of all, that the central committee was no self-appointed Blanquist vanguard. During the siege the formerly middle-class National Guard had been opened up and expanded to include virtually the entire adult male population of the city (roughly 300,000 members compared with 328,000 Parisian voters in the February elections). Thus it comprised, as Marx put it, "all the armed manhood of Paris."[38] Hitherto, the smallest local National Guard units had elected their own officers, a practice which was now extended up the command hierarchy until, on March 15, a central committee was formed out of the elected commanders of all but seven of Paris' twenty *arrondissements*. Marx, aware of these developments from the *Figaro* of March 19, reproduced them in his developing manuscript: "The national guard reorganized itself and entrusted its supreme control to a central committee elected by all the companies, battalions and batteries of the capital, save some fragments of the old Bonapartist formations." Thus he concluded that "the Central Committee, which directed the defense of Montmartre and emerged on the dawn of the 18th March as the leader of the Revolution, was neither an expedient of the moment nor the offspring of secret conspiracy."[39] Neither were there any followers of Marx among these men. To urge that these freshly chosen leaders put off communal elections until after a quick expedition against Versailles, as Marx did in his April letters, is scarcely the same as the traditional Blanquist recipe for postponement of elections until after a radical transformation of the whole nation by a self-appointed committee in Paris.

A great deal would depend, of course, on what the central committee might do *after* an expedition to Versailles that successfully toppled the "usurpatory" Thiers government. In no surviving writing did Marx or Engels conjecture that far ahead. No doubt they were aware of the Blanquist formula. But they were also aware of other, seemingly more widespread opinions. Immediately after the rupture of March 18, according to the *Daily News* correspondent (whose words Marx transcribed in his notebook), "the general opinion among the groups in Montmartre and Belleville is that the National Assembly must be immediately dissolved, and another elected to sit in Paris." An appeal to the provinces accompanied the central committee's call for communal elections: "Let the provinces hasten to imitate the example of the capital by organizing themselves in a republican way and get in contact with the capital as soon as possible, by means of delegates." The communal assembly elected on March 22 behaved on a few occasions as if it were a national government (as in the abolition of conscription) but the bulk of its actions and pronouncements bore a decidedly municipal stamp. Its official program of March 28 called for the radical decentralization of France, leaving only a "central administration" composed of elected delegates from autonomous local communes. "Paris has renounced her *apparent omnipotence*," declared the *Journal Officiel* on April 1, "she has not renounced that moral power, that intellectual influence, which so often has made her victorious in France and Europe in her propaganda." We know from his notebook transcriptions that Marx was aware of all these things, as he was of the Commune's offer in May to dissolve itself and face fresh elections after a two-month campaign period if the National Assembly would do the same.[40] It is true that, while scoring a polemical point toward the end of his *Civil War*, Marx claimed the Commune was "the truly national Government." He meant this in a particular sense we will examine presently.[41] Otherwise there is no positive evidence whatever to suggest he desired a minority dictatorship of Paris over France. Such an enterprise could only produce another swan song. Scarcely a year earlier Engels had commented to his partner, after reading a recently published Blanquist tract: "Comical, the idea that the dictatorship of Paris over France, on which the first revolution foundered, might without further ado be replayed again today and with a different result."[42]

The reason Marx — and Engels as well — called for an early assault on Versailles was essentially a military one: in the days immediately following March 18, the Thiers government was still militarily quite feeble and could easily have been overwhelmed by the 300,000 National Guardsmen of Paris.[43] The other alternative, the more passive course essentially taken by the Communards, was merely to defend their own perimeters in the hope that the Thiers government would leave them alone, and that the rest of France would eventually follow their example. This gave Thiers as much time as he wanted to collect his military forces and proceed — refusing all appeals for compromise and mediation — to smash the Communards with a ferocity that had no equal in all of French history. Perhaps twenty-five thousand (the precise number cannot even be established) were killed, mostly helpless prisoners, while thirteen thousand more were sentenced afterward, many to a slower death in the prison colony of New Caledonia.[44] The defense-mindedness of the Commune, so characteristic of workers' uprisings in general, struck Engels even years later as its biggest failing, and reminded him of his own experiences in the South German insurrections of 1849. From those experiences, the reader may recall, Engels had formulated his two basic rules for insurrection:

> Firstly, never play with insurrection unless you are fully prepared to face the consequences of your play. . . . Secondly, the insurrectionary career once entered upon, act with the greatest determination, and on the offensive. The defensive is the death of every armed rising; it is lost before it measures itself with its enemies.[45]

Marx and Engels had not called forth the Paris Commune; indeed, there is every reason to believe they regretted its untimely appearance as a misfortune. Once it was an accomplished fact, however, whatever small chance of survival it had lay in an offensive strategy that would have overwhelmed the Thiers government immediately. This is why Marx and Engels' manifest caution of September could be followed by such impassioned appeals for action in April. They had not played with insurrection, but once initiated — by others — they called for the offensive.

For such a strategy to have been successful, two other conditions would have to be asumed: first, that the Prussians would not have intervened, since their armies still surrounded the capital and would have tipped the military balance against the Communards. Realizing their vulnerability in this respect, the Communards went out of their way to assure the Prussians that they accepted the peace terms and had no intention of resuming the war. Marx was aware of these efforts, as well as of Bismarck's public statement on his return from the peace negotiations: "The National Assembly would have preferred to see Prussia occupy Paris, disarm the National Guard, and keep the canaille in check; but as the Prussian government had resolved not to sacrifice a single additional man, . . . it could not render this service."[46] Perhaps Marx took hope from these developments as he wrote his April letters, although he allowed in a second letter to Kugelmann that "the presence of the Prussians in France and their position right before Paris" was a "decisive, unfavorable accident" of history. In retrospect, of course, it seems extremely unlikely that Bismarck would have stood by quietly while the "canaille" sallied forth from Paris in numbers sufficient to overpower the National Assembly.[47]

The other condition for any lasting success would have been a more or less immediate rallying of the bulk of the population to the political alternative proposed by the Communards. The workers had to win over their chorus. Hitherto, for Marx, the alliance of the majority classes had involved two partners for the proletariat — the urban petty bourgeoisie and the peasantry — and he included both groups in his would-be reconstitution of that alliance in *The Civil War in France*. As to the former, it seemed an accomplished fact, at least in Paris: "For the first time in history the petty and *moyenne* middleclass has openly rallied round the workmen's Revolution," Marx declared. "It forms with them the bulk of the National guard, it sits with them in the Commune, it mediates for them in the Union Républicaine!" He proceeded to list the several measures taken by the Commune expressly for the benefit of this class. Many non-Marxist historians argue, in fact, that the Paris Commune was really more petty bourgeois than proletarian, both in composition and attitude.[48] The Union Républicaine, in any event, took the most active part in efforts to reconcile Versailles and Paris, and later under Gambetta's resumed leadership would play an important role in the politics of the Third Republic. Evidence of petty-bourgeois sympathy in the provinces could be found in the proclamation of communes in half a dozen cities and towns following March 18, in the numerous provincial delegations that implored the Versailles government to seek a compromise settlement with Paris, and at least to some extent in the results of the April 30 municipal elections.[49]

The more serious task — the crucial test, in fact, of Marx's class-alliance strategy — would have been to win over the conservative peasant majority of France that had voted for Louis Napoleon in 1848, had confirmed his dictatorship in 1851, and had returned the heavy monarchist majority to the National Assembly in 1871. Marx denied, first of all, that the country gentry and provincial aristocrats gathered in that assembly really represented peasant interests. They had been hurriedly chosen to liquidate a lost war, no more. The French peasant could not really desire the rule of those oppressors he had cast off in the Great Revolution and to whom he had been obliged to pay a billion francs indemnity after 1815.[50] But would he prefer the rule of the workers? The first and most extensive draft of *The Civil War,* written in April while Marx still had glimmers of hope for the Commune, allowed that historically there had also existed "a deep antagonism between the townish and rural producers, between the industrial Proletariat and the peasantry." Industrial labor was organized on a grand scale, with centralized means of production; the labor of the traditional peasant remained insulated, his means of production parceled and dispersed. "On these economical differences rests superconstructed a whole world of different social and political views." Yet peasant proprietorship has long since entered its period of decay. Interest payments on his inevitable heavy mortgage, combined with state taxes, judicial fees, and clerical exactions, have made his ownership merely "nominal, leaving to the peasant the delusion of proprietorship and expropriating him from the fruits of his own labor."[51] And now the National Assembly would like to saddle him with the burden of Bismarck's indemnity as well. What can the Commune offer him instead?

> The Commune will abolish Conscription, the party of order will fasten the blood-tax on the peasant. The party of order will fasten upon him the tax-collector for the payment of a parasitical and costly state-machinery, the Commune will give him cheap government. The party of order will continue [to — HD] grind him down by the townish usurer, the Commune will free him of the incubus of the mortgages lasting upon [burdening] his plot of land. The Commune will replace the parasitical judiciary body eating the heart of his income — the notary, the huissier etc. — [by — HD] Communal agents doing their work at workmen's salaries. . . . The party of order will keep him under the rule of the gendarme, the Commune will restore him to independent, social and political life! The Commune

will enlighten him by the rule of the schoolmaster, the party of order force upon him the stultification by the rule of the priest! But the French peasant is above all a man of reckoning! He will find it exceedingly reasonable that the payment of the clergy will no longer [be — HD] exacted from him by the tax-collector, but will be left to the "spontaneous action" of his religious instinct.

A few pages later Marx developed the theme still further:[52]

The Commune . . . is the only power that can give him immediate great loans even in its present economical conditions, it is the only form of government that can secure to him the transformation of his present economical conditions, rescue him from expropriation by the landlord on the one hand, save him from grinding, trudging and misery on the pretext of proprietorship on the other, that can convert his nominal proprietorship of the land into real proprietorship of the fruits of his labor, that can combine for him the profits of modern agronomy, dictated by social wants and every day now encroaching upon him as a hostile agency, without annihilating his position as a really independent producer. Being immediately benefited by the Communal Republic, he would soon confide in it.[53]

Marx's meaning emerged more clearly some three years later in his notes on Bakunin's *Statism and Anarchy*, where he discussed the prospects of workers' revolutions in countries having a peasant majority:

Either the peasants prevent and doom to failure every workers' revolution, as they have done in France up to now, or the proletariat . . . functioning as the government must take steps that will immediately improve his position and thus win him over to the revolution; these steps moreover further the transition from private to communal ownership of land in such a way, that the peasant comes to it of his own accord on economic grounds. But one must not affront the peasant, for instance by proclaiming the abolition of the right of inheritance or the abolition of his property . . . ; still less should one strengthen small ownership by enlarging the plots, by simply transferring the large estates to the peasants, as Bakunin advocated in his revolutionary campaign.[54]

Here we find a clearly expressed opposition to simple redistribution, but also to any program of immediate or forced collectivization. In general, we know that Marx and Engels favored the immediate nationalization only of large estates. These large-scale productive units, reorganized as agricultural cooperatives, would provide the model that would then attract the small peasants, of their "own accord," into associated production with one another. Marx also reiterated here the swan-song theme that minority proletarian revolutions which do not engage peasant support are doomed to failure. "To have any chance of success," he insisted, the workers "must *mutatis mutandis* be able immediately to do at least as much for the peasants as the French bourgeoisie during its revolution did for the French peasants of the time."[55]

Marx seemed convinced during the early weeks of the Commune that such a class alliance could be created. "What separates the peasant from the proletarian is, therefore, no longer his real interest, but his delusive prejudice." And to overcome this prejudice was simply a matter of communication: "Three months of free communication of Communal Paris with the provinces would bring about a general rising of the peasants," a hope that duplicates in its own way the Communards' request for a two-month campaign period leading to fresh National Assembly elections.[56] The Thiers government itself, as we have seen, feared such communication sufficiently to seal off all contact between Paris and the rest of France. Marx's son-in-law, Paul Lafargue, played an active role in trying to mobilize provincial support in the Bordeaux area, venturing at one point into Paris itself "in order to obtain from the Commune 'des pleins pouvoirs' to organize the revolutionary army in Bordeaux," but apparently without success.[57] Marx took hope from the municipal elections of April 30, discussed earlier, as he wrote to the Communard leaders Leo Frankel and Louis-Eugène Varlin: "The provinces are beginning to ferment. Unfortunately the action there is only local and 'pacific.'"[58] As things turned out, of course, it never got beyond the local and pacific stage. "France," as Engels put it many years later, "left Paris in the lurch."[59] The workers' solo had once again become their swan song.

During their brief surge of optimism for the Paris Commune, then, Marx and Engels' strategy was but an adaptation to the given facts of their familiar 1848 strategy involving the alliance of the majority classes— Strategy II. The vocabulary of Marx's first draft in particular betrays such assumptions: the aim of the Communards was termed a "Social Republic" which "disowns the capital and landowner class" and is instead "the representative of all classes of society not living upon foreign labor" (a first-draft Germanism meaning "other people's labor").[60] Hence a victorious "Social Republic" in 1871 would not have been a workers' state

pure and simple, but the instrument of the three familiar partners—
workers, petty bourgeois, and peasants. To be sure, one finds a clear
identification of the proletariat as the senior partner in the alliance, despite the much vaster numbers of the peasantry. The "Communal Constitution," established nationwide, according to Marx, would have
"brought the rural producers under the intellectual lead of the central
towns of their districts, and these secured to them, in the working men,
the natural trustees of their interests."[61] All this is reminiscent of the independent and leading role Marx and Engels assigned to the French and
German proletariat in the struggles of 1849–1850, and raises again the
question whether peasant discontents were not really to be manipulated
and exploited in the interest of minority proletarian rule.

In Marx and Engels' thinking, traditional peasants, however numerous, were incapable as a class of seizing and holding on to the reins of
power in a modern nation-state, whether because of their "lower" cultural level or simply their extreme geographical dispersion. Wherever
the peasantry had appeared on the historical stage as solo actor, typically in jacqueries, their revolts had always been crushed. Only in alliance with another social force, as with the bourgeoisie in the classical
case of 1789, could peasants achieve real success, both for themselves
and for the cause of historical progress generally. The French peasants
had supported the bourgeois revolution—with pitchforks, then votes, and
then army bayonets—not because they were manipulated or swindled
but because it was their revolution too, in their own real and perceived
interest, even though they did not often fill the high positions of state.
So it would be again in Marx and Engels' conception of a model popular revolution, where the majority of peasants would find in proletarian
leaders "the natural trustees of their interests," not because they were
gullible or misguided but precisely because they recognized where their
own real and immediate interests lay. There may well be some lingering Hegelian metaphysics behind this assumption that universal suffrage
would be the "compass needle" that "finally points to this class which
is called upon to rule."[62] Marx and Engels do not appear to have considered what the workers should do next if the peasant majority—to cite
a familiar situation in twentieth-century revolutions—insisted on dividing the great estates and thereafter showed little interest in maximizing
a surplus. Be that as it may, there is nothing in Marx and Engels' writings on the Paris Commune to suggest that they favored forced collectivization, disfranchisement of "reactionary" elements, overrepresentation
of the cities, or anything other than the fully democratic political forms

of the Commune that they praised so highly and that we will examine in the following chapter.

Compromise as an Alternative

Those writers who depict Marx as uniformly enthusiastic about the Paris Commune have always had difficulty with the master's very last words on the subject in 1881. The Dutch socialist, F. Domela Nieuwenhuis, had written Marx asking for his views on the measures a socialist government should take on coming to power. Marx responded that the question could not be answered a priori, since conditions would vary. Then he proceeded:

> One thing you can at any rate be sure of: a socialist government does not come into power in a country unless conditions are so developed that it can immediately take the necessary measures for intimidating the mass of the bourgeoisie sufficiently to gain time — the first desideratum — for permanent action.
>
> Perhaps you will refer me to the Paris Commune; but apart from the fact that this was merely the rising of a city under exceptional conditions, the majority of the Commune was in no wise socialist, nor could it be. With a modicum of common sense, however, it could have reached a compromise with Versailles useful to the whole mass of the people — the only thing that could be reached at the time. The appropriation of the Bank of France alone would have been enough to put an end with terror to the swagger of the Versailles people, etc. etc.[63]

Instead of marching to overthrow Versailles, Marx here recommends a compromise with Versailles, and moreover declares a compromise the "only thing that could be reached at the time."

The whole mood of this letter is reminiscent of Marx and Engels' extreme caution just after the battle of Sedan, when they worked against a rising in Paris, and thus reenforces the idea that they regarded the Commune as untimely, as having little chance of success. Its best chance, moreover, came during the first week or so when a march on Versailles was still militarily promising. One of Marx's acquaintances in Vienna, Heinrich Oberwinder, recalled in his memoirs that "a few days after the outbreak of the March rising in Paris Marx wrote Vienna that the course it had taken precluded all prospects of success."[64] The letter itself has not survived but this account tallies well with the emphasis both Marx and Engels placed on immediate offensive action. It will be remembered that Marx's April 6 letter to Liebknecht began: "It seems the Parisians are succumbing"; and he proceeded to blame their lack of offensive action.

Once this early opportunity had slipped away, about the best the Communards could do militarily was to defend themselves against the predictable assault. Defeat might still be transformed into victory if there were a mass uprising of the provinces against the Thiers government but, given the hermetic seal, this was scarcely the basket in which to place all one's eggs. It would not be surprising to find Marx and Engels contemplating the possibility of a compromise settlement that might at least avert a bloodbath and save the strength of the Paris working class for another day. Beginning in mid-April Marx's newspaper excerpts show considerable interest in mediation efforts, and his treatment of these efforts in *The Civil War* — even in the first April draft — is sympathetic.[65] If he were confident of revolutionary success, it seems more likely he would have denounced mediation as faint-hearted and treasonous, at least in the early drafts.

Marx's specific advice to the Communards, or mainly the lack of it, also suggests that he saw little hope of success after the first week or so. On March 30 Leo Frankel wrote London of his election to the Commune's Commission on Labor and Exchange and, full of optimism, asked what advice Marx could offer: "Your advice on the social reforms to be carried out will be extremely valuable to our Commission."[66] Marx appears to have ignored the request completely. The IWA general council, to be sure, had dispatched Serraillier to Paris again at the end of March, and he played an active role in the Commune, but his letters do not suggest that he served as a conduit for Marx's advice or had much further contact with London at all.[67] Marx later declared that he kept in touch with the Communards "verbally" by means of a German merchant named Eilau, who traveled regularly between London and Paris, but Frankel's second letter to Marx, dated April 25, makes it clear the former still had not received any advice; he repeated his request.[68] The two letters Marx did send to Frankel (and Varlin) during the weeks of the Commune's existence contain not a word on the question of social reform, only advice on how the Commune could sell certain securities on the London Exchange, the counsel to fortify the northern slope of Montmartre, and the recommendation to hide certain documents compromising the Versailles leaders.[69] Not very much direction from the *grand chef* of the International whom the bourgeois press imagined to be pulling all the strings from his London headquarters! And yet the very absence of advice on longer-range issues like social reform suggests Marx's underlying pessimism about the Commune's prospects.

In fact the advice to hide the incriminating documents makes a strong case for the view that Marx wanted to hold open an option for compromise. "Would it not be useful," he wrote, "to put the documents which compromise the Versailles blackguards in a safe place? A precaution of this kind could not do any harm."[70] The documents in question had fallen into the hands of the Communards when they took over the city and, in Marx's opinion, provided "juridical proofs" that prominent Versailles leaders — including Trochu, Jules Favre, Ernest Picard, and Jules Ferry — were guilty of diverse forgeries, embezzlements, and acts of high treason during the Franco-Prussian War, proofs sufficient for the ordinary courts to send them into long years of penal servitude.[71] To recommend the *removal* of these documents for safekeeping would make no sense if Marx anticipated the victory of the Commune; on the other hand they might constitute a valuable bargaining chip in any negotiated compromise with Versailles. Exactly in this sense Marx explained his motives to Edward Beesly on June 12: "I demanded that they should at once send to London all the documents compromising the members of the National Defense, so that by this means the savagery of the enemies of the Commune could to some extent be held in check."[72]

Marx's 1881 letter to Nieuwenhuis, quoted at the beginning of this section, alludes to appropriation of the assets of the Bank of France in very much the same way, as a kind of bargaining chip that would have ended the "swagger" of the Versailles people and perhaps made possible a compromise "useful to the whole mass of the people." Most of the mediation proposals that had been advanced included provision for a broad measure of municipal autonomy for Paris and for the provincial cities and towns as well. Engels spoke retrospectively in the same vein:

> The hardest thing to understand is certainly the holy awe with which they [the Communards] remained standing respectfully outside the gates of the Bank of France. This was also a serious political mistake. The bank in the hands of the Commune — this would have been worth more than ten thousand hostages. It would have meant the pressure of the whole of the French bourgeoisie on the Versailles government in favor of peace with the Commune.[73]

In another writing he went even further, suggesting that "the decision *not* to confiscate the Bank of France . . . was partly responsible for the downfall of the Commune."[74] Clearly Engels was no longer thinking of any revolutionary victory over Thiers; like Marx he was contemplating a compromise peace, one which might even have left the communal government intact with some degree of municipal autonomy. As things actually worked out, of course, Paris fell under the rule of the central government and would not be given even the right to elect its own mayor for more than a century — until 1976.

It is understandable that these retrospective comments should tend to emphasize the alternative of compromise, because after the smoke had cleared away it was obvious that neither of the two conditions for revolutionary success had obtained. On the one hand, Bismarck had not stood by quietly but had given considerable indirect support to the Thiers government, most notoriously through the early release of 20,000 prisoners of war. How much more would he have given if Versailles were under storm by the "canaille"? On the other hand, the peasant masses *had* stood by quietly as passive spectators to the slaughter of the Communards. In fact, they remained basically quiet and d ı le during the rest of Marx and Engels' lives, which must have made the two men realize how unrealistic their April hopes had been. Engels' own last words on the Commune in 1895 equal the pessimism of Marx's Nieuwenhuis letter: "once again it was proved how impossible even then . . . this rule of the working class still was. . . . France left Paris in the lurch, looked on while it bled profusely from the bullets of MacMahon."[75]

If one examines Marx and Engels' diverse comments pertaining to a revolutionary strategy for the Paris Commune in their proper historical context, within the frame of their own chronological development, then they do not appear grossly contradictory. During the Gambetta period of national resistance to Prussia the two men were tempted by the vision of 1792–1793, or a modified version thereof. But otherwise, when Prussian victory and military occupation were imminent (September 1870) or real (February–March 1871), they showed no enthusiasm whatever at the prospect of a proletarian rising in Paris. Once that rising was an accomplished fact, however, its best chance of growing into a national revolution — albeit not a very good one — lay in an immediate offensive to overthrow the usurpatory Thiers government, combined with a simultaneous effort to win over the countryside. Having missed this opportunity, its only remaining option was a compromise that might at least have prevented the bloodbath and preserved municipal self-government for

Paris and the provincial cities. In such a negotiated settlement the Parisians might have used two important bargaining chips—the incriminating documents and the hostage assets of the Bank of France. These changing estimates and recommendations all fit within the general strategy for a democratic revolution by the majority classes.

⟨[5]⟩

The Paris Commune:
Workers' State

IN THE PRECEDING CHAPTER we looked at the Paris Commune to see how it might illuminate Marx and Engels' views on revolutionary strategy. But that is only one facet of the Commune's importance in the political thought of the two men. Since Marx called it "essentially a working-class government" (albeit short-lived and only local), since Engels retrospectively even labeled it a "dictatorship of the proletariat," the Paris Commune acquires enormous significance for understanding Marx and Engels' conception of what the post-revolutionary workers' state would look like. Their abundant commentary on the political structures of the Commune compensates somewhat for the bare-boned generalities we find in most of their other writings. By analyzing this commentary we can get around their usual reluctance to draw blueprints of the future and will be able to flesh out the generalities with considerable detail. As in the case of gentile society, we need not even be too concerned whether they saw the Commune through rose-colored glasses: the more they may have idealized it, the better they must have revealed their own desires, and it is these desires we want to study, rather than the exact degree of correspondence between their factual descriptions and historical reality. Yet, alas, the task is not so easy after all for, quite apart from historical accuracy, what Marx and Engels said about the workings of the Paris Commune appears, prima facie, no less contradictory and subject to suspicion than what they said about its revolutionary strategy. Can we accept as sincere, for example, Marx's public praise of the Communards for "smashing" the state when we know well that, unlike the anarchists, he did not want to see the state dismantled immediately? How are we to understand his praise of the Commune as a democracy, knowing his reputation as an opponent of the separation of powers? And must we not

[125]

disregard completely his praise of the decentralist aspirations of the Communards, knowing his lifelong advocacy of centralization? These are some of the knotty questions we must tackle if the Commune is also to illuminate our understanding of Marx and Engels' conception of the post-revolutionary state.

To Smash or to Use

Marx and Engels' enthusiasm for the Paris Commune could sound positively anarchist sometimes when they depicted it, as Marx did in the First Draft of his *Civil War in France*, as a revolution against all forms of the state: "It was a Revolution against the *State* itself, of this supernaturalist abortion of society." And yet Marx's standard position against anarchism, as he would put it just two years later for example, was to support the workers when, in order to "crush the resistance of the bourgeoisie, instead of laying down arms and abolishing the State they are giving it a revolutionary and transient form."[1] Engels' comments seem equally perplexing. In his 1875 remarks on the Gotha Program, he could declare that the Commune "was no longer a state in the proper sense of the word," but go on in the very next breath to assert the workers' need for the state as "a transitional institution which is used in the struggle, in the revolution, to hold down one's adversaries by force."[2] Or finally, in his well-known introduction to the anniversary edition of *The Civil War* in 1891, Engels again lauded the Communards for not "managing with the old state machine," for their efforts to "do away with all the old repressive machinery," but then in conclusion he invites us to "look at the Paris Commune. That was the Dictatorship of the Proletariat."[3]

Should the state be smashed at once or first used to hold down the class adversary? Are Marx and Engels guilty of duplicity here or are they just confused? For the reader who has followed the development of the two-theories argument up to this point, the response to these questions will be evident: Marx and Engels are using the word "state" in two different senses, apparently without being aware of doing so. The state as parasite was smashed immediately when the Communards came to power, but the state as organized coercive force lingered on in the form of the National Guard. Let us examine the relevant passages on the Commune more closely now in order to appreciate exactly in what ways the state disappeared immediately, as Marx and Engels perceived it, and in what ways it remained in existence.

In *The Eighteenth Brumaire*, it will be recalled, Marx had expressed his alarm and revulsion at the growth of the "appalling parasitic body," the military and bureaucratic apparatus of the French state, which had its origin in the days of absolute monarchy and which reached its zenith of development under Louis Napoleon when it broke completely free of class control and ruled the nation on its own account as a military despotism. During the long course of its emergence, he noted, "all revolutions perfected this machine instead of breaking it." But the next revolution, he went on to prophesy, would bring about "the demolition of the state machine," such that the entire edifice "will fall to the ground."[4] This prediction came back to Marx in April 1871 as he learned about the achievements of the Communards, for he wrote to Kugelmann: "If you look at the last chapter of my *Eighteenth Brumaire*, you will find that I declare that the next attempt of the French Revolution will be no longer, as before, to transfer the bureaucratic-military machine from one hand to another, but to *smash* it, and this is the precondition for every real people's revolution on the Continent. And this is what our heroic Parisian party comrades are attempting."[5] The idea of smashing the state would develop into one of the major themes of *The Civil War in France*, where Marx commenced his description of communal institutions by asserting: "But the working class cannot simply lay hold of the ready-made State machinery, and wield it for its own purposes." It was at this point that Marx, in his First Draft, had used the sharper formulation quoted at the outset: "This was, therefore, a Revolution not against this or that, legitimate, constitutional, republican or Imperialist form of State Power. It was a Revolution against the *State* itself, of this supernaturalist abortion of society, a resumption by the people for the people of its own social life."[6] Here the very vocabulary of 1843–1844 betrays what kind of state Marx had in mind — the state as a "supernaturalist" alienation of social life, the state become divorced from civil society, the state with interests of its own to defend. It is this parasite state the Communards would undertake to demolish.

The Civil War next proceeded to review the historical growth of the parasite state, quite in the manner of *The Eighteenth Brumaire*, including a list of five "ubiquitous organs" of centralized state power that were to be transformed by the Commune — "standing army, police, bureaucracy, clergy, and judicature." As a consequence of the war and the siege, military power in Paris had devolved almost entirely from regular units of the standing army to the militia-type forces of the National Guard. "This fact was now to be transformed into an institution. The first decree of the Commune, therefore, was the suppression of the standing army, and the substitution for it of the armed people."⁷ The First Draft expands upon this crucial point, first by quoting from the decree itself to the effect that the capital will now have "a national militia that defends the citizens against the power (the government) *instead of a permanent army that defends the government* against the citizens." Then Marx enumerated its benefits:

> The people had only to organize this militia on a national scale, to have done away with the standing armies; the first economical *condition sine qua* for all social improvements, discarding at once this source of taxes and state debt, and this constant danger to government usurpation of class rule . . . ; at the same time the safest guarantee against foreign aggression and making in fact the costly military apparatus impossible in all other states; the emancipation of the peasant from the bloodtax and [from being— HD] the most fertile source of all state-taxation and state debts.⁸

First and foremost, then, the "smashing" of the state machine involved getting rid of the standing army, getting rid of full-time soldiers who stood apart from the general population and could be used to beat it into submission, getting rid of the staggering expense of maintaining such an enormous parasitic force.

What was smashed, however, was professionalism in the armed forces and not armed force per se. The full-time army as parasite disappeared, but the part-time National Guard remained as the coercive instrument of the workers' state. Here in sharpest focus one can perceive Marx and Engels' double usage: the parasite state is to be smashed immediately; the state as instrument of class coercion is to remain until the need for it fades away. It is not merely that the revolutionary government discharges an unreliable army and forms a reliable one. Rather, the bearing of arms itself ceases to be the full-time profession of a special body of men and becomes a part-time activity of the entire (male) population. Thus the National Guard was in fact "all the armed manhood of Paris" called up for temporary duty. Marx lauded its democratic organization (election of officers) as well as its subordination to the civilian authority of the Commune: instead of glorifying military leaders as previous governments typically did, "the Commune dismissed and arrested its general whenever they were suspected of neglecting their duties."⁹ He and Engels also praised the fighting qualities of the guardsmen, although of course they lamented that defense-mindedness that prevented them from following up the popular victory of March 18 with an assault on Versailles. Had such a campaign been undertaken successfully, the next task would have been "to organize this militia on a national scale," as Marx put it, but certainly not to dissolve it, as the anarchists seemed to desire in their rejection of all "authority." Thus Engels was led to his classic utterance on the subject in his essay "On Authority" (1873):

> The anti-authoritarians demand that the authoritarian political state be abolished at one stroke, even before the social conditions that gave birth to it have been destroyed. They demand that the first act of the social revolution shall be the abolition of authority. Have these gentlemen ever seen a revolution? A revolution is certainly the most authoritarian thing there is; it is the act whereby one part of the population imposes its will upon the other part by means of rifles, bayonets and cannon — authoritarian means, if such there be at all; and if the victorious party does not want to have fought in vain, it must maintain this rule by means of the terror which its arms inspire in the reactionaries. Would the Paris Commune have lasted a single day if it had not made use of this authority of the armed people against the bourgeois? Should we not, on the contrary, reproach it for not having used it freely enough?[10]

It is in this special sense that the state, although smashed (as parasite standing army), can nevertheless continue to exist (as workers' militia). And although this militia exists in order "to hold down one's adversaries by force," it is nevertheless "no longer a state in the proper sense of the word" — that is, no longer a professional body separated from the mass of the people. The paradox resolves itself as soon as the double meaning of the word "state" is unmasked.

After the standing army, *The Civil War* turned to the police and the bureaucracy. Here Marx sketched the transformation undertaken by the Communards in a passage that is justly famous:

> The Commune was formed of the municipal councillors, chosen by universal suffrage in the various wards of the town, responsible and revocable at short terms. The majority of its members were naturally working men, or acknowledged representatives of the working class. The Commune was to be a working, not a parliamentary, body, executive and legislative at the same time. Instead of continuing to be the agent of the Central Government, the po-

lice was at once stripped of its political attributes, and turned into the responsible and at all times revocable agent of the Commune. So were the officials of all other branches of the Administration. From the members of the Commune downwards, the public service had to be done at *workmen's wages*. The vested interests and the representation allowances of the high dignitaries of State disappeared along with the high dignitaries themselves. Public functions ceased to be the private property of the tools of the Central Government.[11]

The ninety-odd councillors who formed the communal assembly — or the "Commune" in the narrow sense Marx employs here — did their administrative work through ten commissions (for finance, public works, justice, etc.) elected from among their own numbers and responsible to the whole assembly, just as each councillor was in turn responsible to to his popular electorate in the ward, by whom he could be recalled at any time. The intent was to make all administrative posts elective and responsible, which would have the effect, as Marx elaborated in his First Draft, of "doing away with the state hierarchy altogether and replacing the haughteous masters of the people into always removable servants, a mock responsibility by a real responsibility, as they act continuously under public supervision":

> The whole sham of state-mysteries and statepretensions was done away [with — HD] by a Commune, mostly consisting of simple working men, . . . filling all the posts hitherto divided between Government, police, and Prefecture, doing their work publicly, simply, under the most difficult and complicated circumstances, and doing it, as Milton did his Paradise Lost, for a few pounds, acting in bright daylight, with no pretensions to infallibility, . . . making in one order the public functions, — military, administrative, political — *real workmen's functions*, instead of the hidden attributes of a trained caste.[12]

As in the military sphere, "smashing" the state machinery consisted essentially of deprofessionalization. The functions of a "trained caste" of career bureaucrats were now divided among ordinary citizens, elected and recallable at any time. Government by bureaucracy gave way to the authentic *self*-administration of the people. And the new system offered lower taxes as a natural byproduct: "The Commune made that catch-

word of bourgeois revolutions, cheap government, a reality, by destroying the two greatest sources of expenditure — the standing army and State
functionarism."[13]

Another "ubiquitous organ" of the old regime had been the established
church, which had received its major financial support from the state
and had largely controlled the system of public education. Marx reported:
"Having once got rid of the standing army and the police, the physical
force elements of the old Government, the Commune was anxious to break
the spiritual force of repression, the "parson-power," by the disestablish-
ment and disendowment of all churches as proprietary bodies. The priests
were sent back to the recesses of private life, there to feed upon the alms
of the faithful in imitation of their predecessors, the Apostles. The whole
of the educational institutions were opened to the people gratuitously,
and at the same time cleared of all interference of Church and State."[14]
Notice that what Marx applauded here — despite his incidental taunting
of the clergy — was simply the separation of church and state, rather than
any effort to suppress religious belief or observance by force. The whole
issue of freedom of conscience will be dealt with in the next chapter.

Finally there remained the judiciary, where Marx observed: "The
judicial functionaries were to be divested of that sham independence
which had but served to mask their abject subserviency to all succeeding
governments to which, in turn, they had taken, and broken, the oaths
of allegiance. Like the rest of public servants, magistrates and judges
were to be elective, responsible, and revocable."[15] The career of an el-
derly judge in 1871 might have extended through two monarchies, a republic, an empire, and now a new republic — to all of which in succession, like the proverbial Vicar of Bray, he would have sworn and then
broken an oath of allegiance. Such career judges were now to follow the
career bureaucrats and soldiers, and be replaced by nonprofessional,
elected judges. Another "state-mystery" would thus be exploded, another
"trained caste" broken up.

Such were the political institutions set up by the Communards for the
government of Paris, and which they hoped would be imitated throughout the rest of France. Marx described their proposed plan for a national
organization of communes:

> The Commune was to be the political form of even the smallest
> country hamlet. . . . The rural communes of every district were to
> administer their common affairs by an assembly of delegates in the
> central town, and these district assemblies were again to send depu-

ties to the National Delegation in Paris, each delegate to be at any time revocable and bound by the *mandat impératif* (formal instructions) of his constituents. The few but important functions which still would remain for a central government were not to be suppressed, as has been intentionally misstated, but were to be discharged by Communal, and therefore strictly responsible agents.[16]

Thus a national legislature and executive presumably would have been constituted on the same radically democratic principles, each post being filled by a delegate who would have been bound to the instructions of his constituents, by whom he could also be recalled at any time. The important question whether Marx in fact approved such a high degree of decentralization will be treated later in the chapter.

Now, for our purposes, it would be most interesting to ask in what ways this workers' democracy was conceived by Marx to differ from bourgeois conceptions of democracy. Before seeking answers, however, we must recognize that this was *not* the contrast Marx himself sought to present in his *Civil War*. Rather, he was contrasting the Commune with the perfected parasite state. Between his review of the triumph of centralized state power under Louis Bonaparte and his account of how the Communards proceeded to smash its five "ubiquitous organs" we find the following connecting sentence: "The direct antithesis of the *empire* was the Commune" (italics added). Thus Marx was not trying to contrast communal democracy with the "bourgeois democracy" of Thiers and the National Assembly. He never recognized that usurpative government as having democratic intentions of any sort. The Third Republic had only been *proclaimed* (even that as a consequence of "Paris working men's revolution of the 4th of September"); it was not yet *constituted*, and given the conservative monarchist majority in the National Assembly, Marx had every reason to believe it never would be constituted as a democracy. In the meantime Thiers and the National Assembly ruled through the state apparatus they found already in place, which Marx saw as an effort "to restore and perpetuate that old governmental power bequeathed to them by the empire." At all events it was this old apparatus the Communards were praised for smashing and not, it must be recognized, any institutions of bourgeois democracy.[17]

Bearing this in mind we may return to our original query. There appear to be three principal ways in which proletarian democracy, as Marx conceived it, would differ from bourgeois democracy: (1) a much wider use of elections; (2) a radical deprofessionalization of public life; and (3) a different relationship between legislative and executive power. The third is the least important and will be treated in the next section where the separation-of-powers issue will come under general scrutiny.

In any bourgeois democratic republic one might expect all legislators to be elected but only the *chief* executive officers (president, governors, mayors, etc.); in European democracies one would add to this a set of cabinet ministers chosen by and held responsible to the lower chamber of the parliament. Beneath such elected leaders one would expect lesser posts in the civil bureaucracy and — needless to say — all posts in the military to be filled by hierarchical appointment. Judicial positions as well would be staffed by appointees more typically than by elected magistrates. By way of contrast Marx emphasized that "nothing could be more foreign to the spirit of the Commune than to supersede universal suffrage by hierarchic investiture."[18] Not only were judges to be elected but, most of all, administrators at all levels. Marx had always made executive power his prime concern and set forth its radical democratization as the foremost political objective of any popular movement. Thus in the First Draft he declared that the Communards had adapted universal suffrage "to its real purposes" when they used it to choose "their own functionaries of administration and initiation."[19] Such functionaries and indeed all the elected public servants of the Commune would also work under much closer control by their electors, because of the additional safeguards — encountered but infrequently in bourgeois democracies — of *mandat impératif*, the right of recall, and open *executive* proceedings with subsequently published transcripts. Marx had no patience with any institutional devices, checks, or balances whose purpose was to curtail popular influence; he favored a maximum of mass participation in and control over all branches of government. "Freedom," he would write four years later, perhaps thinking of the Paris Commune, "consists in converting the state from an organ superimposed upon society into one completely subordinate to it, and today, too, the forms of state are more or less free to the extent that they restrict the 'freedom of the state.'"[20] Just as bourgeois democracy could be judged much freer, by this yardstick, than Bonapartist despotism, so the Commune could be judged much freer than bourgeois democracy.

The second crucial way in which Marx and Engels conceived that proletarian democracy would be different from its bourgeois counterpart is not simply a matter of forms. A stable bourgeois democracy — America being the only example in 1871 — was likely to be run by professionals almost to the same degree as the Bonapartist state, if one includes as professionals not only the career bureaucrats, judges, and soldiers but also the professional politicians who made a career of holding elective office. In his 1891 introduction to *The Civil War* Engels drew attention, as we saw in chapter 3, to the "two great gangs of political speculators, who alternately take possession of the state power" in the United States and who "dominate and plunder" the nation for their own benefit in quite the same manner as the career officials of the Bonapartist parasite state. Marx and Engels had no desire to see the leaders of the labor movement move into the high positions of state and also govern in the same manner, developing interests as a leadership cadre that would separate them from the masses. What would prevent such a thing from happening? Engels responded:

> Against this transformation of the state and the organs of the state from servants of society into masters of society — an inevitable transformation in all previous states — the Commune made use of two infallible means. In the first place, it filled all posts — administrative, judicial and educational — by election on the basis of universal suffrage of all concerned, subject to the right of recall at any time by the same electors. And, in the second place, all officials, high or low, were paid only the wages received by other workers. The highest salary paid by the Commune to anyone was 6,000 francs. In this way an effective barrier to place-hunting and careerism was set up.[21]

We will scrutinize these safeguards at greater length in chapter 7; for now they serve to document Marx and Engels' desire to be rid of professional politicians, whom they detested as parasites no less than career soldiers and bureaucrats. They wanted all public offices in the proletarian state, from top to bottom, to be *"real workmen's functions"* rather than the spoils of a "trained caste." Nonprofessional service, either short-term or part-time, is the implicit answer to "place-hunting and careerism." Deprofessionalization, in a word, would separate working-class rule as much from any bourgeois state as from Bonapartism.

Combined with radical democratization, that is, the extension of the elective principle into all spheres, this radical deprofessionalization was conceived as the remedy to the parasitic tendency which had existed in all previous forms of the state. It was the essence of what Marx and Engels meant by "smashing" the state machinery.

Separation of Powers

Compared with such radical changes, what Marx and Engels advocated in regard to the separation of powers seems much less significant, but it requires a separate section because their presumed opposition to any separation of powers is sometimes cited as evidence of a totalitarian mentality. It is easy enough to quote Marx's famous line that "the Commune was to be a working, not a parliamentary, body, executive and legislative at the same time." One may even add a few quotations from 1848 expressing contempt for the "worm-eaten theory of division of powers," or reproduce Marx's 1851 rejection of that "old constitutional folly" when he declared categorically: "the condition of a 'free government' is not the *division*, but the *unity* of power."[22] Within the necessary historical context, however, the evidence will show that Marx and Engels always supported the independence of the judiciary, and that they favored a subordination of executive to legislative power mainly in a sense that Europeans nowadays find perfectly normal. Only in the *degree* of subordination desired will we discover a difference here between their conception of proletarian democracy and the traditions of European liberal democracy.

It cannot be emphasized too strongly that Marx and Engels operated within a monarchical tradition and that their political ideas, indeed, took shape as a reaction to the specifically *absolutist* tradition of the Prussian monarchy. Their first sovereign, Frederick William III, not only commanded his army without interference but appointed and controlled the cabinet ministers who ran his civil administration. Without the benefit of any written constitution or parliament he also exercised full legislative power, acting on the advice of his chosen cabinet ministers. He also appointed all royal judges, and their subsequent independence from his interference was but imperfectly protected. What could be more understandable than that the opponents of such a royal absolutism would have a profound aversion to independent executive power? Such a profound aversion, it will be argued, lies at the root of whatever Marx and Engels had to say on the separation-of-powers issue.

Let us begin with judicial power where it is easy enough to reconstruct Marx and Engels' views. Among opponents of Prussian absolutism in the 1840s, three main lines of judicial reform suggested themselves: first, to secure greater independence for judges and judicial processes without necessarily challenging the royal power of appointment; next, to democratize judicial power by the extension of the jury system (used only in the

Rhine Province), and ultimately by the election of *all* judges; and finally, to expand judicial competence sufficiently so as to offer a check, to exert some restraint, upon the omnipotence of the executive. In volume 1 we saw how Marx and Engels had identified themselves with all three prongs of this offensive both before and after they became communists. In his very debut as a journalist, Marx lamented the fact that in Prussian criminal proceedings, "judge, prosecutor, and defence lawyer are *one person*"; he also found it logically necessary that "the independent judge belongs neither to me [as litigant] nor to the government."[23] Engels likewise insisted that "in all states where the separation of powers has been really instituted, judicial and executive powers are quite without any connection"; citing France, England, and America as examples, he went on to one of his favorite themes, "the advantages and guarantees offered by the jury system," insisting "that judicial power is the direct property of the nation, which exercises it through its jurors."[24] Conversion to communism did not seem to affect the young men's views on these subjects. In fact Marx's plans for his never realized book on the modern state exhibit unusually strong interest in the separation of powers. One chapter was to treat the principle of separation while succeeding chapters dealt with each of the three branches — including one on "*Judicial power* and *law*." In 1846 we still find Engels praising the desire in Germany "to introduce the jury, in order to get rid of a separate class of judges, forming a state in the state."[25]

The events of 1848 obliged Marx and Engels to consider problems of judicial power during a democratic revolution against an established authoritarian regime. Marx lashed out at the hypocrisy of those presumably "independent" Prussian judges who nonetheless accommodated themselves to every illegal action of the crown, offering no resistance to such tyrannical acts and therefore providing no check on executive power. Both men called for the temporary suspension of the irremovability principle, as the French revolutionaries had done in 1792 and again in 1848, so as to remove or pension off the most "servile" of the judicial incumbents.[26] Neither man specified any means for choosing replacements: it is plausible to assume they would have preferred election, but would have been happy enough to see the Prussian assembly do the job if it would only bestir itself. They repeatedly urged this assembly to assume responsibility for the exercise of power in *all* spheres during the "revolutionary *Provisorium*" between the collapse of the old regime and the drawing up of a new constitution. Such a *Provisorium*, Engels argued, "even empowers it, if need be, to transform itself into a *court of justice* and to judge without laws!" Here was an allusion to the theory and practice of constituent assemblies in the Great French Revolution, but Engels did not recommend such a union of legislative and judicial power as a permanent feature of government.[27] We will return to the problem of constituent assemblies presently.

During the 1850s, while reporting for the *New York Daily Tribune,* Marx had occasion to touch on the independence of the judiciary again. He lamented that the Prussian counterrevolution had "done away with guarantees even existing at the worst times of the absolute monarchy, with the [formal] independence, for instance, of the Judges of the executive Government."[28] By contrast he pointed to the 1831 constitution of Hesse-Cassel as being, except for its electoral provisions, "the most liberal fundamental law ever proclaimed in Europe." Surely this was high praise from a man who normally took ruthless delight in picking apart the flaws and shams of bourgeois constitutions. Why did he find this document praiseworthy? "There is no other Constitution which restrains the powers of the executive within limits so narrow, makes the Administration more dependent on the Legislature, and confides such a supreme control to the judicial benches." He continued:

> The Prince is divested of the right of grace. He enjoys neither the privilege of pensioning or removing the members of the Administration against their will, there being always open to them an appeal to the courts of law.The latter are invested with the right of final decision in all questions of bureaucratic discipline. . . . In this way, the members of the bureaucracy were emancipated from the Crown. On the other hand, the Courts of law, empowered to decide definitively upon all the acts of the Executive, were rendered omnipotent.

While praising this power to rule on the constitutionality of all executive acts, Marx also had kind words for an 1848 reform of the same constitution which placed "the nomination of the members of the Supreme Court into the hands of the Legislature," thus eliminating the executive power of appointment.[29] Scattered remarks in latter years followed the same pattern. With respect to the draft Gotha Program, Engels complained that it lacked "the first condition of all freedom: that all officials should be responsible for all their official acts to every citizen before the ordinary courts and according to common law." Neither Marx nor Engels, on the other hand, took exception to the program's demand for "administration of justice by the people."[30] The Erfurt Program sharpened this demand to specify "popularly elected judges," again without evoking any protest from Engels.[31] On the contrary, when Jules Guesde wrote against the election of judges in France, Engels protested: "What he says about judges elected by universal suffrage can be applied to universal suffrage generally in the republic, in every political institution. If *Messieurs les francais* do not know how to use this universal suffrage, *tant pis pour eux.*"[32] Through these diverse comments scattered across half a century one perceives the consequence of Marx and Engels' shared Prussian heritage — their consistent desire to see judicial power emancipated from executive tutelage by means of democratization and to see it expanded to include control over unconstitutional acts by the executive. Significantly, the two men were always more concerned with the possibility of unconstitutional executive acts than with unconstitutional legislation.

The treatment of judicial power in *The Civil War in France,* quoted in the previous section, is entirely consistent with the pattern. Marx was happy to see judges "divested of that sham independence" which had masked their "abject subserviency" to executive power, and he rejoiced that such judges were henceforth "to be elective, responsible, and revocable."[33] But nowhere did he call for any merging of judicial with executive or legislative authority. If Marx and Engels can be faulted at all in this sphere, it would be for their insensitivity to the possibility of *too much* democracy, to the threat of lynch justice that hovers around the idea of instantly recallable magistrates. To this danger of mob rule, or the tyranny of the majority, we will return in the next chapter. But nowhere in their writings can one find any suggestion that, as a permanent state of affairs, judicial power be made dependent upon the legislative or executive, or merged together with them.

Whatever the importance of the judiciary, the main political struggles of modern Europe had to do with the respective powers of the legislative and executive branches, of parliaments and kings. In contrast to the American experience where it had been feasible to establish an elected chief executive at the outset (albeit not very democratically elected), virtually all Europeans had to start from the established fact of hereditary monarchy. Indeed, on the Continent the first task was to *create* a representative parliament and the next was to expand its competence as much as possible against the pretensions of divine-right absolutism. These liberal and sometimes democratic objectives unavoidably required massive incursions by elected assemblies into the traditional realm of executive power, usually during periods of revolution, and it is not surprising to find kings and their ministers appealing to the principle of separation of powers in an effort to defend their authoritarian prerogatives. Conversely, in such revolutionary periods, elected representatives were likely to find themselves insisting, like Abbé Sieyès in the classic case of the French National Assembly of 1789, that they incorporate the national will, that sovereignty resides in their assembled ranks, and that the crown has no right to block their actions. Whatever their views on the separation of powers in an ideal constitution, they were obliged to defend temporary legislative dominance for the purpose of drafting a constitution. Constituent assemblies, according to Sieyès' argument, stand outside and above the normal operations of government; momentarily they must exercise supreme power.[34]

When Marx and Engels scorned the "worm-eaten" doctrine of the separation of powers during the German revolutions of 1848, they were defending the rights of constituent assemblies in the same fashion as Sieyès, not advancing some new totalitarian-democratic recipe for government. Thus when a Prussian minister appealed to the doctrine to prevent the Berlin assembly from interfering in his work, Engels fired back the following testy questions:

> Is there in Prussia legally and factually a separation of powers in the sense that you interpret it, i.e. in the constitutional sense? Is not the existing separation of powers the limited, trimmed one which corresponds to the *absolute*, the bureaucratic monarchy? How then can one use constitutional phrases for it before it has been reformed constitutionally? . . . The constitutional separation of powers does not yet exist at all in Prussia; hence there can also be no infringement upon it.[35]

Marx in his turn defended the sovereignty of the Berlin assembly in words that might have been copied from Sieyès:

> It was elected by the people for the purpose of independently enacting a Constitution appropriate to the conditions of life which had come into conflict with the old political organization and laws. It was therefore from the very beginning a sovereign, constituent assembly. The fact that it all the same stooped to entertain the point of view of the agreement [between king and people] was mere for-

mal courtesy towards the Crown, mere ceremony. . . . The King made the concessions which the revolution *compelled* him to make. Neither more nor less.

The crown, Marx went on to argue, strangely demands the respect for the separation of powers before any constitution has been drawn up to establish it, while at the same time recognizing no limit to its own power. "The representatives of the people are expected to play the role of a *constitutional* Chamber confronting an *absolute* monarchy!"[36] But the assembly should not trouble itself with royal pretensions: "The Prussian Crown is within its *rights* in confronting the Assembly as an *absolute Crown.* But the Assembly is in the *wrong* because it does not confront the Crown as an *absolute assembly.*" It must claim and exercise sovereignty even if force is required to overcome royal opposition. Clashes between a constituent assembly and a recalcitrant monarch are not to be grouped with legislative-executive wrangles under an established constitution; they are conflicts between two powers both of which claim sovereignty in a revolutionary *Provisorium.* Only force can resolve such a conflict.[37] In the Prussian case it was the monarch who eventually dispersed the assembly at bayonet point; thereafter Frederick William promulgated his own constitution which granted the most meager powers to a parliament elected through a mockery of universal suffrage.

Once established, European parliaments might continue to contest royal power in any number of areas, but their decisive victory would come with recognition of the principle of "ministerial responsibility," that is, the continual accountability of cabinet ministers to a parliamentary majority which has the power to dismiss them through a vote of no confidence. With the establishment of ministerial responsibility kings lost their traditional right to appoint and dismiss cabinet ministers at their own pleasure and thus lost control over the day-to-day policies and actions of the executive branch. By wresting such control from the hands of the monarch, however, parliaments did not establish a separation of powers in the American sense; on the contrary they created an effective and permanent subordination of executive to legislative power. Such subordination has been a characteristic feature of European democracies ever since.[38]

Nowadays Marx and Engels' putative disciples generally dismiss such bourgeois governmental systems with the phrase "parliamentary cretinism." It must be understood, however, that the masters originally devised that phrase to express contempt for the opposite — for the *absence* of parliamentary rule. The first legislatures so stigmatized were the German and Prussian national assemblies of 1848, whose only efforts to limit the real power of the German princes lay in the paragraphs of the constitutions which they wrote but lacked the courage to impose. As Engels recalled in 1884:

> Finally, we exposed the parliamentary cretinism (as Marx called it) of the various so-called National Assemblies. These gentlemen had allowed all means of power to slip out of their hands, in part had voluntarily surrendered them again to the governments. In Berlin, as in Frankfort, alongside newly strengthened, reactionary governments there stood powerless assemblies, which nevertheless imagined that their impotent resolutions would shake the world in its foundations. This cretinous self-deception prevailed even among the extreme Lefts.[39]

Thus parliamentary cretinism originally referred to the self-deception of "powerless" assemblies that their decisions really mattered so long as they neglected to assert effective control over the "governments," that is over the princes and their ministers, their armies, and their bureaucracies.

The other legislature stigmatized as cretinous was the French Legislative National Assembly in 1851, after it had abandoned any effort to control the army or the ministers of the chief executive, Louis Bonaparte. In a country like France, Marx wrote, the legislature "forfeits all real influence when it loses command of the ministerial posts." Thereafter, the assembly

> took that peculiar malady which since 1848 has raged all over the Continent, *parliamentary cretinism*, which holds those infected by it fast in an imaginary world and robs them of all sense, all memory, all understanding of the rude external world — it took this parliamentary cretinism for those who had destroyed all the conditions of parliamentary power with their own hands . . . still to regard their parliamentary victories as [real] victories.[40]

It is noteworthy that Marx did not apply this epithet to the assembly during the period when it controlled the government, rather labelling this the period of the *"parliamentary republic."* Even more noteworthy is his restriction of the malady to continental Europe: neither Marx nor Engels ever called the British Parliament "cretinous," for by their own standard it was a legislature that, ever since the seventeenth century, had really governed. After his first inspection of the British constitution in 1844, Engels reached the conclusion: "In reality the House of Commons makes the laws and administers them through the Ministers, who are but a committee of the House." A separate royal executive power no longer existed: "The power of the Crown is the power of the Ministers, in other words, of the representatives of the majority of the House of Commons." All that was required to transform Britain into a "pure democracy" was the implementation of the People's Charter. Over and over again Engels and his partner returned to the idea that universal suffrage in Britain would enable the workers to elect a majority to the House of Commons. That victory was not expected to result in an asylum for parliamentary cretins but in the rule of the proletariat.[41]

Engels still had Britain in mind when he lampooned the royally decreed Prussian constitution in 1849:

> In the profane constitutional states, the Chamber rules through its committee, the Government, and the King's only right is that of saying yes and amen, and of giving his signature. . . . But in the royal Prussian constitutional monarchy by the grace of God the exact opposite holds good. The Crown rules through its Ministers, and woe to the Chambers if they venture to do anything but say yes and amen to the effusions of divine grace![42]

Marx similarly deplored the lack of parliamentary control over cabinet ministers in Prussia, despite article 44 of the constitution which declared them "responsible":

> In the paragraph itself, it is not said to whom the ministers are responsible. In practice, on every occasion when the chambers went the length of threatening the ministers with a vote of non-confidence, the latter declared roundly that they were quite welcome to it, ministers being responsible, indeed, but to their royal master only. The question of ministerial responsibility possesses in Prussia, as it did in the France of Louis Philippe, an exceptional importance, because it means, in fact, the responsibility of the bureaucracy. The ministers are the chiefs of that omnipotent, all-intermeddling parasite body, and to them alone, according to Article 106 of the Constitution, have the subaltern members of the administration to look, without taking upon themselves to inquire into the legality of their ordinances, or incurring any responsibility by executing them. Thus,

the power of the bureaucracy, and by the bureaucracy, of the executive, has been maintained intact.[43]

When in the early 1860s Bismarck tried to undercut even the minimal budgetary powers of the Prussian legislature, Engels defended the importance of the issue against the indifference of the Lassalleans:

> Both the bourgeoisie and the workers can only function as a really organized political force through parliamentary representation; and this parliamentary representation is only of value if they can have their say and make decisions. . . . The question must arise whether it lies in the workers' interests for this parliament to be robbed of all political power, this parliament which they themselves hope to enter by gaining universal and direct suffrage and in which they hope to form a majority one day? . . . Hardly.[44]

In these criticisms of the Prussian constitution one can perceive Marx and Engels' admiration for those political systems where ministerial responsibility was really practiced, where parliament "rules through its committee, the Government."

Much the same sort of admiration reveals itself in Marx's praise of the Hessian constitution of 1831, "the most liberal fundamental law ever proclaimed in Europe," which we noted earlier in connection with the judiciary. No other constitution, he asserted in this 1859 article, "makes the Administration more dependent on the Legislature," since the latter "possesses the right of stopping all taxes, imposts and duties, on every conflict with the executive." Then he proceeded:

> The law on Ministerial responsibility, so far from being an unmeaning phrase, enables the representatives to remove, through the State tribunal, every Minister declared guilty of having even misinterpreted any resolution of the Legislature. . . . The Representative Chamber selects out of its members a permanent committee, forming a sort of Areopagus, watching and controlling the Government, and impeaching the officials for violation of the Constitution, no exception being granted on behalf of orders received by subalterns from their superiors in rank.[45]

This form of ministerial responsibility, which held ministers *legally* responsible for the constitutionality of their acts before judicial tribunals when impeached by the "Areopagus," was simply a less developed form of the standard modern practice whereby ministers are held *politically* responsible for all their policies and actions by a parliamentary majority. In both cases what Marx approved wholeheartedly was the subjection of executive power to as many controls as possible. In his most general comment of all on the subject, in *The Eighteenth Brumaire*, Marx asserted that nations express their will through parliaments, through the legislative power, while the executive power expects the nation to renounce all will of its own and submit to an alien will. "The executive power, in contrast to the legislative power, expresses the heteronomy of a nation, in contrast to its autonomy."[46]

Thus, the desire to establish ministerial responsibility, to have a parliament which "rules through its committee, the Government," to have ministers "who are but a committee of the House," these desires place Marx and Engels again squarely in the mainstream of the European liberal-democratic tradition. And it is within this context that one must understand Marx's famous remark from *The Civil War in France* that "the Commune was to be a working, not a parliamentary, body, executive and legislative at the same time."[47] He was not alluding here to some novel fusion of governmental powers but to the standard European practice of parliamentary rule. Executive authority in the Paris Commune was delegated to sub-groups of the communal assembly which were but committees of the "House," its "Government." Their liability to immediate recall by the communal assembly was but another name for ministerial responsibility, recall amounting to dismissal through a vote of no confidence. To perceive insidious totalitarian implications in such practices would occur only to latter-day American scholars brought up in a quite different separation-of-powers traditions.

If all this is true, it must nonetheless be recognized that Marx and Engels wanted to subordinate executive power to the legislature in much more thoroughgoing fashion than did most of their bourgeois European contemporaries. There was an important difference of degree. Firstly, the two men showed no desire to retain an individual chief executive, either in the form of a ceremonial monarch or in the form of a president. In Germany, as late as 1891, Engels founded "unthinkable that our best people should become ministers under an emperor," and even in Britain, Marx and Engels always spoke as if the figurehead monarchy would sooner or later become unpopular and disappear.[48] To substitute an elected president as figurehead would be empty ceremony, while to give a president any real power would be positively dangerous. Europe had had only one experiment with an independent and elected head of state and that had produced the presidency of Louis Bonaparte in December 1848. Marx drew attention to the dangers he perceived:

> While the votes of France are split up among 750 members of the National Assembly, they are here, on the contrary, concentrated on a *single* individual. While each separate representative of the people represents only this or that party, this or that town, this or that bridgehead, . . . *he* is the elect of the nation and the act of his election is the trump that the sovereign people plays once every four years. The elected National Assembly stands in a metaphysical relation, but the elected President in a personal relation, to the nation. . . . As against the Assembly, he possesses a sort of divine right; he is President by the grace of the people.[49]

Within four years President Bonaparte had himself proclaimed Napoleon III, hereditary emperor of the French. Perhaps with this in mind Marx moved in 1866 to abolish the office of president within the International Working Men's Association; he also likened Lassalle to Bonaparte as a would-be "worker's dictator" when the latter created a powerful presidency for himself in the General German Workers' Association.[50] The more stable American presidency never excited so much animus in the two men — Marx even had kind words for Abraham Lincoln during the Civil War — but here too Engels seemed to agree with the Texan socialist who wrote him in 1893 in assuming the office one day would be abolished.[51] To divide executive tasks among responsible committees rather than concentrating them in the hands of one person seemed only natural to Marx and Engels as an antiauthoritarian safeguard: it had been done that way in Periclean Athens; the practice was enshrined in the Constitution of 1793; and it reappeared spontaneously in the institutions of the Paris Commune of 1871.

Secondly, within a proletarian legislature, Marx and Engels seemed to expect that executive tasks would be assigned, not just to a handful of individuals chosen to be ministers, but to most or all the members, each of whom would serve on one committee or another according to his competences. Thus in the Paris Commune, ten "commissions" (nine functional and one executive) were elected by the communal assembly, each having a membership of from five to eight persons, such that sixty-one of the ninety-two original members of the communal assembly were chosen for one or another administrative task.[52] It was because *two-thirds* of its members had such functions that Marx could call the Commune "a working, not a parliamentary, body, executive and legislative at the same time." Few deputies could remain pure parliamentarians, free of responsibility for carrying out the legislative decisions of the group. In approving such practices, Marx was pursuing the goal of maximum democratization of executive power and went well beyond the conventional bourgeois notion of responsible ministries.

Far more radical, however, was Marx and Engels' already discussed desire to see *all* administrative offices made elective and responsible, not only at the top but at all levels and in all departments. This was combined, as we have also seen, with a second expectation that all such functions would be deprofessionalized, would become "real workmen's functions," such that ordinary conscientious persons could take them up for a term and then pass them on, no individual keeping them long enough to acquire a vested career interest. It is really these last two expectations rather than the first two that set Marx and Engels apart from garden-variety nineteenth-century liberal democrats. And in a larger perspective it is these same two expectations, far more than any special attitude toward the separation of powers per se, that makes them profoundly radical when compared to their contemporaries or, for that matter, when compared to present-day social democrats or Communists. What they had in mind was not just to smash the existing bureaucracy of capitalist society but to eradicate the bureaucratic principle itself from all social institutions.

With respect to legislative power per se, most of what needs to be said has already emerged in one context or another — elections based on universal suffrage and secret ballot, bound deputies recallable at any time by their constituents, public legislative proceedings. Only two points need to be added: Marx appeared to endorse the Communards' scheme for a national organization of communes in which each rural commune would send a delegate to a district assembly, which in turn would choose a delegate to send to Paris. This has led many of his disciples to assume he favored an indirect and pyramidal system of national representation. Yet Monty Johnstone has pointed out that nowhere else in Marx or Engels' writings can one find any support for indirect schemes of representation. On the contrary the two men seemed to have accepted as normal the direct representation of geographic constituencies which they encountered in all the advanced parliamentary states.[53] Second, mention should be made of Marx and Engels' suspicion of bicameral legislatures. In their eyes the upper chamber was always included as an oligarchic check upon the more popular lower chamber, and indeed in most nineteenth-century European legislatures the members of the upper chamber sat either by hereditary right (e.g., the English House of Lords) or by governmental appointment (e.g., the German Federal Council). Marx's preferred Hessian constitution of 1831, as he expressly noted, prescribed a unicameral legislature, as did the hallowed Constitution of 1793. It is interesting to note, however, that he spoke with favor of the procedural requirement in Britain and France that bills be considered by the legislature on three separate occasions before a final vote could be taken to make them law. This was conceived as a safeguard against overhasty or rash decision-making.[54]

In short, where institutional checks and safeguards served legitimate purposes, as here or in the independence of the judiciary, Marx and Engels could see their merits; where they served only to frustrate or confine the popular will, or to make the processes of government complex and mysterious, they denounced them time and again. Since these latter motives were far more in evidence than the former in nineteenth-century European constitutions, and since the governing classes appealed to the separation-of-powers principle most frequently in order to thwart mass influence on government, it is understandable that Marx and Engels should be suspicious of the doctrine. "The machinery of government cannot be too simple," Marx declared; "it is always the craft of knaves to make it complicated and mysterious."[55]

Centralism Versus Decentralism

Of all the suspicions about *The Civil War in France*, perhaps the most widespread concerns the praise Marx reserved for the decentralist program of the Paris Commune, its April 1871 proposal to organize the national political life of France in a loose federation of highly autonomous communes. Had not Marx been a lifelong advocate of centralization? Had he not always ridiculed the Proudhonist conceptions that lay behind this April proposal? Scarcely five years earlier in a letter to Engels, he had scoffed at such "Proudhonized Stirnerism. Everything to be dissolved into little 'groups' or 'communes' which will in their turn form an 'association' but no state."[56] Could he really have changed his mind so dramatically? It seems highly improbable. And yet there is considerable evidence in Marx and Engels' mature thought to suggest, if not a complete volte face, at least a certain disenchantment with centralization as a universally benign process and a certain reemphasis of the value of local self-administration. These tendencies, it will be argued, may have made it possible for Marx to sympathize sincerely with the decentralist program of the Commune, though surely not with the absolute local autonomy desired by strict Proudhonists.

Marx and Engels' early advocacy of centralization is too well known to require elaborate documentation, but perhaps it does merit a few words of historical explanation, particularly since it is so often adduced as further evidence of authoritarian values or dictatorial ambitions. A moment's reflection will show how necessary it is to resist the facile equation that centralism equals authoritarianism, and decentralism equals democracy. Under the Confederation of 1815, power in Germany was highly decentralized, yet no one would argue that at any level it was organized democratically. Contemporaneously, in Great Britain power had been highly concentrated in a single parliament, yet surely it was organized more democratically than in Germany. France was still more centralized than Britain and yet, during the momentary flowering of the Second Republic, also considerably more democratic — because of universal suffrage. The same contrast can be found in nineteenth-century American experience: was the formally decentralized government of the Confederacy more, or less, democratic than that of the Union? Although there is no clear consistency on the issue, the forces of "order" in nineteenth-century Europe were probably to be found more frequently in the decentralist than in the centralist camp; the converse would hold for the forces of "progress."

This was true in any event for Germany when Marx and Engels acquired their political education, before the March days of 1848. The desire for national unification was primordially a centralizing aspiration, and the liberals and democrats who championed this cause, however much they might squabble about the *degree* of centralization desirable, all wanted more of it than existed under the Confederation of 1815. Conversely, the defenders of the existing decentralized order were located predominantly in the conservative establishments of the separate states — among the princes, their courts, armies, and bureaucracies. It is not surprising, therefore, to find that both Marx and Engels were centralizers from the beginning, even before they became communists. In September 1842 the twenty-year-old Engels wrote a — rather muddled — article on the issue of "Centralization and Freedom," which is nonetheless worthy of note because he saw no necessary incompatibility between the two:

No state can do without centralization, the federal state no more than the developed central state; . . . Under this centralization, communal administration, everything that affects individual citizens or corporations, can quite well be left free. . . . *Because* centralization is concentrated in a single center, because everything here forms a single unity, its activity must necessarily be general, its competence and powers embracing everything that is of *general* validity, but leaving free everything that concerns only this or that particular individual. From this follows the right of the central power of the state to promulgate laws, to control the administration, to appoint state officials, etc.; from this follows at the same time the principle that judicial power must by no means be connected with the center but must be in the hands of the people — courts of law with juries — and that, as already said, communal affairs, etc., do not come within the competence of the center, and so on.

The central nature of the state does not by the way stipulate that some one person must be the central point, as in an absolute monarchy. . . . The main thing is not the person in the center, but the center itself.[57]

Two sentiments in this passage were to become permanent features of Marx and Engels' centralism: firstly, that the concentration of power in a single center need not mean placing it in the hands of a single person, but only that it be in the hands of a single assembly, like for instance the British Parliament; and secondly, that such a centralization need not and should not destroy local self-administration, individual freedom, or the independence of the judiciary.

Marx and Engels' centralism thus had a natural origin in their German experience and probably would have existed even if the two men had never heard of the Jacobin regime of 1793. No doubt the lessons they drew from the Jacobin example reconfirmed their own centralism, and yet, especially after they became communists, Marx and Engels always stressed the socioeconomic need for centralization more than any directly political need to concentrate force against opponents. This historic link between centralization and socioeconomic modernization is a familiar theme in the *Manifesto;* Engels spelled it out even more plainly in another 1847 writing. Swiss federalism, he argued, represents a backward-looking craft-agrarian localism that everywhere is doomed:

Through its industry, its commerce and its political institutions, the bourgeoisie is already working everywhere to drag the small, self-contained localities which live only for themselves out of their isolation, to bring them into contact with one another, to merge their interests, expand their local horizons, to destroy their local habits, strivings and ways of thinking, and to build up a great nation with common interests, customs and ideas out of the many hitherto mutually independent localities and provinces. The bourgeoisie is already carrying out considerable centralization. The proletariat, far from suffering any disadvantage from this, will as a result rather be in a position to unite, to feel itself a class, to adopt in democracy a proper political point of view, and finally to conquer the bourgeoisie. The democratic proletariat not only needs the kind of centralization begun by the bourgeoisie but will have to extend it very much further. . . . It will not only have to centralize every country separately but will have to centralize all civilized [advanced] countries together as soon as possible.[58]

Here again Engels did not present centralization as antagonistic to democracy but, on the contrary, as a necessary precondition for modern democracy at a national — ultimately international — level.

This same conviction that the proletariat requires a cosmopolitan, not localist, outlook lies behind the often quoted and often misunderstood lines of the March *Circular* of 1850. Throughout the revolutionary period in Germany, Marx and Engels were concerned lest the workers be misled by the seductive backward-looking particularism of so many South German artisans and petty bourgeois, which expressed itself in admiration of Switzerland and in the call for a decentralized federal republic in Germany. In the next revolution, the *Circular* declared, the same petty bourgeois democrats could be expected to renew their agitation for "the utmost possible autonomy and independence for the communities and provinces":

The workers, in opposition to this plan, must not only strive for a single and indivisible German republic, but also within this republic for the most determined centralization of power in the hands of the state authority. They must not allow themselves to be misguided by the democratic talk of freedom for the communities, of self-government, etc. In a country like Germany, where there are still so many remnants of the Middle Ages to be abolished, where there is so much local and provincial obstinacy to be broken, it must under no circumstances be permitted that every village, every town and every province should put a new obstacle in the path of revolutionary activity, which can proceed with full force only from the center. . . . As in France in 1793 so today in Germany, it is the task of the really revolutionary party to carry through the strictest centralization.[59]

Certainly this stands as the most extreme centralist pronouncement associated with Marx and Engels. Even so, one must recognize that its strong words were directed against a particular kind of localist democracy and not against democratic principles in general. The "state authority" in whose hands the *Circular* wanted power centralized could hardly be anything but the freshly elected national assembly referred to elsewhere in the document. (Germany did not yet have a central administration that could be taken over intact by some self-appointed revolutionary committee; it did not even have a single great population center like Paris.) If it were only that Marx and Engels expected local minorities to give way to a national majority in certain matters, few eyebrows would be raised. What is disturbing is the lack of any specified limit on the "most determined centralization of power," as well as the generally shrill tone of the text. This tone undoubtedly reflected Marx and Engels' sharp disillusionment in 1849–1850 with the petty bourgeoisie as an alliance partner, and may also reflect the influence of August Willich and the radical artisans of the Communist League. These matters have been discussed in volume 1, where it was argued that the March *Circular*, a secret unsigned pronouncement of the league's central committee, does not necessarily represent the personal views of Marx and Engels in their purity.[60] It is surely significant that Engels added a footnote to this paragraph when it was published in 1885, which, without repudiating the centralist views outright, softened and modified them almost into oblivion. We will examine this footnote presently, but first it will be useful to inspect some earlier evidences of, and probable reasons for, Marx and Engels' softening on the centralization issue.

The first probable reason for the change has to do with the fate of Ireland in the process of British centralization, the second with the increasingly oppressive and bureaucratic character of French centralization. The second is probably more important and leads directly to *The Civil War in France;* therefore let us tend to the Irish issue first. In the 1840s Marx and Engels seemed to have regarded Ireland's incorporation into the United Kingdom as an accomplished and irreversible fact, part of the historically necessary process of forming great centralized nation-states on a capitalist basis, before which the ethnic sensibilities of the Irish had to succumb just as had those of the Scots, Welsh, and Cornish, or in France those of the Bretons, Basques, and Alsatians. The ethnic oppression of the Irish would come to an end, they thought, only with the general British proletarian revolution that would end all oppression, and not through a prior ethnic revolution that would produce a separate Irish nation-state.[61] In the 1860s, however, after Marx became extensively involved in the British labor movement through the IWA, he changed his mind quite dramatically about the Irish question. "Previously I thought Ireland's separation from England impossible," he wrote Engels in November 1867. "Now I think it inevitable, although after separation there may come *federation*." "The English working class," he added in a later epistle, "will *never accomplish anything* before it has got rid of Ireland."[62] In an IWA pronouncement of 1870 Marx explained succinctly why the antagonism between English and Irish workers "is the *secret of the impotence of the English working class*":

> The average English worker hates the Irish worker as a competitor who lowers wages and the *standard of life*. He feels national and religious antipathies for him. He regards him somewhat like the *poor whites* of the Southern States of North America regard their black slaves. This antagonism among the proletarians of England is artificially nourished and supported by the bourgeoisie. It knows that this scission is the true secret of maintaining its power. . . .
>
> Quite apart from international justice, it is a *precondition to the emancipation of the English working class* to transform the present *forced union* (i.e., the enslavement of Ireland) into *equal and free confederation* if possible, into *complete separation* if need be.[60]

In contrast to Germany, where Marx and Engels opposed federalism in any form, here a federal solution appeared as a desirable goal, with complete separation countenanced as a possible last resort. The historic process of centralization, normally progressive, had become counterproductive where it created divisive fissures within the working class. It was no longer something to be approved automatically.

The other probable reason for second thoughts concerning centralization takes us back to the familiar theme of Bonapartism and the parasite state. We have seen how Marx and Engels generally approved the process of centralization in France, particularly that which was accomplished by the Great Revolution. But they assumed the logical end product of bourgeois political centralization would be — as in Britain — the concentration of power in the hands of a single representative parliament. France seemed to move in this direction throughout the first half of the nineteenth century, but then came the eighteenth Brumaire of Louis Bonaparte. At that point the administrative and military apparatus of the French state, inherited from the absolutist kings, then polished, rationalized, and further centralized by the bourgeoisie to serve its own needs, now broke free of class control and shattered parliamentary supremacy to pursue its own institutional and caste interests, together with those of the adventurer who had inspired the revolt.[64] This was not the sort of centralization Marx and Engels had in mind.

Even in *The Eighteenth Brumaire* itself, Marx began to discriminate between different *kinds* of centralization and to lament that the historically necessary kind accomplished by the French Revolution — "breaking all separate local, territorial, urban and provincial powers in order to create the civil unity of the nation" — had been accompanied by bureaucratic centralization as well, which augmented "the extent, the attributes and the agents of governmental power." Bourgeois rule had thus helped to nurture the appalling parasitic body and now choked French society like a boa constrictor, but the proletarian revolution could do without such a military-bureaucratic apparatus: "The centralization of the state that modern society requires arises only on the ruins of the military-bureaucratic government machinery which was forged in opposition to feudalism. The demolition of the state machine will not endanger centralization. Bureaucracy is only the low and brutal form of a centralization that is still afflicted with its opposite, with feudalism."[65] Here in 1852 was a clear repudiation of centralization in its bureaucratic, and particularly in its Bonapartist, form, yet this was the form that — especially with the advent of Bismarck — seemed the wave of the future for bourgeois Europe. Should centralization be encouraged after all? How could the beneficial and necessary work of centralization be achieved without encouraging its twin — bureaucratization? If there was an answer, it had to lie in some kind of nonprofessional self-administration of localities and departments, right up to the national level. This line of thinking must have disposed Marx to look more sympathetically upon the decentralist schemes of the Communards which he might otherwise have dismissed out of hand. Twenty years of Bonapartism had left their mark.

Already in his preparations for *The Civil War in France* Marx showed especial interest in the decentralization issue, copying down comments on the subject by Montesquieu and Lamenais, as well as the relevant paragraphs of the Jacobin Constitution of 1793. In the First Draft he contrasted the backward-looking decentralism of the provincial aristocrats gathered at Versailles with the forward-looking decentralism of the Communards, and quite obviously read his own desires into the intentions of the latter:

> What they [the aristocrats] really want is to go back to what preceeded the centralized statemachinery, . . . and put into its place the provincial and local domainial influence of the Châteaux. They want a reactionary *decentralization* of France. What Paris wants is to supplant that centralization which has done its service against feodality, but has become the mere unity of an artificial body, resting on gensdarmes, red and black armies, repressing the life of real society, lasting [weighing] as an incubus upon it, . . . to supplant this unitarian France which exists besides the French society — by the political union of French society itself through the Communal organization. . . .
>
> What Paris wants is to break up that factitious unitarian system, so far as it is the antagonist of the real living union of France and a mere means of class rule.[66]

Thus in broad historical terms centralization has already done its service against feodality, and in fact has become an incubus upon the life of French society. The Communards have (that is, Marx has) no desire to break up the underlying accomplished unity of the nation, but only to smash the incubus claiming to represent that unity. They seek to dismantle this centralized apparatus only "so far as it is the antagonist of the real living union of France and a mere means of class rule." To this exact extent Marx could sympathize sincerely and even enthusiastically with the decentralism of the Paris Commune, for it corresponded to his own desire to debureaucratize and deprofessionalize political life.

In the final version of *The Civil War* Marx further clarified what he took to be the desire of the Communards, but which are still more evidently his own desires. They did not wish, he asserted, to go back to the medieval communes which existed before the basic legal, economic, and cultural unity of the nation had been forged, for that unity, "if originally brought about by political force, has now become a powerful coefficient of social production." Neither did they conceive of municipal liberty as a *check* upon the remote and authoritarian central power of the crown, as had the framers of the constitution of 1791. For the central authority proposed by the Communards would not be some alien power but a body of deputies from the communes themselves, chosen from all over the country, "each delegate to be at any time revocable and bound by the *mandat impératif* (formal instructions) of his constituents." Then came the passage cited earlier in this chapter:

> The few but important functions which still would remain for a central government were not to be suppressed, as has been intentionally mis-stated, but were to be discharged by Communal, and therefore strictly responsible agents. The unity of the nation was not to be broken, but, on the contrary, to be organized by the Communal Constitution and to become a reality by the destruction of the State power which claimed to be the embodiment of that unity independent of, and superior to, the nation itself, from which it was but a parasitic excrescence.[67]

"Few but important" is obviously the key phrase here and was perhaps deliberately chosen for its vagueness. In fact the April program of the Communards was itself equally vague, being the product of a compromise between Proudhonist decentralizers and neo-Jacobin and Blanquist elements not exactly friendly to the idea. It spoke of a "great central administration" that would act as the "delegation of the federated communes"; but while the powers of separate communes were itemized at length, no specific central powers were discussed at all.[68] Surely at the very least Marx would have wanted a centralized direction of the economy, as suggested in his remark a few pages later that united cooperative societies were "to regulate national production upon a common plan, thus taking it under their own control."[69] Perhaps Marx also believed that, had the Commune survived and the rest of France followed its example, the Proudhonists would have found themselves compelled to preserve far more central administrative power than they had planned, compelled by the irony of world history (as Engels remarked on a similar issue) to do "the opposite of what the doctrines of their school prescribed."[70] Neither here nor elsewhere did Marx attempt to delineate exactly which functions would devolve upon which levels of the administration, or specify any overall degree of centralization to be achieved, or suggest how the inevitable conflicts and jurisdictional disputes among the various levels would be resolved. This fuzziness makes it possible for Marx's critics to place the passage reproduced above next to the March *Circular*, and charge dissimulation. As we have seen, however, there is good reason to suppose that by 1871 Marx had indeed backed off somewhat from the uncritical centralism of his early years and reemphasized the idea of local self-administration as the antidote to bureaucratic rule. Even in his private 1874 notes on Bakunin, where he had no reason to hide his true feelings, he responded to the anarchist's barbed question whether all forty million Germans would be members of the government by saying: "Certainly, for the thing begins with the self-government of the community."[71]

For additional evidence of a softening on the centralization issue, and important details about it, we may turn to the late writings of Engels, beginning with the promised 1885 footnote to the March *Circular*. This was the only footnote Engels felt a need to add when he published the document for the first time in that year, and it was appended to the anti-decentralization paragraph quoted earlier:

> It must be recalled today that this passage is based on a misunderstanding. At that time — thanks to the Bonapartist and liberal falsifiers of history — it was considered as established that the French centralized machine of administration had been introduced by the Great Revolution and in particular that it had been used by the Convention as an indispensable and decisive weapon for defeating the royalist and federalist reaction and the external enemy. It is now, however, a well-known fact that throughout the revolution up to the eighteenth Brumaire the whole administration of the *départements*, *arrondissements* and *communes* consisted of authorities elected by the respective constituents themselves, and that these authorities acted with complete freedom within the general state laws; that precisely this provincial and local self-government, similar to the American, became the most powerful lever of the revolution and indeed to such an extent that Napoleon, immediately after his coup d'état of the eighteenth Brumaire, hastened to replace it by the still existing administration of the prefects, which, therefore was a pure instrument of reaction from the beginning. But no more than local and provincial self-government is in contradiction to political, national centralization, is it necessarily bound up with that narrow-minded cantonal or communal self-seeking which strikes us as so repulsive in Switzerland, and which all the South German federal republicans wanted to make the rule in Germany in 1849.[72]

Engels' historical account hardly told the *whole* truth about Jacobin government, but his desire to dissociate himself from the ruthless centralism advocated by the March *Circular* was plain enough. He seemed to foresee a desirable "political, national centralization" for legislative purposes, to establish "general state laws," within which elected provincial and local authorities could then operate "with complete freedom." This is a far cry from the original warning against being "misguided by the democratic talk of freedom for the communities, of self-government, etc.," although Engels' distaste for federalism as practiced in Switzerland obviously remained undiminished.

Early the following year Engels read a newly published book, *Hoe ons land geregeerd wordt,* by the Dutch socialist Ferdinand Domela Nieuwenhuis, and wrote a congratulatory letter to the author saying how much he had learned from the book about the administration of Holland. He continued:

> Holland along with England and Switzerland is the only West European country *not* to go through the absolute monarchy of the sixteenth-to-eighteenth centuries, and has many advantages because of it, namely a survival of local and provincial self-government without a genuine bureaucracy in the French or Prussian sense. That is a great advantage for the development of national character and also for later on; with but a few changes the working people can create here a free self-administration that must be our best implement when it comes to transforming the mode of production. In Germany and France all this is lacking and must be undertaken again from the beginning.[73]

Now local self-administration has even become "our best implement" for transforming the mode of production, just as it was "the most powerful lever of the revolution" in France.

More interesting still are the fairly detailed and specific thoughts Engels expressed on the issue in his 1891 critique of the Erfurt Program. The draft demands, he observed, omitted any mention of Germany's curious federal structure, a lopsided construction in which Prussia was twice as large as all the other twenty-four states combined, a mock federation — as Engels jibed — "between Prussia and Reuss-Greiz-Schleiz-Lobenstein, in which the one has as many square miles as the other has square inches." With regard to the socialist restructuring of Germany, he argued:

> On the one hand, *Kleinstaaterei* [petty state particularism] must be eliminated — society can scarcely be revolutionized while Bavaria and Wurttemberg hold onto their special Reserved Rights, and the

map of Thuringia, for example, presents its present woeful aspect. On the other hand, Prussia must cease to exist, must be dissolved into self-administering provinces so that a specific Prussianism ceases to weigh Germany down. . . .

What should take its place? In my view the proletariat can only use the form of a unitary and indivisible republic. In the gigantic territory of the United States a federal republic is still, on the whole, a necessity, although it is already becoming a hindrance in the Eastern States. It would be a step forward in England, where the two islands are peopled by four nations and in spite of a single parliament three different systems of laws still today exist side by side. In little Switzerland, it has long been a hindrance, tolerable only because Switzerland is content to be a purely passive element in the European state system. For Germany federalism of the Swiss type would be an enormous step backward. Two points distinguish such a federal state from a unitary state: that each member state, each canton, has its own separate civil and criminal legislation and judicial system; and then that alongside the popular chamber there is also a chamber representing the states in which every canton, large or small, votes as such. Happily, we have already gotten beyond the first of these and will not be so childish as to reintroduce it. The second we possess in our Federal Council and could very well do without, especially since our so-called "federal state" is already well on the road to becoming a unitary state. It is not our task to reverse the revolution carried out from above in 1866 and 1870, but to give it a necessary supplement and improvement through a movement from below.[74]

Here we find a fairly sophisticated attitude toward federalism, regarded as necessary in the United States, even as a desirable progress in Britain, while at the same time a misfortune for Switzerland and Germany. Engels seemed in particular to favor the centralization of legal systems, consequently of legislatures, but spoke in the same breath of "self-administering provinces" in Prussia — thus again of self-administration under a uniform system of law.

In his next paragraph Engels went on to make the same linkage Marx had made in *The Civil War* between decentralized administration and debureaucratization:

So, then, a unitary republic — but not in the sense of the present French Republic, which is nothing but the Empire established in

1798 minus the emperor. From 1792 to 1798 in France there was complete self-administration on the American model of each local community and each department, and this is what we must have as well. How self-administration is to be organized, and how we can manage without a bureaucracy, has been demonstrated to us by America and the first French Republic, as it is even today by Australia, Canada, and the other English colonies. A provincial and local self-administration of this type is far freer, for example, than Swiss federalism, where the canton is very independent, to be sure, in relation to the central government, but also in relation to the districts (*Bezirke*) and communities. The cantonal governments appoint the district officials and prefects — a feature which is unknown in English-speaking countries, and which we must also ever so politely deny ourselves in the future, along with the Prussian *Landräte* and *Regierungsräte*.

Engels concluded his thoughts by formulating a demand he would like to see added to the program: "Complete self-administration for the provinces, counties and communities through officials elected by universal suffrage. Abolition of all local and provincial authorities appointed by the state."[75]

The proposed demand may serve as an apt final summary of a lifetime's opposition to bureaucratic rule. While Marx and Engels, especially in their early years, favored centralization as a basically progressive tendency in modern society, they never had meant to encourage its twin — bureaucratization. Marx's earliest political passion, as we have seen, was a hatred of bureaucracy, and his antidote always remained the same — nonprofessional, popular self-administration. What changed perhaps, under the impact of Bonapartism, was a greater appreciation of the extent to which centralization irresistibly encouraged bureaucratization in bourgeois society. One cannot help recalling Marx's poignant lament in *The Eighteenth Brumaire* that every common project had been "snatched from the activity of society's members themselves and made the object of government activity, whether it was a bridge, a schoolhouse . . . or the railways."[76] If "the low and brutal form" of centralization indeed undermined such popular self-reliance and encouraged the growth of France's oppressive military-bureaucratic apparatus, then it is not so surprising after all to find Marx and Engels sympathizing in 1871 with *some* of the decentralist values expressed by the Communards, or giving increasing emphasis thereafter to the idea of self-adminstration at the various levels of government.

All the issues examined in this chapter, from "smashing" the state apparatus, to the separation of powers, to decentralization, have turned out to be wound closely around a central thread — namely, the desire to debureaucratize or, more broadly, deprofessionalize public life, to create a democracy without professionals. This is the really crucial and distinguishing characteristic of the workers' state as conceived by Marx and Engels. This is what excited them so about the Paris Commune, rather than any socioeconomic reform. Marx's critics have delighted in pointing out that in the latter sphere the only specific measure he could find to praise was "abolition of the night work of journeymen bakers"; but Marx himself acknowledged in hindsight that "the Commune was in no wise socialist, nor could it be."[77] It was not the socioeconomic but the *political* transformation carried out by the Communards that rekindled Marx's youthful enthusiasm. Most later writers have simply failed to notice what Marx himself said plainly enough. Against the multiplicity of possible interpretations of the Commune, he wrote, "its true secret was this. It was essentially a working-class government, . . . the political format last discovered under which to work out the economic emancipation of labor." Or again: "It supplied the Republic with the basis of really democratic institutions." Or again: "The great social measure of the Commune was its own working existence" ("its own organization," the First Draft had put it).[78] For Victorian respectability the rule of the masses spelled anarchy, violence, and spoliation. "The old world writhed in convulsions of rage," Marx asserted, when it beheld that "plain working men for the first time dared to infringe upon the Governmental privilege of their 'natural superiors,' and, under circumstances of unexampled difficulty, performed their work modestly, conscientiously, and efficiently."[79] For Marx and Engels this example of disciplined self-government by ordinary people was living proof that Victorian political assumptions were wrong, just as the discovery of primitive communal property was tangible proof that Victorian economic assumptions were wrong.

The ultimate significance of the Paris Commune for Marx's thought, then, lay precisely in the political transformation it undertook. As the antithesis of the fully developed parasite state of Louis Napoleon, the total alienation of social power, the Commune represented "a resumption by the people for the people of its own social life." In the Hegelian language Marx still used for the first-draft organization of his thoughts, the Commune involved "the reabsorption of the State power by society as its own living forces instead of as forces controlling and subduing it, by the popular masses themselves, forming their own force instead of the organized force of their suppression." One cannot but think of the young Marx who had written, "only when the real, individual man re-absorbs in himself the abstract citizen, and . . . has recognized and organized his '*forces propres*' as *social* forces, and consequently no longer separates social power from himself in the shape of *political* power, only then will human emancipation have been accomplished."[80] Indispensable to Marx's conception of human emancipation is social ownership of the means of production, but no less indispensable is the self-rule of the masses in a radical democracy without professionals. Deprofessionalization is the remedy to the parasitic tendency which has existed in all previous states. It is exactly what is involved in "smashing" the state machinery and "reabsorbing" state power. It is simultaneously the most distinctive feature of Marx's vision of democracy, rather than any special idea of dictatorship, or any novel system of representation, or any merging of powers, or any other institutional gimmicks, least of all the establishment of a one-party regime. Democracy without professionals, not the dictatorship of the proletariat, is the very essence of Marx's teaching.

❦[6]❧

Individual Rights Versus
Tyranny of the Majority

EVEN IF ONE ACKNOWLEDGES Marx and Engels' attachment to the fundamental democratic idea of majority rule through representative institutions on the basis of universal suffrage, as discussed in the preceding chapter, one may still legitimately doubt their attachment to the idea of individual and minority rights under the rule of such a majority. We are so accustomed nowadays to combining the principles of majority rule and individual rights under the general name of democracy that we are apt to forget they need not go together, indeed were deemed by many political philosophers to be quite incompatible. The rule of the masses, such thinkers held, would inevitably result in the suppression of dissenting individuals and minorities. By depriving dissenters of their core political rights — freedom of expression, assembly, and association — the rule of the majority would become the *tyranny* of the majority, and soon enough would become tyranny pure and simple. We must now inquire what attitude Marx and Engels took toward the question whether individuals should have rights even *against* a ruling majority, specifically in this case, a proletarian majority. To put the question in the sharpest possible form: Would Marx and Engels hesitate, if they thought the workers' revolution threatened, to deprive "counterrevolutionaries" of these basic political rights?

Those who would answer no to this question (and predictably they include both the standard Communist and the standard anti-Communist writers) point to Marx and Engels' talk of crushing bourgeois resistance following the revolution, and their frequent disparagement of "bourgeois" rights as merely formal, negative, and hypocritical, as having emerged historically to serve bourgeois needs. Those who would answer yes to the

[162]

question point to Marx and Engels' lifelong defense of freedom of the press in particular, but freedom of assembly and association as well, all of which the two men argued were valuable — even indispensable — needs of the working class as it strove to organize itself into a decisive political force. This defense of political rights, however, scarcely satisfies our first group, who point out that it is a purely utilitarian one and limited to the pre-revolutionary epoch. In fact both groups are obliged to talk mainly about rights before the proletarian revolution, since Marx and Engels had scarcely anything to say about their fate afterward. Indeed, one is tempted, prima facie, to throw up one's hands, as has a final group of commentators, and declare that the question cannot be answered, that Marx and Engels provide no basis either for the defense or rejection of individual rights after the revolution.[1]

Before yielding to this temptation, however, it will be worthwhile to see if Marx and Engels' silence does not tell us more than it seems to do. What they did *not* say, what they did *not* demand, for example, can be almost as significant as positive evidence if it forms a consistent pattern. And the positive evidence itself is not quite so meager as might be thought, if one looks beyond the most familiar writings. In this chapter, as in the previous one, Marx and Engels' attitude toward the Paris Commune will form a crucially important part of the evidence, since it was the only functioning government they ever regarded as a workers' state. One attractive body of evidence, however, must be excluded at the outset. The pre-communist writings of Marx and Engels can be used very effectively to depict the two men as vigorous defenders of civil rights and liberties, especially freedom of the press, the more so since their argument characteristically proceeded from general principles that would bind any government, and not merely from a desire to bind some existing government.[2] This evidence may legitimately be used to argue that the two men began their careers with liberal rather than totalitarian ideas about rights, but it ought not to be used to establish their later views, for both men appeared to drop any defense of rights based on general moral principles once they became communists. It is true that in 1851 Marx gave some sort of endorsement to his early essays when he had them republished without alteration as a book; nonetheless to allay justifiable skepticism the precommunist writings will be excluded here.

Let us begin by trying to dissect Marx and Engels' rather complex and many-sided attitude toward "bourgeois" rights existing before the proletarian revolution.

Rights Under the Bourgeoisie

Marx's earliest and most extensive attempt to cope with the rights issue after his Kreuznach metamorphosis can be found in his essay "On the Jewish Question" (1843); a comparable effort by Engels appeared in "The English Constitution" (1844). We have examined both in volume 1, but it will be worthwhile here to emphasize how differently each man approached his subject.³ Marx, it will be recalled, began with a crucially important separation between the rights of the citizen and the rights of man, which turned out to be a distinction between political rights and the rights associated in his mind with property ownership. The former were defined, quite respectfully, as "rights which can only be exercised in a community with others. Their content is *participation* in the *community,* and specifically in the *political* community, in the *life of the state.* They come within the category of *political freedom* [*politische Freiheit*], the category of *civic rights.*" But Marx discussed these political rights no further, setting them aside in order to dissect what he contemptuously called the "so-called *rights of man.*" From his carefully selected texts, these emerged as the rights of *liberté,* property, equality, and security. Marx chose the French word, *liberté,* as opposed to *politische Freiheit,* in order to designate the nonpolitical sense of freedom, the right to do anything that does not injure others — "the liberty of man as an isolated monad." The practical application of this right was private property, "the right to enjoy one's property and to dispose of it at one's discretion (*à son gré*), without regard to other men, independently of society." Equality — again Marx specified, in its nonpolitical sense — became only the equal right to *liberté,* as defined above, while security was the "guarantee" of these egoistic rights, the assurance that the police stand ready to protect them. "None of the so-called rights of man, therefore, go beyond egoistic man. . . . He is far from being conceived as a species-being; on the contrary, species-life itself, society, appears as a framework external to the individuals, as a restriction of their original independence." The rights Marx wanted to reject were simply those he associated with private property, with egoism, with man considered as an isolated monad, but not those he associated with citizenship, with participation in the community, with political freedom as opposed to *liberté.*⁴

Returning to the theme in his section of *The Holy Family* (1845), Marx again passed over political rights but elaborated on his understanding of *liberté.* It was established with the reforms that abolished "the *privileges of the trades*, guilds and corporations." These reforms produced a "man freed from privilege" but also a system of trade and industry freed from all restraint. Destroying the ties of tradition in society, they left man "no longer bound to other men even by the *semblance* of a common bond. Thus they produce the universal struggle of man against man." When the smoke has cleared, he prophesied, it will emerge that only property has been genuinely freed; man has been enslaved to his property but imagines its freedom to be his own:

> The *slavery of civil society* is *in appearance* the greatest *freedom* because it is in appearance the fully developed *independence* of the individual, who considers as his *own* freedom the uncurbed movement, no longer bound by a common bond or by man, of the estranged elements of his life, such as property, industry, religion, etc., whereas actually this is his fully developed slavery and inhumanity.[5]

One may witness the culmination of this entire line of thought in the *Communist Manifesto*'s well-known reply to the bourgeois charge that communism would abolish "individuality and freedom":

> The abolition of bourgeois individuality, bourgeois independence, and bourgeois freedom is undoubtedly aimed at.
>
> By freedom is meant, under the present bourgeois conditions of production, free trade, free selling and buying.
>
> But if selling and buying disappears, free selling and buying disappears also. This talk about free selling and buying, and all the other "brave words" of our bourgeoisie about freedom in general, have a meaning, if any, only in contrast with restricted selling and buying, with the fettered traders of the Middle Ages, but have no meaning when opposed to the Communistic abolition of buying and selling.[6]

Here again "bourgeois freedom" was identified with the nonpolitical rights associated with private property; it will come as no surprise to learn that Marx wanted to abolish property rights. But neither here nor elsewhere did he dismiss political rights as "bourgeois" or call for their abolition.

The *Manifesto* did make one comment on the linkage between property rights and other freedoms, a linkage made by many traditional political philosophers who saw private property as the guarantee of free-

dom in general because it gave individuals the independence to stand up
to tyranny or oppression from any quarter. Marx could not resist a sar-
castic observation that the development of capitalism itself had destroyed
such economic independence for the bulk of the population:

> We Communists have been reproached with the desire of abolishing
> the right of personally acquiring property . . . , which property is
> alleged to be the groundwork of all personal freedom, activity and
> independence. . . .
>
> Do you mean the property of the petty artisan and of the small
> peasant, a form of property that preceded the bourgeois form? There
> is no need to abolish that; the development of industry has to a great
> extent already destroyed it, and is still destroying it daily.

What the *Manifesto* promised for the future of freedom was "an association, in which the free development of each is the condition for the development of all." But it remained quite silent about the fate of specific
political rights.[7]

Turning now to Engels' early treatment of the rights issue in "The English Constitution," we find a totally different approach. Engels began
by setting aside the rights associated with property in order to discuss
political rights only. Specifically, he analyzed the rights of free expression, popular assembly, association, habeas corpus, and trial by jury, as
protected in English law. Engels spoke not of egoism and isolated monads
but only of class bias. He did not dismiss these rights as dividing man
from man but only deplored that the poor had such little benefit of them.
For example, "the right of association, in its full extent, is a privilege of
the rich; an association needs money first of all, and it is easier for the
rich Anti-Corn Law League to raise hundreds of thousands than for the
poor Chartist society. . . . And an association which has no funds at its
disposal is not likely to have much effect." Habeas corpus allows the *rich*
to go free on bail; property qualifications for jurors prevent the poor from
being tried by *their* peers, and so forth. Nowhere did Engels suggest that
these rights be abolished; on the contrary he lamented that no Continental country allowed the right of popular assembly. His point was only
that at present such rights benefit the rich primarily and must seem a
hollow mockery to the poor.[8]

In their first really collaborative work, *The German Ideology* (1846),
Marx and Engels made another discrimination which further compli-
cates the issue, since in a muddled version it has entered into the sub-

sequent Marxist tradition. They counterposed what they called the idealist definition of freedom as "self-determination, riddance of the real world, as merely imaginary freedom of the spirit," to their own materialist definition of freedom "as power, as domination over the circumstances and conditions in which an individual lives."[9] Man becomes free, they wanted to insist, "not through the negative power to avoid this or that, but through the positive power to assert his true individuality."[10] This distinction was drawn from Hegel, who had perceived "negative freedom" as the Hindu ideal of pure contemplation, "that pure reflection of the ego into itself which involves the dissipation of every restriction and every content either immediately presented by nature, by needs, desires, and impulses, or given and determined by any means whatever."[11] Thus negative freedom involved the complete retreat of the individual mind into itself; it was a kind of withdrawal Marx and Engels might criticize in the Young Hegelians, especially Max Stirner, but it had little if anything to do with the economic and political freedoms advanced by the bourgeoisie.

Bourgeois freedoms nonetheless made their own separate appearance in *The German Ideology*, and also in contrast to the idea of freedom as power. If materialist freedom meant domination over circumstances, its attainment involved for society as a whole a greater and greater control over the forces of nature, hence over production, as well as a greater and greater conscious control over the organization and functioning of society itself. For the individual it involved the greater and greater cultivation of his own diverse powers and talents in accordance with his own desires. The two processes — social and individual — were inextricably bound together: "Only within the community has each individual the means of cultivating his gifts in all directions; hence personal freedom becomes possible only within the community. . . . In the real community the individuals obtain their freedom in and through their association." Up until now the limited development of the collective powers of mankind has permitted only a minority — the successive ruling classes — to enjoy such freedom in any appreciable degree. "Personal freedom has existed only for the individuals who developed under the conditions of the ruling class, and only insofar as they were individuals of this class."[12] The bourgeoisie has created an illusion of greater freedom, to be sure, by sweeping aside all the diverse fetters of traditional society, but the dissolution of these bonds has left us all separated and alone to face the caprice of the marketplace in competition with all others, thus has left us all subjected to the rule of an impersonal force — capital. "Thus, in imagination, individuals seem freer under the dominance of the bourgeoisie than before, because their conditions of life seem accidental; in reality, of course, they are less free, because they are to a greater extent governed by material forces." Marx and Engels added sarcastically that "this right to the undisturbed enjoyment, within certain conditions, of fortuity and chance has up till now been called personal freedom."[13] Ahead of mankind lies "the task of replacing the domination of circumstances and of chance over individuals by the domination of individuals over chance and circumstances . . . the task of organizing society in a communist way." This can be accomplished by establishment of a collective control over the means of production, "the abolition of private property and of the division of labor," which will create "the only society in which the genuine and free development of individuals ceases to be a mere phrase."[14]

Since freedom as power was contrasted first to "negative freedom," or the idealist "riddance of the real world," and then to the bourgeois freedom to enjoy "fortuity and chance," it was not difficult for subsequent Marxist writers to run the two ideas confusedly together. From Marx's original approach, the economic freedoms established by capitalism could be identified as mere negative freedoms, the clearing away of obstacles, riddance of the fetters of traditional society. The riddance does not in itself produce freedom as power, control over the circumstances that affect our lives, especially as far as the masses are concerned. Engels' critique of bourgeois political rights could be fitted into the same mold. Such rights establish merely formal, negative freedoms, the removal of legal obstacles to free expression or free association. They do not bring with them the positive power to make such association effective, as in the case of the Chartists who lacked the necessary money to make their association as effective as that of the Anti-Corn Law League. Or, to choose another favorite example, the bourgeois right of free press may give a worker freedom from censorship but not the power to write for a newspaper or publish his own. For that he would require money, writing skills, and free time — all of which he is unlikely to enjoy under his existing life circumstances. Following this line of reasoning, twentieth-century Communists could contrast the two notions of freedom as a kind of either-or choice: with bourgeois democracy a worker obtains only the formal right to free press, a negative freedom and for him an empty one; with proletarian democracy he obtains access to education, printing presses, and stocks of paper, all of which give him effective, positive, and meaningful freedom.[15]

But Marx and Engels never spoke of *choosing between* the two kinds of freedom. In the first place, *The German Ideology* used the word "negative" only in relation to idealist withdrawal, not in relation to the removal of obstacles in the real world. "The actual tearing down of restrictions," they asserted, "is at the same time an extremely positive development of the productive forces, real energy and satisfaction of urgent requirements, and an expansion of the power of individuals."[16] Tearing down restrictions has produced all the wonders of capitalist industrial development and all the political rights guaranteed by bourgeois constitutions. If in the course of time economic freedom — or the rights of private property — would become a fetter on the further development of mankind and have to be abolished, nowhere did Marx and Engels suggest that political freedom would likewise become a fetter and have to be abolished. The continued development of positive freedom in the political sphere would seem utterly to *presuppose* those political rights found in bourgeois constitutions. A worker who has access to education, printing presses, and stocks of paper, but who lacks freedom from censorship, remains just as stymied in the free expression of his views as the worker under bourgeois democracy. It cannot be a matter of choosing one or the other kind of freedom. Logically and in practice, freedom as power must include freedom from formal constraints, or else it is not effective freedom after all.

In *The German Ideology* Marx and Engels struck one final theme that would remain a lasting facet of their critique of bourgeois rights, and probably the one most familiar to modern readers. Denying that there is anything God-given, innate, or natural about rights, they pointed to the way in which institutionalized rights and ideas about rights have changed and developed over the course of history. This Hegelian theme received a distinctive twist in their hands with the further assertion that such institutions and ideas form part of a "superstructure" which can be understood only by reference to the real economic foundations of society. Thus the two men berated one adversary for discussing the question of privilege versus equal rights as if it were a struggle between abstract concepts: "In this way he saves himself the trouble of having to know anything about the medieval mode of production, the political expression of which was privilege, and the modern mode of production, of which *right* as such, *equal right*, is the expression, or about the relation of these two modes of production to the legal relations which correspond to them."[17] Any given conception of rights, any given set of legal and political institutions, corresponds to a particular mode of production and satisfies the functional needs of that mode of production, most particularly the needs of its dominant class. Thus the bourgeois conception of rights, both economic and political, emerged historically to serve the needs of the bourgeoisie, especially in its conflict with the myriad forms of privilege embedded in medieval and early modern society. Expressed in the crudest terms, bourgeois rights serve merely as a mask disguising the naked class interest, the greed, of the bourgeoisie.

Once rights are no longer conceived as God-given, innate, or natural, once they are made relative to time and circumstance, even more, once they are exposed as a mask for sordid greed, how can anyone still take them seriously or place any value in them? Does not this historical-ethical relativism of Marx and Engels undercut the foundation for *any* defense of political rights?[18] In response to these questions, one approach might be to argue that Marx and Engels' position was not really relativist, but conceived each successive mode of production as a major advance in development of mankind's collective potential, whose full realization was conceived as the absolute good, the ethical goal of all human striving throughout history. By the same token, each change in the "superstructure" can also be conceived as an "advance" toward that goal. Of political rights in particular, it will be recalled that Marx had written: "*Political* emancipation is, of course, a big step forward. True, it is not the final form of human emancipation in general, but it is the final form of human emancipation *within* the hitherto existing world order." However self-interested and hollow bourgeois political rights might appear to the workers, they still constitute "a big step forward [*ein grosser Fortschritt*]" in the broader scheme of human history.[19] Many years later in *Anti-Dühring* Engels attempted to make the same point in a more positivist vein. As he traced the evolution of moral dogmas over time he allowed that "in this process there has on the whole been progress in morality," and "each step forward in the field of culture was a step towards freedom." Then he added: "A really human morality which stands above class antagonisms and above any recollection of them becomes possible only at a stage of society which has not only overcome class antagonisms but has even forgotten them in practical life." At such a stage, he concluded, "for the first time there can be talk of real human freedom, of an existence in harmony with the laws of nature that have become known."[20] Real human freedom, most recent Marx scholars would probably agree, stands as the absolute good in the Marxist system, and each step in that direction has moral worth whatever the motives of the dominant class.[21] The difficulty is that this argument is too abstract to overcome skepticism: Marx and Engels spent far more energy in exposing the shams of bourgeois rights than they ever did praising the extent to which those rights developed the latent powers of mankind.

Among such exposures in the writings of their later years there is one that adds still another facet to their critique of bourgeois political rights. It was originally developed by Marx in an obscure 1851 essay, "The Constitution of the French Republic Adopted November 4, 1848," but is better known in a shorter version carried over into *The Eighteenth Brumaire.* The freedoms this constitution granted with the right hand, he argued, it consistently took back with the left. Thus, for example, paragraph 3 grandly declared that "the residence of every one on French territory is inviolable," but then added that all homes could be entered "in the forms prescribed by law." Marx commented: "Observe here and throughout that the French constitution guarantees liberty, but always with the proviso *of exceptions made by law*, or which may *still be made!* and all the exceptions made by the Emperor Napoleon, by the restoration, and by Louis Philippe, have not only been retained, but, after the June Revolution, immeasurably multiplied." The rights of free expression, assembly, and association were declared to have no limit save that of "public security." Marx proceeded to review the long list of "public security" laws passed since the June Days which restricted each of these rights almost to the vanishing point. With respect to free expression, for example, caution money and stamps were reestablished for newspapers, effectively destroying whatever remained of the opposition press, while outright censorship was reimposed in the case of stage productions.[22] It is impossible to violate this constitution, Marx fumed, "for every one of its provisions contains its own antithesis — utterly nullifies itself":

> This trick of granting full liberty, of laying down the finest principles, and leaving their application, the *details*, to be decided by subsequent laws, the Austrian and Prussian middle-classes have borrowed from their French prototypes. . . . The middle-class can be democratic in *words*, but will not be so in deeds — they will recognize the truth of a principle, but never carry it into practice.[23]

Whereas Engels stressed the hollowness of rights which ordinary workers lacked the time or money to use effectively, Marx criticized the legal limitations within the guaranteed rights themselves. Beware of the treacherous details, he seemed to be cautioning the English workers in this article for the Chartist press, that lurk behind the grand-sounding freedoms offered by the bourgeoisie. He did not impugn the value of political rights per se, however, but on the contrary, perhaps only for English consumption, spoke of the "truth" of principles.

In fact, for all their criticism of the hollowness and limitations of bourgeois rights, Marx and Engels never drew the practical conclusion that they were not worth having. What is more, they repeatedly castigated those fellow radicals who *did* draw such a conclusion. Against the indifference of the True Socialists in the 1840s, for example, they argued vigorously that bourgeois political rights do benefit the proletariat and consequently must be struggled for, defended, and expanded. The rule of the bourgeoisie in Germany will "place quite new weapons in the hands of the proletariat for the struggle *against* the bourgeoisie," Marx wrote in 1847, citing among these weapons, "trial by jury, equality before the law, . . . freedom of the press, freedom of association and true representation."[24] No one reading the pages of the *Neue Rheinische Zeitung* could doubt the vigor and consistency with which Marx and Engels defended precisely those bourgeois rights that were the all too temporary achievements of the 1848 revolution. Or again in 1865, in a polemic against the Lassallean tendency within the German workers' movement, Engels deplored their inclination to support Bismarck against the strivings of the liberal German bourgeoisie. Bismarck, he argued, would establish a Bonapartist system which "does not tolerate free association, free assembly or a free press." Then he commented: "But without the freedom of the press, and the freedom of association and assembly, *no workers' movement is possible*" (italics added). A bourgeois victory on the other hand offered the following advantages to the workers:

> The bourgeoisie cannot gain political supremacy and express this in the form of a constitution and laws without, at the same time, arming the proletariat. On its banner it must inscribe human rights in place of the old system of social position based on birth. . . . Therefore, for consistency's sake, it must demand universal and direct suffrage, freedom of the press, association and assembly, and the repeal of all emergency laws directed against particular social classes. But this is all that the proletariat need demand from the bourgeoisie. It cannot expect the bourgeoisie to stop being the bourgeoisie, but it can demand that it apply its own principles consistently. The result will be that the proletariat will lay its hands on all the weapons which it needs for its final victory.[25]

Bourgeois rights, then, at least when their principles are consistently applied, are certainly not to be despised. They constitute a major, indeed indispensable, arsenal of weapons that the proletariat requires for its own liberation.

To sum up our findings then, Marx and Engels separated bourgeois rights into political and economic categories. Economic freedom, the rights associated with private property, they depicted as a mask for antisocial egoism, or in the case of freedom of contract, as we saw in chapter 3, as a disguise for the private tyranny of the employer over his workers within the factory.[26] While such rights doubtless helped the bourgeoisie enormously in the development of capitalism, Marx and Engels never suggested they had any positive value for the working class. Doubtless they expected them to disappear after the proletarian revolution. Their attitude toward political rights is more complex. They might criticize such rights as hollow for the masses because the formal freedom from legal restrictions did not include the power to make effective use of them, or as fraudulent in themselves if the details of practice took back what had been granted in principle. On the other hand the two men never argued that such rights were totally without merit. They constitute "a big step forward" in the broader scheme of history, and they have very substantial value for the working class as it struggles to organize itself. Returning to the question posed at the beginning of the chapter concerning the fate of individual political rights after the proletarian revolution, it must be allowed that the evidence presented in this section cannot provide a clear answer. One may argue that Marx and Engels' frequent assaults on bourgeois rights are adequately counterbalanced by their frequent insistence on the value of such rights nonetheless as weapons for the proletariat. But the latter argument is not a defense of rights *in principle*, and says nothing about their fate after the revolution, as has been generally overlooked by those who would present Marx and Engels as friends of individual freedom. Indeed, the military vocabulary employed by both men in this connection suggests an ominously pragmatic attitude. "Weapons" may be discarded, after all, when they are no longer of use; they are commonly *smashed* if they threaten to fall into the hands of the enemy.

Freedom of Conscience

Could it be that Marx and Engels adopted a vocabulary of expediency simply as a forensic device, to win over those who may have been cynical about the rights proclaimed by the bourgeoisie, who would distrust any moralizing and only want to hear about practical advantages? Could it be that, for whatever reason, the two men found themselves unable to use principled arguments to defend individual rights which nonetheless they wanted to see universally respected? Some interesting insights into these matters can be gained if we now look at Marx and Engels' attitude toward a right which is not exactly political or economic, but which they discussed surprisingly often — namely, freedom of conscience, religious freedom. Most importantly for our purposes, they addressed this freedom not only as a right in bourgeois society but also as a right under the rule of the proletariat.

Most religious believers at least until very recently have assumed that Marx and Engels were eager to see religion suppressed by forcible means, as some twentieth-century Communist regimes have attempted to do. It is interesting to discover, then, that the two men consistently defended freedom of conscience and repeatedly denounced those radicals who talked of suppressing religion by force when the workers came to power. At the same time, Marx and Engels could rarely allow themselves, even in private writings, to advance *ethical* reasons for their stand, or to set forth the principle of religious freedom without adding a gratuitous insult to religious sensibilities.

Marx and Engels both renounced any personal religious beliefs well before they became communists. However militant this early atheism, it still did not prevent Marx from attempting as editor of the *Rheinische Zeitung* to defend the Catholic archbishop of Cologne against imprisonment, or from supporting full emancipation of the Jews. Engels also identified himself from the beginning with the cause of Jewish emancipation.[27] But religious issues in general, which had so dominated Young Hegelian intellectual activity, receded from Marx and Engels' consciousness after they became communists. From their new perspective religion was merely a side issue, an otherworldly reflection or by-product of problems located here on earth. Its metaphysical claims, in any event, had already been undermined by the Enlightenment and then given their coup de grace by Young Hegelian criticism. "The criticism of religion ends with the teaching that *man is the highest being for man*, hence with the *categorical imperative to overthrow all relations* in which man is a debased, enslaved, forsaken, despicable being." In this fashion, "the criticism of heaven turns into the criticism of earth," and the point was now to attack the real earthly causes of man's estrangement, after which their "spiritual *aroma*," the religious by-product, could be expected to disappear of itself. People would no longer feel a need for the otherworldly explanations and consolations offered by traditional religion.[28]

This attitude explains the impatience Marx showed in "The Jewish Question" with Bruno Bauer's perverse insistence that Jews (and Christians) would have to give up their religion before they would be entitled to the rights of citizenship in a democratic state. Both Jews and Christians, Marx replied in essence, can be expected to discard their religious illusions by the time human emancipation is complete, but *political* emancipation is only a step toward that goal and by no means requires the abandonment of religion. On the contrary, all democratic constitutions, while effecting a separation of church and state, expressly recognize the right of citizens to be religious if they choose: "The *privilege of faith* is a *universal right of man*."[29] Marx did not treat this right contemptuously, as he did the other "so-called" rights of man, but neither did he transform this descriptive assertion about a right found in all democratic constitutions into a normative assertion that it *ought* to be found there. On the other hand, he did manage to comment on the futility of the Jacobin attempt to bring about "the *abolition of religion*, the *destruction* of religion." Like their parallel attempt to bring about the "abolition" of property rights through confiscations, the law of the maximum, and so forth, it could not succeed because the conditions for full human emancipation had not yet developed. Hence, despite the Reign of Terror, "the political drama necessarily ends with the re-establishment of religion, private property, and all the elements of civil society."[30] Marx could argue that religious persecution is futile, but he could not bring himself to assert a normative right against such persecution.

If we turn next to the *Communist Manifesto*, the same inhibition reveals itself even more plainly. Engels' October Draft had posed the question of the future communist order: "What will be its attitude towards existing religions?" His answer was merely, "remains [*bleibt*]." Since the exciting discovery of the June Draft, we now know what this response was to have been. Possibly hammered out already at the first League congress, the statement nonetheless appears in Engels' hand and bears the unmistakable mark of his thinking: "All religions which have existed hitherto were expressions of historical stages of development of individual peoples or groups of peoples. But communism is that stage of historical development which makes all existing religions superfluous and supersedes them [*überflüssig macht und aufhebt*]."[31] The German verb *aufheben* is used here in its special Hegelian sense of transcending or superseding, rather than in its political sense of abolishing; it does not suggest the idea of forcible suppression. This was the text Marx had before him when he set about the final revision. In place of the straightforward catechism question, he posed the religious issue as an accusation against communism, putting words into the mouth of an indignant bourgeois and using a more explicit verb: "Communism abolishes [*schafft ab*] eternal truths, it abolishes [*schafft ab*] all religion and all morality." In the mouth of the indignant bourgeois the verb *abschaffen* clearly indicates forcible abolition, and Marx did not deny such an accusation. He only repeated Engels' historical argument and concluded: "The Communist revolution is the most radical rupture with traditional property relations; no wonder that its development involves the most radical rupture with traditional ideas."[32] Thus the impression was certainly left that the Communist revolution *will* "abolish" religion in a forcible way.

Marx's reluctance to take an ethical stand here joined forces with his impulse to *épater les bourgeois,* as can be seen in his remarks on several other subjects. We know from the Paris manuscripts, for instance, not to mention from his own private life, that Marx was appalled at the "crude communist" idea of establishing a community of women. Yet in the *Manifesto* he could not bring himself to answer this bourgeois accusation forthrightly. He teased and tormented his hypothetical antagonist, suggesting that the bourgeoisie had already introduced the community of women in the form of prostitution, or in the forced submission of female workers to their employers, or even among the bourgeois themselves in the seduction of one another's wives. Only after this extended taunting did he manage to blurt out: "For the rest, it is self-evident that the abolition of the present system of production must bring with it the abolition of the community of women springing from that system, *i.e.,* of prostitution both public and private."[33] Alas, he did not even manage this much on the religious issue.

About two months after the *Manifesto*'s appearance Marx and Engels formulated the much more specific *Demands of the Communist Party in Germany* and were obliged for once to express their positive desires in normative terms — as demands. Interestingly we find no mention of "abolishing" religion in any sense but only the following call: "Complete separation of Church and State. The clergy of every denomination shall be paid only by the voluntary contributions of their congregations."[34] Here was a straightforward liberal-democratic demand which expressly postulated the continued existence of religious congregations in the future as private associations. It should always be read in conjunction with the more famous tauntings and ambiguities of the *Manifesto.* It was also identical to the position Marx and Engels were to take with respect to the Paris Commune, as we will see shortly.

During the period of the International in the 1860s Marx and Engels had occasion to react to Mikhail Bakunin's religious intolerance. Upon entering that organization in 1868, Bakunin proposed that the IWA adopt a program he had written himself, which included as point 1: "*The Alli-*

ance declares itself atheist; it wants abolition of cults." In repudiating this program Marx commented: "As if one could declare — by royal decree — abolition of faith!"[35] Obviously Marx still regarded the persecution of religion as futile. Bakunin nonetheless persisted, now trying at least to have the organization make atheism a compulsory article of faith for its own members — "*atheism* as a *dogma* dictated to the members," as Marx put it. In a letter to an Italian sympathizer Engels explained his own reaction to this proposal:

> Our strength lies in the breadth with which the first rule is interpreted, i.e., in that all men who aim for the complete emancipation of the working class are admitted. Unfortunately, the Bakuninists, with the narrow-mindedness common to all sects, were not content with this. . . . Atheism and materialism — which Bakunin himself learnt from us Germans — should be made obligatory. . . . Now Marx and I are just as good old atheists and materialists as Bakunin, as indeed are most of our members. . . . But to include all these things in our program would mean to drive away a vast number of members, and to divide instead of uniting the European proletariat.[36]

Both men thus repudiated Bakunin's intolerance but gave only pragmatic reasons for their stand: to suppress religion would be futile; to require atheism would drive away members.

The Paris Commune provides the next opportunity for examining Marx and Engels' views on religious freedom, this time in what they expressly regarded as a workers' state. Marx's remarks in *The Civil War* on the Communards' separation of church and state have already been quoted:

> Having once got rid of the standing army and police, the physical force elements of the old Government, the Commune was anxious to break the spiritual force of repression, the "parson-power," by the disestablishment and disendowment of all churches as proprietary bodies. The priests were sent back to the recesses of private life, there to feed upon the alms of the faithful in imitation of their predecessors, the Apostles. The whole of the educational institutions were opened to the people gratuitously, and at the same time cleared of all interference of Church and State.[37]

It need only be emphasized that Marx's substantive stand was exactly the same here as in the 1848 *Demands of the Communist Party*. Separation was not perceived to require any active suppression of religion, but even postulated that priests would continue their functions, relying on the voluntary "alms of the faithful." His gratuitous sarcasm, however, shows how unwilling he still was to allow religious freedom any real dignity. He could grant the right only while expressing contempt for its exercise.

Engels' comments on the same subject are of more than passing interest. In his 1891 "Introduction," he briefly described the separation of church and state effected by the Communards and characterized it as "the realization of the principle that *in relation to the state*, religion is purely a private matter [*Privatsache*]," a reform which "the republican bourgeoisie had failed to pass solely out of cowardice, but which provided a necessary basis for the free activity of the working class."[38] It should be observed that the separation of church and state, but *not* the suppression of religion, was deemed necessary for the "free activity of the working class." Much more significant were Engels' remarks in his little-known 1874 analysis of the "Programm der blanquistischen Kommuneflüchtlinge," where he took the Blanquists to task for blindly defending the desperate shooting of hostages (including the cardinal-archbishop of Paris) that had occurred during the final blood-drenched days of the Commune, and for preparing a decree to be issued by the *next* commune that would outlaw religion altogether:

> Our Blanquists share the Bakuninists' desire to represent the most far-reaching, the most extreme trend. . . . The point is, therefore, to be more radical than everybody else as far as atheism is concerned. . . . Nothing would be simpler than to have the splendid French materialistic literature of the past century spread on a large scale among the workers. . . . But that cannot be to the liking of our Blanquists. In order to prove that they are the most radical of all, they abolish God by decree as was done in 1793:
>
> "Let the Commune free mankind forever from the ghost of past misery" (God), "from that cause" (non-existing God a cause!) "of their present misery. There is no room for priests in the Commune; every religious observance, every religious organization must be prohibited."
>
> And this demand that men should be changed into atheists *par ordre du mufti* [by orders from above] is signed by two members of the [original] Commune who have really had opportunity enough to find out that, first, a vast amount of things can be ordered on paper without necessarily being carried out, and second, that persecution is the best means of promoting undesired convictions! This

much is certain: the only service that can be rendered to God nowadays is to declare atheism a compulsory article of faith and to outdo Bismarck's *Kulturkampf* laws by prohibiting religion generally.[39]

Religion is dying out of its own accord; if any further effort be required, one should spread materialist literature but certainly not outlaw religion by decree, which would only create martyrdom and prolong the process. Engels' substantive position again is in perfect accord with liberal principles, but when addressing the superradical Blanquists, seemingly he could not take a principled stand without defending it pragmatically, could not say the right thing without giving a cynical reason, as if the only thing wrong with religious persecution were that it is counterproductive.

A reference to Bismarck's *Kulturkampf* also turns up in our next major piece of evidence — Marx's *Critique of the Gotha Program* in 1875. The *Kulturkampf* began as a liberal-supported campaign in Germany to reduce clerical influence in the public schools, but had developed into a wholesale persecution of Roman Catholicism as such, calling into question how liberal the (predominantly Protestant) liberals really were. Commenting on the program's demand for "Freedom of conscience," Marx jibed:

> If one desired at this time of the *Kulturkampf* to remind liberalism of its old catchwords, it surely could have been done in the following form: Everyone must be able to relieve his religious needs, like his bodily needs, without the police sticking their noses in. But the workers' party ought at any rate in this connection to have expressed its awareness of the fact that bourgeois "freedom of conscience" is nothing but the toleration of all possible kinds of *religious freedom of conscience*, and that for its part it endeavors rather to liberate the conscience from the witchery of religion. But one chooses not to go beyond the "bourgeois" level.[40]

In short, "bourgeois" toleration often does not extend far enough to include the tolerance of atheism, but "proletarian" toleration ought to, since atheism is precisely what it wants to encourage. More interesting is the first sentence, where Marx was obliged for once to express a right normatively, *as a right*. He did so with such bad grace, likening religious needs to excretory functions — *"leibliche Notdürfte verrichten"* — that Engels agreed to alter the sentence when he first published the *Critique* in 1891.[41] Taking a cue from Marx, one cannot resist describing this malady as moral constipation, chronic difficulty in expressing a positive moral conviction, a disorder from which both men suffered virtually all their lives.

Marx's last known comments on the subject were published in 1879, in a recently rediscovered *Chicago Tribune* interview. The reporter began:

> "You and your followers, Dr. Marx, have been credited with all sorts of incendiary speeches against religion. Of course you would like to see the whole system destroyed root and branch."
>
> "We know," he replied after a moment's hesitation, "that violent measures against religion are nonsense; but this is an opinion: as Socialism grows, Religion will disappear. Its disappearance must be done by social development, in which education must play a great part."[42]

Here we have Marx's final expression of a lifelong position: education and social development, but no violent measures against religion — as well as his lifelong reluctance to put the argument in terms of rights. Persecution is not *wrong*, it is "nonsense."

One of the things that makes Marx and Engels' stand for religious freedom convincing in spite of their own moral constipation is the consistency with which they criticized intolerance when it appeared among their fellow radicals — from Bruno Bauer to Bakunin to the Blanquist refugees. In 1878 Engels rose to the occasion once more in his polemic against Eugen Dühring, a German academic socialist, not very radical in most respects, who nonetheless wrote in favor of outlawing all religious observance under socialism. Engels again surveyed the history and social function of religion, arguing that it would disappear of its own accord when people are able to understand and control their own destinies. Then:

> Herr Dühring, however, cannot wait until religion dies this, its natural, death. He proceeds in more deep-rooted fashion. He out-Bismarcks Bismarck; he decrees sharper May laws not merely against catholicism, but against all religion whatsoever; he incites his gendarmes of the future against religion, and thereby helps it to martyrdom and a prolonged lease of life. Wherever we turn, we find specifically Prussian socialism.[43]

Prussian socialism, of course, meant authoritarian, state-decreed socialism, pseudosocialism.

Concerning the exact arrangements for separating church from state, we can glean a few details from a letter Engels wrote to Laura Lafargue in 1892, just after her husband had introduced into the French Chamber of Deputies a bill that would complete the separation of church and state begun by the Ferry Laws a few years earlier, laws which eliminated the church's control of public education. Lafargue consciously modeled his bill on the Communards' decree of April 1871. The specific features were: (1) an end to state payment of clerical salaries, (2) confiscation of church property, the proceeds to be used for popular education and social services, and (3) a prohibition of the practice whereby employers often obliged their employees to join religious associations. The most radical feature was obviously the confiscation of church property, and Engels commented:

> The proposition about separation of Church and State in the sense of the Commune was the best thing he could do. . . . Especially now when the French Clergy begin to face the eventuality and try to make it out that they ought to be, in that case, disestablished as the Church of Ireland was, that is to say not only keep all their property, but have the salaries capitalized and bought off in a lump sum. . . . The French Republic, with its revolutionary principles of civil law, cannot *buy off* the Church in the way the English semifeudal monarchy did.[44]

Thus tolerance of religious belief for Engels did not include protection of church property. A socialist government that would confiscate all the great property owners could scarcely be expected to make an exception for the church, especially since the precedent had been so well established all over Europe, not only by bourgeois governments but by assorted monarchs of the Reformation period as well.

Our final text is surely the most interesting of all. It was written about the same time, as Engels reviewed the demands of the German Social Democrats' draft Erfurt program, which included as article 5: "Elimination of all expenditures out of public funds for ecclesiastical and religious purposes. Ecclesiastical and religious bodies are to be regarded as private associations." The next article then went on to demand "secularization of the schools." Since this demand might be interpreted as excluding the possibility of private parochial schools, Engels proposed a reformulation combining both articles into one, then adding a highly revealing parenthetical comment:

> Complete separation of church and state. All religious bodies without exception are regarded by the state as private associations. They

lose all support from public funds and all influence on public schools. (One cannot forbid them, after all, from founding their *own* schools from their *own* funds and there teaching their idiotic rubbish [*Blödsinn*].[45]

Why such restraint? Twentieth-century Communist regimes have not felt any such restraint about the suppression of private religious associations. Nowhere is Engels' underlying liberal and Victorian sense of decency so candidly revealed, combined of course — inevitably — with his need to express simultaneous contempt for religious teachings.

The passages cited in this section include all the significant remarks Marx and Engels made on the subject of religious freedom. They reveal an attitude substantially in accord with the precepts of liberal democracy, in particular a sharp and consistent rejection of any proposal to suppress religious observance and belief under a socialist regime. At the same time, they reveal that peculiar moral constipation that inhibited any straightforward defense of religious liberty on grounds of principle. Thus they should open one's mind to the possibility that this same moral constipation, whatever its causes, may have prevented Marx and Engels from defending on principle those individual *political* rights which in their Victorian decency they may also have taken for granted.

The Rights of Peaceful Opposition

Whatever Marx and Engels' views on religious freedom, our key concern here must be for the core political freedoms which the two men themselves identified often enough as freedom of expression, assembly, and association. Would Marx and Engels have allowed these specific freedoms to the "enemies" of the proletarian revolution? We must now try to answer our question directly, and again the Paris Commune may serve as a key source of insight. In chapter 5 we saw how thoroughly the two men identified themselves with the democratic features of the Commune — democratic, now, in the narrow sense of majority rule and the institutions necessary for such rule. But such institutions do not automatically include protection for dissenting minorities or individuals, and by the same token Marx and Engels' clear support of majority rule does not automatically mean that they supported political rights for dissenting minorities. In fact, if one combines what they said about majority rule in their Commune writings with what they said about the functions of the proletarian state in their polemics against anarchism, the conclusion is easily formed that a tyranny of the majority was precisely what they had in mind, all the more so since their phrase "dictatorship of the proletariat" likewise invites such a conclusion.

We have already encountered in one place or another most of these antianarchist formulations about the repressive functions of the proletarian state. In response to Bakunin's question, over whom the proletariat would rule, Marx noted that "its enemies and the old organization of society do not vanish as a result of its coming to power," and that therefore "as long as other classes and the capitalist class in particular still exist, and as long as the proletariat fights against them . . . it must employ *coercive* measures, that is, governmental measures."[46] More sharply, his essay, "Indifference to Politics," suggested that the workers would "substitute their revolutionary dictatorship for the dictatorship of the bourgeois class," and in this fashion, in order to "crush the resistance of the bourgeoisie, instead of laying down arms and abolishing the State they are giving it a revolutionary and transient form."[47] For his part Engels set down the famous concluding paragraph in "On Authority" where he emphasized the degree to which all revolutions involve authoritarian means — rifles, bayonets, and cannon — and urged that the victorious party "must maintain this rule by means of the terror which its arms inspire in the reactionaries." A decade later he summed up his antianarchist stand as follows:

> The proletarian class will first have to possess itself of the organized political force of the State and with this aid stamp out the resistance of the Capitalist class and re-organize society. . . . It may require adaptation to the new functions. But to destroy that at such a moment, would be to destroy the only organism by means of which the victorious working class can exert its newly conquered power, keep down its capitalist enemies and carry out that economic revolution of society without which the whole victory must end in a defeat and in a massacre of the working class like that after the Paris Commune.[48]

Finally, we may add the strongest remarks of all, from Engels' letter on the Gotha Program concerning the phrase "free people's state":

> As, therefore, the state is only a transitional institution which is used in the struggle, in the revolution, in order to hold down one's adversaries by force, it is pure nonsense to talk of a free people's state:

so long as the proletariat still *uses* the state, it does not use it in the interests of freedom but in order to hold down its adversaries, and as soon as it becomes possible to speak of freedom the state as such ceases to exist.[49]

All these passages may indeed assume democratic government in the sense of majority rule, but all of them stress repressive tasks as the central function of this state, as is evident in the vocabulary itself — employ coercive measures, crush, intimidate, inspire terror, stamp out, hold down. Is not the dictatorship of the proletariat then precisely the unrestrained rule of the majority, or what its critics would surely call the tyranny of the majority?

From one perspective, all this seems to be a consistent extension of the class-state theory fathered by Engels. If coercion is the essence of the state, if *"coercive* measures" are ipso facto "governmental measures," then Marx and Engels at least are being honest to their own theory when they frankly allow that the proletarian state, however democratically organized, is still essentially an instrument of coercion. Just as the essential function of the bourgeois state, however democratically organized, is to "hold down" the class adversary, to "stamp out the resistance" of any rebels, so the function of the proletarian state remains the same. And if freedom requires the absence of external coercion, then *complete* freedom cannot exist until the state, whose essence is coercion, disappears. In this highly abstract sense, by definition state power can never be used "in the interests of freedom." Liberal political philosophy does not place such stress on coercion as the central function of the state but assumes it nonetheless. However generous may be the constitutional guarantees of individual freedom, however democratic the decision-making process, there remain the police to deal with criminals and the army to deal with rebellion. The underlying guarantee of any such government is still the "terror" which arms inspire in potential lawbreakers. Perhaps Marx and Engels were simply being more honest and frank about the necessarily coercive nature of all government.

But, it will be objected (and rightly so), liberal political philosophy presupposes a framework of constitutional law which limits the coercive power of the state. Direct coercion may be used against individual lawbreakers, or even against large minorities that undertake violent rebellion, but not against peaceful dissent or against minorities that exercise their rights and agitate within the law to win support for their views. What is missing from Marx and Engels' various descriptions of the task of the proletarian state is any reference to this limiting framework of law. They seemed to assume a violent suppression of the bourgeois minority in which no quarter need be given, no rights or restraints acknowledged.[50] At this juncture it becomes necessary to recognize that, whereas liberal political philosophy tacitly assumes a framework of preexisting law, Marx and Engels, in all the statements quoted above, assume a revolutionary *Provisorium* in which a proletarian majority has just taken power and in which the dispossessed bourgeoisie continues forcibly to resist the will of that majority. Insofar as liberal political philosophy justifies the suppression of open minority rebellion, there can scarcely be any a priori objection to the coercive measures anticipated by Marx and Engels to deal with violent resistance on the part of the bourgeois minority. And where is the liberal constitution which, under conditions of open rebellion or civil war, guarantees freedom of expression, assembly, or association to the rebels?

Even the most ideal democratic revolution contains a whole Pandora's box of thorny ethical issues, including especially questions of individual rights. If Marx and Engels did not face up squarely to these ethical issues, neither has the bulk of their liberal critics. The initial displacement of old authorities must be followed by the naming of a provisional government to rule temporarily and organize democratic elections for a national assembly — its composition cannot but be arbitrary in a large degree. Once elected, the national assembly itself must take over the tasks of temporary government until it completes the drafting of a new constitution. This new document, when put into effect, will doubtless include guarantees of individual rights and provide the legal machinery to prevent their infringement. But between the collapse of the old legal structure and the erection of a new one there must inevitably be a period of several months' duration at least which forms the revolutionary *Provisorium* so crucial in Marx and Engels' political thinking. During this period individual rights *cannot* exist in the sense of being guaranteed by constitutional law, for the simple reason that no constitution is in effect. Hence the thorny questions: Under what restraints, if any, are the provisional government and the national assembly expected to operate? What are the expectations, in particular, for coping with possible violence inaugurated by supporters of the old regime? Liberal critics cannot fairly expect of Marx and Engels more than they would ask of themselves in such a revolutionary *Provisorium*.

One might on reflection advance the following points as legitimate expectations of democratic revolutionaries: (1) that they have committed themselves publicly and well before the revolution to the establishment of individual rights as a matter of principle, in particular the rights of free expression, assembly, and association; and perhaps also (2) that they have organized themselves — if prerevolutionary organization is possible at all — in such fashion that individual members may criticize their leaders and seek majority support to replace them. Then, most crucially, after the overthrow, one might ask (3) that the same triad of political rights be proclaimed immediately and honored throughout the *Provisorium* by both the provisional government and the national assembly for all peaceful opponents of the new order. If, in spite of this tolerance, a violent counterrevolutionary resistance should develop, one can scarcely ask what no established liberal-democratic constitution recognizes, that violent rebels enjoy the rights of free expression, assembly, and association. What *can* fairly be asked even under such circumstances is (4) that violent rebellion be put down with the minimum force possible and with maximum humanity. Instead of expecting Marx and Engels to endorse eternal rights founded in some conception of natural law they could not honestly recognize, instead of expecting them somehow to provide constitutional rights in a situation where no constitution would exist, let us rather put them to the test on these four more realistic questions, saving the last question for the final section of this chapter.

Beginning with prerevolutionary commitments, it would seem logical to inspect the six official party programs over which Marx and Engels had some influence during the course of their lives. Interestingly, the later three all called expressly for the basic triad of political rights, but the three earlier ones did not. The Erfurt Program of 1891 included as its point 4: "Elimination of all laws which suppress or restrict the free expression of opinion and the right of association and assembly." In his critique Engels passed over this point with no comment. The older Gotha Program of 1875 had included the same point 4 with almost the identical wording: both Marx and Engels had passed over it without comment.[51] This silence is highly significant: since the two men criticized every point they found objectionable and had scarcely a word of praise for anything, it is plausible to take their silence on several points as indicating approval. Such an interpretation is strongly fortified by the appearance of the same demand, almost identically worded, in a draft program for the French Workers' Party, drawn up by Marx and Engels themselves conjointly with Paul Lafargue and Jules Guesde in a session at Engels' residence in May 1880. The only disagreement ever reported at this meeting concerned the demand for a minimum wage.[52] Thus all three of the later party programs associated in some degree with Marx and Engels contained a clear call for the basic political freedoms.

But why then do the earlier ones lack such a call? Several possible explanations present themselves. "One only demands what one has not got," Marx noted with his Gotha commentary.[53] This might explain why the *Demands of the Communist Party in Germany*, written by Marx and Engels in April 1848, included demands for direct universal suffrage and a republic, for example, but ignored the usual political freedoms — the latter had just then been established as a consequence of the March revolution. The same would not apply, however, to the *Communist Manifesto* published just before the revolution. Here a second explanation suggests itself: in any programmatic declaration parties tend to stress what distinguishes them from their competitors, not what they have in common. Marx, Engels, and the league artisans who formulated the ten specific demands listed in the *Manifesto* would understandably want to stress the socioeconomic objectives that set them apart from their principal competitors, the pale democrats. "To win the battle of democracy," on the other hand, was rather taken for granted. One may recall that the earlier drafts stipulated more specifically that the league aimed at establishing a "democratic state constitution." One may also recall the memorable sentiments of the *Kommunistische Zeitschrift* during the same months — probably written by Karl Schapper — declaring the league in favor of "a democratic State wherein each party would be able by word or in writing to win a majority over to its ideas": "We are not among those communists who are out to destroy personal liberty, who wish to turn the world into one huge barrack or into a gigantic workhouse. . . . We have no desire to exchange freedom for equality. We are convinced . . . that in no social order will personal freedom be so assured as in a society based upon communal ownership."[54] Would that Marx and Engels themselves had put the point so forthrightly!

Why did they *not* do so? If they raised no objection to these sentiments and no objection to the inclusion of political rights in the three later programs, why were they so silent themselves? Here the final possible explanation must be invoked — the idea of moral constipation introduced in the previous section. It shows up most demonstrably in Marx's behavior during the drafting of the *Address and Provisional Rules of the Working Men's International Association* in October 1864. Marx and Engels' role in the IWA will be the subject of chapter 8; for now suffice it to say that Marx was elected to a subcommittee to draft a statement of principles, and that another member of this subcommittee came up with an initial proposed draft. Marx described this proposal in a letter to Engels as "an appallingly wordy, badly written and utterly undigested preamble, pretending to be a declaration of principles, in which Mazzini could be detected everywhere." Giuseppe Mazzini was the Italian nationalist leader and pale democrat who was famous for his long-winded and rapturous moralizing, a kind of moral diarrhea in contrast to which Marx's own moral constipation must be understood. Continuing his account to Engels, Marx declared himself "firmly determined that if possible not one single line of the stuff should be allowed to stand." He convinced the subcommittee that he could improve on the draft, and proceeded to do so: "I altered the whole preamble, threw out the declaration of principles and finally replaced the forty rules by ten. . . . My proposals were all accepted by the sub-committee. Only I was obliged to insert two phrases about 'duty' and 'right' into the Preamble to the Statutes, ditto 'truth, morality and justice,' but these are placed in such a way that they can do no harm." "It must be a real work of art," replied Engels laconically.[55] Clearly Marx was very much put off by any Mazzini-style rhapsodizing about the eternal rights of man, preferring phrases like "the emancipation of the working classes." He seemed to equate all talk of rights with empty moralizing and had to be obliged by the others to include any reference to them at all.

What was included was an opening declaration "that the struggle for the emancipation of the working classes means not a struggle for class privileges and monopolies, but for equal rights and duties, and the abolition of all class rule." Marx's thinking still shines through here but not in the second allusion, a later paragraph which declared on behalf of the "undersigned": "They hold it the duty of a man to claim the rights of a man and a citizen, not only for himself, but for every man who does his duty. No rights without duties, no duties without rights."[56] Here the enjoyment of unspecified rights is made conditional upon the performance of equally unspecified duties — a rather ominous but typically Mazzinian formulation that never appeared before or after in any of Marx and Engels' own writings, much to their credit. On one occasion Engels did speak in favor of a simple *association* of rights and duties. The draft Erfurt Program included a variation of the IWA preamble statement, mentioning rights but leaving out duties: "The Social Democratic Party does not fight for new class privileges and prerogatives, but for the elimination of class rule and for equal rights for all without distinction of sex or origin." Engels found no objection to the call for equal rights but suggested: "Instead of 'for equal rights for all' I propose 'for equal rights and equal duties for all,' etc. Equal *duties* are for us an absolutely essential supplement (*Ergänzung*) to the bourgeois-democratic *equal rights* and remove from them their specifically bourgeois connotation."[57] Thus the call for equal rights, the historic slogan of the bourgeoisie, needs to be *supplemented*, not replaced, by the demand for equal duties, in association with which it no longer appears bourgeois. Notice, however, that Engels did not make the enjoyment of rights *conditional* upon the performance of duties, as did the Mazzini-inspired IWA preamble. His statement here also stands as corroborative evidence that he approved the general inclusion of rights in the program, that his earlier noted silence on the specific demand for the rights of free expression, assembly, and association did indeed signify approval.

The value of all these programs as evidence is mitigated, however, by a certain ambiguity that hovers around their specific demands. Are such demands conceived as the first measures the party will carry out after it comes to power, or are some of them at least seen as concessions that might be extracted from the existing government? If the demand for political freedoms belongs to the latter category, then it becomes again a demand for "weapons" against the present regime and not necessarily a call for rights to be recognized permanently. On the other hand, none of the documents suggests that political rights would be curtailed in any way following the revolution. And those radicals who did anticipate serious restrictions on rights after the revolution—like August Willich, Bakunin, or the Blanquist refugees—generally did not hesitate to say so in their public pronouncements. The only repressive measure of *any* sort proposed in our six statements was the *Manifesto's* call for "confiscation of the property of all emigrants and rebels."[58] This demand was left over from the tradition of the Great French Revolution and concerned economic rather than directly political rights. In any event it had disappeared by the time of the Seventeen Demands just four months later, never to turn up again. On the question of prerevolutionary pronouncements, then, Marx and Engels would seem to deserve, if not the highest grades, at least passing ones.

Our second test, perhaps an optional one, had to do with the prior organization of democratic revolutionaries, whether within their party ordinary members had the freedom to criticize leaders and seek majority support to vote them out of office. If such an organization becomes the governing party following a revolution, questions about its internal structure can acquire considerable significance, as we know from twentieth-century experience. In chapter 8 of the preceding volume we examined the structure of the organizations Marx and Engels belonged to up to 1850, especially the Communist League, and in chapter 8 below, we will look at the only organization they joined thereafter — the International. All these organizations pass the above test with flying colors and we need not belabor the point here. Instead let us turn to some correspondence drawn from the period when Engels served as a kind of elder statesman to the diverse socialist parties that were then blossoming across two continents.

When the Danish Social Democratic party summarily expelled a leftist minority in 1889, Engels wrote his protest to the party's leaders:

> Among the socialist workers' parties existing today it would scarcely occur to a single one . . . to treat in this Danish fashion an opposition that has grown up in the bosom of the family. It belongs to the life and growth of every party that in its midst more moderate and more extreme tendencies should develop and even fight with each other, and whoever summarily expels the more extreme tendency thereby only encourages its growth. The workers' movement is founded on the sharpest criticism of existing society, criticism is its lifeblood, how could it shirk criticism of itself and want to forbid debate? Do we demand of others then free speech for ourselves, only to abolish it again within our own ranks?[59]

Noteworthy sentiments indeed. To be sure, Engels sympathized politically with the expellees, but his sincerity on the broader issues of principle was proved the following year when he repeated the same sentiments in the opposite context. At the 1890 party congress the German party leaders, August Bebel and Wilhelm Liebknecht (with whom Engels stood very close), were planning to expel a noisy and critical semianarchist minority, the *Jungen* (with whom Engels disagreed). Nonetheless Engels intervened with Bebel and Liebknecht, as he wrote Friedrich Sorge, "to convince them of the imprudence of all expulsions that are grounded merely on complaints of oppositional activity and not on striking proofs of *acts* injurious to the party. The greatest party in the Reich cannot exist without all shadings within it getting a complete hearing." Engels' letter to Liebknecht went straight to the point: "Show that freedom to criticize prevails, and *if* there must be expulsions, then only in cases where there are quite striking and completely provable matters of fact, overt acts of baseness and betrayal."[60] John Stuart Mill could scarcely have put it better.

Early in 1891 Engels was suddenly obliged to defend *himself*, after having connived with Karl Kautsky to publish the explosive *Critique of the Gotha Program* in the semiofficial organ, *Die Neue Zeit*, without the knowledge of the German party leaders. Bebel wrote Engels a letter of chastisement saying that he (Bebel) would have tried to prevent publication had he known of it in time. Engels responded to this with considerable anger:

> What is the difference between you people and Puttkamer [the Prussian official who administered the Anti-Socialist Law] if you introduce an anti-socialist law within your own ranks? It does not matter much to me personally. No party in the world can condemn me to silence if I am determined to speak. But I think you should reflect whether you would not be wise to be a little less sensitive and in your behavior a little less — Prussian. You — and the Party — *need* socialist science, but it cannot exist without freedom of movement. One must take the disadvantages into the bargain and it is best to do it with decorum, without flinching.[61]

To Kautsky privately Engels complained about the indignation of the party leadership: "It is high time people stop treating party officials — their own servants — with those eternal kid-gloves, and stop standing before them as before infallible bureaucrats, most obediently instead of critically." If the enemies of the party seek to take advantage of such internal self-criticism, Engels declared, the party should reply: "Look how we criticize ourselves — we are the only party that can allow itself such a thing; why don't you imitate us!"[62]

Late in 1892, when his personal interests were *not* involved, Engels wrote again to Bebel to complain about a measure of the last party congress that seemed to him to "nationalize" the party press, that is, to subordinate it to the party executive:

> Your "nationalization" of the press will have great drawbacks if it is carried too far. You *must* absolutely have in the party a press that is not *directly* dependent upon the executive or even upon the party congress; that is to say, a press which is in a position, *within* the program and the accepted tactics, to oppose without the slightest misgivings particular steps taken by the party, and which, within the bounds of party decency, is free to subject even program and tactics to criticism. As the party executive, you people ought to favor such a press, yes, even call it forth.[63]

That "socialist science" required freedom is a recurring theme in these Engels letters. The "magnificent presumption" of Marx and Engels that they were simply dealing in science—so often cited as evidence of their dogmatic intolerance—may account for the arrogant tone of their polemical writings but it was also responsible for the impressive tolerance one finds in these letters.[64] Marx and Engels put forth their own theories as *provisionally* true in the same sense that all scientific knowledge is supposed to be provisional—subject to correction and modification in the light of subsequent discoveries. Such further research would be stultified if the original theories were regarded as dogmatic final truths. Thus Engels repeatedly deplored those "who claimed to be the orthodox Marxists, but who have transformed our concept of movement into a rigid dogma to be learned by heart," a "kind of dogma which alone makes one holy"; those who treat Marx's writings "exactly as if they were texts from the classics or from the New Testament." It was for just this reason that Marx himself declared disgustedly: "All I know is that I am not a Marxist."[65] One cannot really imagine either man wanting to stifle the right to criticize within the party.

Our third and surely most serious test had to do with the willingness of the postrevolutionary government to allow freedom of expression, assembly, and association to those who might oppose its rule peaceably. On this issue the Russian Marxist tradition goes back to Georgii Plekhanov who, as we had occasion to observe in volume 1, "frequently asserted that when 'we' would be in power 'we' naturally would grant freedoms to no one but 'ourselves.'"[66] It culminated in the November Revolution when the Bolsheviks excluded so-called exploiters from all political rights, including even the right to vote. Lenin defended his action by appealing to the concept of proletarian dictatorship:

> A state of the exploited must . . . be a democracy for the exploited, and a means of *suppressing the exploiters;* and the suppression of a class means inequality for that class, its exclusion from "democracy." . . .
>
> The indispensable characteristic, the necessary condition of [proletarian] dictatorship is the *forcible* suppression of the exploiters as a *class,* and, consequently, the *infringement* of "pure democracy," i.e., of equality and freedom, *in regard to* that *class.*[67]

The tradition of German Marxism, however, was quite the opposite, and spokespersons for all three of its branches—left, right, and center—reacted in stunned horror to the Bolsheviks' suppression of political rights. Such a reaction from Eduard Bernstein, intellectual leader of the reformists, and from Karl Kautsky, the leader of the center faction, might be taken as understandable, so it is important to stress that Rosa Luxemburg, leader of the radicals, a cofounder of the German Communist party and a personal friend of Lenin's, repudiated this Bolshevik action with at least equal fervor:

> Freedom only for the supporters of the government, only for the members of one party — however numerous they may be — is no freedom at all. Freedom is always and exclusively freedom for the one who thinks differently. Not because of any fanatical concept of "justice" but because all that is instructive, wholesome and purifying in political freedom depends on this essential characteristic, and its effectiveness vanishes when "freedom" becomes a special privilege.[68]

Luxemburg's posthumously published critique of the Bolshevik Revolution has become a classic indictment of its early development into a one-party dictatorship.

If the traditions of Russian and German Marxism are opposite on this issue, the obvious question is: where did the *founders* of the Marxist tradition stand? Did they think like their Russian followers or like their German followers? On the one hand, one can find nothing in the writings of Marx and Engels that matches the clarity and eloquence of Luxemburg's statement in favor of postrevolutionary freedoms (although Engels' just quoted remarks on *intraparty* freedom strike very similar chords). On the other hand, *they never expressly called for any limitation of rights for peaceable opponents of the workers' state*, as did both Plekhanov and Lenin. And this negative evidence becomes impressive if we consider the two principal situations in which Marx and Engels *might* have called for such a limitation — namely during the 1848 revolutions in Germany and during the Paris Commune.

Throughout their year of revolutionary journalism in 1848–1849 Marx and Engels gave all kinds of advice to the bourgeois liberal German National Assembly in Frankfort as well as to the liberal cabinet ministers in Prussia, advice particularly on how to deal with the developing strength of the counterrevolutionaries. They also advised the more radical Prussian National Assembly, with whose pale democratic majority they felt much more kinship, on how to deal with liberal ministers and the liberal bourgeoisie generally. They urged these assemblies to assert popular sovereignty in a practical sense, to rule themselves instead of leaving the reins of executive power in royal hands. They urged them to exert control over cabinet ministers and over the military, and to replace reactionary officials in a thoroughgoing institutional house-cleaning. These were the desired ingredients in the "energetic dictatorship," as they chose to call it, that should have been exercised by the elected assemblies. But *nowhere* did the two men suggest that opponents of the revolution be denied the core political freedoms or the right to vote. Even during the Prussian counterrevolution, when the temptation must have been strongest, Marx's chosen weapon was tax refusal, not a call for the restriction of rights.[69]

The most radical passage of the most radical document associated with Marx and Engels during this period, the March *Circular* of 1850, did urge league members in the next revolution to "compel the democrats to carry out their present terrorist phrases" (note incidently that the pale democrats did not forswear terror), and specified "popular revenge against hated individuals or public buildings." But even this document made no call for one-party rule or elimination of the rights of peaceable opposition. And the call for terror itself may well have been the inspiration of Willich, as we saw in volume 1, since Marx and Engels never mentioned it in their other 1850 writings. Willich on the other hand subsequently gave repeated directions to his followers concerning the preparation of proscription lists, prevention of emigration, arrest and punishment of all "enemies of the people," and so forth.[70] In an 1854 polemic against this ex-officer of the Prussian army, Marx scoffed at Willich's elaborate plans "to establish an artificially contrived military dictatorship, to introduce a military-social code of laws, to ban all newspapers except *one* which would have to publish daily orders about the prescribed mode of thought and behavior."[71]

If we turn to the Paris Commune the negative evidence becomes even more significant, since we are confronted here not with a bourgeois or petty bourgeois revolution but with one that produced what Marx called "essentially a working-class government," what Engels specifically labeled a "dictatorship of the proletariat."[72] Under the Paris Commune for the first time rights could become so many "weapons" in the hands of the class enemy. When the Central Committee of the National Guard assumed the functions of a provisional government on March 19, its very first decree set a date for municipal elections and lifted the state of siege (martial law) that had been in effect since the war, the latter act having the effect of restoring the rights of free expression, assembly, and association to all Parisians. "An extraordinary measure for a revolutionary government," comments Frank Jellinek in his history of the Commune, "it meant the abandonment of the elementary precaution against counter-revolution."[73] Significantly, however, Marx said no such thing. Neither did he make any such comment a month later as he copied down the newspaper summary of the Communards' program of April 19 which spoke of "the absolute guarantee of individual freedom and freedom of conscience."[74] Not all the Communard leaders were convinced civil libertarians of course, and after Thiers' troops began their assault on the city these elements won a majority on May 1 for the creation of a special executive committee bearing the ominous title, Committee of Public Safety. It existed only during the three final weeks and was but the palest imitation of its famous predecessor. Interestingly neither Marx nor Engels ever praised this step as a necessary one or even mentioned it at all. Indeed, the Paris members of the IWA (including Auguste Serraillier, sent from the general council) formed the backbone of the minority that voted against this measure in the communal assembly, declaring "a Committee of Public Safety will have the essential effect of creating a dictatorial power . . . [which] would be a veritable usurpation of the sovereign rights of the people."[75] Even in the absence of clear positive evidence, then, it surely signifies *something* that neither Marx nor Engels ever said a word in favor of curtailing the rights of peaceful opposition under the Paris Commune.

To be sure Marx reproached the Communards for "an excess of moderation bordering on weakness." We already know how the two men complained of the failure to march immediately on Versailles, and later to seize the assets of the Bank of France. Obviously neither of these complaints concerned rights of peaceful opposition. The phrase, "excess of moderation," actually appeared in the Second Draft and referred more narrowly to the treatment accorded antirevolutionary elements within Paris between March 18 and the time most of them abandoned the city following their poor showing in the March 26 elections.[76] Let us follow this Second Draft account of the period in question, since it treated the ethical and legal issues a bit more straightforwardly and less cynically than the final version that was composed under the immediate impact of the May butchery. The first alleged excess of moderation concerned the *sergents-de-ville*, the much hated Paris policemen who had accompanied the regular army troops in the fateful attempt to purloin the Montmartre cannon. "The sergents-de-ville, instead of being disarmed and locked up, had the doors of Paris flung wide open for their safe retreat to Versailles, while the 'men of order,' left not only unhurt, were allowed to rally quietly [and — HD] lay hold on the strongholds in the very center of Paris." Thus presumably the larcenous policemen should have been locked up, the conservatives prevented from seizing the strongholds.[77]

Marx turned next to the bloody clash at the National Guard headquarters on the Place Vendôme on March 22, the only significant incident of violence within Paris itself prior to the May suppression, and one depicted in the conservative press as a brutal massacre of unarmed demonstrators by the red soldiers. Marx had begun very early to collect newspaper accounts of this incident, and he showed a special interest in reports of hidden weapons carried by the demonstrators and of restraint shown by the guardsmen — it seemed to *matter* to him whether peaceful opposition had been violently suppressed. The Second Draft continued:

> They [the "men of order"] interpreted, of course, the indulgence of the Central Committee and the magnanimity of the armed workmen, as mere symptoms of conscious weakness. Hence their plan to try under the mask of an "unarmed" demonstration the work which four days before Vinoy's cannon and mitrailleuses [machine guns] had failed in. Starting from the quarters of luxury, a riotous mob of "gentlemen" . . . fell in marching order . . . ill-treating and disarming the detached posts of National Guards they met with on their progress. When then at last debouching in the place Vendôme, they tried, under shouts of ribald insults, to dislodge the National Guards from their headquarters, forcibly break through the lines. In answer to their pistol shots the regular sommations (the French equivalent of the English reading of the Riot acts) were made, but proved ineffective to stop the aggressors. Then fire was commanded by the general of the National Guard [killing ten "men of order"] and these rioters dispersed in wild flight. Two national guards [were] killed, eight dangerously wounded and the streets, through which they disbanded, strewn with revolvers, daggers and cane swords, gave clear evidence of the "unarmed" character of their "pacific" demonstration.[78]

Thus from the newspaper evidence available to him Marx concluded that the mob was both armed and riotous and had an essentially military objective — to seize yet another stronghold, the National Guard headquarters. Nonetheless it was handled with considerable initial restraint, even with the proper formalities: the drums rolled for five minutes, Marx noted in his First Draft, and the *sommations* were read ten times before the fatal volley.[79]

What happened to the demonstrators afterward? Here as in many places in *The Civil War*, Marx contrasted the behavior of the Communards with that of the conservatives in power, drawing a parallel to the mass demonstration of June 1849 that he himself had witnessed:

> When, on the 13-th June 1849, the National guards of Paris made a really "unarmed" demonstration of protest against the felonious assault on Rome by French troops, Changarnier, the general of the "party of order" had their ranks sabred, trampled down by cavalry, and shot down. The state of siege was at once proclaimed, new arrests, new proscriptions, a new reign of terror set in. But the "lower orders" manage these things otherwise. The runaways of the 22-nd March being neither followed nor harassed on their flight, nor afterwards called to account by the judge of instruction (juge d'instruction) [equivalent to a public prosecutor], were able two days later to muster again an "armed" demonstration under Admiral Saisset.[80]

Marx seemed proud that the Communards did not behave with the ferocity of the other side. Still he thought they should have been firmer than they were: arrests and proceedings by ordinary public prosecutors are what he suggested. The second demonstration alluded to was Admiral Jean Saisset's menacing effort on March 24 to mobilize all the remaining pro-Versailles guardsmen, perhaps thirty thousand, at the conservative strongholds; then suddenly on the next day he gave up all idea of resistance and fled to Versailles. Marx continued his account: "Even after the grotesque failure of this their second rising they were, like all other Paris citizens, allowed to try their hands at the ballot box for the election of the Commune. When succumbing in this bloodless battle, they at last purged Paris from their presence by an unmolested Exodus."[81] Up through the March 26 elections, then, Marx's complaints about excessive moderation had to do with the failure to arrest and disarm hostile police forces, the failure to prevent the seizure of Communard strongholds, and the failure to prosecute violent demonstrators — nothing more. At the same time, one detects a distinct note of pride when Marx reported that the Communards did *not* resort to martial law. One sees that same pride in his report that, during its entire existence until the suppression began, the Commune "remained so free from the acts of violence in which the revolutions, and still more the counter-revolutions, of the 'better classes' abound" that ordinary crime all but disappeared and "the streets of Paris were safe" for the first time; that the Communards had brought forth the guillotine — primordial symbol of revolutionary terror but long since become the bourgeois state's instrument for executing criminals — only in order to *burn* it in a public ceremony as a relic of barbarism.[82]

In the March 26 elections the wealthier districts of the city returned twenty-one opposition deputies to the ninety-two-man communal assembly, but most of these deputies rejected the role of peaceful opposition, joining the general exodus of the upper classes from the city to await Thiers' military solution. By-elections were held to fill the empty seats, however, and there remained a legal and undisturbed bourgeois opposition group within the communal assembly fluctuating in size from five to fifteen. On the other side, the large pro-Commune majority was by no means a solid block: inspite of fluctuating numbers and very indistinct party lines, modern scholars have identified three general ideological factions of roughly equal size — the nonsocialist neo-Jacobins, the Blanquists, and the Proudhonists.[83] About twenty deputies were, or had been, members of the IWA, but the bulk of these were Proudhonist trade-unionists. Among the Communards generally, only two, or perhaps three, persons have ever been identified who could be called followers of Marx in any narrower sense — Leo Frankel, Auguste Serraillier, and perhaps Elizabeth Dimitrieff. There was no organized Marxist party at all.[84]

How then could Marx possibly describe the Commune in his Kugelmann letter as "the most glorious deed of *our Party* [emphasis added] since the June insurrection in Paris"?[85] He could not have meant the IWA, which did not exist at the time of the June insurrection. How could Engels describe it as a "dictatorship of the proletariat" when the Commune was entirely in the hands of their ideological rivals? The two men were obviously aware of the political complexion of the communal assembly, even if Marx understandably glossed over internal factional divisions when composing his eulogy. In 1891 Engels spoke plainly enough of a Blanquist majority (he lumped the neo-Jacobins together with their Blanquist cousins) and a Proudhonist minority, and this in the very introduction where he called the Commune a dictatorship of the proletariat.[86] So the answer to these questions must be as follows: Marx meant "party" in the broad sense he so often used to describe the entire workers' movement, actual or potential, *regardless of present ideological affiliations*. By "dictatorship of the proletariat" Engels meant the revolutionary rule of the working-class majority, *regardless of present ideological affiliations*.[87] Nowhere does it emerge so clearly that what Marx and Engels had in mind really was the rule of the masses themselves, whether or not they had the "scientifically correct" ideas — and not the rule of scientifically correct ideas whether or not the masses embraced them. From all this it would seem to follow convincingly that Marx and Engels' conception of proletarian dictatorship did not require all the workers to support a single party, much less a Marxist party, still less that all other parties be suppressed. And that is the main point here, for freedom of association involves in the first instance the right to form political parties, or to put it more directly, the right to organize peaceably in opposition to the existing government. No established Communist regime in the twentieth century has found the courage to allow this right which the Communards observed so scrupulously for their bourgeois opponents as well as for their own kind. If Marx and Engels disagreed with the Communards on this matter, there is not a shred of positive evidence to show it.

In fact there is one major piece of positive evidence showing that Marx presupposed a legal bourgeois opposition — an exceedingly interesting passage from the First Draft of *The Civil War*. It was written at a time when Marx still had a flicker of hope that the communal movement might spread to embrace all of France, thus creating a ruling alliance of the majority classes — workers, peasants, petty bourgeois — in a national government. Such a popular government could not have the immediate task of overthrowing capitalism, however, for which the preconditions had yet to be fulfilled. Thus in the First Draft Marx wanted to stress that the Commune is *"the political form of the social emancipation"* and not social emancipation itself. "The commune does not [do — HD] away with the class struggles, . . . but it affords the rational medium in which that class struggle can run through its different phases in the most rational and humane way." Presupposed here is the continued existence of a capitalist class which would struggle to keep its economic power. Communal institutions, thoroughly democratic as they were, would allow the "most rational and humane" development of this struggle to its necessary end in full communism. If this does not mean a legal bourgeois opposition, it means nothing at all. Marx made his presupposition even plainer by adding next: "The communal organization once firmly established on a national scale, the catastrophes it might still have to undergo, would be sporadic slaveholders' insurrections, which, while for a moment interrupting the work of peaceful progress, would only accelerate the movement, by putting the sword into the hand of the Social Revolution."[88] "Slaveholders' insurrections," as we will see in chapter 10, was a code phrase Marx used for rebellions against majority rule by threatened elites. He wanted here to allow for the possibility of such rebellions, which would of course have to be suppressed, accelerating the movement, but notice the implication that the "sword" would *not* be used in ordinary times of "peaceful progress." The workers' sword must be ready to suppress insurrection, not peaceful opposition; the most "rational and humane" resolution of the class struggle was one that takes place peacefully within democratic forms. This must serve as Marx's best statement on the issue of rights under proletarian rule.

After reviewing the entire body of evidence, one may allow that the negative evidence is impressive indeed, but why is the positive evidence — however interesting — so scant and so often indirect and backhanded? If Marx and Engels had essentially the same position on the rights issue as Rosa Luxemburg, why do we find no ringing declarations like hers? The two men were able to describe one-man dictatorship as nonsense, religious persecution as counterproductive, the high-handedness of party leaders as prussianism, a communist regime with only one legal newspaper as ridiculous, and so forth. But it was almost impossible for them to come right out and say these things were *wrong*. Was this because their philosophical views committed them to an ethical relativism which excluded the idea of absolute rights? Yet at the deepest level they were really not relativists at all, and in any event Luxemburg presumably shared the same philosophical views. Was their moral constipation then perhaps more a matter of personality than of weltanschauung? Let us keep this in mind as we put the last of our four questions.

The Rights of Civilized Class Warfare

We opened the previous section with a barrage of familiar quotations drawn from Marx and Engels' antianarchist polemics, all of which stressed the repressive functions of the future workers' state. As we have now seen, this evidence may *not* legitimately be cited as proof that the two men wanted to deny the rights of peaceful opposition; but it can and should be cited as evidence that they *anticipated* a violent resistance, anticipated that the bourgeoisie would refuse to accept the role of peaceful opposition within democratic restraints. Such a pessimistic anticipation is not really surprising if one remembers how long the European propertied classes in the nineteenth century resisted the introduction of completely democratic institutions, and in particular, of course, how they acted to suppress such institutions in the revolutions of 1848. In the German case one finds it difficult even to keep track of all the popularly elected assemblies that were dispersed at bayonet point, all of which seemed a textbook example of what happens when democratic revolutionaries do *not* prepare for the possibility of violent counterrevolution by maintaining some kind of loyal armed force in readiness. This lesson could scarcely be lost on Marx and Engels, themselves so passionately involved in that revolution, and so it is understandable that Marx should praise the Communards first and foremost for the "new feature" that distinguished their revolution: "that the people, after the first rise, have not disarmed themselves and surrendered their power" to their social betters.[89] The National Guard, "the armed manhood of Paris," was the ultimate guarantee of the Commune's existence, not against peaceful opposition, which it allowed, but against violent opposition and as a deterrent to such violent opposition.

Armed force may be used either to fight or to deter, of course, and the latter use seems to have been contemplated in some of the aforementioned passages. It is the obvious sense of Engels' remark that in any revolution the victorious party must "rule by means of the terror which its arms inspire in the reactionaries." The Paris Commune would not have lasted a single day, he went on, "if it had not made use of this authority of the armed people against the bourgeoisie."[90] The National Guard was never used actively to attack the bourgeois civil population; the "terror" which its arms inspired was a passive sort of terror, a kind of deterrent, as when conservative authorities make a massive show of military force in a tense city as a deterrent to rioting and insurrection. In the same deterrent vein Marx once spoke of a need for "intimidating" or "throwing a scare into" the mass of the bourgeoisie ("*ins Bockshorn zu jagen*").[91] Other passages countenance the actual use of force, and some even employ harsh verbs like "crush" and "stamp out." In each of these cases, however, Marx and Engels specified that it was the *resistance* of the bourgeoisie that must be crushed or stamped out and not the bourgeoisie per se.[92] It is curious that the presumably more radical anarchists seemed unconcerned about such resistance, leading one to wonder if they did not tacitly assume that the class enemy would be physically exterminated at the outset. And perhaps not even tacitly. Bakunin published one slogan that called for "peace for the workers, liberty for all the oppressed and death to rulers, exploiters and guardians of all kinds"; similar verbal excesses can be found scattered throughout his writings.[93] Of course one is never sure whether the flamboyant anarchist leader literally meant every extravagant thing he wrote. What should be emphasized is that blood-curdling proclamations such as this are nowhere to be found in Marx and Engels' public or private writings. If their antianarchist polemics stressed the repressive tasks of the proletarian state, that very emphasis also presupposes the continued physical existence of a bourgeoisie whose violent resistance needs to be suppressed.

These polemics alone do not exhaust our sources, however, and it is quite misleading to quote them without qualification as universal Marxist principles. If Marx reproached the Communards for excesses of moderation, for example, and Engels wanted them to use their authority more freely, it does not necessarily follow that the two men would have preferred *unrestrained* brutality. In fact, we have now examined *all* the specific ways in which Marx and Engels themselves suggested that communal authority ought to have been used more freely. The one they repeated most often concerned the seizure of the assets of the Bank of France — scarcely a matter requiring a Nuremberg Tribunal. In fact, Engels linked this failure very interestingly in his 1891 "Introduction" with the most serious inhumanity with which the Communards *can* be charged: "The hardest thing to understand is certainly the holy awe with which they remained standing respectfully outside the gates of the Bank of France. This was also a serious political mistake. The Bank in the hands of the Commune — this would have been worth more than ten thousand hostages. It would have meant the pressure of the whole of the French bourgeoisie on the Versailles government in favor of peace with the Commune."[94] Did Engels mean to suggest that it was wrong to take the hostages, that the Bank was a better "hostage"? How did he and Marx respond generally to this least humane action of the Paris Commune — the arrest of hundreds of hostages and the eventual shooting of some sixty to seventy of them? Did they argue that in open class warfare, no quarter need be given, nothing is forbidden; or did they see a need for restraints even here, for some mutually accepted rules of civilized class warfare?

The bloodshed between Paris and Versailles began, of course, with the March 18 killing of two army generals by an enraged mob on the heights of Montmartre. Marx did not deny that this was an act of "wild lynch justice," but he noted that the National Guard Central Committee had vainly tried to stop it and in any event was "as much responsible" for these spontaneous mob actions "as the Princess of Wales was for the fate of the people crushed to death on the day of her entrance into London."[95] Apart from the Place Vendôme affair which we have already examined, there was no further significant violence within Paris itself until the bloody May week. "The Paris Workmen's Revolution," Marx wrote in the Second Draft, "made it a point of honor to keep the proletarian [revolution] clean of . . . crimes." Not so the Versaillese, however, who began immediately to mistreat the prisoners they took, shooting many of them. The First Draft quoted the London *Daily Telegraph* for April 4 when twenty-five prisoners were mowed down in a single episode: "Every man wearing the uniform of the regular army who was captured in the ranks of Communists was straightaway shot without the slightest mercy. The governmental troops were perfectly ferocious." In outrage Marx exclaimed that Thiers was denying the Communards "all the rights and customs of civilized warfare."[96] Presumably Marx wanted these rights applied to the class war as well.

It was in response to the shootings that the Commune passed its Law of Hostages on April 7 and arrested several hundred people deemed "guilty of complicity with the Versailles Government," threatening to execute three of them for every prisoner subsequently shot by Thiers. In his First Draft, Marx judged this a measure of "self-defense against the savage atrocities of the Versailles Government," but once again he seemed to take pride that "the Commune was too humane to execute its decree of reprisals," even after Thiers resumed his brutal shootings. Instead of urging the Communards to carry out their reprisals Marx declared: "the Commune has refused to soil its hands with the blood of these bloodhounds!"[97] These comments were written before the final week. The published version of *The Civil War* was written immediately after it, which explains the tone of controlled, brittle rage that pervades Marx's new treatment of the same issue:

> Hardly, however, had Thiers and his Decembrist generals become aware that the Communal decree of reprisals was but an empty threat, that even their gendarme spies caught in Paris under disguise of National Guards, that even *sergents-de-ville*, taken with incendiary shells upon them, were spared — when the wholesale shooting of prisoners was resumed and carried on uninterruptedly to the end.

In the last days of the fighting, after all semblance of central direction had broken down among the Communard resisters, between sixty and seventy hostages were shot by small groups acting on their own initiative. Marx commented:

> The bourgeoisie and its army in June, 1848, re-established a custom which had long disappeared from the practice of war — the

shooting of their defenceless prisoners. . . . On the other hand, the Prussians, in France [during 1870–1871], had re-established the practice of taking hostages—innocent men, who, with their lives, were to answer to them for the acts of others. When Thiers, as we have seen, from the very beginning of the conflict, enforced the humane practice of shooting down the Communal prisoners, the Commune, to protect their lives, was obliged to resort to the Prussian practice of securing hostages. The lives of the hostages had been forfeited over and over again by the continued shooting of prisoners on the part of the Versaillese. How could they be spared any longer after the carnage with which MacMahon's praetorians celebrated their entrance into Paris?

Marx concluded that "the bourgeois of our days considers himself the legitimate successor to the baron of old, who thought every weapon in his own hand fair against the plebeian, while in the hands of the plebeian a weapon of any kind constituted in itself a crime."[98]

Thus the bourgeoisie had to expect that the workers would respond to brutality with brutality, to the shooting of prisoners with the shooting of hostages. Yet both practices were (in those innocent Victorian days) reversions to barbaric practices which had "long disappeared from the practice of war." Even in the class war, "the only justifiable war in history," Marx seemed to be saying, there are certain "rights and customs of civilized warfare." Our side began by respecting them, making it a "point of honor" to keep its revolution clean of crime; despite considerable provocation it did not want to "soil its hands," and so forth. But if driven to the extreme, he seemed to argue, you cannot expect our side to observe the rights of civilized class warfare unless your side does so as well. Here was the idea of an implicit contract, a kind of tacit understanding that certain restraints ought to be observed even in the class war.[99]

This same idea turned up again in Marx's remarks on the other notable repressive act of the Communards. On April 18, two weeks after Thiers' troops had begun their attack on the fortresses surrounding Paris and their artillery bombardment of the city itself, the Commune began to suppress a series of pro-Versailles newspapers that had been allowed to publish freely up to that point. These suppressions thus belong to the present section on belligerent rights rather than the previous section on the rights of peaceful opposition, as Marx himself made clear in his commentary:

While the Versailles Government, as soon as it had recovered some spirit and strength, used the most violent means against the Commune; while it put down the free expression of opinion all over France . . . ; while it burned by its gendarme inquisitors all papers printed at Paris, and sifted all correspondence from and to Paris; while in the National Assembly the most timid attempts to put in a word for Paris were howled down in a manner unknown even to the *Chambre introuvable* of 1816; with the savage warfare of Versailles outside, and its attempts at corruption and conspiracy inside Paris — would the Commune not have shamefully betrayed its trust by affecting to keep up all the decencies and appearances of liberalism as in a time of profound peace? Had the Government of the Commune been akin to that of M. Thiers, there would have been no more occasion to suppress Party-of-Order papers at Paris than there was to suppress Communal papers at Versailles.[100]

Notice first of all Marx's matter-of-fact assumption that there are "decencies" one allows one's opponent in peacetime, such as freedom of speech, decencies that must be withdrawn, however, during a condition of "savage warfare," that are not "compatible with the state of a besieged town."[101] The rather convoluted final sentence presumably means that, given the initial condition, there would have been no Party-of-Order newspapers to be suppressed in Paris, since pro-Paris sentiments at Versailles were stifled from the outset. The converse is implied: if Versailles had allowed Paris to govern itself in peace, if Versailles had not suppressed pro-Commune sentiments all over the country, then there would have been no "occasion" for the commune to suppress the Party-of-Order press — again the idea of contract.

While Marx used these arguments to defend the repressive acts of the besieged Commune, he never gloried in the acts themselves as did, for example, some of the Blanquist survivors from their London refuge in 1874. Engels took these refugees to task for the callous eagerness with which they claimed "responsibility" for the shootings and incendiarism of the Commune's final days:

In every revolution all sorts of stupidities unavoidably occur, just as in any time, and when afterwards enough calm has been restored so that the critical faculties may work again, one necessarily comes to this conclusion: we have done much that we should not have done, and we have failed to do much that we should have done, and that is why things went wrong. But what a lack of critical faculties to declare the Commune to be sacred and infallible, to assert that every house burnt and every hostage shot represented an exact justice down to the dot over the "i." Is this not the same as maintaining that, during that week in May, the people shot exactly those persons it was necessary to shoot, and no others; that they burnt exactly those buildings it was necessary to burn, and no others? Is it not the same as saying that in the first French Revolution justice was done to every single guillotined person—first to those whom Robespierre had guillotined, and then to Robespierre himself? It comes to such childishness when basically well intentioned people give free rein to their urge to appear fearsome.[102]

"To appear fearsome" was an urge Marx and Engels had not always resisted themselves, but here at least Engels recognized it as something that ought to be resisted. More importantly, after three years of calm, what had seemed like justified reprisals in 1871 now began to look like "stupidities" (*Dummheiten*). This rarely noticed article appeared just six months after the famous suggestion in "On Authority" that the Communards should have used their authority more freely—the two texts ought always to be quoted together.

Another text should also receive its due, a letter that may surprise those who imagine that Marx and Engels' private correspondence must contain the bloodthirsty plans they discreetly left out of their public writings. Back in 1870, just after Engels learned the news of Sedan, he was convinced the war was over and France would have to make peace. Thus he discounted the restlessness in Paris and the hue and cry of those neo-Jacobins who called for a new *levée en masse*, and a new reign of terror. All this represented, as Engels perceived it, only a terrified unwillingness to admit France's defeat:

> These perpetual little panics of the French—which all arise from fear of the moment when they will really have to face the truth—give one a much better idea of the Reign of Terror. We think of it as the reign of people who instill terror; but quite the contrary, it is the reign of people who are themselves terrified. Terror consists mostly of useless cruelties perpetrated by frightened people in order to reassure themselves. I am convinced that the blame for the Reign of Terror, Anno 1793, falls almost exclusively on the overnervous bourgeois acting the patriot, on the little philistine petty bourgeois who is scared shitless, and on the mob of riff-raff who make a business out of terror. The present little terror comes from precisely the same classes.[103]

How interesting to find Engels, when for once allowing himself a moral judgment, speaking of "useless cruelties" and apportioning not the credit but the "blame" for the original Reign of Terror!

The idea of a tacit understanding concerning the rules of civilized class warfare appears in Marx and Engels' writings in either of two logically complementary ways. On the one side it was used to emphasize to the bourgeoisie that it must expect brutality as the response to brutality, as we have observed in the case of the Communard hostages. Back in 1845 Engels had cited with approval a left-wing Chartist maxim which expressed this idea in normative terms: "The oppressed has the right to use all means against his oppressor that the oppressor employs against him."[104] On the other side, there was at least a tacit promise that restraint would be matched by restraint and the implication that such restraints on inhumanity would be in the interest of both parties — the more of them the better. It is not usually noted, for example, that Marx's famous remark about lessening the "birth-pangs" in the preface to *Capital* was addressed not to some revolutionary vanguard but to the ruling classes of the European continent. Their own interest, he suggested, should show them the value of English-style factory legislation, honest parliamentary investigating commissions, and so forth, for such things can reduce the brutality of the coming social transformation:

> It will take a form more brutal or more humane, according to the degree of development of the working-class itself. Apart from higher motives, therefore, their own most important interests dictate to the classes that are for the nonce the ruling ones, the removal of all legally removable hindrances to the free development of the working-class. For this reason, as well as others, I have given so large a space in this volume to the history, the details, and the results of English factory legislation. One nation can and should learn from others. And even when a society has got upon the right track for the discovery of the natural laws of its movement . . . it can neither clear by bold leaps, nor remove by legal enactments, the obstacles offered by the successive phases of its normal development. But it can shorten and lessen the birth-pangs.[105]

When Marx wrote these lines he was aware of two major new bills then pending before the House of Commons, one promising to limit child labor more seriously and the other to extend voting rights to the working class.[106] To recommend such measures to the ruling classes as being in their own interest, as likely to make the coming transformation less brutal and more humane, was seemingly the only form in which Marx could allow himself to propose restraint for restraint — that is, he predicted it rather than proposing it outright. Nonetheless, if threatened with brutality as a response to brutality, the existing rulers were also told it lay within their power to lessen the birth pangs of the coming social transformation. Indeed, as we will see in detail in chapter 10, they were told it lay within their power to keep it entirely peaceful and legal. All that was required were fully democratic institutions — the removal of legal hindrances — and a willingness to submit to the will of an eventual proletarian majority, especially on the issue of socialization of the means of production. Even here Marx and Engels seemed ready to be flexible: although they rejected any legal or moral claim to financial compensation for expropriated owners, Engels wrote in 1895, "we by no means consider compensation as impermissible in any event; Marx told me (and how many times!) that in his opinion we would get off cheapest if we could buy out the whole lot of them." It would depend, he added, upon "the circumstances under which we obtain power, and particularly upon the attitude adopted by these gentry . . . themselves."[107] Here most directly and clearly Engels promised restraint in exchange for restraint.

This notion of a tacit contract, with its double implication — brutality for brutality, restraint for restraint — explains much that is otherwise problematic in the masters' writings. There is no reason to quote an extreme pronouncement next to a moderate pronouncement and throw up one's hands at the "ambiguous legacy," or to probe for deep psychological ambivalences, as has lately become the fashion, in order to explain what is a fairly commonsensical ethical standpoint.[108] What is necessary is to pay some attention to context. As we saw in volume 1, the famous "terror" passages of the *Neue Rheinische Zeitung* were written in a *context* of massive and brutal counterrevolutionary repression and promised red terror as the retaliation for the white terror just then being carried out. A half century later, within a *context* offering some hope that the old rulers might submit peacefully to majority will, Engels could even hold out the prospect of financial compensation — restraint as the reward for restraint. The same kind of thinking reveals itself in Engels' public response to an Irish terrorist bombing in 1885. Comparing the deed to the assassination of Czar Alexander II four years earlier, he declared "the tactics of the Russian revolutionaries are prescribed by necessity and *by the actions of their enemies*" (emphasis added). He went on to repudiate sharply "the gentlemen who produce pointless schoolboy parodies of this struggle in Western Europe."[109] Thus the relative degree of extremism or of restraint in popular movements should depend on the behavior of the other side.

In a parallel way the relative degree of extremism and restraint in Marx and Engels' language reflected the fluctuating behavior of the other side. Major acts of repression tended to evoke violent and bitter language, as we have already observed. On a few occasions — very few — their bitterness might even lead Marx and Engels to say things they did not really mean, the most obvious and provable being Engels' revolting call in 1849 for the extermination of the South Slavic "ethnic trash" which was then providing the brute force of the Hapsburg counterrevolution, when in other writings both before and after 1849, he treated these peoples more respectfully and allowed some room in his future scheme of things for their independent national development.[110] Another example may be Engels' pessimistic conclusions regarding the backwardness of the French peasantry in November 1848, jotted down as he himself was in flight from the counterrevolution and tramping through the French countryside on his way to an uncertain Swiss exile. "The French proletariat, before it enforces its own demands, will first have to put down a general peasants' war," he predicted gloomily — an idea that stands in flat contradiction to *everything else* Marx and Engels wrote about the relation of peasants to the anticipated revolution in France.[111] A final example may be Marx's cynical remark in *Class Struggles in France* when he described the culminating installment of the bourgeois counterrevolution in 1850 — the curtailment of voting rights. "Universal suffrage had fulfilled its mission. . . . It had to be set aside by a revolution or by the reaction." Just prior to this remark, in his running account, Marx made it clear that he would have preferred to see the French masses take up arms and fight in order to *save* universal suffrage, but something in his psychological makeup would not allow him to be outdone in cynicism by the other side. If the bourgeoisie hypocritically abolished universal suffrage, he felt compelled to suggest that the revolutionary side had thought of it first, was planning to do it all along, and so forth.[112]

This psychological observation can be extended to include relations with various superradicals like the Blanquists, Willich, and the Bakuninists. When such worthies adopted a pose of "fearsomer-than-thou," Marx and Engels did not want to appear tender-minded and, especially when they were in fact urging a more moderate course, the two men were apt to dress up their moderation in strong language that suggested "no-less-fearsome-than-thou." We have seen in volume 1 how Marx countered

Willich's insistence on immediate revolution in 1850 by arguing that the workers would have to "go through 15, 20, 50 years of civil war"—a horrendous-sounding process that Engels described under less stressful circumstances simply as a "long and vicissitudinous period of revolution" or even "a series of revolutionary *journées*."[113] We have seen how, in united fronts with Blanquist groupings, Marx and Engels could adopt fearsome-sounding slogans like "permanent revolution" and "dictatorship of the proletariat" they they did not use under normal circumstances, and by which they meant something quite different than their partners. The same need to sound no-less-fearsome-than-thou surely prompted them to use the "dictatorship" slogan again when countering the professedly more radical anarchist demand for the immediate abolition of the state.[114] Finally, it must be significant that one finds the harsh-verbed appeals to "crush" and "stamp out" the resistance of the bourgeoisie *only* in the anti-anarchist polemics of the Bakunin period.[115]

If psychological factors help to explain occasional excesses of violent language, they may also help to explain the infrequency of assurances offered to the class antagonist, particularly assurances about postrevolutionary rights and freedoms. Marx and Engels had little reason, as we have noted, to suppose that the overwhelmingly antidemocratic European upper classes would allow a working-class majority to rise to power legally, much less that they would peaceably bow to the confiscation of their property by such a majority. It is unreasonable on the face of it to expect that the two men would devote much ink to a possibility that seemed so remote, the possibility of a purely peaceful opposition to the workers' government. Beyond this, however, we have also seen evidences of that moral constipation that made it almost impossible for them to speak of rights at all in normative terms. Once in a half-serious parlor-game questionnaire administered by his daughter, Marx declared that "servility" was the vice he detested most, while "strength" was his favorite virtue and "to fight" was his idea of happiness.[116] Psychologically, it would seem, for Marx to assure an overbearing antagonist that one intended to treat him according to rules of fair play (if he would but observe them himself) was to be intolerably solicitous. All moralizing about rights and restraints smacked of weakness and toadying. To be strong was to put on an air as tough and cynical as that of one's antagonist. Thus Marx could speak privately to Engels about the possibility of compensation for expropriated owners (and how many times!), but never managed to express such sentiments even once in his millions of words of published writings.

This reluctance to speak about moral questions has perhaps been explained most eloquently by one of Marx's most formidable twentieth-century critics — Karl Popper. However total Popper's rejection of Marxism as a system, he acknowledged a certain respect for Marx the man, as he revealed in the following passage:

> Marx, I believe, avoided an explicit moral theory, because he hated preaching. Deeply distrustful of the moralist who usually preaches water and drinks wine, Marx was reluctant to formulate his ethical convictions explicitly. The principles of humanity and decency were for him matters that needed no discussion, matters to be taken for granted. (In this field, too, he was an optimist.) He attacked the moralists because he saw them as the sycophantic apologists of a social order which he felt to be immoral; he attacked the eulogists of liberalism because of their self-satisfaction, because of their identification of freedom with the formal liberty then existing within a social system which destroyed freedom. Thus, by implication, he admitted his love for freedom; and in spite of his bias, as a philosopher, for holism, he was certainly not a collectivist, for he hoped that the state would 'wither away.' Marx's faith, I believe, was fundamentally a faith in the open society.

In this generous appraisal of his antagonist, Popper recognized the two main points that have been stressed in this chapter — Marx's underlying respect for the freedom of the individual, combined with his extreme reluctance to talk about it, his moral constipation.[117]

Surely this moral constipation, whatever its deeper roots, has been a misfortune for us all. The entire body of evidence we have now examined, private as well as public, negative as well as positive, in deeds as well as words, all points to the conclusion that underneath the tough cynicism they so often affected Marx and Engels did respect the rights of peaceful opposition and would have allowed those Victorian "decencies" to their class antagonists after the revolution just as consistently as they demanded them for themselves before it. But their inability to say so clearly enough, loudly enough, and often enough has made it all too easy for their putative disciples to ignore the difference between peaceful and violent opposition and to adopt a real — rather than affected — cynicism about rights in general.

❧[7]❧

The Classless Society as a Polity

No PICTURE of Marx and Engels' political ideas would be complete that did not treat the political features of the future classless society, of communism. It may seem paradoxical to talk about the "political" features of a society that was to have no "state" and no "political" institutions as Marx and Engels understood those words, yet the classless society was to be organized as a polity (to use a looser word than state), which they preferred to call a "commonwealth," "*commune*," or "*Gemeinwesen*." And it was to have a structure for making and carrying out collective decisions, which they chose to call an "administration," but which we may examine as a political structure in a broader, more conventional sense of the word. It may also seem paradoxical to spend time on a subject that Marx and Engels themselves persistently refused to speculate about in detail, since they held the drawing up of blueprints for an ideal society to be the very essence of utopianism. Yet, despite their reticence, they always allowed that "science" could predict the broad outlines of the future society. Their underlying philosophical conception of man included an idea of man's ultimate destiny, moreover, which implies a good deal about the character of communist society. And perhaps most importantly, in less guarded moments, both men dropped revealing hints about their personal anticipations for the future. From all these sources it is possible to reconstruct a reasonably complete picture of what Marx and Engels expected and desired the future society to be like.

The main questions to be asked would appear to be: What socio-economic changes did they think would provide the foundation for a "stateless" society? In particular, what did they mean by their enigmatic talk about "abolishing" the division of labor? In what sense was the state supposed to "wither away" and what would remain thereafter? Were Marx and Engels merely playing with words, making the state disappear semantically but not in reality? Why did they not foresee the probable emergence of a new ruling class under communism?[1]

Transcending the Division of Labor

We must begin by stepping back temporarily from political questions in order to look at mankind's evolution and destiny, as Marx and Engels conceived them, in more cosmic terms. One central characteristic of communist society — *the* central characteristic, it will be argued here — was to be what they termed *"die Aufhebung der Teilung der Arbeit,"* the abolition/transcendence of the division of labor. Perhaps the most misunderstood of all their ideas, the notion of "abolishing" the division of labor has been mostly forgotten, or ignored, or misrepresented, or trivialized, or dismissed by subsequent writers (recently there have been a few notable exceptions).[2] As we will see, it explains most of what is problematic in Marx and Engels' conception of the classless society.

When the two men first set down their materialist conception of history in *The German Ideology,* they devoted much attention, to be sure, to changing modes of production, class struggles for political power, and so forth, but underneath all this, at the deepest level, they presented human history as a progressive development of the combined talents of mankind made possible by the progressive division of labor. How far any given people had developed was "shown most manifestly by the degree to which the division of labor has been carried,"[3] from the simplest tribal organization in which there was scarcely any permanent division of labor, in which the whole tribe successively hunted as a group, fashioned tools as a group, regulated its internal affairs as a group, and so on, down to the most advanced nineteenth-century capitalist country with its incredibly intricate division of labor, in which a man might spend his entire active life performing the same routine task over and over again. This progressive subdividing of tasks, this process of occupational specialization, underlies and explains the increasing productivity of man, not only in the material sense but also in the products of the mind — science, the arts, and so forth. It is through the unfolding division of labor that mankind develops the powers that slumber within it, that people as individuals develop their own talents and skills — but not without paying a price.

Marx and Engels' view of human evolution was never a rose-colored tale of progress pure and simple. Indeed, we saw in chapter 1 how Engels could present gentile society attractively as a kind of golden age of primitive communism. To describe its eventual dissolution he even used the word "*Sündenfall*," the Fall of Man.[4] By eating of the apple Adam gained knowledge but was condemned to a life of unrewarding toil. By the dividing of labor tasks primitive men opened up a world of human potentialities but condemned themselves at the same time to alienated labor, labor in which "man's own deed becomes an alien power opposed to him, which enslaves him instead of being controlled by him. For as soon as the division of labor comes into being, each man has a particular, exclusive sphere of activity, which is forced upon him and from which he cannot escape. He is a hunter, a fisherman, a shepherd, or a critical critic, and must remain so if he does not want to lose his means of livelihood." Marx and Engels went on, as we also saw in chapter 1, to cite this same primeval division of labor as being responsible for the emergence out of tribal society of private property, social classes, the state, the antagonism between men and women, and the division between town and country.[5] The Curse of Adam pales by comparison.

The progressive division of labor reappeared as one of the principal themes of *Capital*, which lays particular stress on its negative side. Labor, Marx suggested, is not inherently unpleasant from the outset:

> Labor is, in the first place, a process in which both man and Nature participate, and in which man of his own accord starts, regulates, and controls the material re-actions between himself and Nature. He opposes himself to Nature as one of her own forces, setting in motion arms and legs, head and hands, the natural forces of his body, in order to appropriate Nature's productions in a form adapted to his own wants. By thus acting on the external world and changing it, he at the same time changes his own nature. He develops his slumbering powers and compels them to act in obedience to his sway.

Far from resenting such labor as an imposition, "he enjoys it as something that gives play to his bodily and mental powers." But not all labor is enjoyable: "Constant labor of one uniform kind disturbs the intensity and flow of a man's animal spirits, which find recreation and delight in mere change of activity." The more labor is subdivided, the more it becomes repetitive and uninteresting — a process which culminates in the modern factory that "converts the laborer into a crippled monstrosity, by forcing his detail dexterity at the expense of a world of productive capabilities and instincts; just as in the States of La Plata they butcher a whole beast for the sake of his hide or his tallow."[6] In his moving final summary Marx drew a bitter contrast between gained productivity and lost humanity:

> Within the capitalist system all methods for raising the social pro-
> ductiveness of labor are brought about at the cost of the individual
> laborer; all means for the development of production transform
> themselves into means of domination over, and exploitation of, the
> producers; they mutilate the laborer into a fragment of man, de-
> grade him to the level of an appendage of a machine, destroy every
> remnant of charm in his work and turn it into a hated toil; they
> estrange from him the intellectual potentialities of the labor-process
> in the same proportion as science is incorporated in it as an inde-
> pendent power.[7]

All these themes were taken up at length again by Engels in *Anti-Dühring*, where he emphasized that factory workers, though their sufferings are the most palpable, are not the only victims of the division of labor. This "stunting of man" affects all social classes. It has "condemned the rural population to thousands of years of mental torpidity" by isolating peasants from the higher culture of the towns and making them creatures of the land they cultivate. "And not only the laborers, but also the classes directly or indirectly exploiting the laborers are made subject, through the division of labor, to the tool of their function: the empty-minded bourgeois to his own capital and his own insane craving for profits; the lawyer to his fossilized legal conceptions, which dominate him as an independent power."[8] The dividing of labor into permanent life-long professions, skills, trades, and tasks stunts the potential of all people, then, and their calling becomes a cage which entraps them and molds their growth and conceptions according to *its* needs rather than their own spontaneous ones.

But are not these disadvantages the price that must be paid for the increased productivity, knowledge, and culture that are the benefits of occupational specialization? What is the alternative? A person who reads Marx and Engels' critique of the division of labor and then learns of their desire to "abolish" it might well conclude that the two men wanted to turn their backs on modernization itself, to go back to a time when work was more varied and provided more satisfaction, when a master cabinet-maker, for example, could feel some pride in a fine piece of furniture he had conceived with his own brain and made with the skill of his own hands. But one will look in vain in Marx and Engels' writings for the slightest hint of such a desire. On the contrary, they pilloried without mercy those socialists like Proudhon who were genuinely attracted by the charms of a craft-agrarian society. Such a system, Marx wrote, which excludes concentration of the means of production, cooperation and the division of labor, the application of science and technology, is compatible only with a society "moving within narrow and more or less primitive bounds"; to perpetuate it would be "to decree universal mediocrity."[9] Engels was even more vociferous in a direct attack on Proudhon:

> A reactionary streak runs through the whole of Proudhonism; an aversion to the industrial revolution and the desire, sometimes overtly, sometimes covertly expressed, to drive the whole of modern industry out of the temple — steam engines, mechanical looms and the rest of the business — and to return to old, respectable hand labor. That we would then lose nine hundred and ninety-nine thousandths of our productive power, that the whole of humanity would be condemned to the worst labor slavery . . . — what does all that matter if only . . . "eternal justice" is realized?[10]

On the one hand, Marx and Engels condemned the effects of the division of labor but, on the other hand, they praised the modern industrial system that rests inevitably upon it. It seems they wanted to have their cake and eat it too!

Just so. This is at once the most radical and most misunderstood ingredient in their vision of communist society. They did not call for the "abolition" of the division of labor in the sense of undoing or going back; they called rather for its *Aufhebung*, our familiar Hegelian term which means abolish only in the sense of supersede or transcend. The phrase "transcendence of the division of labor," then, meant in essence that each individual would develop several skills, as many of his own latent talents as he possibly could, so that he could be active in many occupations and pastimes, in combination or in sequence, without being entrapped or limited by any of them. It was not *skills* that would disappear but lifelong confinement to a particular skill, or *professionalism*. And if we want to replace Marx and Engels' rather awkward terminology with a social-science neologism, we might introduce the word "deprofessionalization," bearing in mind that this term does not really convey the full import of the transformation Marx and Engels anticipated. In order to appreciate just how radical an idea it was, let us now draw out its major implications for the organization of the future communist society.

Its first ingredient would be found within the factory itself — job rotation. In *Anti-Dühring* Engels harked back to Fourier and Owen: "Labor should recover the attractiveness of which the division of labor has despoiled it, in the first place through this variation of occupation, and through the correspondingly short duration of the 'sitting' — to use Fourier's expression — devoted to each particular kind of work."[11] The factory system itself invites such rotation, according to *Capital:* "Since the motion of the whole system does not proceed from the workman, but from the machinery, a change of persons can take place at any time without any interruption of the work." In addition to providing relief and variety, such job rotation would familiarize those involved with the various phases and aspects of the whole productive process, allowing them to grasp it conceptually and perhaps take a pride in their collective finished product akin to the pride of the master craftsmen noted above. Marx argued further that such rotation, far from reducing efficiency would produce a versatility that is more and more needed as industrialization advances:

> Modern Industry . . . is continually causing changes not only in the technical basis of production, but also in the functions of the laborer, and in the social combinations of the labor-process. At the same time, it thereby also revolutionizes the division of labor within the society, and incessantly launches masses of capital and of workpeople from one branch of production to another. . . . Modern Industry . . . imposes the necessity of recognizing, as a fundamental law of production, variation of work, consequently fitness of the laborer for varied work, consequently the greatest possible development of his varied aptitudes. . . . [It] compels society, under penalty of death, to replace the detail-worker of to-day, crippled by life-long repetition of one and the same trivial operation, and thus reduced to a mere fragment of a man, by the fully developed individual, fit for a variety of labors, ready to face any change of production, and to whom the different social functions he performs, are but so many modes of giving free scope to his own natural and acquired powers.[12]

Job rotation, then, was a major and essential step in transcending the division of labor, but a step only, for it does not go beyond the factory gates. In our own time job rotation no longer seems even necessarily a socialist measure, since it has been undertaken by privately owned firms — notably automobile factories in Sweden — simply to improve worker productivity. The setting of job rotation is the factory, but the factory itself must be superseded as the exclusive workplace.

Transcending the division between town and country, between industry and agriculture, was the second ingredient, and a favorite theme of Engels. *The German Ideology* had already deplored this "subjection which makes one man into a restricted town-animal, another into a restricted country-animal, and daily creates anew the conflict between their interests," which produces especially "the isolation and consequent crudity of the peasants."[13] Engels' November Draft of the *Manifesto* included a demand obviously inspired by Owen and Fourier: "The erection of large palaces on national estates as common dwellings for communities of citizens engaged in industry as well as agriculture, and combining the advantages of both urban and rural life without the one-sidedness and disadvantages of either." Overcoming the contrast between town and country, having agricultural and industrial work done by the same people instead of by two distinct classes, all this Engels presented as "an essential condition of communist association."[14] It was not just a matter of erecting model communities, however, in an otherwise unchanged landscape, but of eliminating both cities and rural existence as we have known them. *The Housing Question* (1872) was quite categorical:

> Only as uniform a distribution as possible of the population over the whole country, only an intimate connection between industrial and agricultural production together with the extension of the means of communication made necessary thereby — granted the abolition of the capitalist mode of production — will be able to deliver the rural population from the isolation and stupor in which it has vegetated almost unchanged for thousands of years.[15]

Make no mistake about it, he added in *Anti-Dühring*, with no apparent regret, "the great cities will perish." Sounding astonishingly contemporary, he went on to argue that "the present poisoning of the air, water and land can be put an end to only by the fusion of town and country; and only such fusion will change the situation of the masses now languishing in the towns, and enable their excrement to be used for the production of plants instead of for the production of disease."[16] No cities, then, and no sparsely populated countryside, but rather a more or less uniform distribution of communities which combine agriculture and industry. The word "community" in this sense conjures up visions of Brook Farm or the religiously inspired communistic colonies with which Americans are familiar, so it is important to emphasize that Engels was not talking about handicraft industries but modern factory production, not traditional *petite culture* but collective farming with the latest scientific techniques, not communities isolated from the rest of society but intricately interlaced together, enjoying the higher culture and collectively constituting the *whole* of society. In place of the term "community," in many ways the ancient term *"polis"* would be more adequate. As we will see shortly, there is more than an accidental resemblance between the communist society of Marx and Engels' conception and the culture of the ancient Greek city-states.

The third ingredient had to do with transcending the traditional division of labor between the sexes. *The German Ideology* spoke of the ultimate source of the division of labor as "originally nothing but the division of labor in the sexual act, then the division of labor which develops spontaneously or 'naturally' by virtue of natural predisposition (e.g., physical strength)." It spoke further of the "natural division of labor existing in the family" and the "slavery latent in the family." This latent slavery developed slowly in conjunction with private property. Indeed, the very first possessions of men were their wives and children: "The first form of [private property] lies in the family, where wife and children are the slaves of the husband. This latent slavery in the family, though still very crude, is the first form of property, but even at this stage it corresponds perfectly to the definition of modern economists, who call it the power of disposing of the labor-power of others."[17] By the time of *The Origin of the Family* in 1884 Engels had modified this picture substantially to allow for early forms of group marriage and most importantly for the high status of women in gentile society. "Among all savages and all barbarians . . . the position of women is not only free, but honorable." Since the family unit was defined in matrilineal terms and consisted of all the female descendents of a common ancestress, together with their husbands and children (except married male children), households were necessarily large and housekeeping was a public function. Such "communistic households" provided "the material foundation for that supremacy of women which was general in primitive times." *The Origin of the Family* then went on to link the degradation of women with the emergence of private property and the transition to the monogamous family:

It is based on the supremacy of the man, the express purpose being to produce children of undisputed paternity; such paternity is demanded because these children are later to come into their father's property as his natural heirs. . . .

Household management lost its public character. It no longer concerned society. It became a *private service;* the wife became the head servant, excluded from all participation in social production. . . . The modern individual family is founded on the open or concealed domestic slavery of the wife.

From all this Engels drew the same conclusion he and Marx had drawn back in 1846: "the first condition for the liberation of the wife is to bring the whole female sex back into public industry, and . . . this in turn demands that the characteristic of the monogamous family as the economic unit of society be abolished."[18]

The communist alternative here is already partly implicit in the reorganization of society into communities, as described above, with "large palaces" where housekeeping and child rearing could once again become public functions: "With the transfer of the means of production into common ownership, the single family ceases to be the economic unit of society. Private housekeeping is transformed into a social industry. The care and education of the children becomes a public affair."[19] Women and, in some degree, children too would perform socially necessary work outside the family unit, as was more and more required anyway, Marx observed in *Capital,* by the advance of modern (nineteenth-century) industry:

> Modern industry, by assigning as it does an important part in the process of production, outside the domestic sphere, to women, to young persons, and to children of both sexes, creates a new economic foundation for a higher form of the family and of the relations between the sexes. . . . It is obvious that the fact of the collective working group being composed of individuals of both sexes and all ages, must necessarily, under suitable conditions, become a source of humane development.[20]

Marx and Engels expected such practical work to form part of every child's education and to liberate both wife and children from the economic domination of the *paterfamilias.* Finally, communism "will make the relation between the sexes a purely private relation which concerns only the persons involved, and in which society has no call to interfere." Engels anticipated that monogamy in some form would continue, "but what will quite certainly disappear from monogamy are all the features stamped upon it through its origin in property relations; these are, in the first place, supremacy of the man and secondly, the indissolubility of marriage."[21] Overcoming the division of labor between the sexes thus anticipated many of the ideas of today's radical feminists. While Marx and Engels might well fail some present-day tests for residual male chauvinism, they did recognize the authoritarian nature of the traditional family and understood that women's liberation required more than legal rights; it required a change in the basic relationship that made the wife economically dependent on her husband. They also envisaged a liberation that would include all women, not just the educated or unusually talented.[22]

The fourth and probably most important ingredient had to do with transcending the division between mental and manual labor, between the brain that conceives and organizes the process of production (and distribution) and the hand that carries it out. "Division of labor only becomes truly such," declared *The German Ideology*, "from the moment when a division of material and mental labor appears," for this more than anything else gives rise to a dominating class. And in the modern factory, "a separation of the intellectual powers of production from the manual labor," according to *Capital*, results in "the conversion of those powers into the might of capital over labor," into that private despotism we examined in chapter 3.[23] Here transcendence must involve a job rotation that extends beyond the assembly line, fall harvest, and kitchen, to include kinds of work we would call white-collar, technical, and especially managerial, a transcendence in which the manual worker would acquire intellectual skills and take on intellectual tasks, while the intellectual worker would acquire manual skills and take on manual tasks, such that the two would soon become indistinguishable, the one from the other, in terms of education, status, and power. Engels found it absurd that Dühring would pay identical wages in building construction to architects and porters—but not because architects deserved higher wages. Rather, for Engels, it was because neither skill would exist any longer as a "profession":

To the mode of thought of the educated classes which Herr Dühring has inherited, it must seem monstrous that in time to come there will no longer be any professional porters or architects, and that the man who for half an hour gives instructions as an architect will also act as a porter for a period, until his activity as an architect is once again required. A fine sort of socialism that would be — perpetuating the professional porters!

The man who had been a professional porter would have developed new skills and talents, say among others, in bookkeeping, medical aid, and choral singing, such that his old manual work only occupied part of his time. The old professional architect might have a half-dozen activities as well, but they would include his share of manual labor:

> Society cannot free itself unless every individual is freed. . . . The former division of labor must disappear. Its place must be taken by an organization of production in which, on the one hand, no individual can throw on the shoulders of others his share in productive labor, this natural condition of human existence; and in which, on the other hand, productive labor, instead of being a means of subjugating men, will become a means of their emancipation, by offering each individual the opportunity to develop all his faculties, physical and mental, in all directions and exercise them to the full — in which, therefore, productive labor will become a pleasure instead of being a burden.[24]

If there remained any kind of labor for which no one spontaneously volunteered — cleaning tasks, for instance — then following out Engels' reasoning, the only alternative to having a permanent class of "menials" would be to divide up such work universally so that it would be a minor chore for everyone and an all-day, lifelong burden for no one.

Marx and Engels did not deny the need for highly specialized skills (quite the contrary), what they denied was any need to transform such expertise into "mysteries," akin to the craft secrets of the traditional guilds, known only to the initiated, who alone have the right to practice them and to choose their successors in the art.[25] If everyone had the opportunity to develop his talents to the maximum, not everyone would learn architecture, to be sure, but architectural knowledge would become sufficiently widespread so that society would not have to depend on a small self-interested group of professionals. At the same time, the adepts in the field would not have to defend a narrow craft monopoly as their sole means of livelihood. *The German Ideology* deplored the condition in which a person is "exclusively a painter, sculptor, etc.; the very name amply expresses the narrowness of his professional development and his dependence on division of labor." Then it concluded: "In a communist society there are no painters but only people who engage in painting among other activities."[26] By substituting any series of skills, we may employ this latter sentence as a general formula for the idea of deprofessionalization. Thus, in a communist society there are no railroad engineers but at most people who run locomotives among other activities; no dentists but people who perform dentistry among other activities; no garbage collectors but people who collect garbage among other activities, and so forth.

In much the same way, Marx and Engels did not deny the need for leadership. "All combined labor on a large scale requires, more or less, a directing authority," Marx wrote in *Capital*. "A single violin player is his own conductor; an orchestra requires a separate one."[27] What they did deny is any need for a "mystery" of management, a monopoly of managerial power exercised by a cadre of career executives who co-opt their own successors. Multiple occupations and job rotation were to apply here too, for in a communist society there would be no factory managers but only people who manage a factory (for a term) among other activities. Not everyone in the community need be interested in, or capable of, managing a community factory, so long as the job changed hands often enough to prevent any individual from acquiring a vested interest. We will return later to the important question of how managers would be selected, but the foregoing will serve to illuminate the radical sense in which Marx and Engels anticipated the division between mental and physical labor — this prime source of antagonistic classes — would be superseded.

The fifth ingredient in this general *Aufhebung* will already have been anticipated by the reader, for it proceeds directly out of the foregoing and has already been discussed at length in chapter 5. The public-service functions of the entire polity — its "administration" — would similarly be performed on a part-time or short-term basis at every level and in all spheres — legislative, executive, judicial. Indeed, from all indications, Marx and Engels anticipated that literally everyone would be involved in such activity, but no doubt in varying degrees and in different periods of time. For, while not everyone need be interested in architecture, or capable of making shoes, the *res publica* was by definition the concern of all, as Marx had emphasized already back in 1843: "In a rational state, to sit an examination should be demanded of a shoemaker rather than an executive civil servant. For shoemaking is a skill without which one can be a good citizen of the state and social human being; whereas the necessary 'political knowledge' is a requirement without which a person in the state lives outside the state, cut off from himself, from the air." Hegel's "universal class," or "general estate" (*allgemeiner Stand*) of public servants had to become "really general — that is, to be the estate of every citizen."[28] We have observed how the Communards exploded the "state-mystery" by converting the functions of a "trained caste" into ordinary tasks that masses of citizens could perform, on a short-term basis, subject to recall. It was precisely through such deprofessionalization that the state as parasite was to be *aufgehoben*.[29]

The final ingredient would involve the "transformation of labor into self-activity,"[30] or transcending the division between vocation and avocation, between directly productive labor and pursuits that are associated with leisure time. For if human activities are organized in the way just described, then we have arrived back at the beginning, where man finds enjoyment and fulfillment in his labor, "as something that gives play to his bodily and mental powers," through which he "develops his slumbering powers and compels them to act in obedience to his sway." Then, as Engels put it, productive labor itself will offer "each individual the opportunity to develop all his faculties, physical and mental, in all directions. . . . Productive labor will become a pleasure instead of being a burden."[31] If work could become satisfying, even pleasurable, nonetheless it could never become simple amusement, as Fourier had imagined. In the *Grundrisse* Marx chose his ground rather carefully *between* Fourier's conception and the traditional view of work as a curse, exemplified in Adam Smith's assertion that with every hour of labor the worker "must always give up the *identical portion of his tranquility, his freedom*, and his *happiness*." Marx commented on this assertion:

And this is labor for Smith, a curse. . . . It seems quite far from Smith's mind that the individual . . . also needs a normal portion of work, and of the suspension of tranquility. Certainly, labor obtains its measure from the outside, through the aim to be attained and the obstacles to be overcome in attaining it. But Smith has no inkling whatever that this overcoming of obstacles is in itself a liberating activity — and that, further, the external aims become stripped of the semblance of merely external natural urgencies, and become posited as aims which the individual himself posits — hence as self-realization, objectification of the subject, hence real freedom, whose action is, precisely, labor. He is right, of course, that, in its historic forms as slave-labor, serf-labor, and wage-labor, labor always appears as repulsive, always as *external forced labor;* and not-labor, by contrast, as "freedom, and happiness.' . . . [But under communism] labor becomes attractive work, the individual's self-realization, which in no way means that it becomes mere fun, mere amusement, as Fourier, with *grisette*-like naïveté, conceives it. Really free working, e.g. composing, is at the same time precisely the most damned seriousness, the most intense exertion. The work of material production can achieve this character only (1) when its social character is posited, (2) when it . . . appears in the production process not in a merely natural, spontaneous form, but as an activity regulating all the forces of nature.[32]

Thus work cannot be mere amusement, but need not be a curse either. Properly organized it can become "attractive," a "liberating activity," "the individual's self-realization."

However attractive such work might become, still it belongs to the realm of necessity in the sense that it *must* be done to satisfy the physical needs of the community. Beyond it lies another realm of activity which is not under any compulsion at all. Marx made the distinction eloquently at the end of the third volume of *Capital:*

The realm of freedom actually begins only where labor which is determined by necessity and mundane considerations ceases; thus in the very nature of things it lies beyond the sphere of actual material production. Just as the savage must wrestle with Nature to satisfy his wants, to maintain and reproduce life, so must civilized man, and he must do so in all social formations and under all possible modes of production. With his development this realm of physical necessity expands as a result of his wants; but, at the same time, the forces of production which satisfy these wants also increase. Freedom in this field can only consist in socialized man, the associated producers, rationally regulating their interchange with Nature, bringing it under their common control, instead of being ruled by it as by the blind forces of Nature; and achieving this with the least expenditure of energy and under conditions most favorable to, and worthy of, their human nature. But it nonetheless still remains a realm of necessity. Beyond it begins that development of human energy which is an end in itself, the true realm of freedom, which, however, can blossom forth only with this realm of necessity as its basis. The shortening of the working-day is its basic prerequisite.[33]

The ultimate and freest form of human activity is that which takes place under no compulsion whatsoever. To expand that realm of freedom, not just for a privileged leisure class, but for everyone in equal measure, is the final goal of communism.

This well-known passage ought not to be interpreted, as some have done, to mean that in his maturity Marx returned to the traditional view of necessary work as a curse, that his only solution now was to shorten such drudgery as much as possible so as to allow the worker maximum leisure for the development of his mind. Such a view confines satisfying activity to leisure time and probably assumes the division of labor can be transcended, if at all, only during leisure hours. Clearly this was not Marx's intention. In the first place he did not separate off leisure in a watertight compartment as something totally divorced from productive work. In the *Grundrisse*, which also stressed the need to maximize leisure time, Marx made it clear that such leisure included at least the following: (1) time to be idle (rest, etc.); (2) time for artistic endeavor; and (3) time for scientific pursuits. Most science was done in leisure time during Marx's day, including the social "science" he did himself. A continuing development of scientific knowledge would have obvious return benefits in rationalizing the processes of production. The growth of leisure time in general would produce a more knowledgeable and versatile work force: "Free time — which is both idle time and time for higher activity — has naturally transformed its possessor into a different subject, and he then enters into the direct production process as this different subject."[34] Marx's last commentary on these matters is to be found in the *Critique of the Gotha Program*, written in 1875, a decade after the third volume of *Capital*. Here we find the striking passage which confirms that the radical vision of *The German Ideology* remained consistent in Marx's mind to the end — under communism work will be attractive ("life's prime want"), and the division of labor will be totally overcome:

> In a higher phase of communist society, after the enslaving subordination of the individual to the division of labor, and therewith also the antithesis between mental and physical labor, has vanished; after labor has become not only a means of life but life's prime want; after the productive forces have also increased with the all-round development of the individual, and all the springs of cooperative

wealth flow more abundantly—only then can the narrow horizon of bourgeois right be crossed in its entirety and society inscribe on its banners: From each according to his ability, to each according to his needs![35]

For Marx and Engels, then, communism was never equated simply with nationalization of the means of production. From beginning to end, their writings stress the transcendence of the division of labor as integral to the classless society. It was not some queer, extraneous, or easily discardable part of their system of ideas. It was the division of labor, after all, that first created private property—not vice versa—along with social classes, the state, the antagonism between the sexes, alienated labor, and the separation of town and country. If the dividing of labor was original sin, its *Aufhebung* alone would mark the redemption of mankind. Nationalization of the means of production, in and of itself, overcomes none of the aforementioned evils, but only enhances the power of the state, making it a single giant monopoly corporation. Later generations of Marx's followers, Communists and social democrats alike, increasingly misunderstood, trivialized, or simply forgot this aspect of the masters' teaching, surrounded as they were by a world in which occupational specialization gained ground every day in every sphere, quite regardless whether the local economic system was communist, socialist, or capitalist. The relentless dividing of labor tasks seemed as inevitable as death and taxes. Only quite recently have some radicals begun to reconsider this whole issue seriously.

If we inquire where Marx got the idea of transcending the divison of labor, at one level it appears to be his reinterpretation of the general liberal call for "the free development of the individual personality," especially in its specifically German incarnation as the ideal of *Bildung*—maximum cultivation of the talents of the individual, especially the "higher" faculties and sensibilities, into a well-proportioned whole.[36] Marx reinterpreted this ideal first by reminding the liberals that the free development of the individual personality does not occur on a desert island: "Only within the community has each individual the means of cultivating his gifts in all directions; hence personal freedom becomes possible only within the community." But mainly he democratized the liberal ideal which had always tacitly presupposed the existence of "lower orders" to look after the "lower" needs of each free personality. By transcending the division of labor in society at large, "the genuine and free development of individuals ceases to be a mere phrase."[37] In the renowned words of the *Manifesto*, "the free development of each is the condition for the free development of all."[38] Of course the *Bildung* ideal itself was based on Renaissance models and above all on the Greek ideal of personal well-roundedness, suggesting once again the extent of Marx's underlying debt to the values of classical antiquity.

Marx's other obvious debt in this respect, equally evident in Engels, and which both men acknowledged often enough, was to preceding socialist thinkers — Owen, Proudhon, above all, Fourier. It was the eccentric genius, Fourier, after all, whose supreme message was that work should be attractive, that it must be varied, and that the diverse talents and inclinations of individuals could be fitted together without coercion to meet all the labor needs of the community — a doctrine the young Engels had labeled "unassailable," and "the great axiom of social philosophy."[39] In nineteenth-century Europe the ideal of a well-rounded individual was not merely the aristocratic ideal of the "gentleman amateur," or the product of a university education. Neither Owen, nor Fourier, nor Proudhon had upper-class origins; none had a university education. In broader social terms the latter two especially spoke for a preindustrial handicraft and peasant mode of life in which work *was* more varied and more under the control of the individual. It was precisely this mode of life that was threatened by the processes of modernization, most particularly the relentless advance of the division of labor. It is surely no accident that both Fourier and Proudhon were hostile to large-scale industry per se — in some sense, they gave voice to a profound, if amorphous, lower-middle-class resistance to modernization. Marx and Engels' attitude toward occupational specialization, as we have seen, was by no means one of simple resistance. Just as they democratized the liberal ideal of *Bildung*, so they reinterpreted the craft-agrarian ideal of varied and satisfying labor, control over the production process, and so forth, so as to make it compatible with large-scale undertakings. If their anticipations proved correct, if deprofessionalization actually worked in practice, then mankind could indeed have its cake and eat it too.

Many observers, however, find deprofessionalization the least realistic, the most dewy-eyed of all Marx and Engels' ideas. Eyebrows are almost always raised at the passage in *The German Ideology* which grandly declares: "In communist society, where nobody has one exclusive sphere of activity but each can become accomplished in any branch he wishes, society regulates the general production and thus makes it possible for me to do one thing today and another tomorrow, to hunt in the morning, fish in the afternoon, rear cattle in the evening, criticize after dinner, just as I have a mind, without ever becoming hunter, fisherman, shepherd or critic."[40] The obvious problems are, first, that "society regulates" but nonetheless I can somehow do "just as I have a mind." What about conflicts between the two? And, second, the occupational examples seem drawn from a bucolic wonderland. Moving into the real world, could anyone seriously imagine, even in 1846, rebuilding a power loom in the morning, projecting five-year national production goals in the afternoon, and performing surgery after dinner? Would anyone trust his gall bladder to a surgeon of this stripe?

On the first point, Marx and Engels may well have swallowed too uncritically the Fourierist notion of a natural harmony of inclinations. They never dealt directly with the question who would do the work for which no volunteers might be found — collecting the garbage for instance. It was all too easy to evade such questions by associating them with utopian blueprints and fantastic speculations. On the other hand, Engels formulated the question somewhat better when he spoke of people passing from one task to another "according to the needs of society *or* their own inclinations" (emphasis added), suggesting that the two might not always be identical.[41] Both men recognized, as we have seen, that certain kinds of work belonged to the "realm of necessity" in the sense that they *must* be done. In this sense society as a collectivity of individuals cannot do "just as it has a mind." Even if the bulk of such necessary labor became attractive and rewarding, it seems more than likely there would remain a residue of tasks for which no one would spontaneously volunteer. But Engels also spoke of a "uniform obligation to work," and his dictum that "no individual can throw on the shoulders of others his share in productive labor" might plausibly be extended to include the idea that each individual must accept his equal "share" of the tasks for which no volunteers are found.[42]

The second problem is bound to seem more serious to present-day observers, confronted as we are with an additional century's accumulation of knowledge and technical expertise. Marx and Engels' vision seems to take insufficient account of time economy. Even supposing an ideal organization of society, there are still only so many hours in a day, only so many years in a lifetime. Can any person really develop *all* his talents in every direction to the fullest extent? If it takes many years of *full-time* effort to develop the skills of a brain surgeon, how many such skills can a person develop? Perhaps Marx and Engels would point out that not all the talents and inclinations of an individual are likely to require such effort to develop — even today it is not too hard to imagine a brain surgeon who also enjoys tinkering to keep his sports car in a high state of tune, serving on the local medical board, and occasionally cooking a gourmet dinner for friends. No doubt, if it fell to his lot, he would also be capable of cleaning hospital floors. Within the absolute limits imposed by time, then, the cultivation of at least several skills and talents is not at all inconceivable. What one must presuppose, as Marx and Engels did, is a society prosperous enough so that people would not be constrained as they are now to give over every possible hour to the exercise of their *highest-level* skill — or in present-day society to whichever skill is the best paid. Also, the system of rotation suggested in *The German Ideology* (morning-afternoon-evening) need not be taken as a rigid formula: occupations requiring more intensive concentration might be rotated weekly, seasonally, or even in periods lasting several years. Certainly the two men conceived the process of education to be a lifelong process that would develop fresh talents in later life, just as they themselves undertook to study the language and culture of Russia when in their fifties and educated themselves in anthropology when in their sixties. Indeed, one could scarcely find better examples of what Marx and Engels had in mind than in their own lives. Engels was perfectly capable, for example, of managing a textile mill in the morning (which he did!), commanding an army in battle in the afternoon, and presenting a learned paper on comparative linguistics after dinner. Perhaps the nineteenth century's most impressive autodidact, Engels also "dabbled" in the natural sciences, just as Marx "dabbled" in literature and advanced mathematics. While Marx had demonstrated that he could edit a daily newspaper or help lead a mass workers' organization, his principal talents seem more purely cerebral. But what a cornucopia of cerebral powers, whose published products are still read and held to be worth reading by economists, philosophers, historians, sociologists, political scientists, and anthropologists! Few men if any could so justly claim the maxim Marx chose as his own: "*Nihil humani a me alienum puto.*"[43]

Perhaps Marx and Engels unwittingly overestimated the potentials of ordinary people because of what they found in themselves. They did acknowledge "unequal individual endowment," that "one man is superior to another physically or mentally." (Marx added: "they would not be different individuals if they were not unequal.")[44] It is not ultimately clear, however, whether they acknowledged any *hereditary* basis for such differences. The great stress in their writings is certainly upon environmental factors: just as the "idiocy of rural life" produced the "mental torpor" of the traditional peasantry, so the sons and daughters of those peasants who migrated to become urban proletarians also acquired far greater cultural and political sophistication. As to the potential of such people, Marx included in *Capital* the poignant report of a French worker who had gone to California to seek his fortune: "I never could have believed, that I was capable of working at the various occupations I was employed on in California. I was firmly convinced that I was fit for nothing but letterpress printing. . . . Once in the midst of this world of adventurers, who change their occupation as often as they do their shirt, egad, I did as the others. As mining did not turn out remunerative enough, I left it for the town, where in succession I became typographer, slater, plumber, etc. In consequence of thus finding out that I am fit for any sort of work, I feel less of a mollusk and more of a man." Surely this is what Marx had in mind when he wrote that, by acting on the external world and changing it, man "at the same time changes his own nature. He develops his slumbering powers and compels them to act in obedience to his sway."[45]

The Disappearance of the State

We are now in a position to appreciate the disappearance of the parasite state, as discussed in chapter 5, in its larger context, as one facet of a broader, a universal process of deprofessionalization. But the disappearance of the state as parasite in turn is only one facet of a broader process in which the state was expected to disappear. For, as we have already seen in a limited way, the state disappears for Marx and Engels in two distinct senses corresponding to the two conceptions of the state — it disappears as an alien cadre of professionals and it disappears as organized coercion. To complicate matters further, it will be argued here that where the workers' state is a dictatorship, its *dictatorial* character disappears according to a third timetable. All three facets of disappearance must be understood as separate, semiautonomous processes which need not all reach completion simultaneously.

Let us begin with the facet Marx and Engels apparently thought would have the shortest timetable, the smashing of the parasite state, which the Communards seemed to have accomplished in a matter of weeks. Here, the basic task was to disband the professional army, dismiss the professional bureaucrats, politicians, and judges, and replace them all with ordinary people serving on a part-time or short-term basis. It is just such a deprofessionalization of state functions that constitutes the *Aufhebung* of the division of labor in public life, which is the *Aufhebung* of the state as a self-serving hierarchy of professional administrators divorced from civil society, the reabsorption by the people of its alienated social power. It was Marx rather than Engels who first talked about the state in these terms, and it is extremely interesting to discover that nowhere in Marx's own writings prior to late 1847 can we find any clear call for the rule of the proletariat, or any reference to a postrevolutionary *state* at all! He spoke rather of the "emancipatory" mission of the proletariat and of an *Aufhebung* of the state that would take place immediately. Until late 1847, then, he was still thinking of the state primarily as an alien structure to be dismantled rather than as an instrument of organized coercion to be taken over and used. More importantly for our immediate purposes, he clearly conceived the former as a task that could be accomplished straightaway.

Marx planned during one period in 1844 to write a history of the French revolutionary National Convention of 1792, and it is almost certainly the deprofessionalizing reforms of this body that provided the model in his mind of what needed to be done and how long it might take. The convention came into being after a popular attack on the Tuileries Palace in August 1792 which forced the government of the recently established constitutional monarchy (an oligarchy of wealth) to step aside in favor of a new constituent assembly to be elected this time on the basis of universal manhood suffrage. Held in September, these elections produced the National Convention, which met and immediately abolished the monarchy altogether, assuming itself the responsibility for all executive functions through committees chosen from its own ranks. Meanwhile the Parisian *sans-culottes*, organized in the various sections of the city, had taken over the municipal government as well, dismissing the old bureaucrats and reorganizing the entire administration as a community self-help operation, all with a monumental effervescence of civic-mindedness and popular participation. In the military sphere, a National Guard had already been formed at an earlier stage in the revolution, but it was the convention, mortally threatened by invading armies in August 1793, that inaugurated the famous *levée-en-masse* (universal conscription), a measure which, combined with the opening up of the officer corps to "talent," transformed the old professional standing army into a mass citizen army. The convention did not attack private property, of course, or tamper with the division of labor outside the sphere of government, but it did accomplish a fairly massive deprofessionalization within that sphere, and all in a matter of weeks for the civil side, about a year later for the military side — although there was no inherent reason why the latter could not have been undertaken in 1792 as well. Most of these changes, it must be added, did not prove very lasting.[46]

All this must have produced a model in Marx's mind when in 1843 he spoke of the *Aufhebung* of the state for the first time in his Kreuznach *Critique*, linking it to the attainment, almost certainly through revolutionary action, of universal suffrage, and by implication the election of a new National Convention:

> It is therefore self-evident that *elections* are the chief political interest of actual civil society. Civil society has *really* raised itself to abstraction from itself, to *political* being as its true, general, essential mode of being only in *elections unlimited* both in respect of the franchise and the right to be elected. But the completion of the abstraction is at the same time the transcendence [*Aufhebung*] of the abstraction. In actually positing its *political existence* as its *true* existence, civil society has simultaneously posited its civil existence, in distinction from its political existence, as *inessential;* and the fall of one side of the division carries with it the fall of the other side, its opposite. *Electoral reform* within the *abstract political state* is therefore the demand for its *dissolution*, but also for the *dissolution of civil society.*[47]

Note that the political state will be dissolved, not used temporarily. Within the context of Marx's initial communist thought, the achievement of what he then called "true democracy" required an end to the egoism of civil society (abolition of private property) and the egoism of the state (deprofessionalization and democratization) such that civil society and the state would be transcended in a higher unity. The two tasks appear as simultaneous rather than sequential, and it is noteworthy that even after his stay in Paris, when outlining the chapter titles for his never finished book on the modern state, Marx concluded with a chapter called "Suffrage: the Struggle for the *Aufhebung* of the State and Civil Society"— still no allusion to a proletarian state or proletarian rule.[48]

To be sure, the proletariat does make its first appearance in the Paris period—not as ruler, however, but as emancipator. In the Paris "Critique" of 1844, Marx wrote: "The role of *emancipator* therefore passes in dramatic motion to the various classes of the French nation one after the other until it finally comes to the class which implements social freedom," a class "which cannot emancipate itself without emancipating itself from all other spheres of society and thereby emancipating all other spheres of society."[49] There was no mention in this essay of any post-revolutionary state at all. Even more pointedly Marx wrote in another 1844 essay, "Critical Marginal Notes on the Article 'The King of Prussia and Social Reform'": "*Revolution* in general—the *overthrow* of the existing power and *dissolution* of the old relationships—is a *political act.* But *socialism* cannot be realized without *revolution.* It needs this *political* act insofar as it needs *destruction* and *dissolution.* But where its *organizing activity* begins, where its *proper object,* its *soul,* comes to the fore—there socialism throws off the *political* cloak."[50] What is political about the proletarian revolution is the overthrow and dissolution of the old state; its constructive activity requires no state at all.

In *The German Ideology,* as we have seen, Marx and Engels merged their two theories of the state, but the only reference to its ultimate disappearance is almost surely a reference to the parasite state: "Previous revolutions within the framework of division of labor were bound to lead to new political institutions; . . . the communist revolution, which transcends the division of labor, gets rid of political institutions at last."[51] Getting rid of the state here still means deprofessionalization and is linked to the general *Aufhebung* of the division of labor which previous revolutions (i.e., the French) did not carry out. Revolutions which do not overcome the general division of labor, Marx and Engels wanted to insist, are bound to wind up with a new state run by professionals, regardless of the intentions of the revolutionaries.

As late as *The Poverty of Philosophy* in 1847, Marx summarized the development of the class struggle up to the anticipated revolutionary climax and then asked: "Does this mean that after the fall of the old society there will be a new class domination culminating in a new political power (*pouvoir politique*)?" The "correct" answer, Engels' answer, would have been: "Yes, but only temporarily, etc., etc." Marx responded with an unambiguous and unadorned "No." He went on to add that the working class "will substitute for the old civil society an association which will exclude classes and their antagonisms, and there will be no more political power properly so-called, since political power is precisely the official expression (*résumé officiel*) of antagonism in civil society."[52] Here was Marx's last allusion to his own original theory of the state as the product (*résumé officiel*) of the general egoism of civil society, rather than the specific instrument of its dominant class. And that state, the state conceived as parasite, was still to be dismantled straightaway. By the end of 1847 Engels' views on the state assumed the dominant position in Marx's thinking and he began for the first time in his own writings to use the phrase "rule of the working class."[53] The *Communist Manifesto* employed the same concept, of course, and defined political power — in neat contrast to the definition just quoted — as "the organized power of one class for oppressing another."[54] Prior to the final triumph of Engels' thinking, however, it is clear that Marx conceived the disappearance of the state as an immediate *Aufhebung* involving deprofessionalization, rather than as a "withering away" that would take place only later on, after the proletariat no longer required organized coercive force against the bourgeoisie. The two kinds of disappearance are not incompatible, of course, but one should at least be clear that they are distinct and separate processes, and that the first takes place immediately.

We have seen previously how the idea of the parasite state appeared anew in Marx's thinking after Louis Bonaparte carried out his Eighteenth Brumaire and constructed a parasite state *par excellence*, and also how the dismantling of such a state no longer seemed just a theory after the Communards came to power in March 1871. There is no need to repeat here everything that was said in the first section of chapter 5, only to underscore that "smashing" the state meant deprofessionalization, and that it was accomplished in a matter of weeks, just as in the earlier model of 1792. The Communards did not do away with organized coercion (what else was the National Guard?), but they did get rid of the *professional* army, professional bureaucrats, professional judges, and so forth, showing that it was the state as parasite, the state run by professionals, that Marx had in mind when he wrote: "It was a Revolution against the *State* itself, of this supernaturalist abortion of society, a resumption by the people for the people of its own social life." One recognizes again the Marx of the early years when he defined their accomplishment as "the reabsorption of the State power by society as its own living forces instead of as forces controlling and subduing it."[55]

If in Marx's writings of the 1848 period Engels' class state temporarily eclipsed his own original view, so in revenge Marx's parasite state was ascendent in Engels' writing on the Paris Commune. Surely it was unique for Engels to write that the Commune, in spite of its 300,000 National Guardsmen, "was no longer a state in the proper sense of the word." But now he was thinking of the state as an alien cadre of professionals, not in his more habitual manner as organized coercive force, and the same conception underlies his famous 1891 remark that the state is "at best an evil inherited by the proletariat after its victorious struggle for class supremacy, whose worst sides the victorious proletariat, just like the Commune, cannot avoid having to lop off at once *(sofort möglichst zu beschneiden)*." He also referred to the same process as the "shattering *(Sprengung)* of the former state power."[56] For neither Marx nor Engels, then, does the state as parasite "wither away" slowly in some extended process; it is *aufgehoben*, dissolved, thrown off, *beseitigt*, smashed, reabsorbed, lopped off at once, shattered—the verbs tell the whole story.

By contrast the state as an instrument of class coercion, as a special repressive force, lingers on for a time. That a state could both be smashed and yet still linger on—as Marx said in effect of the Paris Commune, and Engels too, almost within a single sentence—most convincingly reveals the existence of two distinct conceptions of the state at some level in their minds. But since a repressive force can be deprofessionalized without being disbanded, there is no inherent logical inconsistency. As we saw in chapter 5, "the first decree of the Commune . . . was the supression of the standing army, and the substitution for it of the armed people." The bearing of arms ceased to be a full-time profession for a special body of men (parasitism) and became a part-time activity for virtually the entire male population. But since the National Guard manifestly remained an instrument of coercion, a special repressive force, it was still a state in Engels' original conception of the word.[57]

In contrast to Marx, it will be remembered, the young Engels believed the essence of the state to lie in force and coercion; as a special repressive force it passed from hand to hand down through the social classes, changing its form along the way but not its essential character. The Chartists' demand for democracy was really a demand for the rule of the proletariat. But democracy as a form of *state* is still a coercive institution— "the force of the majority oppresses the weakness of the minority"—and in the longer run "democracy, as well as every other form of government, must ultimately break to pieces." In the end, "what we want is anarchy."[58] The classless society was for the young Engels primordially a society without coercion, just as for the young Marx it was primordially one without alienation.

How long would the coercive workers' state linger on before it disappeared? Neither Marx nor Engels ever specified any measure of time, although obviously, from what has already been said, they expected it to exist longer than the parasite state. Thus the two men praised the Communards precisely because they did *not* lay down their arms after the first uprising—the National Guard survived the dismantling of the parasite state. If not a measure of time, what Marx and Engels did specify was a condition, or set of conditions, that would have to be met before the class state could disappear. Sometimes the condition appears as an economic one: "Do away with capital, the appropriation of the whole means of production in the hands of the few, and the state will fall away of itself."[59] Sometimes it was social: "[Social classes] will fall as inevitably as they once arose. The state inevitably falls with them."[60] Sometimes it was directly political: "The state is only a transitional institution which is used in the struggle, in the revolution, in order to hold down one's adversaries by force, . . . [after which] the state as such ceases to exist."[61] Most frequently, however, two, or all three, of these conditions appear together, as in the familiar lines of the *Manifesto:*

> When, in the course of development, class distinctions have disappeared, and all production has been concentrated in the hands of a vast association of the whole nation, the public power will lose its political character. Political power, properly so called, is merely the organized power of one class for oppressing another. If the proletariat during its contest with the bourgeoisie is compelled, by the force of circumstances, to organize itself as a class, if, by means of a revolution, it makes itself the ruling class, and, as such, sweeps away by force the old conditions of production, then it will, along with these conditions, have swept away the conditions for the existence of class antagonisms and of classes generally, and will thereby have abolished its own supremacy as a class (*hebt . . . seine eigene Herrschaft als Klasse auf*).[62]

The proletariat must become the ruling class in order forcibly to sweep away the "old conditions of production" and, as we saw in the last chapter, in order to put down any violent resistance that might develop during this process. In an 1871 letter Engels elaborated on the first of these coercive steps:

> We must liberate ourselves from the landowners and capitalists, putting in their place the associated classes of rural and industrial workers, and taking possession of all the means of production — land, tools, machines, raw materials, and enough goods to sustain life during the time necessary for production. Therewith inequality must fall away. In order to carry this through to an end, we need the political supremacy of the proletariat.[63]

On the second point — suppressing violent resistance — Marx put the argument most clearly as he responded to Bakunin's question why the state should continue to exist:

As long as other classes, and the capitalist class in particular, still exist, and as long as the proletariat fights against them (for its enemies and the old organization of society do not vanish as a result of its coming to power) it must employ *coercive* measures, that is, governmental measures; so long it is still a class itself, and the economic conditions which give rise to the class struggle and the existence of classes have not yet disappeared and must be forcibly removed, or transformed in a process accelerated by force.

He added a bit later: "With its complete victory, therefore, its rule also comes to an end."[64]

If governmental measures are coercive measures by definition, if "political" and "state" are equated with rule based ultimately on force, then in this exact sense the proletariat requires the state only for its coercive measures — expropriating the means of production and "crushing" any violent resistance to this expropriation that may develop. This is the sense of Marx and Engels' carefully formulated statement of 1850: "The abolition of the state has meaning with the Communists, only as the necessary consequence of the abolition of classes, with which the need for the organized might of one class to keep the others down automatically disappears."[65] In this same sense, to draw the obvious conclusion, the proletarian state has no reason for existence after the last capitalist property has been expropriated and the last capitalist resistance has melted away. The *positive* tasks of socialist construction emanate from the masses themselves; they are not imposed upon the masses by governmental, that is, coercive, measures.

Marx and Engels never specified any *international* conditions for the disappearance of the state; they never seriously addressed the question whether a workers' state might need to maintain organized force against an *external* threat. This of course has been the principal argument used by the Soviet state to justify its own continued existence for more than six decades after the revolution. The two men generally assumed that the advanced countries would achieve socialism at more or less the same time, that they would pose no threat to each other, and that they would form a block of nations economically too powerful to be menaced by less developed nonsocialist countries. On two occasions Engels touched on the issue in passing and justified defensive war, should the need arise. The first — very early — allusion appears in one of his Elberfeld speeches of 1845, when he dealt with the question of standing armies under communism. There would be no need for any, he stated simply, either to put down internal unrest or to fight a war of aggression. For a war of defense, on the other hand, a militia would meet the need perfectly well: "It will be easy to train every fit member of society, in addition to his other occupations, in real, not barrack-square handling of arms to the degree necessary for the defense of the country." Here, then, the state might be needed (in the limited form of the workers' militia) to fight a defensive war, but it could only be fought, Engels added, against "*anti-communist nations,*" since no communist nation would attack another.[66] His other allusion, in an 1882 letter to Kautsky, formally took the same position, as he speculated about the fate of European colonies after the revolution:

> In my opinion the colonies proper, *i.e.,* the countries occupied by a European population, Canada, the Cape, Australia, will all become independent; on the other hand the countries inhabited by a native population, which are simply subjugated, India, Algiers, the Dutch, Portuguese and Spanish possessions, must be taken over for the time being by the proletariat and led as rapidly as possible towards independence. How this process will develop is difficult to say. India will perhaps, indeed very probably, produce a revolution, and as the proletariat emancipating itself cannot conduct any colonial wars, this would have to be given full scope. . . . We shall have enough to do at home. Once Europe is reorganized, and North America, that will furnish such colossal power and such an example that the semi-civilized countries will follow in their wake of their own accord. Economic needs alone will be responsible for this. . . . One thing alone is certain: the victorious proletariat can force no blessings of any kind upon any foreign nation without undermining its own victory by so doing. Which of course by no means excludes defensive wars of various kinds.[67]

Thus Engels categorically excluded the idea of spreading socialism by the sword. While he again acknowledged the possibility of defensive wars, the obvious question arises — against whom? With Europe and North America reorganized as socialist societies, what backward country would dare attack this "colossal power"? For all his interest in military questions, Engels never dealt seriously with the external military needs of socialist societies — and for the obvious reason that in his mind it was not a serious problem. He never imagined that less developed *socialist* countries would be menaced by more advanced *capitalist* countries. As we will see in chapter 9, it was inconceivable to him that backward countries could achieve socialism before its achievement in the West, and without substantial help *from* the West.

Thus, in general, while the proletarian class state was to linger on after the parasite state had been smashed, while Marx and Engels never specified an exact measure of time, it is abundantly clear that they were thinking in terms of years rather than decades or generations. There are only three passages that suggest anything *other* than a rapid process — all of them written by Engels, late in his life, and with a special meaning. The first is the most famous and merits the closest attention. In *Anti-Dühring* Engels sketched the broad development of mankind up to the point where *"the proletariat seizes political power and turns the means of production in the first instance into state property."* Then he added immediately: "But, in doing this, it abolishes itself as proletariat, abolishes all class distinctions and class antagonisms, abolishes (*hebt auf*) also the state as state" — seemingly a quick sequence. He then went on to characterize the state predictably enough as the coercive instrument of successive ruling classes, and continued:

> When at last it becomes the real representative of the whole of society, it renders itself unnecessary. As soon as there is no longer any social class to be held in subjection; as soon as class rule, and the individual struggle for existence based upon our present anarchy in production, with the collisions and excesses arising from these, are removed, nothing more remains to be repressed, and a special repressive force, a state, is no longer necessary. The first act by virtue of which the state really constitutes itself the representative of the whole of society — the taking possession of the means of production in the name of society — this is, at the same time, its last independent act as a state.

Now the first act and the last act are even simultaneous! But immediately thereafter Engels added the well-known lines:

> State interference in social relations becomes, in one domain after another, superfluous, and then dies out of itself (*schläft dann von selbst ein*); the government of persons is replaced by the administration of things, and by the conduct of the processes of production. The state is not "abolished." *Er stirbt ab* (it dies out; it withers away).[68]

If expropriation, the first act of the proletarian state, is also "its last independent act as a state," what are these other "interferences" which die out more slowly?

Obviously they should not have to do with the noncoercive "administration of things," or the "processes of production"; logically they ought to refer to coercive measures which are not directly related to the class struggle. While Marx and Engels often exaggerated for effect in describing the coercive state as "merely" an instrument of class oppression, whenever they — especially Engels — formulated the matter more carefully, we find qualifiers like "the *main* object," or in the very passage under scrutiny, "had need of the state . . . *especially* for the purpose" (emphasis added).[69] Earlier in *Anti-Dühring*, as we observed in chapter 1, Engels described the origin of the state in terms of "certain common interests the safeguarding of which had to be handed over to individuals"; among his examples were "adjudication of disputes" and "repression of trespasses on the part of individuals who went beyond their rights." He concluded that such "delegations of office . . . are naturally endowed with a certain measure of authority and are the beginnings of state power."[70] If state power began, in Engels' conception, with such coercive measures against individuals, even before classes arose, it is entirely plausible to conceive it fading away in the same fashion, after the class struggle is essentially settled but before each and every individual may have internalized social rules to the extent that no institutionalized coercion whatsoever would be required.

The other two passages support this interpretation: in 1891 Engels referred to the state as "at best an evil inherited by the proletariat after its victorious struggle for class supremacy, whose worst sides the victorious proletariat, just like the Commune, cannot avoid having to lop off at once as much as possible until such time as a generation reared in new, free social conditions is able to throw the entire lumber of the state on the scrap heap."[71] This is the only passage to speak of an entire generation, but Engels seems again to be thinking of occasional individual infractions that would not require any elaborate institutions of repression. At all events he makes no reference to any external need. The remaining statement, written in 1883, is brief and adds nothing; it simply alludes to "the gradual dissolution and ultimate disappearance of that political organization called *the State*."[72] Since Engels regarded the workers' militia as the only coercive force required to handle the main brunt of violent capitalist resistance, and praised the Communards for "lopping off" the other repressive appendages of the old state, one can imagine how trivial an amount of coercion he had in mind for this later period when even the militia would be in a process of "gradual dissolution."

A final note should be added concerning the famous phrase "withering away," which suggests a long process and which the English-speaking world universally associates with Marx and Engels' ideas. The phrase derives from Engels' above quoted sentence in *Anti-Dühring, "er stirbt ab,"* which was translated for the first English edition of *Socialism, Utopian and Scientific* in 1892 as "it withers away." While *"absterben"* in a figurative sense can mean "atrophy," "wither," or "fade away," its primary and literal meaning is "die out," and it is so translated in almost all subsequent editions of the same work.[73] Since "withers away" is a dubious translation, since even *"er stirbt ab"* was used only once (never by Marx), one ought really to pay more attention to the other verbs used by the two men in conjunction with the disappearance of the class state. If not so dramatic as "smashed" and "shattered," nonetheless they suggest a fairly rapid process: breaks to pieces, falls away of itself, ceases to exist, is *aufgehoben*, comes to an end; also: disappears, dissolves, falls asleep, and is surmounted.[74] Taken together the verbs again tell the whole story.

There remains to consider whether the rule of the proletariat was conceived as coextensive with the dictatorship of the proletariat, whether Marx and Engels would call all proletarian rule dictatorial. The Leninist tradition has imbued almost everyone — not merely its followers — with certain standard assumptions about the masters' labels and expectations. Thus Lenin presumed that Marx and Engels regarded all class government as inherently dictatorial; he also declared that proletarian rule, ergo dictatorship, lasts until the achievement of "full" communism, which is to say, throughout the long initial period of "socialism."[75] The distinction between a lower phase of "socialism" and a higher phase of "communism" is based on Marx's *Critique of the Gotha Program*, but even the most cursory inspection of this document will show that it does not say at all what Lenin wanted it to say. In the economic section of the *Critique*, Marx rather distinguished between two phases *within* communist society, according to the standard by which individuals would derive their income:

> What we have to deal with here is a communist society, not as it has *developed* on its own foundations, but, on the contrary, just as it *emerges* from capitalist society; which is thus in every respect, economically, morally and intellectually, still stamped with the birthmarks of the old society from whose womb it emerges. Accordingly, the individual producer receives back from society — after the deductions [for reinvestment, insurance, services, etc.] have been made — exactly what he gives to it.

Marx went on to explain that, under this standard, one worker might still receive more than another, and that further inequities would remain because the standard makes no allowance for the worker with a large family, and so forth. Then he continued:

> But these defects are inevitable in the first phase of communist so-
> ciety as it is when it has just emerged after prolonged birthpangs
> from capitalist society. Right can never be higher than the eco-
> nomic structure of society and its cultural development conditioned
> thereby.
>   In a higher phase of communist society, . . . society [can] inscribe
> on its banners: From each according to his ability, to each accord-
> ing to his needs![76]

In three separate uses here, Marx consistently referred to different phases of *communist* society, and nowhere used the word "socialist."

The issue becomes more than a quibble over labels if we now turn to the political section of the *Critique*, a few pages later, where Marx made his most famous reference to the dictatorship of the proletariat:

> *Between* capitalist and communist society [emphasis added] lies a
> period of the revolutionary transformation of the one into the other.
> There corresponds to this also a political transition period in which
> the state can be nothing but *the revolutionary dictatorship of the
> proletariat.*[77]

Thus, in the writing that most carefully and thoughtfully distinguishes future stages of development, Marx said very plainly that the dictatorship of the proletariat lies *between* capitalist and communist society generally; he did not say it lasts until the end of its lower phase. Lenin's motives in restricting the label "communist" to the higher phase are painfully transparent; what is harder to understand is the uncritical acceptance of this obfuscation by virtually everyone else.

If the dictatorship of the proletariat was not to last until the higher phase of communism, how long was it to last? Is it possible that it might end before the coercive institutions of the workers' state had been thrown entirely on a scrap heap of history, perhaps even before capitalist resistance had completely faded away? The existing evidence indeed points this way, although it is not conclusive enough for a categorical answer. We have seen in volume 1 how Marx and Engels employed the phrase "dictatorship of the proletariat" very infrequently and principally to make certain factional distinctions in their minor polemical writings.[78] It was surely *not* the essence of their teaching. They did seem to have a fairly clear idea of what they meant by dictatorship, proletarian or otherwise, when they spoke of something apart from individual dictators. They meant extralegal government, government outside or beyond the framework of normal law — thus most obviously revolutionary government and government under martial law. Lenin to the contrary, they did not regard all government as inherently dictatorial: they never referred to ancient or feudal governments in these terms, or even to the bourgeois governments of Britain and the United States. In fact they used the word most frequently to describe the post-June government of the Second French Republic that had labeled *itself* a "dictatorship," that is, a government of martial law, a government which — as Marx put it — declared the workers "*hors la loi.*"[79] Even the phrase "dictatorship of capital" follows the same logic, alluding to the private, *unrestricted* command power of the capitalist within the factory gates. Marx's early legal training, after all, could not but have left some trace.

By logical extrapolation, the dictatorship of the proletariat would refer to the unavoidably extralegal rule of the proletariat after the overthrow of capitalist legality but before the establishment of any new legality, a new constitution drawn up and put into effect by the workers' representatives. Except for one ambiguous reference, Marx and Engels never spoke of such a constitution.[80] And yet, while it is conceivable that in the distant future they imagined mankind could do without written law, surely the emergent workers' state would have to set down, as soon as it could, some general rules of government that could be called a constitution, a new legality. But then, by Marx and Engels' own consistent use of the term, the *dictatorship* of the proletariat would cease when that new constitution went into effect, even though its *rule* might extend somewhat longer. Coercion, the use or threat of force, they held to be the essence of all government, yet they acknowledged the elementary distinction between a government of law (*Rechtsstaat*), where coercion may be used only within legally prescribed limits, and a government not so restricted. Revolutionary dictatorships and governments of martial law belong in the second category. Where else but in the first category could one place a workers' government after the adoption of a new legality (and after any periods of martial law under it)? Insofar as force or the threat of force would still be the ultimate sanction, albeit now within the law, we would still be dealing with a state, with the *rule* of the proletariat, but no longer with its *dictatorship*. Only when institutionalized coercion, even within the law, disappeared could one logically speak of the *Aufhebung* of the state as such.

Other considerations add plausibility to this interpretation. Our discussion so far has rested on the assumptions of Strategy I, the classic model of the majority proletarian revolution against a bourgeois oligarchy that formed the standard or ideal type in Marx and Engels' minds. But Strategy I was not the only path to communism. We will see in chapter 10 that both Marx and Engels allowed for the possibility of a completely peaceful and legal transition to the new society. They never referred to such a legally elected proletarian government as a dictatorship, nor would it have made any sense by their own understanding of the word, even though such a government manifestly would be the *rule* of the proletariat, even though it might well have to use coercive means, under law, against some individual capitalist lawbreakers, or any other lawbreakers for that matter. Only if it were obliged to resort to martial law to quell a violent capitalist insurrection could one logically speak of dictatorship.

The peaceful path was not the only exception to the classical model of proletarian revolution. In volume 1 we saw how the conditions of less advanced countries like France and Germany called forth Strategy II, revolution against bourgeois oligarchy by an alliance of the majority classes—workers, petty bourgeois, peasants—to establish a democratic republic; no *inevitable* violence was foreseen thereafter. Where is the dictatorship of the proletariat in such a scenario? One might say, as Marx seemed to say in *Class Struggles in France*, that the provisional government of the allied classes is in effect the dictatorship of the proletariat, since the workers were expected to play the leading role. Thus Marx said of the French peasant in 1849: "*The social-democratic, the Red* republic, is the dictatorship of his allies"—that is, of the workers and petty bourgeois.[81] Is this how Marx would have regarded a communal revolution that had spread throughout France in 1871? Although such a national government might be called dictatorial while it was still provisional, would Marx really have applied the label throughout the subsequent period when it "affords the rational medium in which the class struggle can run through its different phases in the most rational and humane way"? At most he might have applied it to those moments when "sporadic slaveholders insurrections . . . [put] the sword into the hands of the Social Revolution"—that is, martial law—but these insurrections would only be distractions "for the moment interrupting the work of peaceful progress."[82] We will also see in chapter 10 how the aging Engels anticipated a popular revolution in Germany that would establish a democratic republic in which the petty bourgeoisie would rule first, but in which the Social Democrats would soon win majority support and take over the government.[83] At which point, then, would dictatorship of the proletariat be established? The provisional government would not be in the hands of the workers; and the eventual workers' government would not be extralegal. What all this really shows is that Marx and Engels envisaged a mass revolution to *establish* democratic institutions, preferably in the radically deprofessionalized form suggested by the Paris Commune, but once established in any event, there was no further need for violence unless provoked by the other side, and no further need for dictatorship unless to deal with such insurrections through martial law. Dictatorship was not an inherent part of workers' rule—perhaps this is one reason they used the term so infrequently.

To sum up, then, Marx and Engels expected the state as parasite to disappear immediately through deprofessionalization, the state as dictatorship, if required initially, to disappear by definition with the establishment of a new legality, and the state as coercive power to disappear substantially with the end of expropriations and bourgeois resistance, but only completely and absolutely after a new generation had so internalized the rules of social intercourse that no external coercion whatsoever would be required. If the first transcendence would be marked by the formation of the workers' militia to replace the standing army, the last would be marked when no one remembered any longer the procedure for mobilizing that militia.

What Remains

Assuming the state has really disappeared in all these senses, what if anything would be left? Marx himself posed this question in the familiar lines of the Gotha *Critique* but then—unfortunately for us—declined to answer it: "The question then arises: what transformation will the polity (*Staatswesen*) undergo in communist society? In other words, what social functions will remain in existence there that are analogous to present functions of the state? This question can only be answered scientifically, and one does not get a flea-hop nearer to the problem by a thousandfold combination of the word people with the word state."[84] Certainly Marx never imagined human beings could live together like herds of animals without any conscious organization at all. In a communist polity there would remain, as these Gotha questions made clear, social functions "analogous" to those of a present-day state. In *The Civil War in France*, Marx similarly distinguished between the "legitimate functions" and the "merely repressive organs of the old governmental power."[85] And in the *Manifesto* Marx and Engels expressed the same thought by saying "the public power will lose its political character."[86] Note the "public power" itself would not disappear, but only lose its "political," that is, coercive, character. Just as primitive people organized themselves in a polity before the emergence of classes, before their social organization could be called a state, so communist society would retain a "public power" performing "legitimate functions" that would be "analogous" in some respects to those of the state. But it should not be called a state because it would lack the two crucial qualities Marx and Engels attributed to all states properly so called: it would not be manned by professionals, a "trained caste," set apart from the community at large; and it would not possess instruments of coercion (police, prisons, armed forces, etc.) or have any need of them.

In order to discriminate between the coercive power to command others against their will and the "legitimate functions" of a communist public power, Marx and Engels generally fell back on a Saint-Simonian formula which spoke of the "future conversion of political rule over men into an administration of things and a direction of processes of production."[87] In communist society, presumably one does not command men, one administers things. This is why the word "administration" was preferred to "state." And yet, as any number of critics have pointed out, it is impossible to conceive of a public power having the authority to direct the processes of production and administer things which does not thereby have the authority to command men.[88] What is more, Engels acknowledged as much in his essay "On Authority." The anarchists imagine, he wrote, that one can get rid of authority as such, that is, "the imposition of the will of another upon ours." But all "combined action" requires organization and all organization requires some kind of an authority to which "the will of the single individual will always have to subordinate itself." He offered several examples of such unavoidable authority, of which the most extreme was on board a ship in danger of sinking where "the lives of all depend on the instantaneous and absolute obedience of all to the will of one."[89] Pointing to this essay, many critics — liberals as well as anarchists — have accused Marx and Engels of being authoritarians after all, of abolishing the state merely through semantic tricks and not in real life, and thus deceiving us and perhaps themselves as well about its continued existence under communism.

But this would not be fair. While all authority involves the power to command, in some degree, the will of others, not all authority includes *coercive* power, the power to command others *against their will* by the use or threat of force. The elected president of a local bowling club and the commander of conscript soldiers both possess some measure of authority, but the former has no military police, court-martial, stockade, or firing squad to compel the obedience of his flock. He relies instead on their voluntary acceptance of the principles associated with majority rule, the delegation of offices, and so forth. The authority of officials in a state, Marx and Engels wanted to argue, is akin to that of the military commander, and so is that of the capitalist within his factory, although here the threat of starvation replaces the threat of confinement or physical punishment. The authority of leaders in communist society would be akin to that of the president of a voluntary association whose members willingly subordinate themselves to their own collective decisions, their own elected leaders. Authority is still involved, and Engels is rather to be commended for *not* playing with words, or not pretending that everyone can enjoy the absolute autonomy of a hermit while living within society, even communist society.

Do not liberal critics who cite Engels' essay as proof of his authoritarianism find themselves obliged to take the same stand, using all the same arguments, when they themselves address the anarchist position? Can they differentiate their stand by arguing that, as opposed to Engels, they want such public authority to be confined to the narrowest possible bounds and exercised only by duly elected officials? But Engels says the same thing! On the issue of restriction for example: "If the autonomists confined themselves to saying that the social organization of the future would restrict authority solely to the limits within which the conditions of production render it inevitable, we could understand each other; but they are blind to all facts that make the thing necessary and they passionately fight the word." On the issue of election, all of Engels' examples presuppose a democratic process of decision-making. In a cotton factory, for example, he pointed out that all the machinery powered by the same steam engine must be worked during the same hours. Thus:

> The workers must, therefore, first come to an understanding on the hours of work; and these hours, once they are fixed, must be observed by all, without any exception. Thereafter particular questions arise in each room and at every moment concerning the mode of production, distribution of materials, etc., which must be settled

at once on pain of seeing all production immediately stopped; whether they are settled by decision of a delegate placed at the head of each branch of labor or, if possible, by a majority vote, the will of the single individual will always have to subordinate itself.

Thus majority vote where time permits; decision by a delegate where it does not. That such delegates were to be democratically elected is evident from Engels' next example, a railway, where the need to prevent accidents requires primordially "a dominant will that settles all subordinate questions, whether this will is represented by a single delegate or a committee charged with the execution of the resolutions of the majority of persons interested." For the anarchists, as Engels observed in a contemporaneous letter, "the authority of the majority over the minority also ceases. Every individual and every community is autonomous; but as to how a society of even only two people is possible unless each gives up some of his autonomy, Bakunin again maintains silence."[90] Thus the reputation of "On Authority" is quite undeserved. Engels envisaged a radical extension of democratic principles into the work place which few liberals think possible, and a totally noncoercive organization of public life such as no liberal philosophy countenances. Liberals may label the essay unrealistic and utopian, but only the strictest anarchists have the right to call it authoritarian.

Marx's views on these matters appear to be identical to those of his partner. We have already noticed how he likened all cooperative labor to an orchestra, which cannot do without a conductor. But necessary managerial functions need not be organized as despotic power, and Marx repeatedly pointed to workers' cooperative factories as an alternative model in which the members organize their own work discipline, choose their own manager, hold him accountable, and so forth. While Marx never believed in producers' cooperatives as a *strategy* for supplanting capitalism, he praised them lavishly as *organizational models*. In his *Inaugural Address* to the IWA (1864) he asserted that "they have shown that production on a large scale, and in accord with the behests of modern science, may be carried on without the existence of a class of masters employing a class of hands."[91] Two years later he formulated the resolution on the subject that was accepted by the Geneva Congress of the IWA, declaring the producers' cooperative movement to be an attack on the very "groundwork" of the capitalist system because it substituted "republican" principles of organization within the factory for the despotism of the capitalist. "Its great merit is to practically show that the present pauperizing and despotic system of the subordination of labor to capital can be superseded by the republican and beneficent system of the association of free and equal producers."[92] In the third volume of *Capital*, where he could have had no need to please IWA cooperative enthusiasts, Marx still asserted that producers' cooperatives "represent within the old form [of society] the first sprouts of the new": "Co-operative factories furnish proof that the capitalist has become no less redundant as a functionary in production as he himself, looking down from his high perch, finds the big landowner redundant. . . . In a co-operative factory the antagonistic nature of the labor of supervision disappears, because the manager is paid by the laborers instead of representing capital counterposed to them."[93] Such a manager, chosen and paid by the workers themselves, exercises a quite different sort of authority than that of the capitalist despot.

In *The Civil War in France*, where Marx spoke of the "legitimate functions" of public power, he praised the Communards for having "restored" them "to the responsible agents of society": "Universal suffrage was to serve the people, constituted in Communes, as individual suffrage serves every other employer in the search for workmen and managers in his business. And it is well known that companies, like individuals, in matters of real business generally know how to put the right man in the right place, and, if they for once make a mistake, to redress it promptly. On the other hand, nothing could be more foreign to the spirit of the Commune than to supersede universal suffrage by hierarchic investiture."[94] Leadership functions, then, whether in a factory or for society at large, were to be performed by "public servants," in the real sense of the word, chosen by the public to perform necessary tasks, but held accountable by them as well, and dismissed by them whenever necessary.

Perhaps the most candid thoughts of all on the organization of the classless society come from Marx's 1874 conspectus on Bakunin's *Statism and Anarchy*, which was quoted at length in volume 1. Bakunin had expressed doubt whether the "Marxists" would allow mass participation in future decision-making:

BAKUNIN: There are about forty million Germans. Will all forty million be members of the government?

MARX: Certainly, for the thing begins with the self-government of the communities.

BAKUNIN: The whole people will govern and there will be no one to be governed.

MARX: When a man rules himself, then, according to this principle, he does not rule himself, for he is only himself and nobody else.

BAKUNIN: It means that there will be no government, no State, but if there is a State in existence there will be people who are governed, and there will be slaves.

MARX: That is simply to say, when class rule has disappeared a state in the now accepted political sense of the word no longer exists.[95]

Thus the state as a "political" institution, that is, a coercive institution, would disappear, but the people would still require arrangements through which to *rule themselves*, as a man rules himself, without any external coercion being involved. Such arrangements would rest on a foundation of self-governing communities.

Above the local level there opened up the real gap between Bakunin's thought and Marx's, for the former was not prepared to allow any elections for delegation of authority, arguing that all such deputies are corrupted by their office and become tyrants over the people. But not all elections are "political," Marx insisted; they do not always have to do with *coercive* institutions:

Elections are a political form which exists in the smallest Russian commune and artel. The nature of the elections is determined not by the name, but by the economic basis, the economic interrelations of the voters, and from the moment when the functions have ceased to be political ones (1) governmental functions no longer exist; (2) the distribution of general functions becomes a routine matter and does not entail any domination; (3) elections completely lose their present political character.

A Russian village commune or an artel provide examples of a delegation of authority through elections where no coercive power is involved, where leadership does not entail domination. To renounce all such delegation of authority would be to require continuous decision-making by the whole collectivity:

BAKUNIN: Will the proletariat as a whole be at the head of the government?

MARX: In a trade union, for instance, does the whole union constitute the executive committee? Will all division of labor in a factory disappear and also the various functions arising from it? And
in Bakunin's construction "from the bottom up," will everybody be
up at the top? Then there would be no "bottom."

Notice that Marx did not object to such a division of labor; here as elsewhere the division of labor was to be transcended, not undone. If the
people working in a cooperative factory select one of their own number
to serve a term as manager, they have not thereby submitted to an alien
domination. "If Herr Bakunin understood at least the position of a manager in a workers' co-operative factory, all his illusions about domination
would go to the devil." But would not such workers-turned-leaders acquire domineering ways and really cease to be workers? "No more than
does a manufacturer today cease to be a capitalist upon becoming a city
councilman."[96]

Thus Marx and Engels, despite their own strictures against detailed
blueprints of the future, set down enough of their personal speculations —
or desires — to reveal broadly how public power would be organized in
the classless commonwealth, and we easily recognize the same radically
democratic forms they praised so lavishly in the Paris Commune, or at
a less sophisticated level in the tribal organization of the Iroquois. While
they occasionally noted that democracy was a form of government too,
and thus would disappear like the others, they were merely being punc-
tilious about the word.[97] Democracy as a form of rule (Greek: *kratía*),
that is, coercion, by a proletarian majority over a bourgeois minority,
would indeed disappear, but democratic *forms* — the majority principle,
elections to delegate authority, and so on — manifestly would not disappear, as both men made abundantly clear. No doubt they left many
questions unanswered, or only barely answered. Did they, for example,
imagine *all* antisocial acts would cease, even crimes of passion or youthful vandalistic pranks, for example; and if not, how would such acts be
dealt with, particularly in the absence of any coercive apparatus? Or,
granted some measure of autonomy for each local community, how
would conflicts be resolved between a community and the central "administration"?

The list could probably be extended at length, but surely the question
most frequently put, and by the most diverse observers, is this: why did
Marx and Engels not foresee the probable emergence of a new ruling class
following the disappearance of the old one, a class that might be com-

posed of officials of the central administration, factory managers, party leaders, intellectuals generally, or some combination of these groups? The new-class question is entirely legitimate; it is essentially the same question Bakunin was trying to raise about the corruptibility of leaders. Most people who raise the question today of course have in mind the experience of the Soviet Union and the other Communist countries. This time, however, an answer can be found in the masters' writings, or at least the better part of an answer, one almost universally overlooked by those who pose the question.

A hint to the answer is given in Marx's just-cited example of the manufacturer-city councilman. It grows out of the concept of transcendence of the division of labor, which has been so little understood, and particularly out of its application to the realm of public power, the overcoming of the state as parasite by means of radical deprofessionalization. A new class composed of high administrators would not have occurred to Marx and Engels because they never allowed that there would be high administrators to start with. In communist society — to reintroduce the formula of *The German Ideology* — there are no high administrators but only people who administer among other things, no factory managers but only people who manage a factory among other things, no intellectuals but only people who are intellectually active among other things. A fine sort of socialism that would be, to paraphrase Engels, perpetuating professional administrators, managers, intellectuals, and so on. Can a factory be managed on a part-time basis? From his personal experience Engels would doubtless have answered in the affirmative. And the manufacturer pointed to by Marx who also served as city councilman surely divided his time between at least these two activities. If one expands the idea to include essentially full-time work done for a short term, one can begin to imagine how Marx and Engels thought leadership could be provided without creating a professional class of leaders. No person would serve long enough in one capacity to develop a vested interest in his job; no special group of people could be identified as an administrative class because it would have become the class of all citizens. In a word, communist society would be a democracy without professionals.

The twentieth-century observer is likely to throw up his hands immediately at the impossibility of such a thing, so accustomed have we become to professional leadership and to bureaucratic principles of selection and advancement, where even our elected political leaders are professionals in every sense of the word. To give Marx and Engels a fair hearing, we must consider that they did have a real-life model in their minds.

If we were to read of a society in which there existed a "union of town and country"; where "civil rights implied civil duties"; whose ideal of democracy "requires that all citizens not only shall be the sovereign power but shall in fact rule"; where this goal was accomplished by making all offices "generally accessible and by constantly changing the holders"; where "all officials were elected" and there resulted "the greatest possible turn-over within the citizen body in the holders of office"; where as a consequence there was no "bureaucratic hierarchy" but "every official was no more than a citizen, accidently, as it were, for a limited period engaged in some special service for the state"; where all these practices created a "political life that was the very life and nature of the citizens," an "identity of citizens with the state," an "identity of state and society" — if we were to read these things, we might be sure it was Marx describing the classless society. But in fact it is a description of Periclean Athens written by the German-educated classicist, Victor Ehrenberg.[98] The fact that Ehrenberg expressly rejects the Marxist interpretation of antiquity makes it all the more astonishing that his descriptive phrases could almost have been written by Marx with the classless society in mind. It is testimony to that veneration of ancient Greece that permeated German academic life for more than a century, and specifically to the admiration of Athenian society in its golden age as a model of the harmonious fusion of public and private life.

It has been argued in volume 1 that Marx shared this veneration of classical antiquity and used Periclean Athens as a model for the political functioning (if he would forgive us the word) of a classless society. He never quite acknowledged the model, though we saw how he ridiculed the Prussian civil service examination by commenting: "One does not hear that the Greek or Roman statesmen passed examinations."[99] In the *Grundrisse* he came closer to an acknowledgment as he praised the humanistic values of antiquity. They struck him as "loftier" than the mammonism of modern bourgeois society:

> Do we never find in antiquity an inquiry into which form of landed property etc. is the most productive, creates the greatest wealth? Wealth does not appear as the aim of production. . . . The question is always which mode of property creates the best citizens. . . . Thus the old view, in which the human being appears as the aim of production, regardless of his limited national, religious, political character, seems to be very lofty when contrasted to the modern world, where production appears as the aim of mankind and

wealth as the aim of production. In fact, however, when the limited bourgeois form is stripped away, what is wealth other than the universality of human needs, capacities, pleasures, productive forces etc., created through universal exchange? The full development of human mastery over the forces of nature, those of so-called nature as well as of humanity's own nature? The absolute working-out of his creative potentialities, with no presupposition other than the previous historic development, which makes this totality of development, i.e. the development of all human powers as such the end in itself, not as measured on a *predetermined* yardstick? Where he does not reproduce himself in one specificity, but produces his totality? Strives not to remain something he has become, but is in the absolute movement of becoming?

Here one sees the direct link between the humanism of the Ancients and Marx's own ethic of collective self-realization. It should not be thought, however, that Marx dreamt nostalgically of re-creating the golden age of a simpler society. He defined his attitude on this point in an earlier passage of the *Grundrisse*, as he posed the question why Greek art should continue to exercise such a fascination on the modern mind:

A man cannot become a child again, or he becomes childish. But does he not find joy in the child's naïveté, and must he himself not strive to reproduce its truth at a higher stage? Does not the true character of each epoch come alive in the nature of its children? Why should not the historic childhood of humanity, its most beautiful unfolding, as a stage never to return, exercise an eternal charm?[100]

Modern man, then, should not and cannot expect Greek art to return again, but should "reproduce its truth at a higher stage." In just the same sense the classless society would reproduce Athenian political forms at a higher stage.

Engels did not have a university education and seems to have been less influenced by the veneration of Greece, yet even he acknowledged Hellenism to be "the flowering of the ancient world." And he had some kind words for Athenian democracy in particular, as we have already seen, in *The Origin of the Family*. "It shows a very highly developed form of state, the democratic republic, arising directly out of gentile society," he noted, and its various self-governing townships, or demes, were "the prototype of the self-governing American township. The modern state in its highest development ends in the same unit with which the rising state in Athens began."[101] The American town meeting was closer to hand, but Engels admired it for the same reasons both he and his partner admired Athenian democracy.

It will be objected — and Marx and Engels would be the first to agree — that Athenian democracy never transcended the level of a city-state (numbering in its prime perhaps one hundred fifty thousand citizens, including wives and children); that it rested on a technologically unsophisticated society; and that the attractively high level of citizen participation in public life presupposed the existence of a slave population, at least equal in size, to perform the menial work of the polis. Marx and Engels perceived a critical linkage, however, between a low-productivity economy and the existence of an exploited class. Engels stated it best in *Anti-Dühring:*

> All historical antagonisms between exploiting and exploited, ruling and oppressed classes to this very day find their explanation in this same relatively undeveloped productivity of human labor. So long as the really working population were so much occupied with their necessary labor that they had no time left for looking after the common affairs of society — the direction of labor, affairs of state, legal matters, art, science, etc. — so long was it necessary that there should constantly exist a special class, freed from actual labor, to manage these affairs; and this class never failed, for its own advantage, to impose a greater and greater burden of labor on the working masses. Only the immense increase of the productive forces attained by modern industry has made it possible to distribute labor among all members of society without exception, and thereby to limit the labor-time of each individual member to such an extent that all have enough free time left to take part in the general — both theoretical and practical — affairs of society.

Thus leisure and knowledge would be socialized along with the means of production. "What is really worth preserving in historically inherited culture," Engels observed in 1872, would be "converted from a monopoly of the ruling class into the common property of the whole of society." And the decisive point, he concluded, was this: "As soon as the productive power of human labor has risen to this height, every excuse disappears for the existence of a ruling class."[102]

Marx expressed the same thoughts in different language when he wrote in the *Grundrisse:*

> *The creation of a large quantity of disposable time* apart from necessary labor time for society generally and each of its members (i.e. room for the development of the individuals' full productive forces, hence those of society also), this creation of the not-labor time appears in the stage of capital, as of all earlier ones, as not-labor time, free time, for a few. What capital adds is that it increases the surplus labor time of the mass by all the means of art and science. . . . It is thus, despite itself, instrumental in creating the means of social disposable time, in order to reduce labor time for the whole society to a diminishing minimum, and thus to free everyone's time for their own development. . . . The mass of workers must themselves appropriate their own surplus labor. Once they have done so — and *disposable time* thereby ceases to have an *antithetical* existence — then, on one side, necessary labor time would be measured by the needs of the social individual, and, on the other, the development of the power of social production will grow so rapidly that, even though production is now calculated for the wealth of all, *disposable time* will grow for all.

He went on to indicate that such disposable time would be "both idle time and time for higher activity," and that the latter "then corresponds to the artistic, scientific etc. development of the individuals in the time set free, and with the means created, for all of them."[103]

Both Marx and Engels, then, considered high-level technology and high labor productivity to be absolute prerequisites for a communist society. Thus they would not likely have been impressed with the arguments of those who point to the Soviet Union and other Communist countries as evidence of the necessary emergence of a new ruling class. "So long as it is not possible to produce [in great abundance]," Engels had written in 1847, "so long must there always be a ruling class disposing of the productive forces of society, and a poor, oppressed class."[104] Engels of course did not have the Soviet Union in mind, but his argument applies well enough to any backward country that experiences revolution. It is not the intentions of the revolutionaries that matter, after all, any more than the labels they give themselves. If the level of labor productivity is too low, then by the argument of Marx and Engels, there will not be sufficient disposable time for the mass of the population to take a really active part in economic management and public affairs, to educate itself in the process, and thus to govern itself effectively as a participatory democracy. Where the masses are unable to do this, where the revolution was organized and carried out by a Leninist-style vanguard party, it is predictable enough that the party will replace the masses in the tasks of economic management and political governance, that it will become, in the words of Lenin himself, "the teacher, the guide, the leader of all the working and exploited people in organizing their social life."[105]

Marx and Engels themselves never said anything about the role of political parties after the revolution. A good deal can be surmised, nonetheless, from what they said about related issues. First, in the period leading up to the revolution, as we have seen in volume 1 and will see again below, Marx and Engels consistently rejected the idea of a vanguard party, as Lenin would come to define it; they rather conceived the party ideally and potentially as coextensive with the proletariat itself, that is, as coming to embrace the majority of the whole population. Second, while a single party would obviously serve the proletariat as a stronger weapon than several parties in the struggle against the bourgeoisie, Marx and Engels never insisted that a single party alone was acceptable. On the contrary, the fact that the Paris Commune contained three distinct factions — none of them Marxist! — did not prevent it from being a glorious deed of "our Party" or from being, on Engels' authority, a "dictatorship of the proletariat." Third, Marx and Engels' historical conception of the function of political parties in class-divided society includes as a *logical* conclusion their complete disappearance under communism. Although they never argued that *all* historically existing parties represented distinct social classes, nonetheless they would surely hold this true for the important parties, the "historically necessary" ones, whose function is to fight in the political arena for their respective classes. With the final defeat of the bourgeois "party," however, the proletarian "party" would become redundant; in a society where everyone is obliged to accept his share of productive labor, a "workers' party" would be the party of everyone, hence a logical absurdity, because party *means* "part" of the whole. Just as there were no permanently organized parties alternating in office in the classical *polis*, or necessarily in the classical New England town meeting, so most likely Marx and Engels imagined that the citizens of the classless society would divide on successive specific issues, but not in such recurring patterns as to provide the basis for new parties. One must remember how recent the general acceptance has been that democracy requires permanently organized parties that alternate in power — even the American founding fathers hoped such parties could be avoided.[106]

It is not difficult to imagine, however, disagreements even in a classless society that might lead to the formation of such parties, disagreements that concerned, for example, what proportion of the gross national product should be reinvested in capital goods rather than consumed directly. It is not at all clear that Marx and Engels would have *opposed* postrevolutionary parties that grew up on some such basis. All that does seem clear is that they would have opposed the existence of a *single* party which ruled by denying all others the right to existence, and which purported to be "the teacher, the guide, and the leader" of the masses. Such a party by definition sets itself above the masses, and we know what choice epithets Marx reserved for those who wanted to "uplift" the great unwashed. From beginning to end, surely the central and most distinctive ingredient in Marx and Engels' radicalism was the idea that there is no authentic emancipation save *self*-emancipation, that the masses must teach themselves, guide themselves, lead themselves. The grammar of freedom knows only the reflexive form.

If we return to the new-class problem within the context Marx and Engels would have recognized as appropriate — highly productive labor, a generous measure of disposable time available for all, no vanguard party — then it would still be legitimate to raise skeptical questions, for example, about the dispensability of all professionals. As early as 1851 Engels himself seems to have become disillusioned with the military effectiveness of the pure Swiss-style militia he had advocated in 1845. His own military expertise led him to appreciate the need for more professional "cadres" around which militiamen could muster in time of need. He expressed these thoughts concisely in an 1868 letter to Marx commenting on Gustave-Paul Cluseret's proposals for a militia:

> The American [Civil] War — militia on both sides — proves nothing. . . . What would have happened to the Yankees if, instead of the Southern militia, they had faced a solid army of a couple of hundred thousand men? Before the North organized itself, this army would have been in New York and Boston and dictated a peace. . . . [Cluseret] is rich when he says the main point is to have good officers and the trust of the men in these officers, both of which being precisely what is unobtainable in a militia system. What impresses people generally about the militia idea is the large mass of men im-

mediately available and the relative ease with which they can be trained, especially in action itself. . . . But for that, good cadres are required, and for that something other than the Swiss-American militia system. . . . Which is not to say that a rational military organization does not lie somewhere in the middle between the Prussian and the Swiss — but where? That depends on individual circumstances. Only a society established and *educated* on communist lines can closely approach the militia system and even that only asyncopically.[107]

By the time such a system were perfected, presumably it would no longer be needed. Yet Engels' practical-minded recognition of the need for military "cadres" may be taken as paradigmatic of the pressure toward professionalism in every field. In theory, of course, there is no necessary contradiction between the need for expertise and the desire to transcend the division of labor — Engels' own military expertise did not make him a professional soldier. But would there be sufficient expertise in a sufficient number of people so that *professional* cadres could be dispensed with?

In another letter, written in 1890, Engels touched on the subject again as he responded — in a rather irritated tone — to the parlor-pink question put by an aristocratic sympathizer in Breslau, whether the socialist idea would not have to wait until the masses were more highly educated:

I see no difficulties. That our workers are able to do it is proved by the many producers and consumers' cooperatives which . . . are better and more honestly administered than bourgeois corporations. I cannot understand how you can speak of lack of education among the German masses after the brilliant proof of political maturity furnished by our workers in their victorious struggle against the Anti-Socialist Law. . . . To be sure we still lack technicians, agronomists, engineers, chemists, architects, etc., but at the worst we can buy these, just like the capitalists do, and if a couple of traitors — which there will certainly be in such company — are made a good example of, the rest will find it in their interest not to cheat us any longer. Apart from such specialists, however, among whom I would add schoolteachers, we can manage very nicely without the rest of the "educated" classes. . . .

The large estates of the East Elbean Junkers can be given over without difficulty, under appropriate technical guidance, to the present-day laborers (or tenants, as the case may be) and cultivated in association. If there are excesses, the Herren Junkers will be responsible, since, contrary to all existing school legislation, they have left the people there in such a raw state. . . .

When we have a sufficient number of supporters among the masses, as soon as we have political power, then big industry and big agriculture can be socialized very quickly. . . .

You speak of the lack of equal insight [between the educated and uneducated]. This exists — but on the side of the educated people stemming from aristocratic and bourgeois circles who haven't the faintest idea how much they still have to learn from the workers.[108]

Several observations here: Engels separates managerial from technical expertise and holds the workers immediately capable of the former if not the latter; while not everyone need be an expert in engineering or agronomy, everyone ought to have his share, in some way and to some degree, in the general control decisions, in executive tasks. Engels is prepared to "buy" some technicians and keep close watch over them; but he also seems to anticipate a certain amount of disorganization, or "excesses," which must be accepted as the price for the practical self-education of the masses. Again he is assuming a high-productivity economy which might better be able to afford such temporary inefficiencies.

Even assuming the new society could be constructed without relying — unduly — on existing professionals, another legitimate question may be raised concerning the possibility that future socialist experts in any given field might tend to *become* professionals, might *want* to devote themselves exclusively to one field instead of being "well-rounded." Engels might deplore those unfortunates who had "sunk so low that they *rejoice* in their own subjection and one-sidedness," yet the person who devotes himself single-mindedly to one pursuit possesses all the advantages that a professional athlete has over an amateur athlete, a professional manager over administrative amateurs, and so forth. Marx himself seemed to acknowledge, at least in the direction of the British East India Company, that amateurs are no match for professionals. Thus he noted in 1853 that the twenty-four nominal "directors" (really merchants, bankers, etc.) devoted only a small portion of their time to the management of the East India Company. Further, they divided themselves into three functional committees:

These Committees are every year appointed by rotation, so that a *financier* is one year on the Judicial and the next year on the Military Committee, and no one has any chance of a continued super-vision over a particular department. The mode of election having brought in men utterly unfit for their duties, the system of rotation gives to whatever fitness they might perchance retain, the final blow. Who, then, govern in fact under the name of the Direction? A large staff of irresponsible secretaries, examiners and clerks at the India House, . . . the permanent and irresponsible *bureaucracy*.[109]

Is not Marx his own best critic? Even allowing for all the obvious differ-ences, would not the upright well-rounded citizens of the classless society soon fall victim to those who had "sunk so low" as to pursue, let us say, administrative and managerial expertise with single-minded devotion?

In response one can only point to the "safeguards" Marx and Engels mentioned in connection with the Paris Commune. To become an offi-cial in a communist society, one would have to be elected; it would not be a matter of preparing for such a career and then rising through a bu-reaucratic hierarchy step-by-step. If the voters were attracted by the su-perior expertise and zeal of a single-minded specialist, they might also suspect his motives and one-sidedness. In any event they could get rid of him at any time by simple recall. Election and recall, then, not merely of "political" leaders but of all officials in every sphere of society — this was the first of the two "infallible means" by which the Communards safeguarded themselves against their own officials. Marx and Engels seemed to assume that this measure alone would insure a healthy turn-over of leaders, although the history of democratic institutions, including those within the European socialist movement itself, would not seem to bear this out.[110] The two men never stressed any limitation in the *right* of reelection, such as one finds for the American presidency or much more radically in Periclean Athens, which would most directly insure the turn-over they desired, although at the price of "wasting" acquired compe-tence and constantly having to build it anew, as Marx made clear in his East India example.

The second "infallible means" was to pay all officials only "workmen's wages," so that leaders would not be distinguished from others by a higher standard of living.[111] It is worth emphasizing this point because in recent decades there has been a tendency to soft-pedal Marx and Engels' dis-tributive egalitarianism. First it was Stalin and his defenders who needed to justify growing inequalities of income in the Soviet Union, but more recently it has been non-Communist Western scholars who want to stress that Marx was more concerned with how people *produce*, with their self-realization through productive labor, than with how they *consume*, or whether they consume in exactly equal shares.[112] This latter emphasis is doubtless correct so long as it does not obscure the essential egalitarianism both men espoused in the sphere of consumption. It is certainly true that they opposed any *ascetic* egalitarianism that aspires to level down everyone's consumption to the minimum conceived as necessary for a "simple" life. Marx reacted to such ideas in his Paris manuscripts of 1844: "Crude communism is only the culmination of this envy and of this leveling-down proceeding from the *preconceived* minimum"; it is a "negation of the entire world of culture and civilization, the regression to the *unnatural* simplicity of the *poor* and crude man who has few needs."[113] When dealing with socialists of this sort Engels was apt to stress that "the *idea of equality* is *itself a historical product*" and ought not to be represented as "the highest principle and ultimate truth"; Marx also insisted that "between one country and another, one province and another and even one locality and another there will always exist a *certain* inequality in the conditions of life, which it will be possible to reduce to a minimum but never entirely remove."[114]

On the other hand, when dealing with socialists who seriously *opposed* distributive equality, Marx and Engels' emphasis was quite the opposite. Thus the young Engels found the economic principles of the Saint-Simonians "not unexceptionable":

> The share of each of the members of their communities in the distribution of produce was to be regulated, firstly, by the amount of work he had done; and, secondly, the amount of talent he displayed. A German Republican, Boerne, justly replied to this principle, that talent, instead of being rewarded, ought rather to be considered as a natural preference; and, therefore, a deduction ought to be made from the share of the talented, in order to restore equality.[115]

In *The German Ideology* Marx and Engels attacked the obscure True Socialist, Georg Kuhlmann, for confusing "the *diversity* of faculties and capacities with the *inequality* of *possessions* and of *enjoyment*":

> But one of the most vital principles of communism, a principle which distinguishes it from all reactionary socialism, is its empirical view, based on a knowledge of man's nature, that differences of *brain* and of intellectual ability do not imply any differences whatsoever in the nature of the *stomach* and of physical *needs;* therefore the

false tenet, based upon existing circumstances, "to each according to his abilities," must be changed, insofar as it relates to enjoyment in its narrower sense, into the tenet, "*to each according to his need*"; in other words, a *different form* of activity, of labor, does not justify *inequality,* confers no *privileges* in respect of possession and enjoyment.[116]

A half century later Engels still insisted that under communism, "the means for existence, for enjoying life, for the development and employment of all bodily and mental faculties will be available *in an equal measure* and in ever-increasing fulness" (emphasis added).[117]

This would apply, to be sure, to the higher phase of communist society, separated off by Marx in the Gotha *Critique* from a lower phase in which each individual would receive a "certificate" for "such and such an amount of labor" he had performed. With this certificate he would be able to purchase an equivalent amount of consumer goods — "a given amount of labor in one form is exchanged for an equal amount of labor in another form." Marx went on to explain that "one man is superior to another physically or mentally and so supplies more labor in the same time, or can labor for a longer time; and labor, to serve as a measure, must be defined by its duration or intensity, otherwise it ceases to be a standard of measure."[118] Thus certain inequalities of income would be unavoidable in this lower phase. Differences in the *duration* of labor could scarcely produce gross inequalities, however; it was intensity that provided the loophole through which Stalin was able to justify differences of income greater than in most capitalist countries. Did Marx only mean to allow that in a given hour's labor one person might produce six finished goods while another produced eight, or did he mean to suggest that all skilled labor was more "intense" than unskilled, all managerial labor even more "intense," etc.? It is doubtful he meant the latter, for only a few years later he listened to and presumably approved Engels' categorical pronouncement in *Anti-Dühring:*

> How then are we to solve the whole important question of the higher wages paid for compound [that is, skilled] labor? In a society of private producers, private individuals or their families pay the costs of training the qualified worker; hence the higher price paid for qualified labor-power accrues first of all to private individuals. . . . In a socialistically organized society, these costs are borne by society,

and to it therefore belong the fruits, the greater values produced by compound labor. The worker himself has no claims to extra pay.[119]

This also accords very neatly with Marx's praise of the Communards for paying their own officials only "workmen's wages" for what they hoped was skilled labor. In the higher phase of communism, of course, wages would disappear altogether, and, as Engels put it, "anyone who pedantically insists on being given his equal and just share of the products is laughed to scorn by being given twice as much."[120]

⟨[8]⟩

The International Working Men's Association

MARX AND ENGELS' reactions to the Paris Commune have helped pin down their ideas on revolutionary strategy, the workers' state, individual rights, and the classless society, but we have been obliged temporarily to by-pass their participation in the organization whose history (1864–1872) bridges over the period of the Commune — the International Working Men's Association, called simply the International or the IWA. This is not the place to attempt a general history of the International, of course, but it will be appropriate to analyze Marx and Engels' activity within it, especially since it was the only political organization they ever chose to join during their later years.[1] We may pose the same kinds of questions as were posed in volume 1 concerning the Communist League and the other organizations of that period.[2] The first set of questions concerns *internal* matters, how the organization was structured, how Marx especially (Engels was much less involved) conceived his personal role in the organization, what patterns can be discerned in his actual behavior as a leader, and so on. The second set of questions looks *outward* from the organization itself, to what Marx and Engels conceived to be the tasks of the IWA, its relationship to the unorganized masses, to other organizations, and so forth. A large portion of our attention will be given over to the conflict with Mikhail Bakunin and his anarchist followers, which dominated the later history of the IWA and eventually caused its demise. In this protracted struggle we will find some of the best answers to both sets of questions.

Marx's Role in the International

So widespread is the post-Commune tabloid image of Marx as the *grand chef* of the International, the man who could raise forth revolutions or put whole cities to the torch with a nod of his head, that it is

[266]

necessary to emphasize how small a role he actually played in the early years of the IWA, particularly in its founding in 1864. By coincidence his former disciple, Ferdinand Lassalle, was involved at almost the same time in founding the organization that later became the German Social Democratic party. Lassalle's behavior may serve as a convenient foil by which to measure Marx's leadership role, particularly since the conventions of the Cold War have served to make the former into a hero of "democratic" socialism as opposed to the alleged authoritarianism of Marx. Early in 1863 the leaders of the German Workers' Educational Associations invited Lassalle to express his views on the idea of creating a working-class political association. He answered with his famous "Open Reply Letter" outlining his personal views on how to achieve socialism and inviting them to accept these ideas and his leadership on a take-it-or-leave-it basis. They accepted. At the founding convention of the General German Workers' Association in May 1863, Lassalle became president (for a five-year term) of an organization in which he named his own vice-president, disposed of the party funds, controlled the party press, and appointed a deputy for each branch to preside over the meetings of the local comrades and acquaint them with the leader's wishes.[3] In a letter to his acquaintance, the Prussian prime minister, Otto von Bismarck, Lassalle revealed with embarrassing exactness how he interpreted the statutes of the new organization. "Enclosed you will find," he wrote, "the constitution of *my* empire. From this miniature picture you will be able to see clearly how true it is that the working classes are instinctively inclined to dictatorship, if they can be justly convinced that this dictatorship is exercised in their interests."[4] That he hoped eventually to expand this personal sway over Germany at large is revealed in another letter the following year to his prospective fiancée: "Believe me, it would be a proud moment to be acclaimed 'President' of a Republic, chosen by the people. To rest secure on the good-will of a nation, more securely than to be 'King by the Grace of God' and to sit upon a rotten worm-eaten throne. . . . 'Ferdinand, the chosen of the people,' is a proud name, and if all goes well, it shall be mine."[5] Lassalle's fantasies were cut short when he was killed in a duel in 1864. Marx and Engels were thoroughly aware of Lassalle's personal ambitions and, in private letters during this period, frequently expressed concern that his attitude was quite that of a "future workers' dictator."[6]

Like Lassalle, Marx could have seized an opportunity to impose himself on some workers' organization on a take-it-or-leave-it basis, but until 1864 he chose to maintain a lonely independence through the long years of exile that followed the collapse of the Communist League. He had had his "fill" of parties, as he wrote his friend, Ferdinand Freiligrath, and he turned down all invitations to become involved.[7] Why then did he change his mind in 1864 and take part in the founding of the IWA? Do the sources give any evidence of the kind of personal ambitions that drove Lassalle?

The IWA grew most directly out of contacts that were established when a group of French labor delegates, mostly Proudhonists and led by the engraver, Henri Tolain, met with British trade unionists while visiting the London International Exhibition in 1862. On the British side, the prime movers were George Odger, a shoemaker by trade and secretary of the London Trades Council, and William Cremer, also on the Trades Council and a leader of the carpenters' union. Odger and Cremer not only were active unionists but had been prominent in mobilizing working-class support for political causes, such as Italian unification and the anti-slavery campaign in the American Civil War. Thus when a major Polish insurrection broke out in 1863, it seemed only appropriate for them to invite back Tolain and his comrades for a joint Anglo-French meeting to express moral support for the Polish cause. At this 1863 meeting a decision was also taken to establish a permanent international organization. Apart from broader questions of international solidarity, the British workers were particularly concerned to combat the common entrepreneurial practice of importing scabs from the Continent in order to break strikes. So it was that a year later, on September 28, 1864, the interested parties, including also a few Italian and German émigrés, met at St. Martin's Hall in London to found the IWA.[8]

Marx was not involved in any of the preliminaries to this meeting, and Engels of course still lived in Manchester. In a long letter on November 4, Marx summed up the events and indicated his own role in them. He was first contacted on behalf of the meeting's organizers perhaps a week in advance: "A certain *Le Lubez* was sent to ask me if I would take part on behalf of the German workers, and especially if I would supply a German worker to speak at the meeting, etc. I provided them with Eccarius, who came off splendidly, and ditto was present myself as a mute figure in the platform. I knew that this time real "powers" were involved both on the London and Paris sides and therefore decided to waive my usual standing rule to decline any such invitations."[9] Georg Eccarius, it may be remembered, was a German tailor exiled in London who had played a prominent role in the Communist League during the second phase of its existence. He remained close to Marx thereafter until 1871.

Engels' reply to Marx's letter was unenthusiastic, but he agreed that the organization represented the mainstream of the French and English working class: "It is good that we are coming again into contact with people who at least represent their class, which is the main thing in the end."[10]

Even though Marx did not speak at the meeting, he was well known enough to be elected, along with Eccarius, as the two German representatives on the thirty-four-man provisional committee, charged with drawing up provisional statutes and a program for the organization, as well as chartering affiliates in various countries and preparing for a general congress to be held the next year. At the first meeting of this committee, Marx was further elected to a nine-man subcommittee assigned to produce a draft for the statutes and program. He was ill during the first subcommittee session, where an old Owenite, John Weston, came forth with an extremely wordy and sentimental draft program, while Mazzini's friend, Major Luigi Wolff, produced as a model statute the forty rules of the Italian working men's associations. Marx also missed the next meeting of the full committee on October 12, where there was general dissatisfaction with these proposals. Eccarius reported back to Marx in a letter written the same evening: "After the meeting, Cremer said privately that Weston ought to have nothing to do with the matter, that the editing of the draft must be turned over to a commission of three at most, which could make use of the available material or could not as they saw fit. Odger and the others agreed. 'The right man in the right place' will undoubtedly be Dr. Marx."[11]

Further subcommittee work, still in the absence of Marx, improved the draft sufficiently so that the full committee on October 18 approved the "sentiments" contained therein but sent it back again for further subcommittee "editing." It was at this point that Marx managed to have the documents left with him. As he reported to Engels:

> I saw that it was impossible to make anything out of the stuff. In order to justify the extremely strange way in which I intended to present the "sentiments" already "voted for," I wrote *An Address to the Working Classes* (which was not in the original plan: a sort of review of the adventures of the Working Classes since 1845); on the pretext that everything material was included in this *Address* and that we ought not to repeat the same things three times over I altered the whole preamble, threw out the declaration of principles and finally replaced the forty rules by ten. . . . My proposals were all accepted by the sub-committee.

Marx went on to explain how he was obliged to insert the phrases about "truth, morality and justice," which we examined in chapter 6, but then, "at the meeting of the general committee my address, etc., was agreed to with great enthusiasm (unanimously)." The minutes of the November 1 meeting confirmed Marx's report, except that one word, "profitmongers," was excised from the *Address* by an amendment carried eleven to ten.[12] That the subcommittee had twice been sent back to improve its work shows that the full committee was not ready to approve just anything, while the immediate and unanimous endorsement of Marx's work shows how cautiously he had drafted the documents so they would be acceptable both to the English trade unionists and to the French Proudhonists. Far from imposing himself on the group, Marx drastically softpedaled his own personal views, offered his work for subcommittee and then committee approval, accepted amendments, and so forth, all within a perfectly normal democratic organizational process.

The provisional statutes themselves offer further testimony of Marx's democratic values and modest personal ambitions within the IWA. Interestingly — and ironically in light of the later conflict with Bakunin — he found the forty rules of Mazzini's group too *centralized.* They "aim at something which is in fact utterly impossible," he wrote Engels, "a sort of central government of the *European* working classes."[13] Marx's ten rules, on the other hand, transformed the existing committee into a "provisional central council" (later called general council) and assigned it the following tasks: "To connect the different national working men's associations, enlist members in the United Kingdom, take the steps preparatory to the convocation of the General Congress, and discuss with the national and local societies the main questions to be laid before that Congress." That Congress was to meet in 1865 and consist of "representatives of such working men's societies as may have joined the International Association": "The Congress will have to proclaim before Europe the common aspirations of the working classes, decide on the definitive rules of the International Association, consider the means required for its successful working, and appoint the Central Council of the Association. The General Congress is to meet once a year." Each annual congress was to receive for its approval a public account of the council's "transactions"and elect a new council for the following year.[14]

The central council was to sit in London, to "consist of working men belonging to the different countries represented," and to elect from among its own members "the officers necessary for the transaction of business, such as a president, a treasurer, a general secretary, corresponding secretaries for the different countries, etc." Marx retained for the central council a power given the original committee at St. Martin's Hall, that of adding to its own numbers through co-optation between congresses. Article 6 further delineated the council's functions:

> The Central Council shall form an international agency between the different co-operating associations, so that the working men in one country be constantly informed of the movements of their class in every other country; that an inquiry into the social state of the different countries of Europe be made simultaneously, and under a common direction; that the questions of general interest mooted in one society be ventilated by all; and that when immediate practical steps should be needed, as, for instance, in case of international quarrels, the action of the associated societies be simultaneous and uniform. Whenever it seems opportune, the Central Council shall take the initiative of proposals to be laid before the different national or local societies.

Membership in the IWA was open to individuals, to local societies, and to national organizations as well, but members were urged to "use their utmost efforts to combine the disconnected working men's societies of their respective countries into national bodies, represented by central national organs." In many Continental countries, however, such organization at the national level was illegal, and, the statutes added, "apart from legal obstacles, no independent local society shall be precluded from directly corresponding with the London Central Council." No specific requirements or expectations of membership were set down, nor any arrangements for expulsion either of individuals or of affiliated societies. These structural arrangements became permanent when the 1866 Geneva Congress accepted Marx's statutes with only minor modifications.[15]

Within the central council, the English trade unionists predominated both in numbers and in offices held. Of the thirty-four original members, twenty-seven were English, and Odger was soon elected president, Cremer general secretary, and George Wheeler treasurer. Eccarius was elected vice-president in November 1864, while Marx was merely corresponding secretary for Germany, one of five such secretaries, the others being for Italy, France, Switzerland, and Poland. Since the St. Martin's Hall meeting had authorized the executive body to co-opt new members at its own discretion, the council grew rapidly during its initial months of existence, numbering sixty-six by the end of the year, with the following national distribution — thirty-seven English, nine Germans, eight French, seven Italians, two Swiss, two Poles, and one Dane.[16] Apart from Eccarius, Marx would count as his own followers at most Pfänder, Lessner, and Lochner among the Germans, Dupont among the French, and Jung among the Swiss — a total of seven votes (including his own) among the sixty-six. The original drafting subcommittee evolved into a kind of informal standing executive committee, whose membership included all the officers and corresponding secretaries, and which met every week to prepare the business of the main body. The "Marx party" numbered only three (Marx, Eccarius, Jung) among the ten members of this committee at the end of 1864.[17]

Thus Marx threw in his lot with an organization he did not control, nor did he make any concerted effort at direct control before the Bakunin conflict changed the stakes of the game in 1869. Until that time he never attended the annual congresses himself. Following the 1866 congress he was nominated for the presidency of the general council by several English trade unionists, but he declined and himself renominated Odger instead.[18] It is true that in September 1867, he wrote the widely quoted letter to Engels remarking that "in the next revolution, which is perhaps nearer than it appears, *we* (i.e., you and I) will have this powerful engine *in our hands*." Although Engels had joined the IWA as an individual member in Manchester, he remained for some time lukewarm and skeptical about its prospects, so that Marx needed to impress his partner with the importance of the organization.[19] But in fact Marx was still only corresponding secretary for Germany, and of the twenty-eight members just elected to the new general council by the Lausanne Congress only six belonged to the "Marx party," including Marx himself.[20] On the other hand there were seventeen English trade unionists, the bulk of whom were not even socialists, and who surely were not in Marx's hands, most particularly if he had tried to turn the organization in an openly revolutionary direction.

Marx did initiate one step, shortly after his letter to Engels, that indirectly increased his influence on the general council. George Odger had become more and more involved in activities and organizations associated with the Liberal party, and hence less and less active as president of the IWA's general council. Since the beginning of 1867 he had shown up to chair the weekly meetings only five times; he had not appeared at all since June and did not attend the Lausanne Congress. Meanwhile, in July the vice-president, Eccarius, had been moved over by unanimous vote

to fill the vacant post of general secretary, leaving the chair entirely vacant and making it necessary for each weekly meeting to elect its own
chairman.[21] Such was the situation when the newly elected general council met on September 24 to choose its officers. Marx proposed at this point
that the office of president be abolished in favor of the rotating chair-
manship which was already the de facto practice. Dissatisfaction with
Odger was such that this proposal carried unanimously.[22] The move
clearly had its tactical side, since the "jealous Odger" was more and more
objectionable to Marx, and by abolishing the presidency, as he explains
to Engels, "'President' Odger is also abolished."[23] And yet the move was
more than just a power play, for Marx passed over the obvious alternative of having himself elected president in Odger's place, just as he did
the previous year.

In October 1868, Marx referred back to the event in a highly interesting letter to Johann Baptist von Schweitzer, Lassalle's successor as authoritarian president of the General German Worker's Association.
Schweitzer had written for Marx's comments on the statutes of a new
trade-union association he had just established, and which was modeled
on the centralized and dictatorial structure of its parent organization.
Marx commented:

> As to the draft of the rules, I regard it as fundamentally mis-
> guided. . . . The *centralist* organization, no matter how valuable
> it may be for secret societies and sectarian movements, contradicts
> the essence of trade unions. . . . [In Germany,] where the worker
> is subject to bureaucratic discipline from his infancy and believes
> in officialdom and higher authority, it is above all a question of
> teaching him to *walk by himself.*

Among other specifics, Marx zeroed in on a provision for a "President
(a completely superfluous figure in this context) elected by *all members*,"
declaring: "Lassalle made a big blunder when he borrowed the *'president elu du suffrage universel'* from the French Constitution of 1852. And
now the same sort of thing in a trade-union movement! Such a movement is largely concerned with questions of money, and you will soon
discover that in such a situation all dictatorship has to come to an end."
Most interesting was his parenthetical note: "In the rules of the International Working Men's Association a president also figures. But in reality
he never had any function other than chairing the meeting of the Gen-

eral Council. At my suggestion the office, which I turned down in 1866, was abolished completely and replaced by a chairman, who is elected at each weekly meeting of the General Council."[24] In later years too, Marx referred back proudly to the fact that the IWA had no president. And at the Basel Congress of 1869, on the proposal of the general council, a resolution was adopted asserting that "it is not in accordance with the dignity of a workers' society to maintain within its ranks a monarchical or authoritarian principle," and recommending therefore that all affiliated organizations likewise abolish the office of president.[25] In these ways Marx separated himself both in words and in deeds from the dictatorial conceptions of Lassalle.

Certainly Marx enjoyed a strong *intellectual* influence over the general council and a personal influence over its general secretary, Georg Eccarius, until the latter broke with him in 1871. In the absence of a president, the general secretary had an obvious importance, particularly since he was the only full-time paid officer. Still, he had no unusual powers and had to be reelected every year, first by the congress and then by his fellow general council members. The charge of a "German dictatorship" in the general council was first raised by an English member in 1867, but there was no point at which the substantial majority of English trade unionists could not have removed Eccarius and eradicated the influence of his gray eminence.[26] Marx himself responded to the charge in 1871 when raised by the Bakuninists: "This refers to the *unpardonable* fact that *I* am by birth a German and actually do exercise a decisive intellectual influence on the General Council. (Notabene: the *German* element in the Council is two-thirds weaker *numerically* than either the *English* or the *French*. The crime therefore consists in the fact that the English and French elements are ruled *theoretically* (!) by the German element and find this rule, *i.e.*, German science, very useful and even indispensable.)"[27] If the overwhelming English and French majority reelected Eccarius year after year, and accepted the influence of his gray eminence, it was because they perceived their own interests to be served thereby, and because Marx fenced in his own desires sufficiently to retain their support.[28] But most emphatically, it was not because Marx or his personal followers exercised any secret or sinister power within this perfectly ordinary democratic organization. From the beginning to the end of the IWA, the corresponding secretary for Germany was obliged to work under the Damoclean sword of all democratic leaders — that he could be voted out of office at any time by a majority he did not control.

The Conflict with the Anarchists

We have now gained an adequate vantage point from which to examine the famous conflict between Marx and Bakunin which dominated the last years of the International and ultimately destroyed it. Although this conflict involved differences on a number of general political issues — attitudes toward the state, the right of inheritance, and so forth — our focus here will be on the organizational questions that were an integral and crucially important part of it, and that do much to illuminate both Marx and Bakunin's conception of what the IWA should be and how leaders should function within it.

While Marx and Engels had a slight acquaintance with Bakunin in the 1848 period, there was no contact between them again until Bakunin emerged from long years of imprisonment and Siberian exile to take up revolutionary activity once again from a base in Italy. It was Marx who took the initiative, paying a visit to Bakunin while the latter was passing through London in November 1864. Apart from curiosity about the fate of his old acquaintance, Marx seems to have hoped that Bakunin might work for the cause of the IWA in Italy, where he could form a useful counterweight to the influence of Mazzini. In a letter to Engels, Marx reported: "I must say I liked him very much better than formerly. . . . He is one of the few people whom after sixteen years I find to have developed further instead of backwards." For his part Bakunin expressed his determination to devote himself in the future exclusively to the socialist cause. He evidently gave Marx reason to believe he would work for the IWA in Italy (although he did not join), for Marx shortly sent him copies of the newly printed *Address* and *Rules*. It is obvious from Marx's letter that no serious enmity existed as yet between the two men. Bakunin also responded favorably to the *Address* and *Rules* in a letter beginning "carissimo amico" and suggesting that the two families exchange photographs.[29]

It was not in Bakunin's nature, however, to work patiently in an open mass organization, or in one he did not personally control. Ever since his revolutionary experiences of 1848, Bakunin had been convinced of the need for a secret cadre organization through which the prospective leaders of the revolution, under his own benign guidance, could invisibly coordinate the work of the masses. Wherever he went in subsequent years he repeatedly created such organizations, most of which had only a handful of members and a shadowy existence, but all of which were formed from the same conspiratorial mold. Of his first such secret society, created to mastermind a Czech revolution in 1848, Bakunin himself had written:

> The society was to consist of three separate independent societies under different names and unacquainted with one another: one for the *bourgeois,* one for the students, and one for the villages. Each was subject to a strict hierarchy and to unconditional obedience. . . . These societies were to be limited to a small number of people and were to include as far as possible only able, experienced, energetic and influencial men who, in strict obedience to a central control, would in their turn work invisibly on the masses. All three societies were coordinated by a central committee, which would have consisted of three, or at most five members: myself, Arnold, and others whom we should have had to select. . . . If my plan had been carried out, all the chief threads of the movement would have been concentrated in my hands, and I could have been sure that the intended revolution in Bohemia would not stray from the lines I had laid down for it.[30]

Thus the champion of decentralization, of organization from below, of full local autonomy, saw no contradiction in the fact that his own secret societies all required "strict hierarchy," total centralization, and "unconditional obedience" to his own dictates. The results would have been more sinister — and more damaging to his reputation as an antiauthoritarian — were it not for Bakunin's childlike inability to devote himself consistently to any project for more than a few weeks. Thus his secret societies tended to fade away as quickly as they had been created.

It is not surprising, then, that when Bakunin returned to Italy in 1864 following his interview with Marx, he ignored the IWA and proceeded to establish, first in Florence and then in Naples, the most long-lived of his secret societies — the International Brotherhood. The provisional rules, drawn up by Bakunin personally, divided the group into "National Families," within which each member owed unquestioning obedience to a "National Junta," while the latter in turn took its directions from a "Central International Directorate." Members swore an elaborate oath of fidelity, taken on a dagger, and were threatened with "unsparing vengeance" if they ever violated it. Bakunin wrote into the statutes a promise that when the membership reached seventy, a congress would be held to make these provisional rules permanent, but needless to say this never took place.

He did find occasional new recruits, however, among whom perhaps the most impressive was the Swiss schoolmaster, James Guillaume. In 1867 Bakunin moved to Switzerland himself, where he began looking about for a larger organization which the Brotherhood could enter and capture.[31]

Such an opportunity to capture a larger organization seemed to present itself in September 1867 when some six thousand people attended the founding congress in Geneva of the League of Peace and Freedom, whose initiators had included such notables as John Stuart Mill, Victor Hugo, Alexander Herzen, and Giuseppe Garibaldi. While the organization was bourgeois democratic and pacifist in its substantial majority, Bakunin nonetheless managed to have himself elected as a Russian delegate to the permanent central committee headquartered in Berne. His friends and International Brothers made up the rest of the Russian and Polish delegations, giving him a base from which subsequently to influence the more conservative majority of the central committee. Remarkably enough, by sheer force of his indomitable personality, he seems to have won over sufficient members so as to steer the committee in the direction he wanted during the spring and summer of 1868, only to come to grief when the next congress, meeting in September, restored a more moderate leadership. During these few months, however, Bakunin entered round one of his fateful struggle with Marx.[32]

At some point Bakunin had become convinced that the International rather than the League was destined to play the leading role in any general European revolution, and he hastened to make good his earlier neglect by joining the Geneva section of the IWA in June or July of 1868. But he had no intention of remaining a humble individual member of an organization that, as he imagined, "belonged" to Marx. Instead, as his biographer, E. H. Carr, put it:

> His entry into the International must be a dramatic and significant event. He conceived the bold plan of concluding an alliance between the League and the International which would make him, the prime mover in the League, co-equal with Marx, the directing spirit of the International. The League would thus serve him as a stepping-stone to that position in the International to which his personality and record entitled him.[33]

So it was that in August, Bakunin induced the League's central committee to recommend to its approaching congress a close alliance with the IWA. "In order to become a beneficial and active force, our League ought to become the purely political expression of the great social-economic interests and principles which are now being so triumphantly developed and disseminated by the great International Association of Working Men."[34] In the meantime the central committee sent greetings to the Brussels Congress of the IWA convening in early September and invited its members to attend the League congress in Berne later the same month. If all went well, some kind of merger might result that would give Bakunin his "rightful" influence in the International.

When the League for Peace and Freedom was first created in 1867, Marx had regarded it as essentially a bourgeois undertaking with which the IWA should have no official connection, although individual members might participate if they chose. A resolution to this effect was passed by the general council in August 1867.[35] He remained unaware of Bakunin's growing influence in the League and did not learn of its merger overtures in time to influence the vote taken at the IWA congress meeting in Brussels. There, in Marx's absence and against only three dissenting votes, the delegates adopted a tersely worded resolution declaring that the League "has no *raison d'etre* in the presence of the efforts of the International Working Men's Association," and inviting its members instead to join the IWA.[36] Although Marx was not in the least responsible for the congress's rebuff and at this time still spoke of Bakunin as an "old personal friend," the latter was quick to attribute his rejection to the "malevolence of a certain clique" whose center was Marx. He now began more and more to regard Marx as a dangerous rival.[37]

Bakunin immediately suffered a second humiliation when the League's own congress in Berne repudiated his ideas, leaving him little choice but to secede from that organization along with about twenty of his supporters. One might have supposed he would now urge these supporters to join the International, but he still had no intention of entering except as a general at the head of his own officer corps. Consequently, on the very day he resigned from the League, he and his fellow secessionists formed a brand new organization — the International Alliance of Socialist Democracy. The new group unilaterally declared itself to be a branch of the IWA, accepting all its general rules, but with the idea of serving as a special cadre, "having a special mission to study political and philosophical questions." The Alliance was to have its own central bureau in Geneva (the founders graciously appointed themselves to this body), as well as national bureaus and local branches in each country, and annual congresses that would meet simultaneously with — but in a separate building from — the IWA congresses. In December 1868 the Alliance wrote officially requesting recognition of this status by the IWA general council.[38]

Something of Bakunin's motives may be divined from a curious conversation he had at this time with Charles Perron, one of the three IWA delegates to vote for Bakunin's cause at the Brussels Congress, and a Swiss craftsman whom the anarchist leader now brought into his circle of supporters by the following remarkable steps. According to Perron, Bakunin declared the IWA to be an excellent institution in itself but there was something better he should also join — the Alliance. Perron agreed. Then Bakunin added that even the Alliance was not as purely revolutionary as it might be, and in back of it stood a more dedicated secret cadre which he should likewise join — the International Brotherhood. Perron again agreed. A few days later Bakunin explained further that the Brotherhood was in turn operated by a directorate of three men, of which he, Perron, should be one. Perron once more agreed, but said Bakunin never mentioned the Brotherhood again.[39] How much of this was serious conspiracy, how much a figment of Bakunin's fecund imagination, is difficult to say. But at least in his private fantasy, the anarchist leader seems to have imagined that through the directorate he would control the Brotherhood, through the Brotherhood the Alliance, and through the Alliance the International at large.

Marx followed the creation of the Alliance in the press, at first hoping it would prove stillborn. Only when the official request for recognition arrived in December was he moved to take action. The other members of the general council agreed that the Alliance must be repudiated; they were particularly incensed at the claim that the new organization was necessary to make up for the inadequate "idealism" of the IWA.[40] Marx was appointed to draft the reply. He sent the pertinent documents off for Engels' inspection and for the *first* time expressed suspicion of Bakunin's motives: "*Herr Bakunin* — in the background of this business — is condescending enough to be ready to take the workers' movement under *Russian* direction." What the Alliance proposes, replied Engels with considerable justice, "*c'est l'Etat dans l'Etat*, and from the first moment conflict would burst out between the practical council in London and the theoretical, 'idealistic' council in Geneva. . . . These gentlemen, having no constituents except for themselves, want the International to transform itself into their rank and file."[41] Thus the first serious ill will on Marx and Engels' side came from their understandable objection to Bakunin's desire to work for the IWA only under conditions that would make his Alliance a state within a state, and his self-appointed central bureau a kind of co-equal power alongside the general council. From this point on Marx's suspicions grew geometrically. In another letter to Engels he referred sarcastically to the "anarchist collectivism" Bakunin claimed to stand for: "Anarchy at all events in his head, where there is room for only one clear idea — that B[akunin] must play first fiddle."[42] Thus Marx remained unimpressed when Bakunin tried to win his support in a letter that has often been quoted and was possibly sincere:

> I have come to understand better than ever how right you were when you followed, and invited us all to follow, the great high road of economic revolution, and abused those of us who were losing themselves in the by-roads of national, or purely political, adventures. I am doing now what you began to do twenty years ago. . . . My country is now the International, of which you are one of the principal founders. You see then, dear friend, that I am your disciple and proud to be one.[43]

On the very day this letter was being written, December 22, 1868, the general council unanimously adopted Marx's draft reply. It sharply repudiated the "self-appointed" central council of the Alliance which "takes upon itself the right of admittance to the *International Association*," declaring such pretensions to be "null and void" and stating that the Alliance "may not be admitted as a branch of the *International.*" In justifying this decision, the reply asserted that IWA rules did not allow for the admission of other *international* organizations, that the presence of such a body within the IWA would be "the most infallible means of its disorganization," and would make it a "plaything for intriguers of every type and nationality."[44] While the original intention of the general council had been to make this decision public, Engels' advice seems to have been followed to minimize the whole issue and distribute the reply only within the IWA itself. The following January, Marx reported happily to his partner that all the intraorganizational responses had been positive, without a single voice raised on behalf of Bakunin's group.[45]

The ball was now once again in Bakunin's court. At the end of February the Alliance wrote the IWA general council again saying it stood ready to dissolve itself as a separate international organization if its local sections could be enrolled as sections of the IWA, and if the general council would approve its "radical" program. Bakunin now seemed ready to make do with much less of a grand entrance than he had hoped. Marx regarded the Bakuninist program as an abomination, knew that relatively few people were actually involved, and was highly suspicious of the anarchists' motives. "It really would have been better for us," he wrote Engels, enclosing the new proposal, "if they had kept their 'uncounted legions' in France, Spain, and Italy for themselves." Nonetheless, it is highly significant that Marx did not suggest excluding them from the IWA — surely the best move if he felt his personal ambitions threatened — nor did such an idea cross Engels' mind in his reply.[46] On March 9 the general council unanimously approved Marx's draft response declaring that there was now "no obstacle to the transformation of the sections of the Alliance into sections of the Int. W. Ass." As for the approval of their program, the policy of the IWA was "to let every section freely shape its own theoretical program" so long as "its *general tendency* does not run against the *general tendency* of the Int. W. Ass., viz., *the complete emancipation of the working class.*" In this connection, the Alliance was asked to repair one phrase in its statement which called for the "equalization of classes." The general council found this "logically impossible" and probably "a mere slip of the pen." The offending phrase was duly transformed and the Geneva section of the Alliance was admitted to the IWA in July, the other sections apparently dissolving themselves entirely.[47] We will return later to the vexed question whether Bakunin *really* dissolved the Alliance as an international organization, but those who see Marx as the jealous dictator of the IWA have difficulty explaining why he admitted the Trojan horse within the gates in the first place.

Meanwhile the arena of conflict shifted to the IWA congress held in Basel in September 1869. If Bakunin was not allowed to enter as a general at the head of his own officer corps, at least he could make his congress debut as a great socialist theoretician and orator, and perhaps win over a majority of the delegates for one of his pet demands, "that the right of inheritance ought to be completely and radically abolished." Although Marx did not attend the congress, he had drafted a statement opposing this demand which had been accepted unanimously by the general council and was now read to the congress by Eccarius.[48] The substance of the debate may be passed over. Suffice it to say that Bakunin's eloquence won his proposition an impressive thirty-two votes but not enough to carry it against the twenty-three negative votes and thirteen abstentions (which counted as negatives votes under congress rules). On the other hand, the statement drafted by Marx was then voted down as well by a resounding thirty-seven to nineteen with six abstentions. For the very first time a stand taken by the general council had been repudiated by a congress—herein lay Bakunin's relative victory. Marx himself did not seem terribly disturbed.[49]

The Basel Congress also voted for some significant additions to the authority of the general council, assigning it the power: (1) to admit or deny admission to new groups seeking affiliation, subject to repeal by the next congress; (2) to suspend any local sections pending final disposition by the next congress, and leaving to each federal and regional organization the right of excluding sections from its own fold; and (3) to decide differences between branches of the same national group, or between groups of different nationalities, again with a right of appeal to the next congress. Ironically in view of their later opposition to anything that augmented the power of the general council, Bakunin and his friends supported all these changes at the Basel Congress. Indeed, Bakunin personally introduced the first two! His public explanation was that he wanted the general council to act firmly against "reactionary" sections; it seems equally likely, as Carr suggests, that at this stage he still hoped to capture the general council rather than destroy it. There seems to be no substance, however, to the charge later made by Marx that Bakunin connived at the Basel Congress to have the seat of the general council moved to Geneva.[50]

Following the congress a period of mutual sniping ensued, set off by a series of attacks on the general council published in two Swiss newspapers controlled by the Bakuninists. Marx wrote a circular letter on behalf of the general council responding to these complaints and suggesting that they should have been communicated through the organization instead of being exposed to the outside world.[51] Marx's reply was restrained in tone and did not mention names. During the next few months, however, he also sent out a number of private communications to his friends in Germany, France, and Belgium for the first time denouncing Bakunin personally as the intriguer responsible for the attacks and charging that the Alliance had not really been dissolved at all, but was being used secretly "to prepare for the dictatorship of Bakunin over the International."[52] From Bakunin's correspondence of this same period we may single out a remarkable letter to his old friend, Alexander Herzen, who had written inquiring why Bakunin was attacking Marx's disciples but not the master himself. Bakunin replied:

Marx is unquestionably a useful man in the International. He has been hitherto one of the strongest, ablest, and most influencial supporters of socialism in it, one of the most powerful obstacles to the infiltration into it of any kind of *bourgeois* tendencies or ideas. I should never forgive myself if, from motives of personal revenge, I destroyed or diminished his undoubtedly beneficial influence. It may happen, and probably will happen, that I shall have to enter into conflict with him, not for a personal offence, but on a matter of principle, on a question of state communism, of which he and the party led by him, English and German, are fervent supporters. Then it will be a life and death struggle. But all in good time.

After this initial generosity, however, Bakunin proceeded to assume the conflict to be already engaged, for he explained his attack on the disciples as an application of the principle *"divide et impera.* If I now declared war on Marx, three-quarters of the International would turn against me, . . . but if I begin the war by attacking his rabble, I shall have the majority on my side."[53] Presenting himself alternatively as high-minded man of principle and Machiavellian intriguer, Bakunin must have confounded his friends not less than he aroused the suspicions of his antagonists.

The general council was soon called upon to make use of its new powers in order to settle a pair of disputes, one in France, the other in Switzerland. However immoderate his attack on Bakunin in private communications, Marx's behavior in the resolution of these disputes was tempered by what can scarcely be called anything but a sense of fair play. Anti-anarchist elements in the Lyons section of the IWA, taking encouragement from Marx's above-mentioned circular letter, had moved to expel Albert Richard, Bakunin's principal friend there, and both sides in the dispute appealed to the general council. In a letter to Engels, Marx commented that Richard had been "very active" for the IWA: "Apart from his attachment to Bakunin, with its accompanying pretentiousness, I know of nothing with which he can be reproached. Our last circular letter seems to have made a great sensation, and in Switzerland and France a witch-hunt against the Bakuninists has begun. But everything has its measure and I will see that no injustice occurs." Two weeks later the executive committee produced a judgment, unanimously accepted by the general council, declaring the accusations against Richard to be "without the least foundation" and reaffirming his position in the Lyons section. The accusers' conduct was "energetically" censured.[54]

The Swiss case was more complicated and involved the so-called Romance Federation, which represented all the IWA sections in the French-

and Italian-speaking areas of Switzerland. At a congress of this federation in April 1870, a split developed over the question whether Bakunin's Alliance of Socialist Democracy, already admitted to the IWA generally, should also be admitted—since it was located in Geneva—to the Romance Federation. There was a clear geographic and social basis for the split: the highly skilled craftsmen of the Geneva sections opposed Bakunin's radicalism and political abstentionism, while the semiskilled workers of the remote Jura Mountain area found them attractive. When the latter carried the day by a narrow margin of twenty-one to eighteen, the Geneva-centered delegates seceded to hold their own congress. This left the twenty-one the opportunity to elect an anarchist-dominated Romance federal committee and move its headquarters to their geographic stronghold in La Chaux-de-Fonds in the Jura Mountains. The minority then charged that some of the majority's mandates had been falsified, and that in any event its own eighteen delegates represented two thousand members, whereas the twenty-one represented only six hundred. They demanded a membership referendum to settle the issue, but in the meantime elected their own federal committee to sit in Geneva, so that the Romance Federation now had two committees claiming to speak for it. Both appealed to the general council in London.[55]

The latter body first requested additional documentation from each side and, when it arrived, Marx sent it as usual for his partner's judgment. Engels allowed that the Bakuninist majority was "formally right" and suggested temporizing until the proposed referendum could be carried out. If the Bakuninists refused to take part, as seemed likely, they would at least place themselves morally in the wrong. But the general council eventually struck upon another solution which seems as fair-minded as it was ingenious. Quite apart from animosity toward Bakunin, no one wanted to drive away the two thousand Geneva members who from the beginning had formed the backbone of the IWA in Romance Switzerland. The general council's decision in June 1870 thus referred to the "nominal" character of the anarchists' majority and declared that since the Geneva federal committee had always fulfilled its obligations to the IWA and acted in conformity with its rules, "the General Council does not have the right to relieve it of its title." The general council did not disband or expel the Chaux-de-Fonds committee, however, but requested that it simply "select another, local title of its own choosing."[56] At first the anarchist committee would have nothing to do with this decision, but eventually it complied and would reemerge in the second phase of the Marx-Bakunin struggle as the Jura Federation. In the summer of

1870 Bakunin was obliged for quite personal reasons to abandon Geneva for the relative isolation of Locarno. This coincided more or less with the outbreak of the Franco-Prussian War in July, and brought a temporary lull to the internecine conflict.

During this first phase, the worst Marx can be accused of were some intemperate and not always accurate charges against Bakunin in private communications. On the other hand, his behavior on the general council would appear to have been as restrained and fair-minded as one could ask. At the same general council meeting which pronounced on the Swiss quarrel, Marx even took the extraordinary initiative of seeking, in effect, a vote of confidence or no confidence in the London leadership. He proposed that the next congress, scheduled to meet in Mainz in September 1870, move the seat of the general council to Brussels (where Marx himself obviously would not be a member). "We must not let it crop up as a privilege," he said, "that the Council sits in London." A confidential communication was sent out to all sections asking them to instruct their delegates specifically on this issue. The outbreak of the Franco-Prussian War made it impossible to hold the Mainz Congress, but various responses received by mail expressed confidence in the London general council. There was not a single suggestion that it be moved.[57]

The Final Struggles

Following the suppression of the Paris Commune in May 1871, the supporters of Marx and of Bakunin within the IWA found time once again for the factional battles that mark the second phase of this internecine struggle. The war of words reached a new crescendo in the wake of the London Conference of September 1871, when the Bakuninists published a formidable indictment, usually called the Sonvilier *Circular*, denouncing the general council for various sins of "authoritarianism" since the time of the Basel Congress in 1869. To this the general council responded with a lengthy defense brief in the form of a pamphlet, written by Marx and Engels, called *Fictitious Splits in the International* (1872).[58] The actual minutes of the weekly general council meetings, combined with those of the London Conference, can help us judge the merits of the accusations and of Marx and Engels' defense brief, all of which will give us still further insight into the structure and functioning of the IWA and the leadership roles of Marx and Engels within it.

The Sonvilier *Circular* first charged that the right enjoyed by the IWA congress to elect the general council was purely perfunctory: "One voted by an act of faith for lists that were presented to the congress and which bore names the majority of which were absolutely unknown to the delegates." The result was a general council "composed of the same men, always reelected, for five years in a row."[59] While it is not too startling that the Swiss mountaineers making this complaint, most of them relatively recent recruits, would not have recognized all the names of the predominantly English list of nominees, still there is some justice to the charge of perfunctoriness. General council elections do not appear to have been contested, and the names which appeared on the lists were probably placed there by the outgoing general council, perhaps after informal consultation with the various national delegations represented, a practice that was common in the European labor movement. The result was not really an unchanging oligarchy, however, for only eight of the sixty-six persons on the 1864 general council reappeared on the one elected by the Basel Congress in 1869. Five of these eight, to be sure, were members of the "Marx party," but precisely because they were long-termers, these five were the most likely to be known to the delegates and thus to serve as lightning-rods for any widespread rank-and-file discontent. Thus there is an element of truth in Marx and Engels' otherwise limp retort that the reelection of an old group "would seem to prove that it had done its duty."[60] At least the statutes provided a *means* for the rank and file to vote out unwanted leaders, which is more than can be said of Bakunin's secret societies.

The *Circular* went on to attack the practice of co-optation which permitted the general council to add to its own numbers, and thus "to change completely the nature of its majority and its tendencies," and which resulted in a body most of whose members "are not even our regular mandatories, not having been elected by a congress."[61] Interestingly enough the latter part of the charge was quite true, inasmuch as the Basel Congress had elected twenty-one persons to the general council in 1869, of whom sixteen still appear as members by the time of the London Conference in 1871, while in the meantime the council had added no fewer than thirty-eight new members! But the first part of the charge is manifestly false, for there was no perceptible packing on a factional basis. Of the thirty-eight co-opted members, only four belonged to the "Marx party" (Engels and Frankel were added for the first time; Pfänder and Lochner were old members who had temporarily dropped out of the general council and were now picked up again by co-optation). The anarchists, on the other hand, had *no* representation on the general council elected by the rank-and-file delegates at Basel, but two Bakunin supporters were co-opted by the "authoritarian" enemy (Robin, nominated by Marx himself, and Bastelica), along with two Proudhonist Communards (Theisz and Chalain) who supported Bakunin on many issues, and a fifth (Herman) who became an anarchist by the time of the Hague Congress. Apart from these identifiable antagonists, the bulk of the co-opted members — fifteen — were English trade unionists; eight were quasi-honorary members who were not active or who had dropped away by the time of the London Conference; and nine were refugee Communards added in the summer of 1871.[62] As Marx and Engels plausibly explained, the sizeable turnover had to do mainly with the various insecurities of working-class existence, and not with factionally inspired packing.[63] It should also be noted that the custom of co-optation derived from the original St. Martin's Hall meeting of 1864, thus antedating Marx's influence on the organizational structure. Eventually Marx and Engels themselves would move to limit the practice, as we will see shortly.

The Sonvilier *Circular* went on to deplore the "blind confidence" with which the Basel Congress had voted the general council the right to admit and suspend sections and to resolve disputes within the IWA — a rather awkward charge inasmuch as Bakunin himself had introduced most of these powers and all of his friends had voted for them.[64] Marx and Engels responded that the power over admission was necessary to keep out *agents-provocateurs* and cited concrete examples from France and Austria, but, they pointed out, it had only been used where local groups sought direct affiliation through the general council and never to interfere in cases where locals sought affiliation through an existing national federation. Similarly the right to suspend sections was "necessary for extreme cases" but had never been used to date, and finally in disputes within the association the general council had "only acted as arbiter at the request of the two parties." General council minutes bear out these claims and the minutes of the London and Hague assemblies contain no record of any appeal from a general council decision.[65]

The *Circular* next charged the general council with perpetuating its own "authoritarian" rule by failing to convene a congress in 1870, using the war as a pretext, and by convening a "secret conference" in 1871 instead of a full and open congress. Such a conference was not provided for in the statutes and "certainly did not offer a complete representation of the International since numerous sections, our own in particular, had not been invited."[66] The statutes did manifestly provide for congresses every year, allowing the general council in case of need to change the place but not the time of these gatherings. But the Franco-Prussian War, which broke out seven weeks before the scheduled Mainz Congress, created a quite unforeseen situation, and one may follow the sometimes pained discussions within the general council as its members tried to decide what to do. At first there was some consideration of changing the place from belligerent Germany to some neutral country, but even then the German and French delegates would not likely be permitted to leave their countries. At length Marx proposed that all the sections be written, requesting permission to postpone the congress. This was done, and when a number of answers had been received, all favorable, the council passed a resolution — on an evening when Marx himself was away on vacation — postponing the congress "till the earliest opportunity."[67] The war was followed by the Paris Commune, which in turn was followed by an intensified persecution of the IWA, not only in France but in other Continental countries as well. To hold a public congress, even in a safe country, would be to expose many of its delegates to arrest when they returned home. Not wanting still another year to pass by without any gathering at all, Engels proposed that a conference be held in London in September 1871, with each section sending its representative as to a public congress, but that the meeting be private (to protect the delegates) and confine itself to organizational questions. While the statutes did not provide for such a private conference, there had been a precedent in 1865; and organizational matters, even at regular congresses, were handled in closed session.[68] While the Bakuninists later objected to this procedure, at the time their spokesman on the general council, Paul Robin, who had been pressing for such a gathering since March, rose to second Engels' motion. He even agreed that the conference should be private and held in London.[69] It is true that the Bakuninist federation which issued the Sonvilier *Circular* was not invited, but it had denounced the June 1870 request of the general council that it choose a new name, and had not been in regular communication with London since that date. There is no record that any other section complained about not receiving an invitation to the London Conference.[70]

On the other hand, one cannot help but sympathize with the next Sonvilier complaint, which concerned the overrepresentation of the general council at the London Conference.[71] The council traditionally had been represented at congresses: for example, it chose six of its own members to take their places among the seventy-eight delegates to the Basel Congress. In the case of the London Conference, however, the police repression on the Continent permitted finally only Belgium, Switzerland, and Spain to send their delegates, nine in all. After this situation became known, the general council resolved that the missing countries would be represented by their corresponding secretaries, but then still insisted on its "regular" six delegates, the result being a lopsided gathering in which thirteen delegates were general council members chosen by that body itself, and only nine were authentic elected delegates. The Bakuninists could scarcely be blamed for thinking the deck had been stacked against them. On the other hand, these thirteen included not simply the faithful old guard of the "Marx party" but six recently co-opted members, including two Communards and even Bakunin's friend, André Bastelica, who had been chosen by his "enemies" as one of the six council representatives.[72]

As to the work of the London Conference, the Sonvilier *Circular* put its case eloquently:

> This conference, which absolutely could not consider itself invested with the rights of a congress, has nonetheless passed resolutions which undermine the general statutes and tend to transform the International from a free federation of autonomous sections into a hierarchical and authoritarian organization with disciplined sections placed entirely under the thumb of the general council which can, at its pleasure, refuse their admission or suspend their activities. And to crown this edifice, the conference decided that the general council itself will fix the time and place of the next congress, *or of a conference to replace it*, so that we are threatened by the suppression of general congresses, those great public assizes of the International, and their replacement, at the whim of the general council, by secret conferences similar to the one that has just taken place at London.[73]

Of the specific charges made, Marx and Engels were quick to point out that the power to admit and suspend had not been granted at London, but at Basel, on the initiative of Bakunin and his friends. But they had no ready answer to the second charge.[74] In fact, since the rules required that each congress prescribe the time and place of the next one, there was no correct statutory way for the London Conference to proceed, and the hastily conceived resolution turning the matter over to the general council was introduced in a late session by Cesar DePaepe (certainly no friend of Marx's at this point) and passed hurriedly by *unanimous* vote. The genuine dangers alluded to by the *Circular* were obviated, however, when the general council fixed a regular public congress for September 1872 in the Hague, and introduced there (on Engels' proposal) a permanent change in the rules, allowing the council to substitute a private conference for a congress only with the sanction of a majority of the federations, and prescribing that it must be within three months of the time originally set by the previous congress.[75]

Of the other organizational changes made at London, the only ones that could conceivably be called "hierarchical and authoritarian" were the efforts undertaken to regularize contributions to the chronically insolvent general council, and the permission given it to "publicly denounce and disavow" any IWA publication which—like the two Bakuninist newspapers in Switzerland—discussed internal organizational matters before the bourgeois public.[76] On the other hand, the most consequential measure taken at London—to sanction a federal council for Britain—was manifestly a decentralizing one, and had been opposed hitherto by Marx on the ground that the English trade unionists were not sufficiently radical to be left to themselves. The changeover was now introduced by Marx himself.[77] The general council was also "invited" by the London Conference to limit the number of its co-opted members, and to hear advice from the appropriate sections before electing the corresponding secretary for each country—neither measure seems a step *toward* authoritarianism.[78]

With respect to the disputes in Switzerland, after hearing both sides, the conference confirmed the general council's decision of June 1870 recognizing the Romance Federal Committee in Geneva, but there was still no move to expel the rebellious Bakuninist federation, even though Marx manifestly had the votes to do it. Instead, it appealed to their "feelings of fraternity and union" and invited the "brave working men of the mountain sections" to rejoin their Geneva comrades, but, if that should not be practicable, to take the name "Jura Federation" for themselves.[79] The other perennial conflict, concerning Bakunin's Alliance of Socialist Democracy (whose Geneva center had been admitted by the general council but never by the Romance Federation), now seemed to solve itself, as the handful of surviving members, probably disheartened by their founder's long absence in Locarno, announced the dissolution of the group in August 1871. The London Conference happily declared the problem "settled," but with an eye toward the future also declared that "no branches, section, or groups will henceforth be allowed to designate themselves by sectarian names such as Positivists, Mutualists, Collectivists, Communists, etc., or to form separatist bodies under the name of *sections of propaganda*, etc., pretending to accomplish special missions, distinct from the common purposes of the Association."[80]

It was in reaction to the London Conference that the uninvited Jura sections called their own federal congress at Sonvilier in November 1871 and there issued the *Circular* we have been examining. Its conclusion included the sharp demand that the next IWA congress divest the general council of its "dictatorial" powers and "restore" it to "its normal role, which is that of a simple bureau for correspondence and statistics."[81] It became the Bakuninist objective for the next congress to emasculate the general council completely. Marx and Engels responded with the confidential pamphlet, *Fictitious Splits*, but still made no move to expel the Jura group. On the contrary, until the following spring, they seemed to feel confident that the worst was over. In a January 1872 letter to one of their younger supporters, Engels reviewed the strength of the anarchist legions, pointing out in particular that the Jura Federation no longer had more than two hundred members, and then concluded: "As long as these individuals stay within the legal bounds [that is, the IWA statutes], the General Council will gladly allow them freedom of action, and this coalition of quite heterogeneous elements will soon fall apart itself. But as soon as they undertake anything contrary to the statutes or the resolutions of the congress, the General Council will do its duty."[82] It was not until Marx and Engels had proofs of secret conspiratorial activity, as we will see, that they proposed any expulsions.

With respect to the Hague Congress of 1872 the principal anarchist complaints were, first, that Marx pushed through further rules changes to consolidate the "dictatorship" of the general council over the organization and second, that he packed the congress with his own supporters so as to insure passage of these changes and the expulsion of the anarchists.[83] Let us examine these charges in turn. Of the two rules changes adopted, one granted a specific new power to the general council — the right to suspend not merely sections but federal councils, and even entire federations (like the Jura Federation) until the next congress. The idea was first broached by Marx within the general council in June 1872, although the Jura Federation was not his immediate concern. He pointed to a farcical situation that had developed in the United States, where the millionaire sisters and eccentric reformers, Victoria Woodhull and Tenni Claflin, had recently managed to take over the New York federal council by creating enough local sections on paper to swing the majority their way.[84] Engels then produced a draft which surrounded the proposed new power with safeguards:

> In case of the dissolution of a Federal Council, the General Council shall, at the same time, call upon the branches composing such federation to elect a new Federal Council within thirty days.

In case of the suspension of a whole federation, the General Council is bound to inform thereof immediately all the remaining federations. If the majority of the federations should demand it, the General Council shall convoke an extraordinary Conference composed of one delegate for each federation, which Conference shall meet within a month and decide finally on the matter.

Some members of the general council thought these safeguards too cumbersome and "parliamentary," but Engels insisted that "for every increase of power . . . there should be a safeguard provided." His wording was finally adopted, both here and then at the Hague.[85]

The other rules change was fuzzier, but perhaps for that reason more ominous for the anarchists. It stated that "the General Council is bound to execute the Congress resolutions and to see to it that in every country the principles, rules, and general regulations of the I.W.A. are strictly observed."[86] In the eyes of Marx and his friends, this article was probably conceived in the first instance as a defensive move, to reaffirm the powers of the general council against the express anarchist desire to transform it into a "simple bureau of correspondence and statistics." The statutes had always required the general council to carry congress resolutions into effect, and why else did it have the power to admit and suspend if not to insure *some degree* of conformity to the principles and rules of the organization? The past record of the general council showed that it had behaved responsibly and never used its suspension power in any narrowly sectarian way. Even so, the words "strictly observed" were new and suggested a greater degree of discipline than heretofore. Moreover, the Hague Congress was also asked to reaffirm the antianarchist political action resolution adopted by the London Conference, declaring that "to conquer political power has become the great duty of the working classes," and that to accomplish this the workers should everywhere form their own political party.[87] If the general council now intended to require strict observance of principles such as these, then the anarchist sections obviously could no longer remain within the International.

Still, at the congress itself, the critics of centralization made scarcely any attack on these new powers specifically. One could scarcely think they perceived them as marking any radical change in the organizational structure; in their view the general council already exercised overweening power. The Belgian printer, Désiré Brismée, expressed their common sentiment "that it is futile to discuss the powers of the General Council; we (the Belgians) do not wish the General Council to have any power;

this is a question of principle about which we in Belgium all agree; the delegates of the Vesdre valley even demand complete abolition of the General Council." What the critics objected to, then, was not excessive power versus delegated and circumscribed authority, but any authority whatsoever. This prompted Marx to rejoin: "We would rather abolish the General Council than follow Brismée's wish and transform it into a letter box. . . . the General Council has no army, no budget, but only a moral force and always will be impotent unless it has the consent of the entire Association."[88]

Most anarchist writers also omit to mention that Marx and Engels chose the very moment of their triumph, the alleged consolidation of their dictatorship, to announce . . . their resignations! In May 1872 they had spread word of their intention to withdraw from the general council at the close of its term. "It will be the end of my slavery," Marx wrote to DePaepe; he found the IWA consuming more and more of the energies he wanted to devote to the completion of *Capital*.[89] As they made clear their own intention to step down, Marx and Engels also supported a reform in the composition of the council to meet complaints about co-optation and the overrepresentation of certain nationalities. The creation of the British federal council removed all justification for the traditional preponderance of Britishers (although Bakunin's friends imagined a *German* preponderance), so Marx and Engels proposed that each nationality be given an equal representation on the council, with the practice of co-optation limited strictly to the filling of vacancies.[90]

As for the charge of packing the congress, most older accounts have relied on the factually detailed but highly partisan memoir-history of the Swiss anarchist, James Guillaume, whose chief allegations were: (1) that Friedrich Sorge arrived from America with a "dozen" blank mandates that were then passed out to loyal Marx followers; (2) that Serraillier also arrived "with his pockets full" of similar French mandates from sections whose very existence could not be checked by the other delegates, since all sections within France were necessarily secret in 1872; (3) that nine delegates purported to represent IWA "sections" in Germany, although it was well known that the law there allowed no formal sections and that the Basel Congress of 1869 had ruled that informal representatives from Germany would have no voting rights at IWA congresses; and (4) that various other delegates had obscure and improbable mandates, like Frederic Cournet, the Blanquist exiled in London who represented Denmark! All in all, Guillaume calculated that thirty-one of Marx's forty supporters had phony mandates—only nine were indisputably entitled to vote. As against these nine, the anti-Marx forces had a real majority of twenty-five authentic delegates.[91]

Since the publication in 1958 of a full transcript of the Hague Congress, as well as other related documents, we are in a better position to judge the allegations of packing. Scarcely any of Guillaume's charges were raised at the congress itself. Two supporters of the minority were placed on the credentials committee and had a chance to inspect the secret credentials of the French delegates that were withheld from the congress at large, yet the two raised no question — either on the floor or in any minority report — as to the authenticity of the French mandates. Neither was the authenticity of the German sections challenged, or the voting rights of their delegates. The existence of the thirty-one phony delegates in Guillaume's memoirs obviously rested on arguments thought up by the anarchists afterward, for only five pro-Marx delegates were challenged at the time. After extensive discussion of each case by the full congress, Vaillant was accepted "almost unanimously," Barry was accepted with only two contrary votes, Dereure and Sorge with only one apiece, and Lafargue with none. Surely a determined minority of twenty-five, sincerely convinced it was being swindled, could have done better than this. In truth the five challenges had as much to do with personal and local animosities as with any fears of systematic packing. On the other side, the majority-dominated credentials committee challenged eight delegates, and a ninth was added during the plenary discussion, but eventually opposition was dropped against six, one was admitted over Marx and Engels' personal opposition by a vote of thirty to twenty, one was temporarily "suspended" until the case of the Alliance was resolved, and only one was denied admission altogether. This was William West, who represented the Woodhull element in America and found no one to vote for his credentials. Opinion at the Hague Congress seems to have been rather less neatly polarized than most writers have assumed.[92]

It is certainly true that Marx and Engels made greater efforts than ever before to mobilize their supporters in preparation for the congress. They had reason to believe the Bakuninists were doing the same thing, and not necessarily by legitimate means. As Engels wrote to Theodor Cuno:

Bakunin & Co. will make every effort to beat us at the congress, and as these gentlemen have no scruples about methods, we must take precautionary measures. They will send delegates from a hundred different societies, which don't even belong to the International, and try to obtain a seat and a vote for these persons as delegates of the International, in order — with help from a coalition of the most heterogeneous elements — to place the General Council in the minority.

In another contemporaneous letter Engels totaled up the various phony mandates he anticipated and produced a figure well over one hundred, showing how greatly he — like the anarchists on their side — overestimated the organizing ability and unscrupulousness of the other side.[93] The anarchists did manage to organize some twenty new sections in Italy, and these proceeded — without ever having been formally admitted by the general council — to elect delegates to the Hague Congress. But a month before the gathering opened, these delegates, perhaps anticipating that they would not survive the credentials fight, announced their secession from the IWA and called for a creation of a new "anti-authoritarian" international.[94]

Given these anticipations and the conviction that Bakunin had used similar tricks to overrepresent his forces at earlier gatherings, Marx and Engels understandably wanted to mobilize their own forces fully. The question is whether they used underhanded means to do so. Marx's most famous effort in this regard was a letter to Friedrich Sorge in New York, later made public, in which he implored: *"At this congress it will be a matter of life and death for the International. You and at least one other, if not two, must come. As for those sections that do not send their own delegates directly they can send mandates."* Marx proceeded to list a dozen friends already in Europe in whose names the mandates might be made out. Then he concluded: "Every section, of course, what ever its strength, unless more than five hundred, is entitled to only one delegate."[95] The practice of allowing sections to choose delegates from outside their own membership was perhaps inevitable in a workers' organization, where many sections were simply too poor to send one of their own members to the often distant congresses. Both factions had previously made use of this device (at the Basel Congress, Bakunin represented Naples and Lyons, although he then resided in Switzerland). So long as the section itself chose the outsider to represent it, there could be no complaint. And this is obviously what Marx intended by including the list of — well-known — names which might be chosen by various pro-Marx sections in America. His desire to remain within the statutes is also indicated by the last sentence — nowhere in any surviving letter did he or Engels suggest manufacturing fictitious sections of any other unstatutory device. To be sure, Sorge seems to have gone Marx one better and brought over signed mandates from a number of sections with the delegate left unspecified, so the name could be added in Europe. But if he indeed brought a dozen, as Guillaume alleges, they were not used very efficiently for packing purposes: only four were actually distributed and three of those were given to delegates who already held at least one other valid mandate, like Marx who was a representative of the general council as well as of the Leipzig section. Because multiple mandates did not entitle a delegate to multiple votes, the Marx forces gain exactly one vote (Barry) from Sorge's famous manipulation! The evidence in favor of packing—by either side—is skimpy indeed.[96]

A further allegation is that Marx secured the expulsion of Bakunin at the Hague by introducing trumped-up charges against him, and this seems at least partially true. Prior to 1872 Marx and Engels made no move to expel the Bakuninists, and Engels' letter of January 1872 will be recalled in which he acknowledged their "freedom of action" so long as they did not "undertake anything contrary to the statutes."[97] In April 1872, however, Paul Lafargue reported just such an undertaking from Spain—the continued existence of the supposedly dissolved Alliance of Socialist Democracy as a secret cadre organization within the IWA. When the written proofs arrived in London, including a copy of its statutes and a letter of encouragement from Bakunin himself, Marx and Engels secured general council approval for an indictment to be laid before the impending Hague Congress proposing the expulsion of all Alliance members. This indictment, composed by Engels, declared: "Need we say that the very existence of such a secret society within the International is a flagrant breach of our General Rules? These Rules know only one kind of members of the International, with rights and duties equal for all; the Alliance separates them into two classes, the initiated and the profane, the latter destined to be led by the first, by means of an organization whose very existence is unknown to them."[98]

At the Hague Congress a five-man committee of inquiry was chosen, including one supporter of the minority, to investigate the charges. It listened to Engels and scrutinized the documents he presented, and then to the Spanish delegates, who freely admitted that the Alliance *had* existed in Spain, but, they insisted, it had since been dissolved. Having no means of delving further into the matter, the committee seemed to have drawn up the first two articles of its final report, stating rather limply that the Alliance clearly had existed, but that there was "insufficient proof of its continued existence," and that the Bakunin letter showed that he had tried to establish the Alliance, "and perhaps had succeeded."[99] On such conclusions one could scarcely expel anybody, and Marx appears to have decided to use his secret weapon, held in reserve till then in hope that the expulsions could be based on objective evidence alone.

The story is a familiar one. Two years earlier, Bakunin had contracted with a St. Petersburg publisher to do a Russian translation of *Capital*, and had accepted a substantial advance. Characteristically, he soon tired of the project, but not before having spent all the money. When the publisher began to make inquiries, Bakunin explained his predicament to his young nihilist disciple, Sergei Gennadyevich Nechayev, little realizing that the totally amoral Nechayev, on his own initiative, would take drastic action. In the name of an imaginary revolutionary committee Nechayev wrote the publisher threatening unpleasant consequences should he press Bakunin further for either the translation or the return of the money. Marx became aware of this letter and contrived to obtain it just prior to the Hague Congress. Although he knew Bakunin was not personally responsible for it, Marx must have led the committee to believe the contrary, which would explain the third article of its final report, declaring Bakunin guilty of fraud and threats against another individual, and calling for his expulsion. The committee report also called for the expulsion of the two Jura leaders, James Guillaume and Adhémar Schwitzguebel, "in the conviction that they still belong to the society Alliance," that is, to the society whose continued existence remained unproven according to article 1 of the same report. Clearly Marx's appearance before the committee, his use of the relevant but damning Nechayev letter had been the major factor in producing the expulsion recommendation. The full congress then voted to expel Bakunin and Guillaume but drew the line at Schwitzguebel.[100] Marx and Engels had to content themselves with only two actual expulsions. They had never sought to expel all opponents of the general council, however, or even all anarchists, but only those who belonged to a secret cadre organization within the IWA, and only after written proofs of its existence had been discovered.

Marx and Engels have also been accused of killing the International by transferring the seat of the general council to New York rather than seeing it fall into the hands of their enemies. We have already taken note of their own decision the previous spring to withdraw from the council at the end of its term. What would happen to it thereafter? Given the crucial votes at the Hague Congress, it is unlikely Marx and Engels were concerned about an anarchist takeover; the anarchists now seemed certain to follow the example of their Italian confreres and split from the old International to form a new one of their own. There were scarcely any anarchist leaders in London anyway. More to the point was the existence of a new anti-Marx faction in the British Federation under the leadership of John Hales, and the large number of Blanquists among the French exiles in London. If the general council remained in that city without Marx and Engels' participation, a Blanquist preponderance seemed the most likely consequence. Hence their fateful action. But an IWA controlled by the Blanquists would not likely have lasted any longer than the one directed from New York. The short and melancholy history of Bakunin's secessionist international similarly points to the conclusion, embraced by most recent authorities, that the 1870s were singularly unpropitious for *any* international working-class organization.[101] If this is true, then Marx and Engels' contribution to the demise of the IWA was only a modest one. The responsibility must also be shared by the majority of the Hague Congress delegates, who were independent enough to reject Marx and Engels' leadership on at least two votes (the accreditation of Sauva and the refusal to expel Schwitzguebel), but who nonetheless voted for the "suicidal" transfer to New York.

Judged as a whole, there is no doubt that the IWA became in the course of its history a more centralized organization, but not necessarily a less democratic one for that reason. Even after the Hague revisions, the powers of the general council could scarcely be called dictatorial. Its most abusable power — the right to refuse admission and the right to suspend — had rarely been used in fact and were both subject to appeal to the next congress. The absence of such appeals over the years seems to indicate that the general council made use of these powers in ways the great bulk of the membership approved. As for Marx and Engels personally, neither one exercised any *formal* powers that could possibly be called dictatorial (in contrast to those enjoyed by Lassalle and Bakunin in *their* organizations). The worst provable offense of Marx and Engels was their use of the Nechayev letter. Otherwise, the charges made against them tend on close inspection to have little real substance. Their behavior overall remained well within the limits of the democratic tradition.

❧[9]❧

Strategy III:
Skipping Stages

IT IS NOW TIME to turn back to a subject that occupied much of our attention in volume 1 — Marx and Engels' strategies for attaining communism. In the years before 1850 we saw how they elaborated two distinct revolutionary strategies for two different kinds of situations. In advanced countries where the working class was already a majority, where its development was held back by a class oligarchy of the bourgeoisie, such as in Britain, it sufficed for the workers to organize their numbers as a political force and overthrow bourgeois rule in a mass democratic revolution. This always remained for Marx and Engels the classic path to communism, the ideal type as it were, and we have labeled it Strategy I. Strategy II was worked out to deal with less developed but still essentially bourgeois countries, like France and Germany, where the workers were not yet numerous enough to do the job alone and were counseled to seek allies among the older middle strata — the peasants and the urban petty bourgeois. Such an alliance of the majority classes, as we have called it, was expected to lead to communism only through a more extended process with distinct stages, but would still begin with a mass revolution to establish democratic institutions. This strategy remained appropriate for most Continental countries during the rest of their lives, as we saw most dramatically in the case of the Paris Commune.

In the 1870s, however, political and social developments led Marx and Engels to consider two new paths to communism. With the emergence of stable democratic institutions in parts of Western Europe, the two men began to speak for the first time of a possible peaceful and legal assumption of power by the workers in the most advanced countries. At the other extreme and perhaps more surprisingly, for very backward countries with remnants of primitive communist institutions, most notably Russia, they

[299]

began to speak quite seriously of the possibility of skipping over the capitalist stage of development entirely. Both these new ideas are eminently worthy of our examination since the first in part anticipated twentieth-century social democratic thinking, and the second in part anticipated Bolshevik ideas. In both cases, however, we will try to make clear what still separated Marx and Engels profoundly from the twentieth-century ideologies.

Saving the question of peaceful revolution for chapter 10, we will examine here Marx and Engels' thinking on the possibility of skipping stages, primarily in reference to Russia, but with an eye toward the obvious implications for all backward countries.[1]

Changing Assessments of the Obshchina

The idea that Russia might find its own unique path to communism, one that avoided capitalism altogether, was not invented by Marx and Engels of course; it was the common heritage of several generations of Russian revolutionaries and can be traced back mainly to the writings of Alexander Herzen in the 1840s. Herzen's argument rested on the conviction that Russia's vast peasant population was uniquely ripe for communism because it already held property in common through the distinctively Russian institution of the communal village, called the *mir* or *obshchina*, the latter term being technically more exact. The peasant lands of each village were conceived as belonging to the community as a whole and were redistributed every ten years to preserve a rough equality among its member families. The village was also collectively responsible for the payment of taxes, and administered many of its own affairs collectively, including agricultural decisions such as when to plow, to plant, and so forth. Those who advocated an agrarian communism in Russia based on the *obshchina* came to be called populists, and Herzen along with Mikhail Bakunin became the mentors from whom succeeding generations of rebellious Russian students and intellectuals imbibed these ideas. For the populists it was not a matter of skipping stages (that would presuppose a Marxist conception of historical development), but of avoiding the moral degeneration they associated with Western capitalism, and of providing through Russia's providential uniqueness a grand example for the moral regeneration of mankind.[2]

One can imagine the reaction of those arch-Russophobes, Marx and Engels, to this holier-than-thou belief in Russia's uniqueness and special mission to redeem mankind. Up to the 1870s they had nothing but scorn for populist fantasy-mongers who imagined that communism could be established in a backward country without the necessary material and human preparation. In the 1848 period as well, it will be recalled, Marx and Engels had repeatedly spoken out against those impatient radicals in Germany who thought it possible to skip over the necessary period of bourgeois-sponsored economic development.[3] In 1859 Marx summed up these thoughts classically in his *Critique of Political Economy:* "No social order is ever destroyed before all the productive forces for which it is sufficient have been developed, and new superior relations of production never replace older ones before the material conditions for their existence have matured within the framework of the old society. Mankind thus inevitably sets itself only such tasks as it is able to solve."[4] In the preface to *Capital* he expressed a similar thought by saying: "The country that is more developed industrially only shows, to the less developed, the image of its own future." Or even more categorically: "A society . . . can neither clear by bold leaps, nor remove by legal enactments, the obstacles offered by the successive phases of its normal development."[5] Thus at least as of 1867 Marx would appear to have allowed no possibility for skipping stages in Russia or any other country.

The Russian nation and people meant little to Marx and Engels in their early years; for them Russia was simply the autocracy — the expansionist colossus of the East, the reserve army of European reaction. By the early 1850s they had become familiar with the writings of Herzen and Bakunin touching on the *obshchina*, and Engels at least became sufficiently interested at this time to learn the Russian language and study other Slavic languages. But he made his motivation quite clear in an 1852 letter to Marx:

> Apart from the linguistic interest, there is also the consideration that at least one of us, when the next great fuss begins, should know the languages, history, literature, and social institutions of precisely those nations with which we will immediately come into conflict. Bakunin really became a somebody for the simple reason that nobody knew any Russian. And the venerable Panslav dodge about transforming old Slavic communal property into communism, and presenting the Russian peasant as a born communist, will be harped upon all over again.[6]

Ironically then, Engels set about learning Russian in order to *refute* the populist notion that the *obshchina* could be the direct basis for a communist society. Marx certainly must have shared these sentiments; as late as 1868, when he read G. L. Maurer's famous study proving the existence of communal villages among the early Germans, Marx commented to his partner:

> It's interesting just at this moment, that the *Russian* practice of redistributing the land at fixed intervals (in Germany initially every year) survived in Germany here and there until the 18th and even the 19th century. Though Maurer knew nothing of the view I have put forward, i.e. that the Asiatic or Indian forms of property constitute everywhere in Europe the beginning, he provides further proof of it. The Russians lose even the last traces of a claim of originality, even in this line. All that is left to them is that they are still stuck today in the forms which their neighbors have long since cast off.[7]

The *obshchina* appears here not only as unoriginal but as a vestige that long since should have been "cast off." In another 1868 letter he added that the only features distinguishing the Russian communal village from its historical German counterpart were negative ones: "(1) the *nondemocratic, patriarchal,* character of the commune leadership, and (2) the *collective responsibility* to the state for taxes, etc. It follows from the second point that the more industrious a Russian peasant is, the more he is exploited for the purposes of the state. . . . The whole foul mess is now in the process of collapse."[8] Marx seemed not at all unhappy at the prospect.

How then can we account for the evident change of attitude about the prospects of the *obshchina* by the mid-1870s? There is very little direct evidence from which to construct an answer, partly because after 1870 Engels took up residence in London, bringing to an end the almost daily interchange of letters between the two men that offers such a marvelous insight into their thinking. Nonetheless it is reasonable to begin with the early signs of social ferment they saw emanating from Russia. Apart from one flight of fancy in an 1851 Engels letter, their first perception of social revolutionary possibilities in Russia came in the wake of that country's defeat in the Crimean War, which brought growing pressure for domestic reform, especially for the emancipation of the serfs. The assembling of a committee of nobles in St. Petersburg in 1858 to consider the latter question convinced Marx momentarily that "in Russia *the revolution has begun*," as he reported to Engels, recalling the French Assembly of Notables called in 1787 on the eve of the Great Revolution.[9] Marx followed the various emancipation proposals closely and kept his *New York Daily Tribune* readers well informed. He pointed to the strong aristocratic resistance to emancipation, stressing that the nobles were in no mood for a "4th of August" style voluntary renunciation of their manorial privileges:

> The nobility are sure to resist; the Emperor, tossed about between state necessity and expediency, between fear of the nobles and fear of the enraged peasants, is sure to vacillate; and the serfs with expectations worked up to the highest pitch, and with the idea that the Czar is for them, but held down by the nobles, are surer than ever to rise. And if they do, the Russian 1793 will be at hand; the reign of terror of these half-Asiatic serfs will be something unequalled in history, . . . and finally place real and general civilization in place of that sham and show introduced by Peter the Great.[10]

It is important to note that neither here nor elsewhere did Marx speak of this as a bourgeois revolution. His parallels to the French Revolution concern its agrarian side exclusively. Both Marx and Engels spoke expressly of an "agrarian revolution" in Russia.[11] While Marx seemed confident that it would ultimately advance the cause of "civilization" in that country, he offered no further speculations on its character or on what role the *obshchina* might play in it. The emancipation of Russia's serfs was actually accomplished in 1861 without producing any sort of revolution. The final form of emancipation, Marx judged at the time, actually strengthened the czarist autocracy, and during most of the next decade he again lost interest in Russia's domestic situation.

That interest revived dramatically at the end of the 1860s with the appearance of a single book — N. Flerovsky's *The Situation of the Working Class in Russia*. So intrigued was Marx by reports of this massive first-hand empirical study by a populist writer mainly of Russian peasant conditions that he now learned the Russian language in order to read it. "I read the first 150 pages of *Flerovsky's* book," he reported to Engels in February 1870: "This is the first work to tell the truth about Russian economic conditions. . . . One can see that the man has traveled around everywhere and seen everything for himself. . . . No socialist doctrine, no mysticism about the land (although in favor of the communal form of ownership), no nihilistic extravagance. . . . This is the most important book which has appeared since your *Condition of the Working Class*."[12] One of Flerovsky's main themes was the deterioration of peasant conditions *since* emancipation, in particular the undermining of communal property in the villages. In a second letter to Engels, Marx drew his own conclusions: "From his book it follows irrefutably that the present conditions in Russia can no longer be maintained, that the emancipation of the serfs only, of course, hastened the process of disintegration and that a fearful social revolution is approaching."[13] In another letter to his daughter and son-in-law Marx noted Flerovsky's predictable belief in "the infinite perfectability of the Russian nation and the providential principle of *communal property* in its Russian form," and then went on: "But never mind that. After studying his work one is firmly convinced that an extremely frightful social revolution — naturally in the lower forms that correspond to the present Moscovite stage of development — is inevitable and imminent in Russia. That is good news. Russia and England are the two great corner pillars of the present-day European system."[14] Here again we find the expectation of a revolution neither bourgeois nor proletarian but in the form of an elemental peasant outburst, to be welcomed first and foremost because it would destroy the czarist state. But without support from any urban class, could such an "extremely frightful" revolution produce anything positive for Russia? Would it not be doomed to failure like the historic risings of Stenka Razin and Pugachev? Marx never had much confidence, after all, in peasant *jacqueries*.

On these questions Marx, and to a somewhat lesser extent Engels, appear to have been significantly influenced by the newer generation of Russian populists. The doctrine they hitherto identified with the ethnocentricism and aristocratic dilettantism of Herzen and Bakunin now became intellectually more imposing and politically less objectionable in the writing of Flerovsky. Marx was almost equally impressed with another empirically inclined younger populist writer — Nikolai Gavrilovich Chernyshevsky. These two men, Marx commented, "really do the Russians honor and prove that their country is also beginning to participate in the general movement of our century."[15] During this same period of time in 1870 a group of Russian revolutionary émigrés in Switzerland broke away from Bakunin's tutelage, renounced his Panslavism, and declared themselves in favor of Polish independence. Under the leadership of Nikolai Issaakovich Utin they formed a Russian branch of the IWA in Geneva and invited Marx to represent them in the general council. Happy to have such allies in the struggle against Bakunin, Marx accepted, commenting to Engels that it was "a funny position for me to be functioning as the representative of young Russia!"[16] In the radical migration to London that followed the suppression of the Paris Commune, Marx also made the acquaintance of Pyotr Lavrovich Lavrov, destined to become the foremost of all populist writers in the 1870s. Finally, these positive contacts with Russian revolutionaires led to the early translation and publication in Russian of Marx's *Capital* by Nikolai Frantsevich Danielson, a St. Petersburg populist economist with whom Marx and then Engels would continue to correspond for the rest of their lives. All these were men Marx and Engels could not help but respect, and all of them believed in the vitality of the *obshchina*, its potential as a basis for communism in Russia. Thus Marx and Engels could not help but themselves consider more seriously the potential of the communal village. Marx in particular became more and more engrossed in Russian social and economic studies, promising Danielson in 1872 that "in volume II of *Capital*, in the section on landownership, I will occupy myself very extensively with its Russian form."[17] Occasional comments Marx now made on the *obshchina* began to take on a more positive tone, as when he wrote Kugelmann that the *obshchina* was not the cause of peasant poverty, as some believed, but rather "the only thing that eases it"; or when he commented to Danielson that the communal village did not likely originate from some czarist ukase, "when everywhere else it arose spontaneously and formed a necessary phase in the development of free peoples." Such were the changes that may help to explain Marx's first revisionist pronouncement on the *obshchina* in 1877.[18]

Two years before Marx, however, Engels wrote his own first pronouncement on the subject, expressing his views far more extensively and forthrightly than Marx himself would do. We can only speculate that Engels was influenced by the same considerations that altered his partner's views, although there is reason to believe the two differed significantly on the issue, as we will see shortly. Engels' essay grew out of one of his innumerable polemics against Bakuninism, in which he chanced to criticize an essay by one Pyotr Nikitich Tkachev, whom he supposed— mistakenly as it turned out—to be an anarchist disciple. The issue of the *obshchina* was not initially involved, but Tkachev responded by publishing an open letter rebutting Engels' charges and arguing at some length that Russia was closer to a social revolution than Western Europe because her peasantry was already "permeated with the principles of common ownership."[19] The open letter evoked a second and more sustained blast from Engels, published in April 1875, under the title, "On Social Relations in Russia."

The opening paragraphs sounded most uncompromising as Engels reminded his readers that "only at a certain level of development of the productive forces of society, an even very high level for our modern conditions, does it become possible to raise production to such an extent that the abolition of class distinctions can be a real progress." Attempting to abolish them under backward conditions brings about "stagnation or even decline in the mode of social production." Tkachev had argued that Russia, having no significant bourgeoisie, would be easier to transform in a socialist direction, overlooking what Engels found to be crucial — the vast modernizing role of the bourgeoisie. "A man who will say that this [socialist] revolution can be more easily carried out in a country, because *although* it has no proletariat, it has no bourgeoisie *either*, only proves that he has still to learn the ABC of Socialism."[20]

Engels then turned to the condition of the peasantry, pouring water in Tkachev's wine by reminding him that common ownership of peasant land was by no means unique to Russia; that Russian peasants no longer even *worked* their land in common but only redistributed it periodically; that these isolated village communities, far from promoting a revolutionary outlook, were everywhere the "natural basis for oriental despotism"; and that Russian peasants, though they had occasionally risen against the nobility, had never rebelled against the crown. The emancipation of 1861, by giving the best land to the nobles and saddling the peasants with crushing redemption payments on top of their already crushing tax burden was really a death sentence for the *obshchina*. Nonetheless, Engels allowed, it was also turning the peasants for the first time against the state as such, and thus creating a real revolutionary situation. It was at this point that he made the central observation we are concerned with and it deserves to be quoted in full:

> It is clear that communal ownership in Russia is long past its period of florescence and to all appearances is moving towards its disintegration. Nevertheless, the possibility undeniably exists of raising this form of society to a higher one, if it should last until circumstances are ripe for that, and if it shows itself capable of development in such manner that the peasants no longer cultivate the land separately, but collectively; of raising it to this higher form without it being necessary for the Russian peasants to go through the intermediate stage of bourgeois small holdings. This, however, can only happen if, before the complete breakup of communal ownership, a proletarian revolution is successfully carried out in Western Europe, delivering to the Russian peasant the pre-conditions requisite for such a transition, particularly the material conditions which

he needs if only to carry through the revolution necessarily connected therewith of his whole agricultural system. It is, therefore,
sheer bounce for Mr. Tkachev to say that the Russian peasants, although "owners," are "nearer to Socialism" than the propertyless
workers of Western Europe. Quite the opposite. If anything can
still save Russian communal ownership and give it a chance of growing into a new, really viable form, it is a proletarian revolution in
Western Europe.[21]

In this fashion Engels managed to reconcile the populist dream of avoiding capitalism with his own just repeated insistence on a high-productivity
foundation for communism, while incidently offering a jab at Tkachev's
Russocentrism. He was not insisting that the Russians simply wait for the
proletarian revolution in the West, for in at least three other writings
he suggested that Russia might indeed give the signal, that the overthrow
of czarism as the ultimate bastion of European reaction might unleash
the workers' revolution in the West.[22] What he *was* insisting upon was
the presence of socialist regimes in Western Europe if the *obshchina* was
to be rescued and transformed as the basis for a modern agrarian socialism in Russia. The West would have to "deliver" to the Russians the "preconditions," presumably capital goods ("material conditions") and technological expertise for carrying out a modernizing revolution of the "whole
agricultural system."

In an 1894 "Afterword" to this essay Engels added some interesting
detail to his argument. Even more categorically than before, he insisted
that the *obshchina* "has existed for centuries without ever having produced any stimulus to develop out of itself a higher form of communal
property. . . . The initiative for such a possible transformation of the
Russian village community can only originate, not in the community itself, but solely among the industrial proletariat of the West. . . . How
could it acquire the gigantic productive forces of capitalist society in the
form of socially owned property and instruments of production before
capitalist society itself has brought about this revolution? How could the
Russian communities show the world how to operate heavy industry collectively when they have already forgotten how to cultivate their lands
for their common good?" By 1894 capitalist institutions were already
firmly implanted in Russia and it was no longer possible to think of avoiding capitalism altogether, but Engels was still willing to consider a drastic "shortening" of the capitalist period, given help from a socialist Western Europe:

After the victory of the proletariat and the transfer of the means of production to common ownership among Western European peoples, the countries which have just entered the stage of capitalistic production and have still preserved institutions of gentile society or remnants of them will derive from the remnants of common ownership and the corresponding folkways a powerful means of appreciably shortening their process of development to a socialist society and of escaping most of the sufferings and struggles through which we in Western Europe have had to labor. But in this process the example and the active support of the formerly capitalistic West is an unavoidable prerequisite. Only when the capitalistic economy has been overcome in its homeland and the countries of its flowering, only when the backward countries see by this example "how the job is done," how modern industrial productive forces can be made to serve the collectivity as socially owned property — only then can they tackle this shortened process of development. But then they will also be certain of success. And this goes for all countries in a pre-capitalistic stage of development, not merely for Russia.[23]

In the last sentence Engels made it clear he was not granting a specific concession to Russian populism but putting forth a general possibility for all societies with remnants of gentile institutions. He specifically mentioned the South Slav household community, or *zadruga*, which he elsewhere described enthusiastically as "a splendid starting place for development into communism, exactly like the Russian *mir*."[24] To skip over or foreshorten the stage of bourgeois domination did not under such circumstances violate Engels' deeper assumptions about societal development. Would not a proletarian government in Britain have to carry along, for example, the more remote regions of the Scottish Highlands, and a similar government in France, the backward peasants of Gascony? Western Europe as a whole would be able to carry along backward Russia, not against its will of course, but because surviving gentile traditions would dispose the vast Russian peasantry in the same direction. Russia thus could achieve socialism by hanging on to the coattails of the proletarian revolution in the West. Any other backward country could do the same if its gentile institutions and traditions were still sufficiently vital.

Marx's Differences from Engels

Marx approached the problem more abstractly than his partner, and much more hesitantly, but in a way that suggests some rather different underlying assumptions. His earliest surviving writing on the subject dates from 1877 (thus two years after Engels' article) and takes the form of a letter he intended to send to the editors of the St. Petersburg journal, *Otechestvenniye Zapiski (National Review)*. An article had appeared in this journal by the populist writer Nikolai Konstantinovich Mikhailovsky, which cited *Capital* and asserted it to be Marx's view that Russia must undergo capitalism and the consequent dissolution of the *obshchina* before it could attain socialism. Marx wanted to protest this was not necessarily his view, that his ideas on historical development were not so rigid: "In the chapter on primitive accumulation I claim only to trace the path by which the capitalist order in Western Europe developed out of the feudal economic order," a process which did indeed involve the separation of most peasants from their land, transforming them into proletarians. If Russia becomes a capitalist country, as seems to be happening, then it "will have to submit to the implacable laws of such a system." But must Russia inevitably become a capitalist country in the first place, as Mikhailovsky asserts? "For him it is absolutely necessary to change my sketch of the origin of capitalism in Western Europe into an historical-philosophical theory of a Universal Progress, fatally imposed on all peoples, regardless of the historical circumstances in which they find themselves. . . . But I must beg his pardon. This is to do me both too much honor and too much discredit." At the end of his letter Marx insisted again that "one will never succeed with the open sesame of an historical-philosophical theory, of which the supreme virtue consists in its being *supra-historical*."[25] Clearly he wanted to say that Russia was *not* fated to follow the same path as Western Europe, and his remarks suggest once again a more open-ended and flexible conception of historical development than he is usually credited with having.

With regard to the issue at hand, however, Marx seemed reluctant to go very much further. He contrasted the view of Herzen, in whose hands "the Russian village community serves merely as an argument to prove that Europe, old and decadent, ought to be regenerated by the victory of Panslavism," with those of Chernyshevsky, for whom Marx obviously had more sympathy: "In several remarkable articles the latter has considered the question of whether Russia should begin by destroying the rural commune in order to pass to the capitalist system, as the liberal economists want it, or whether, on the contrary, without experiencing the hardships of this system, it can appropriate its benefits while developing its own historical conditions. He takes his stand in favor of the last solution." Marx then noted his own developing interest in the question and his own conclusion:

In order to be able to judge the economic development of contemporary Russia from the knowledge of its causes, I learned Russian, and then for many years studied the official and other publications concerning this subject.

I arrived at this conclusion: If Russia continues to move in the path followed since 1861, it will lose the finest chance that history has ever offered a people, and undergo all the fatal vicissitudes of the capitalist system.[26]

Marx was clearly impressed by Chernyshevsky's arguments: Russia did have at least a chance to skip over capitalism, indeed "the finest chance that history has ever offered a people." But Marx also seemed unsure of his own opinions, which he expressed in curiously roundabout fashion, for he elaborated no further and in fact finally decided not to send the letter at all. It was not published until after his death.[27]

There is another noteworthy feature in this letter. While Marx spoke of appropriating the "benefits" of Western capitalism, he did not stipulate a Western proletarian revolution as a prerequisite for Russian success as Engels had done. This might be dismissed as an oversight, but the Western revolution is missing again in Marx's next and most extensive treatment of the issue—his 1881 letter to Vera Ivanovna Zasulich. This young Russian revolutionary, exiled in Geneva, had written Marx in February 1881 posing once again the question we have been examining here. Some Russian socialists were quoting *Capital* as proof the *obshchina* was doomed, she wrote, in which case there was little for the Russian comrades to do but calculate "in how many decades the land of the Russian peasant will pass from his hands into those of the bourgeoisie, and in how many centuries Russian capitalism will attain perhaps a development similar to that of Western Europe." Is that really what Marx wanted? The other possibility was "that this village community, if freed from the immoderate exigencies of the fisk, the payments to arbitrary landlords and administrators, is capable of developing in a socialist path, that is, of organizing stepwise its production, and the distribution of its products on a socialist basis; in this case the revolutionary socialist must sacrifice all his powers to the freeing and further developing of the community."[28] Here was an appeal Marx could scarcely ignore, and he dropped everything to write a lengthy response, revising it through three drafts, all of which have fortunately survived. On the main issue at hand there are only small differences of nuance among the drafts, moving if anywhere in the direction of greater confidence in the socialist potential of the village community.[29]

Marx began by placing the Russian *obshchina* at a point of social evolution somewhere between the gentile society he had recently been studying in Lewis Henry Morgan's work and more modern forms based on private property. With the former type it shared the institution of collective possession of the soil, but it had already lost other important characteristics of gentile society — kinship as the basis of community organization, a common dwelling for the whole group, and collective tilling of the soil. The result was a "deep-seated dualism" which made it possible to foresee the *obshchina's* developing in either of two directions. On the one hand the emergence of private property in dwellings as well as domestic animals, money, and other movable goods showed that "the community carries in its own bosom elements of its own destruction." Moreover, the *obshchina* was externally threatened, particularly since emancipation, by "a conspiracy of powerful interests": "It is stamped under foot by the exactions of the state, pillaged by commerce, exploited by large landowners, internally sapped by usury."[30] As in his previous letter, then, Marx stressed that Russia *seemed* to be headed toward capitalism and the consequent dissolution of the village community.

On the other hand, "its innate dualism permits an alternative development," for "communal ownership of the land and the social relations deriving from it" offered the *obshchina* "a natural basis for collective appropriation," and most importantly, "it occupied a unique situation, without precedent in history."[31] Marx proceeded to explain why the situation was so unique:

If Russia were isolated in the world, then it would have to work out by its own forces the economic advances which Western Europe has achieved only by passing through a long series of evolutions from its primitive communities to its present state. There would be, at least in my opinion, no doubt that its communities would be condemned to inevitable disappearance with the development of Russian society. But the situation of the Russian community is fundamentally different from that of the communities of the West. Russia is the only European country in which communal property has been preserved on a vast nation-wide scale. But, at the same time, Russia finds itself in a modern historical environment. It is contemporaneous with a superior civilization, it is tied to a world market in which capitalist production predominates.

By appropriating the positive results of this mode of production, it is in a position to develop and transform the yet archaic form of its village community, instead of destroying it. . . .

If the patrons of the capitalist system in Russia deny the possibility of such a combination, let them prove that in order to use machinery, Russia was forced to pass through the early stages of production by mechanical means! Let them explain how they succeeded in introducing in Russia in a few days, so to speak, the mechanism of exchange (banks, credit institutions, etc.), the elaboration of which has taken centuries in the West![32]

Marx offered but a few more comments: the *obshchina* could borrow from the capitalist model "all the ready made material conditions of cooperative labor, organized on a vast scale." "It can gradually supplant the tilling of the soil by lots," he added, "by collective agriculture, with the aid of machines, the use of which the physical configuration of the Russian soil invites." In such fashion the *obshchina* might modernize itself in socialist form, and "cast off its old skin without first committing suicide."[33]

We find Marx here no less willing than Engels to allow Russia the possibility of skipping over capitalism. While both men tied this possibility expressly to the existence of more developed countries in the West, Marx nowhere mentioned any proletarian revolution as a prerequisite. The Russian peasants need only appropriate the "positive results" of *capitalism* in order to transform their own mode of production. He made his meaning even clearer in a later passage, starting from the premise that "only a Russian Revolution can save the Russian village community": "If such a revolution takes place in time, if it concentrates all its forces to assure the free development of the rural community, this latter will soon become the regenerating element of Russian society, and the factor giving it superiority over the countries enslaved by the capitalist system."[34] To imagine socialism being constructed in Russia while the West remained "enslaved" by capitalism was to venture far beyond what Engels had envisaged, and attribute to the backward Russian peasants an initiative and capacity at which Engels surely would have frowned, if not gasped. While the latter stressed that "the Russian village community has existed for centuries without ever having produced any stimulus to develop out of itself a higher form of communal property," its isolated units serving only as the passive basis for despotism, Marx offered his impression that "this isolation which originally was foisted on the Russian communities by the vast extension of the territory can easily be eliminated, once the governmental fetters have been cast off." External fetters are stressed again and again in the Zasulich drafts as the barrier to the *obshchina*'s development: "After having been put temporarily in a normal state of functioning [i.e., without fetters] in its present form, it can become the *direct point of origin* of the economic system towards which modern society develops." Or again in the final version of the letter: to build socialism out of the *obshchina*, "it is necessary to eliminate first the pernicious influences which attack it from all sides, and then to assure it of *normal conditions for a spontaneous development*" (emphasis added).[35]

Although he did not say so, the logic of Marx's argument would seemingly extend this same possibility to the South Slavs, at least if he judged the *zadruga* to be preserved on a sufficiently wide basis, and perhaps to any other peoples around the world whose gentile institutions and traditions were still strong enough. All of this opens up a remarkable vista for different paths of development. When combined with the theory of Oriental despotism and the *Grundrisse*'s flexibility concerning variant roads out of the primitive tribal community, it seems to leave in ruins the picture of Marxism as a rigid unilinear schema obliging all peoples to tread the same stepping stones. It also suggests that Marx himself was more flexible in these matters than was Engels, although the latter was clearly more flexible than his present-day detractors allow. Indeed, both men are themselves partly to blame for the caricatures of vulgar Marxism: if they actually wanted to allow for multiple paths of development, they also wrote the occasional sweeping generalization, such as the ones quoted at the beginning of this chapter, which seem to stand in flat contradiction to the idea.

Subsequent Marxist writers have usually taken the view that Marx and Engels had purely "tactical" motives for making this "concession" to populism. Certainly everyone acknowledges how much they wanted to see the autocracy destroyed, both to end the threat of czarist expansionism and to eliminate Europe's reserve army of reaction. Since the populists were the only serious Russian revolutionary movement in sight during this period, the argument runs, they had to be encouraged, even at the price of a harmless verbal concession about the *obshchina*. However plausible at first glance, this interpretation will not stand up to close examination: there was no need for Marx to spend months and years learning the Russian language and digesting mountains of documents and studies if the object were simply to make a harmless verbal concession. Moreover the "concession" appears in too many different contexts to have been insincere — including one private letter to a non-Russian (Eduard Bernstein).[36]

What *can* fairly be observed is that Marx seemed unusually hesitant and uncertain about the issue and that Engels eventually changed his mind. As in the case of his 1877 epistle, Marx finally decided not to send this letter to Zasulich, at least not in the form he had developed so laboriously through the three successive drafts. Inexplicably, Marx abandoned his labors in the middle of a sentence, and then sent off an entirely new, extremely brief, and quite vague response. It stated simply that the historical laws described in *Capital* applied only to Western Europe, and then continued: "The analysis presented in *Capital* thus gives reasons neither for nor against the vitality of the village community, but the special study which I have made of it . . . has convinced me that this community is the strategic point of social regeneration in Russia. But before it can function as such, it is necessary to eliminate first the pernicious influences which attack it from all sides, and then assure it of normal conditions for a spontaneous development."[37] That was all. So little was Zasulich impressed by this response that she later could not remember having received it.

Moreover, within a year Marx seemed to have been won over to — or to have acquiesced in — Engels' position on the *obshchina*, for in a preface they wrote jointly for the new Russian edition of the *Communist Manifesto* in January 1882, they addressed the question as follows: "Today only one answer is possible to this question. If the Russian revolution sounds the signal for a proletarian revolution in the West, [the decomposition of the communal ownership of the land in Russia can be evaded] so that each complements the other, the prevailing form of communal ownership of land in Russia may form the starting-point for a communist course of development."[38] Had Marx been convinced by Engels' argument about the need for socialist help from the West? Did he find Engels' formulation intellectually safer, in any event, than his own hesitant and surprising speculations? Of did he simply accept Engels' formulation without reflecting how much it differed from his own? We can never know, for this was Marx's last word on the *obshchina* before his death the following year. Engels maintained ever after that Marx agreed with him on the need for a socialist model in the West; he seemed to overlook the fact that Marx never mentioned such a model in his own individual comments on the subject.

In his later years Engels became progressively more pessimistic about Russia's chances of avoiding capitalism, until by the end of his life he spoke of her "now inevitable transition through the capitalist system."[39] In his letters to Danielson one can follow the progress of his thought, as he watched the *obshchina* wither away more and more under the cumulative impact of the 1861 settlement and the mushrooming growth of a state-subsidized capitalist economy. "If we in the West had been quicker in our own economic development," he wrote in 1893, "if we had been able to upset the capitalistic regime some ten or twenty years ago, there might have been time yet for Russia to cut short the tendency of her own evolution towards capitalism. Unfortunately we are too slow," he concluded, and "with you the commune fades away."[40]

Shortly before his death in 1895 Engels summed up the evolution of his and Marx's views on Russia in a postscript written for the republication of his 1875 essay, "Social Relations in Russia." He did not repudiate the views expressed there or in the writings of 1877 and 1882 concerning the possibility of building socialism directly on the basis of the village community, although he did reiterate strongly his insistence that the "initiative" could "only originate, not in the community itself, but solely among the industrial proletariat of the West." But then he turned to the developments of the intervening years: "In a short time all foundations of the capitalist mode of production were laid in Russia. However, the axe had also been taken to the roots of the Russian village community. Any regrets about this are now useless." Russia's transition to capitalism is now held "inevitable." All Engels would allow to the old populist dream was the idea of "shortening" the period of capitalism's existence, as described earlier.[41] So the matter rested at the time of Engels' death.

A Russian popular revolution that stimulates Western workers to action but then turns to them for help; a revolution in which the peasantry plays a crucial part; a revolution which begins more or less immediately the building of socialism — all these ideas expressed by Marx and Engels were to become standard Bolshevik assumptions by 1917. On the other hand, and ironically, the Russian Marxists under Georgii Plekhanov came into existence as a distinct political current with the decisive repudiation of the populist scheme for Russia. Lenin's own polemical debut in 1894, *Who Are the "Friends of the People,"* was a long attack on populism which asserted that Russia's salvation lay in her emerging proletariat rather than in the peasantry. The early Russian Marxists either forgot about Marx and Engels' idea of skipping stages, or dismissed it as a "concession" to the older generation of populists. Yet the Bolsheviks' underlying drive to justify the earliest possible revolution, and the earliest possible construction of socialism, strangely led them back to all of these ideas, albeit in an increasingly distorted form. After the experience of the 1905 Revolution, Lenin for the first time appreciated the revolutionary potential of the peasants and allowed for a major peasant role in the next workers' revolution — but not for the now defunct *obshchina*. By April 1917 he had also accepted Trotsky's hitherto heretical idea that, with help from a Western proletarian revolution, the Russian revolutionaries could begin the construction of socialism almost immediately — even though the gentile survivals posited as necessary by Engels no longer existed. Finally, after the Western revolution failed to materialize, in the grossest perversion of all, Stalin came back to Marx's idea that the Russian economy might be modernized in socialist form even without proletarian help from the West. His program for "Socialism in One Country," involving the brutal collectivization of agriculture, was a cruel mockery of Marx's hesitant speculation, a program carried out not as a "spontaneous development" of the peasants themselves through their own surviving gentile institutions but as an ukase imposed from above by a directing vanguard party. Such a party, it deserves repeating now in a specifically Russian context, also had no place whatsoever in either Marx or Engels' thought.

A Revolutionary Vanguard?

Apart from concern for the *obshchina*, if there was another specifically Russian characteristic in its revolutionary tradition, it was surely the idea of the revolutionary vanguard, which manifested itself across a full century in virtually all groups and writers from the Decembrists to Herzen, from Bakunin to Tkachev, from Chernyshevsky's *What Is to Be Done?* to Lenin's famous pamphlet of the same name. It is now increasingly recognized that the Bolshevik notion of the vanguard party, only dubiously tied to Marx and Engels' teachings, had its profound roots in the general Russian revolutionary tradition. It was the logical, though perhaps not inevitable, outgrowth of a movement nourished by generations of alienated intellectuals who found themselves unable to establish any lasting contact with the great illiterate mass whose plight inspired their sacrifice and good intentions.[42] Marx and Engels did not live long enough to encounter the Leninist version of this well-intentioned Russian revolutionary elitism, but they had more than their fill of its nineteenth-century antecedents. Their own vision of social revolution in Russia left no room for any sort of vanguard.

Off and on for a period of over thirty years Marx and Engels anticipated the imminent outbreak of a Russian revolution. What we have observed earlier in a different context must now be emphasized: in none of these many anticipations did they speak expressly of a *bourgeois* revolution; they spoke rather of an "agrarian revolution" or a "social revolution" springing out of peasant discontent. The parallel Marx drew in his 1859 article to the Great Revolution in France reappears frequently in later anticipations and has led most writers to assume the masters therefore had a bourgeois revolution in mind. But if we inspect these allusions to France more closely, we find them used rather to convey the idea of a two-stage revolution in which the first stage accomplishes the overthrow of absolutism and creates an elite-sponsored constitutional oligarchy, while the second pushes beyond, in an explosion of the masses, and establishes a more radical and popular regime. Neither phase was presented as particularly bourgeois in the Russian case.[43] In his 1875 article Engels speculated about a revolution "which, started by the upper classes of the capital, perhaps even by the government itself, must be rapidly carried further, beyond the first constitutional phase, by the peasants."[44] The two men repeatedly pointed to the discontent of *all* social groups under the czarist parasite state, including the nobility and intelligentsia. Only in Engels' last writings did the Russian bourgeoisie — understandably — figure more significantly, although he showed little confidence in its revolutionary capacity. He commented to Bebel in 1891 that in Russia

> the young bourgeoisie flourishes as nowhere else; it gradually approaches the point where it must come into conflict with the bureaucracy, but that can take years still. The Russian bourgeoisie, created out of drunken kulaks and state-plundering army suppliers, is what it is because of the state — protective tariffs, subsidies, graft, state permission and protection for the most oppressive exploitation of the workers. Things will have to become very hard indeed before this bourgeoisie, which far exceeds our own [German bourgeoisie] in abjectness, will assail the Tsarist autocracy.[45]

From beginning to end Marx and Engels showed far more interest in the second phase — the Russian peasant revolution, its equivalent to 1793.

This was the peasant upheaval Marx first described as "half-Asiatic" and "frightful" but eventually conceived as holding the potential for immediate socialism, as we have seen, though neither man ever judged it to be more than a possibility. The upheaval might fail just as the original attempt at plebeian rule had failed in 1794, but there can be no doubt that what they had in mind was a revolution made by the masses themselves and not simply made in their name by some self-appointed vanguard. In a recently rediscovered 1879 newspaper interview for the *Chicago Tribune* Marx was asked the inevitable question about "bloody revolution":

> "No socialist," remarked the Doctor, smiling, "need predict that there will be a bloody revolution in Russia, Germany, Austria, and possibly in Italy. . . . That is apparent to any political student. But those revolutions will be made by a majority. No revolution can be made by a party, but by a Nation."[46]

Engels too spoke of the coming upheaval when "Czarism is overthrown and the Russian people takes the center of the stage." Both men referred frequently to the calling of a national assembly as the crucial act in the development of such a revolution and the principal instrument through which the peasant masses could exercise their power. "As soon as a national assembly gives the vast majority of the Russian people, the peasant population, an opportunity to raise its voice, very different things will be heard," declared Engels.[47] He explained further in an 1883 discussion with Hermann Alexandrovich Lopatin, as reported by the latter,

> that in Russia the task of a *revolutionary* party of *action* at this time does not consist in propagating some new socialist ideal, and still less in trying to realize this scarcely worked out ideal by means of a provisional government composed of our comrades. Rather it consists of gathering all forces in order (1) to force the tsar to convene a *Semski Sobor* (estates general), or (2) through intimidation of the tsar, etc., to call forth such strong unrest that it would lead to the convening of the Sobor or something like it. He believes, as I do, that a Sobor of that sort will lead *inevitably* to a radical social— not merely political—transformation. He is convinced of the extraordinary importance of the campaign period which will make possible an incomparably more successful propaganda than all our books and verbal efforts. According to his opinion, a purely liberal constitution without a deep-going economic transformation is impossible—he doesn't worry about such a risk. He believes that existing conditions of popular existence have assembled sufficient materials for the reordering of society on a new basis. Naturally he doesn't believe in the immediate realization of communism, or anything like that, but only of that which is already ripened in the life and soul of the people. In his conviction the people will understand

how to find eloquent spokesmen for its needs and strivings. He is certain that this revolutionary transformation, once begun, cannot be halted by any force on earth.[48]

Engels' confidence in the capacity of the Russian masses to find their own leaders and work out their own destiny is much in evidence here.

Only two years later in 1885, however, Engels wrote a letter to Vera Zasulich that has often been quoted as evidence of underlying Blanquist tendencies, for he described Russia as a "charged mine which only needs a fuse to be laid to it," and then continued:

> This is one of the exceptional cases where it is possible for a handful of people to *make* a revolution, *i.e.*, with one small push to cause a whole system, which (to use a metaphor of Plekhanov's) is in more than labile equilibrium, to come crashing down, and thus by one action, in itself insignificant, to release uncontrollable explosive forces. Well now, if ever Blanquism — the fantasy of overturning an entire society through the action of a small conspiracy — had a certain justification for its existence, that is certainly in Petersburg.

If this passage is quoted, however, the rest of the letter should be examined as well, for Engels went on to make clear that vanguard rule and educational dictatorship were not what he had in mind at all. The small conspiratorial groups which existed in Russia — quite independent of Engels' will, needless to say — might indeed provide the spark, but thereafter "the people who laid the spark to the mine will be swept away by the explosion, which will be a thousand times as strong as themselves." Even if they imagine they will create an educational dictatorship, subjective intentions, Engels mused, matter little in social conflagrations:

> Supposing these people imagine they can seize power, what does it matter? Provided they make the hole which will shatter the dyke, the flood itself will soon rob them of their illusions. But if by chance these illusions resulted in giving them a superior force of will, why complain of that? People who boasted that they had *made* a revolution have always seen the next day that they had no idea what they were doing, that the revolution *made* did not in the least resemble the one they would have liked to make. That is what Hegel calls the irony of history. . . .
>
> To me the most important thing is that the impulse should be

given in Russia, that the revolution should break out. Whether this fraction or that fraction gives the signal, whether it happens under this flag or that flag matters little to me. If it were a palace conspiracy it would be swept away tomorrow. . . . When 1789 has once been launched, 1793 will not be long in following.[49]

Engels allowed that revolutionary groups might provide the spark, but a palace conspiracy would do the job just as well. Their role was quite incidental: "1789 draws near — even without the nihilists," he remarked in another letter.[50] In general Engels made it clear that the social revolution would go its own way according to the great social forces that impelled it, sweeping aside those who might have set the spark with special schemes in mind. Blanquism was still only a fantasy, a self-deception, even in those exceptional cases where it might unwittingly and incidentally perform a useful service.

The most famous action designed to bring down the Russian autocracy during these years was the assassination of Czar Alexander II in March 1881 by a group of populist terrorists — Narodnaya Volya. It is generally accepted that Marx and Engels never advocated nor encouraged such acts of political terrorism against an existing regime. In this case they maintained a discreet silence, allowing the event to pass without any public comment at all. When the assassins were put on trial in April, however, in a private letter to his daughter Marx expressed admiration for the stoic dignity with which the defendants accepted their deed. "They want to inform Europe," he commented, "that their modus operandi is a specifically Russian, historically unavoidable method of action, about which it is as useless to moralize — for or against — as about the earthquake in Chios."[51] If Marx thus privately condoned the act, a few years later Engels left no doubt that such "specifically Russian" methods were not appropriate for Western Europe. When Irish extremists exploded three bombs in London in 1885, injuring more than a dozen people indiscriminately, Engels responded immediately with an article comparing the event to Russian terrorism:

The tactics of the Russian revolutionaries are prescribed by necessity by the actions of their enemies. They are responsible to their people and to history for the means they employ. But the gentlemen who produce pointless schoolboy parodies of this struggle in Western Europe, . . . direct their weapons not even against the real enemy but against the general public, these gentlemen are in no way followers or comrades of the Russian revolutionaries, but their worst enemies.[52]

Thus Engels seemed to agree that the uniquely oppressive character of the autocracy made extremist methods inevitable in Russia, but nonetheless wanted to keep them out of Western Europe. Where the class struggle could be conducted on more humane terms, he seemed to be saying, it should be. Where the government closed all legal avenues of protest, it had to expect extremism in return.

Among the Russian revolutionaries who espoused the vanguard idea, none aroused Marx and Engels' ire more than Mikhail Bakunin, in part no doubt because of the threat he posed within the IWA, but also because of the evident hypocrisy — the gap between Bakunin's sanctimonious public antiauthoritarianism and his private schemes and dreams of manipulating the social revolution himself. Nothing would be more appropriate than to conclude this section with some extracts from a long neglected text, the culminating document in the protracted Bakunin-Marx feud — *The Alliance of Socialist Democracy and the International Working Men's Association,* published in 1873 under instruction from the Hague Congress as a report on the expulsions carried out there.[53] Marx and Engels wrote this long and in large part tedious indictment, which laboriously reiterated the entire history of the conflict, but which also reproduced the secret statutes of Bakunin's Alliance as well as extensive extracts from his writings published in Russian, both sources being used adroitly to unmask the anarchist leader's profoundly elitist and authoritarian assumptions. It will be recalled from the previous chapter how Bakunin had established within his public Alliance a secret International Brotherhood which was supposed invisibly to control the Alliance; and through the Alliance the IWA; and through the IWA, he hoped, the social revolution at large. In one of his Russian language writings he referred darkly to this secret International Brotherhood as an "already existent, already active organization, which is made strong by its discipline, the passionate dedication and self-sacrifice of its members, and by the blind obedience they give to *a single committee* which knows all and is known by none." "*Like the Jesuits,*" he continued in his enthusiasm, "each of them has renounced his own will, but for the sake of emancipating rather than subjugating the people."[54] This inauspicious allusion to the Jesuits provided Marx and Engels with the leitmotif for their own critique.

First the two men analyzed the secret statutes, arguing — not without justification — that their convoluted paragraphs actually placed control of both the public Alliance and the secret Brotherhood in the hands of a small central committee whose members were effectively chosen by Bakunin himself — this was the all-knowing committee referred to above. The statutes also expatiated at some length on the purpose of the secret Brotherhood:

> "It is necessary that in the midst of popular anarchy, which will make up the very life and all the energy of the revolution, *the unity of revolutionary thought and action should be embodied in a certain organ.* That organ must be the *secret and world-wide association of the international brothers.*
>
> "This association arises from the conviction that revolutions are never made either by individuals or by secret societies. . . . The only thing a well-organized secret society can do is first to assist the birth of the revolution by spreading among the masses ideas that accord with the instinct of the masses, and to organize not the army of the revolution — that army must always be the people" (cannonfodder) "but *a revolutionary General Staff* composed of devoted, energetic and intelligent individuals who are above all sincere — not vain or ambitious — friends of the people, capable of serving as intermediaries between the revolutionary idea" (monopolized by them) "and the popular instincts.
>
> "The number of these individuals should not therefore be too large. For the international organization throughout Europe *one-hundred serious and firmly united revolutionaries would be sufficient.* Two or three hundred revolutionaries would be enough for the organization of the largest country."[55]

The parenthetical comments belong to Marx and Engels and expressed their revulsion at a program which divided the movement into those who monopolized the revolutionary idea and those who served as cannon fodder. Further commentary followed:

> So everything changes. Anarchy, the "unleashing of popular life," of "evil passions" and all the rest is no longer enough. To assure the success of the revolution one must have *"unity of thought and action."* The members of the International are trying to create this unity by propaganda, by discussion and the public organization of the proletariat. But all Bakunin needs is a secret organization of one

hundred people, the privileged representatives of the *revolutionary idea*, the general staff in the background, self-appointed and commanded by the permanent "Citizen B." Unity of thought and action means nothing but orthodoxy and blind obedience. *Perinde ac cadaver*. We are indeed confronted with a veritable Society of Jesus.

To say that the hundred international brothers must "serve as intermediaries between the revolutionary idea and the popular instincts," is to create an unbridgeable gulf between the Alliance's revolutionary idea and the proletarian masses; it means proclaiming that these hundred guardsmen cannot be recruited anywhere but from among the privileged classes.[56]

Here Marx and Engels struck at the essence of the vanguard idea, which implicitly or explicitly denies the capacity of the masses to emancipate themselves and therefore assigns the responsibility for thinking and leading to a self-appointed general staff drawn — inevitably — from the educated classes. Note the image of the vanguard as the "general staff" of the revolution, made famous by Lenin, was expressed clearly here by Bakunin several decades earlier, and was just as clearly repudiated by Marx and Engels.

Next Marx turned to the publications Bakunin and his disciple Sergei Gennadyevich Nechayev addressed to their Russian readers, which contained some of their most extravagant utterances — extolling brigandage as an "honorable" form of popular resistance, declaring that all forms of destruction were sanctified by the revolution, and calling for death lists to be drawn up. Aimless propaganda not followed by deeds was declared intolerable: "'We shall silence by force the chatterers who refuse to understand this.'" There was also to be no room for the faint-hearted: "'He who has ears and eyes will hear and see the men of action, and if he does not join them his destruction will be no fault of ours, just as it will be no fault of ours if all who hide behind the scenes are cold-bloodedly and pitilessly destroyed.'" The new society was to be organized with communal dormitories and communal eating places; education was to be minutely regulated from above; everyone was enjoined to produce as much and consume as little as possible; antisocial elements would "'have no alternative but work or death.'" Finally: "'The ending of the present social order and the renewal of life with the aid of the new principles can be accomplished *only by concentrating all the means of social existence in the hands of* Our Committee, *and the proclamation of compul-*

sory physical labor for everyone.'"[57] Marx and Engels could not contain their scorn: "What a beautiful model of barrack-room communism! Here you have it all: communal eating, communal sleeping, assessors and offices regulating education, production, consumption, in a word, all social activity, and to crown all, *Our Committee*, anonymous and unknown to anyone, as the supreme director. This is indeed the purest anti-authoritarianism."

At length the two men summed up their entire indictment in the following conclusion:

> This same man who in 1870 preaches to the Russians passive, blind obedience to orders coming from above and from an anonymous committee; who declares that jesuitical discipline is the condition *sine qua non* of victory, the only thing capable of defeating the formidable centralization of the State — not just the Russian State but any State; who proclaims a communism more authoritarian than the most primitive communism — the same man, in 1871, weaves a separatist and disorganizing movement into the fabric of the International under the pretext of combatting the authoritarianism and centralization of the German Communists. . . . If the society of the future were modelled on the Alliance, Russian section, it would far surpass the Paraguay of the Reverend Jesuit Fathers, so dear to Bakunin's heart.[58]

With these biting words Marx and Engels denounced the Russian revolutionary elitism of their own day. We can only imagine how they would have reacted to its twentieth-century counterpart. In backward countries no less than advanced ones, under despotism no less than democracy, they held to their oft-repeated idea that popular emancipation must be the work of the masses themselves. It cannot come as the gift of some revolutionary vanguard, however well intentioned that vanguard might be. Whatever the possibilities for skipping stages in backward countries where gentile institutions survive, whatever the possibilities for popular revolution in backward countries generally, Marx and Engels appear to have made *no* special exceptions for situations where vanguards might be appropriate.

⦃10⦄

Strategy IV:
Legal Revolution

OF THE TWO STRATEGIES developed by Marx and Engels in their later lives, the one we have just examined was applicable to very backward countries; the one we must address now pertained to the most advanced. If the Bolsheviks later adopted — in distorted form — most of the ideas contained in the strategy of skipping stages, European social democratic parties later adopted — also in distorted form — most of the ideas contained in Marx and Engels' thoughts about a possible legal and peaceful revolution.[1]

Right at the outset it will be useful to discriminate among four pairs of terms that are often used synonymously and too casually to contrast the social democratic vision of change with what is assumed to be the opposite alternative — legal versus illegal, peaceful versus violent, democratic versus undemocratic, gradual versus abrupt. While these neatly paired opposites may all fit together well enough in certain cases, it is by no means logically necessary that all the modifiers be clustered thus — it presupposes too much. One of the principal arguments of this book has been that Marx and Engels, throughout most of their lives, advocated a violent, illegal, fairly swift, but nonetheless *democratic* revolution against the then existing authoritarian governments. Where the masses could not vote, the rule of the majority — democracy — could only be imposed violently and illegally. Even the existence of legal structures for carrying out the majority will gives no absolute guarantee of peaceful development, as the American Civil War reminds us; it required a great deal of violence to enforce legality as well as the majority will upon the secessionists of 1861. Conversely, not all illegal actions need be violent, as the civil disobedience campaigns of the twentieth century bear witness. Finally, it should be just as obvious that there is no *necessary* correlation between gradual and legal-peaceful-democratic change (consider the rise of early modern absolutism), any more than between swift and illegal-violent-undemocratic change (e.g., the British Labor Government of 1945–1951). In the discussion which follows, each set of opposites — democratic versus undemocratic, legal versus illegal, peaceful versus violent, gradual versus abrupt — will be treated as separate and distinct, for only in this way can Marx and Engels' real views be understood and discriminated from those of later generations. These separations will be especially necessary in the case of Germany, where it will take a special section to untangle Marx and Engels' almost universally misunderstood views on the socialist road to power.

The Democratization of Capitalist Countries

Some of the best known phrases in the Marxist tradition are ones associating communism with violent revolution: *"Revolutions are the locomotives of history,"* declared *The Civil War in France.* "Force is the midwife of every old society pregnant with a new one," according to *Capital.*[2] The *Communist Manifesto* made perhaps the most famous declaration of all: "The Communists disdain to conceal their views and aims. They openly declare that their ends can be attained only by the forcible overthrow of all existing social conditions. Let the ruling classes tremble at a Communistic revolution." This stirring call for violent revolution occurs in the same document which proclaims that "the proletarian movement is the self-conscious, independent movement of the immense majority, in the interest of the immense majority."[3] Even if Marx and Engels were immodestly anticipating here the mass support their movement did not yet actually have, still there is no contradiction, for at the beginning of 1848 there was not a single country in Europe where the "immense majority" could have voted itself into power legally. The masses could scarcely have asserted their will against the entrenched oligarchies except by "forcible overthrow." While Marx and Engels never systematically addressed the ethical side of their advocacy of revolution, the latter at least managed to leave us a paragraph touching on the issue. In his own draft of the *Manifesto* Engels had posed the question: "Will it be possible to bring about the abolition of private property by peaceful methods?" His answer:

It is to be desired that this could happen, and Communists certainly would be the last to resist it. The Communists know only too well that all conspiracies are not only futile but even harmful. They know only too well that revolutions are not made deliberately and arbitrarily, but that everywhere and at all times they have been the necessary outcome of circumstances entirely independent of the will and the leadership of particular parties and entire classes. But they also see that the development of the proletariat is in nearly every civilized country forcibly suppressed, and that thus the opponents of the Communists are working with all their might towards a revolution. Should the oppressed proletariat in the end be goaded into a revolution, we Communists will then defend the cause of the proletarians by deed just as well as we do now by word.[4]

The proletarian majority forced into revolution by the oppression of the other side—this was the image Engels presented. Can his declared preference for "peaceful methods" be taken seriously? The point was academic in Europe, but Engels' phrase "nearly every" country seems to have been designed to allow room for the United States. There he recognized that "a democratic constitution has been introduced," and there, most significantly, he did not speak of revolution but rather urged that "the Communists must make common cause with the party that will turn this constitution against the bourgeoisie and use it in the interest of the proletariat, that is, with the national agrarian reformers."[5] In these words we find the first implicit allowance for the possibility of a legal road to power and the first elements of a strategy for achieving power through democratic institutions. Alas, the thought was destined to remain an undeveloped embryo for the next twenty years. The United States produced no mass labor movement during that period and, in any event, the Civil War that broke out there in 1861 did not offer much reassurance that democratic institutions could guarantee the peaceful resolution of vital conflicts.

The question of a peaceful and legal achievement of communism therefore remained academic and rather theoretical until the most advanced capitalist countries of Western Europe began to permit the introduction of genuinely democratic institutions, a process of democratization that reached its apex in the decade 1867–1877—as we have already seen in a different context in chapter 3. In Great Britain parliamentary government had long insured the control of the propertied electorate over the monarch but only the Reform Act of 1867 gave the majority of male industrial workers the right to vote (universal suffrage did not arrive until after World War I). In France, after the momentary flowering of the Second Republic, universal manhood suffrage served only as a manipulative device designed to cloak the repressive dictatorship of Louis Napoleon, and it was well into the 1870s, following the bloody suppression of the Paris Commune, before the democratic institutions of the Third Republic became at all firmly rooted. In Germany, Bismarck's version of Bonapartism involved a unique and perplexing mixture. From 1867 on there was a Reichstag elected by universal manhood suffrage, and under somewhat freer conditions than Napoleon generally allowed, but the Reichstag did not control the executive through any system of ministerial responsibility and could at most harass the bureaucratic and military machine that actually governed the country. Germany, then, was only partially and superficially carried along in this decade of capitalist democratization.

How did Marx and Engels react to these changes? If they really held liberal-democratic values, as has been argued throughout this book, one would expect them to drop any insistence on violent revolution in those countries where a legal road to power was opened up for a movement that expected to achieve majority support. Let us now examine and analyze their various statements on the issue, which, interestingly, begin to appear in swelling numbers after 1867.

Marx himself contributed in a very modest way to start the ball of democratization rolling. In 1865 the IWA helped to found the Reform League which spearheaded renewed agitation for universal suffrage in Great Britain. Marx actively supported this agitation and took pride in the leadership given by the IWA. In a letter to his friend Ludwig Kugelmann he explained why he chose not to return to live in Prussia: "I prefer a hundred times over my agitation here through the *International Association*. Its influence on the English proletariat is direct and of the greatest importance. We are making a stir here now on the General Suffrage Question, which of course has a significance here quite different from what it has in Prussia." That significance, of course, lay in the sovereign power of the British Parliament; as Marx had declared in 1852, "Universal Suffrage is the equivalent of political power for the working class of England."[6] Although the actual extension won in the Reform Act of 1867 fell far short of universal suffrage and left Marx and Engels disappointed, still a path was now opened to develop the power of the working class in Parliament. Very possibly this is what Marx had in mind when he remarked in an 1867 public speech: "It is possible that the struggle between the workers and capitalists will be less fierce and bloody than the struggle between the feudal lords and the capitalists in England and France. Let us hope so."[7]

This was also the year Marx completed volume 1 of *Capital*, and in his preface, as we saw in chapter 6, he held up British factory legislation to the Continental ruling classes as a model. While he did not specifically mention political rights, his central point applies equally well to them. The coming social transformation, he declared,

> will take a form more brutal or more humane, according to the degree of development of the working-class itself. Apart from higher motives, therefore, their own most important interests dictate to the classes that are for the nonce the ruling ones, the removal of all legally removable hindrances to the free development of the working-class. For this reason, as well as others, I have given so large a space in this volume to the history, the details, and the results of English factory legislation. One nation can and should learn from others. And even when a society has got upon the right track for the discovery of the natural laws of its movement . . . it can neither clear by bold leaps, nor remove by legal enactments, the obstacles offered by the successive phases of its normal development. But it can shorten and lessen the birth-pangs.[8]

In addition to factory legislation, Continental rulers could scarcely find a better means of lessening the birth-pangs than by granting full and meaningful rights of citizenship to their toiling masses. This would remove the "hindrances" to the free political development of the working class and thus help to ensure, Marx now ventured to predict, a less brutal, more humane, social transition.

Four years later Marx found himself obliged to deal with these questions much more directly. His role as public champion of the Paris Commune, not to mention the image created of him as its mastermind and gray eminence, made him a serious object of attention for the bourgeois press. When interviewed by reporters he was inevitably asked about his stand on bloody revolution. His reply to the *New York World* interviewer included the following crucial differentiation: "In England, for instance, the way to show political power lies open to the working class. Insurrection would be madness where peaceful agitation would more swiftly and surely do the work. In France a hundred laws of repression and a mortal antagonism between classes seem to necessitate the violent solution of social war."[9] Here is the basic distinction we will find used from this point on: where the way to power lies "open," insurrection would be "madness"; where it is closed, violence will be inevitable. Marx even proposed to make this a matter of IWA policy. In September 1871 he suggested the following formulation to the delegates at the London Conference: "We must declare to the governments: we know that you are the armed power directed against the proletariat; we will agitate against you in peaceful ways where that is possible for us, and with arms where it is necessary."[10]

The following year, 1872, saw Marx's most famous pronouncement on peaceful means. Following the Hague Congress of the IWA he made a public speech in Amsterdam to review and explain its major resolutions. One of those resolutions had repudiated the anarchist appeal for political "abstention," and called for the workers, as Marx summarized it, "one day to take over political supremacy in order to establish the new organization of work." He continued:

> Of course we do not pretend that the means to this end will be everywhere the same.
>
> We know the special attention that must be paid to the institutions, customs, and traditions of the various countries; and we do not deny that there are certain countries, such as America and England — and if I knew your institutions better I might add Holland — where the workers can achieve their ends by peaceful means. If that is true, we must also recognize that in most Continental countries force must be the lever of our revolutions; it will be necessary to turn to force eventually in order to establish the reign of labor.[11]

There are a number of noteworthy features in this statement. For one thing the United States was mentioned expressly along with Great Britain, harking back to Engels' 1847 remarks. It would continue to be mentioned, as we shall see, in every subsequent listing. On the other hand France did not appear, even though the democratic Third Republic had been formally established for two years. Furthermore, Marx did not specify what it was about the "institutions, customs, and traditions" of the two Anglo-Saxon countries (and perhaps Holland) that made peaceful means possible there while being impossible in "most Continental countries."

These circumstances made it easy in later years for Lenin to insert his own principle of distinction and to place an interpretation on these remarks that has become accepted even by a great many non-Leninists. It was the absence in the 1870s of a powerful executive state apparatus, the military-bureaucratic machine, in the two Anglo-Saxon countries, Lenin declared, that separated them from most of the Continent, including France, and thus made it possible for Marx to contemplate peaceful means. After the 1870s, he went on to argue, both the Anglo-Saxon countries developed such a military-bureaucratic machine, thus putting an end to any dream of peaceful change even there.[12] Very neat. Without denying the authenticity of Marx's 1872 statement, Lenin adroitly nullified its significance for his own time.

Too neat however. If Britain lacked a developed military-bureaucratic machine in the 1870s, the same was presumably true in the earlier decades, yet it was not until 1867, the year most British workers got the vote, that Marx showed any optimism about a peaceful development there, and he specified it was because "the way to show political power lies open to the working class." He made the point even more sharply in an 1878 fragment (to be introduced later in its full context) when he wrote: "If, for example, in England or the United States, the working class were to win a majority in Parliament or Congress, if could legally put an end to laws and institutions standing in the way of its development."[13] In fact, nowhere in their writings that touch on the issue did either Marx or Engels draw any link between the peaceful possibility and the absence of a military-bureaucratic apparatus. Whenever they made any linkage at all they associated the peaceful possibility with the presence of democratic institutions — not just universal suffrage to be sure, but universal suffrage combined with a competent legislature, a democratically controlled executive branch, and the usual political freedoms.

The absence of France from Marx's 1872 list is not really so surprising if one recalls his reference the previous year to "a hundred laws of repression and a mortal antagonism between classes" in that country. The memory of the martyred Communards was still too fresh in 1872. The same uncompromising National Assembly still sat as France's legislature; its majority still regarded the Republic as a bridge to monarchist restoration. It would not have been too surprising to find this National Assembly finally creating a phony parliament like the one with which Napoleon ornamented his dictatorship during the previous twenty years, a parliament in which, if universal suffrage survived at all, it would again be merely an instrument of dupery, giving the workers only the right of "deciding once in three or six years which member of the ruling class was to misrepresent the people in Parliament." (Too often it is forgotten that Marx directed this famous sarcasm at Napoleon's sham legislature, not at real parliaments.)[14] In succeeding years, however, the Third Republic consolidated itself as a parliamentary democracy, and Marx and Engels gradually became more optimistic about its future. Engels greeted the election of a prorepublican legislature in 1876 with real enthusiasm.[15] By 1878, in an aforementioned interview with the *Chicago Tribune*, Marx conspicuously left France *off* his list of Continental countries where "bloody revolution" could be predicted.[16] By 1880, in his capacity as ghost writer of the preamble for the draft program of the new Workers' Party in France, Marx coaxed the French proletariat to overcome its long suspicion of universal suffrage. That institution, he asserted, could be "transformed from an instrument of dupery, which it has been up to now, into an instrument of emancipation."[17]

The crowning piece of evidence came a decade later in Engels' much neglected critique of the draft Erfurt Program. Engels was concerned to repudiate as sharply as he could the notion that Germany could achieve socialism peacefully (a subject we will address later) and so drew the following sharp distinction:

> It is conceivable that the old society can grow peacefully into the new in those countries where all power is concentrated in the popular representative body, where, as soon as a majority of the people stands behind you, you can do what you want constitutionally. This is the case in democratic republics such as France and America, and in monarchies such as England where the imminent buying off of the dynasty is discussed everyday in the press and where this dynasty is powerless against the popular will. But [it is ridiculous] to proclaim such a thing in Germany, where the government is practically all-powerful and the Reichstag and other representative bodies are without real power.[18]

Here Engels left no room for doubt. What separates Germany from countries where the peaceful possibility exists is not a military-bureaucratic apparatus (which according to Lenin *all* these countries possessed by 1891) but the lack of a sovereign parliament, of a democratically controlled executive. In countries where such institutions do exist, where parliaments are not impotent and voting rights not a fraud, a peaceful road to socialism may be found. And those countries now explicitly include France, whose republican institutions Engels even declared three years later to be the "*ready-made* political form for the future rule of the proletariat."[19]

How should the workers organize themselves in democratic countries? And, as they strive to develop mass support, what policies should they pursue in bourgeois-dominated legislatures, or in the streets? The former question was answered most concisely in Engels' reaction to the first appearance in 1886 of a mass workers' movement in the United States. He welcomed this appearance as a sign that American workers now realized that they formed a distinct and permanent class in modern society, with common grievances and interests that gave them a feeling of "solidarity as a class in opposition to all other classes." He continued: "In order to give expression and effect to this feeling, they should set in motion the political machinery provided for that purpose in every free country," namely "form themselves into a distinct political party, independent of, and opposed to, all the old political parties formed by the various sections of the ruling classes." The next step, he went on, would be to develop a program for such a party. This program would evolve over time with the expanding consciousness of the workers:

> The platform of the American proletariat will in the long run coincide, as to the ultimate end to be attained, with the one which, after sixty years of dissensions and discussions, has become the adopted platform of the great mass of the European militant proletariat. It will proclaim, as the ultimate end, the conquest of political supremacy by the working class, in order to effect the direct appropriation of all means of production — land, railways, mines, machinery, etc. — by society at large, to be worked in common by all for the account and benefit of all.[20]

In private letters to his American correspondents Engels emphasized that such a consciousness could not be expected to emerge overnight. He saw the Knights of Labor as forming the "still quite plastic" basis of the American movement, despite its theoretical backwardness; and he had little patience for the tiny German-speaking Socialist Labor party, despite its greater theoretical sophistication. "The Germans have not understood how to use their theory as a lever which could set the American masses in motion," he complained to Friedrich Sorge. "They do not understand the theory themselves for the most part and treat it in a doctrinaire and dogmatic way as something that has to be learned by heart." He continued:

> The first great step of importance for every country newly entering into the movement is always the constitution of the workers as an independent political party, no matter how, so long as it is a distinct workers' party. And this step has been taken, much more rapidly than we had a right to expect, that is the main thing. That

the first program of this party is still confused and extremely defi-
cient, . . . these are unavoidable evils but also merely transitory
ones. The masses must have time and opportunity to develop, and
they can have the opportunity only when they have a movement
of their own — no matter in what form so long as it is *their own*
movement — in which they are driven further by their own mistakes
and learn through their mistakes.[21]

He reiterated the same themes to Florence Kelley Wischnewetzky, adding the following thoughts on the proper role of the more militant few:

> They ought, in the words of the *Communist Manifesto*, "to repre-
> sent the future of the movement in the present of the movement."
> But above all give the movement time to consolidate; do not make
> the inevitable confusion of the first start worse confounded by forc-
> ing down people's throats things which, at present, they cannot
> properly understand but which they soon will learn. A million or
> two of workingmen's votes next November for a *bona fide* working-
> men's party is worth infinitely more at present than a hundred thou-
> sand votes for a doctrinally perfect platform.[22]

The more militant few, then, should not separate themselves off as a vanguard party but should work patiently within the broader movement,
pointing the way toward its future.

Marx and Engels never showed any sympathy for those radicals who
used violence in democratic countries. Following Marx's injunction, "we
will agitate against you in peaceful ways where that is possible for us,
and with arms where it is necessary," they condoned the assassination
of Czar Alexander II in tyrannical Russia, but Engels excoriated those
Irish terrorists "who produce pointless schoolboy parodies of this struggle
in western Europe."[23] Engels likewise condemned the 1886 Haymarket
bombing in Chicago and similar acts as "stupidities" and "anarchist fol-
lies."[24] The same year he even condemned the London leaders of the Social Democratic Federation who, fancying themselves to have become
real revolutionaires, had transformed a peaceful Hyde Park meeting into
a violent demonstration, complete with window-smashing, looting, and
general rioting. "They have done irreparable damage to the movement
here," he declared.[25] One will search the writings of Marx and Engels
in vain to find any advocacy, either specific or in general, of the use of
political violence as an offensive weapon in stable democratic countries.

Even in Germany, during the years when the Social Democratic party was illegal, the two men opposed any deliberate violent initiative, while at the same time encouraging all sorts of illegal nonviolent activities— underground organizing, printing and distributing of illegal literature, and so forth.[26]

Further, as the movement gathered mass support in the various democratic countries, but before it won a majority, it could expect to wrest concessions from the existing rulers. Marx and Engels never opposed the winning of reforms in this sense. Their enthusiasm for the campaign to win the ten-hour day in Britain is well known. Political reforms likewise could advance the workers' cause, and would be granted in proportion as the bourgeois parties came to respect the power of the workers' party. In Britain the very act of forming the Independent Labor party in 1893, Engels noted, "put a match to the [Liberal] government's backside." The latter promptly introduced two bills — subsequently emasculated — that would have eliminated *all* remaining property qualifications, transferred certain election expenses to the public treasury, begun salaries for members of parliament, and so forth. Engels jubilated:

> In short, the Liberals recognize that, to make sure of governing at the present time, there is nothing for it but to increase the political power of the working class who will naturally kick them out afterwards. The Tories . . . will realize that there is nothing for it but to enter the lists to gain power, and to that end there remains but one means: to win the working-class vote by political or economic concessions; thus, Liberals and Conservatives cannot help extending the power of the working class.[27]

To accept such concessions, to mobilize pressure inside and outside Parliament in order to win more of them — these activities Marx and Engels found eminently legitimate.

On the other hand they cautioned against any illusion that socialism would come into being simply as the cumulative result of such piecemeal reforms within the capitalist system. Engels wrote in 1894 that as long as the French Republic remains controlled by the bourgeoisie, "we can wring concessions from it, but never look to it to carry out our job."[28] Was there a difference between wringing concessions and following a reformist path to socialism? Thus far the evidence presented in this section might all be judged as demonstrating that Marx and Engels, by the end of their lives, had stepped over into such a reformist path, at least for democratic countries. But this would be a premature conclusion. Certainly the two men never perceived any such change in themselves. Repeatedly and consistently over a period of thirty years they deplored whatever signs of reformism and opportunism they perceived in the German Social Democratic party. Engels lived long enough to witness the establishment of the Fabian Society in Britain — he never had so much as one kind word for it. Perhaps most clearly of all, in France the aging Engels had a neat choice between two separate parties — Jules Guesde's militant Workers' party and the reformist "Possibilist" socialists. He supported and encouraged the former as consistently as he denounced and deplored the latter. No one would be more surprised than Engels himself to learn that so many twentieth-century scholars have pronounced him a reformist in his last years.[29] But if Marx and Engels allowed for a peaceful and legal "revolution" in democratic countries, if they advocated the formation of an open mass party that aimed at winning an electoral majority, if they rejected political violence as an offensive weapon and sought reform through legislation — then why should they *not* be considered reformists? In the next two sections we will seek some answers to that question.

A Pro-Slavery Rebellion?

If democratic institutions opened up the possibility of a peaceful path to socialism, there is no way they could *guarantee* such a development. Marx and Engels rarely spoke of the possibility without adding a word of caution about probabilities. Marx set the tone during his 1871 *World* interview, cited earlier. After he had allowed that "insurrection would be madness where peaceful agitation would more swiftly and surely do the work," the American interviewer pressed again for specific reassurances, suggesting that "the English system of agitating by platform and press until minorities become converted into majorities is a hopeful sign." This time the reporter had pressed too far, however, and Marx gave the following retort: "I am not so sanguine on that point as you. The English middle class has always shown itself willing enough to accept the verdict of the majority so long as it enjoyed the monopoly of the voting power. But mark me, as soon as it finds itself outvoted on what it considers vital questions we shall see here a new slaveowner war."[30] The final allusion of course was a barbed one to the American Civil War. "Slaveowner war" and "pro-slavery rebellion" would become Marx's code phrases ever after for violent capitalist resistance to a legal workers' government. This idea, when all its implications are understood, will explain the greater part of what still separated Marx and Engels on issues of strategy from the garden variety of reformist social-democratic thinking.

Marx developed the idea at somewhat greater length in 1878 in notes for an article he intended to write on Bismarck's outlawing of the German Social Democratic party. We may now inspect the full passage whose key sentence was quoted earlier:

> An historical development can remain "peaceful" only so long as no forcible hindrances are put in its way by the existing rulers of a society. If, for example, in England or the United States, the working class were to win a majority in Parliament or Congress, it could legally put an end to laws and institutions standing in the way of its development, although even here only so far as societal development permitted. For the "peaceful" movement could still be turned into a "violent" one by the revolt of those whose interests were bound up with the old order. If such people were then put down by force (as in the American Civil War and the French Revolution), it would be rebels against the "lawful" power.[31]

Here Marx envisaged a legal and peaceful electoral victory for the workers that would make them the "lawful" power. A rebellion by the displaced old elite, however, might oblige the new government to use violent means against it, a use of force to uphold legality and the will of the majority which is provided for in every democratic constitution. The legal path is thus not necessarily or automatically a peaceful one. Engels expressed the same thought in 1885 when he reminisced that Marx's lifelong study of England led him "to the conclusion that, at least in Europe, England is the only country where the inevitable social revolution might be effected entirely by peaceful and legal means. He certainly never forgot to add that he hardly expected the English ruling classes to submit, without a 'pro-slavery rebellion,' to this peaceful and legal revolution."[32] Like his partner Engels needed to use the adjectives "peaceful" and "legal" separately in order to characterize a development that would begin both legally and peacefully with the workers' electoral victory, but which might very well end in the forcible suppression of a "pro-slavery rebellion." As in the case of the three revolutionary strategies discussed previously, violence would be exercised by a majority in order to carry out its will against a minority unwilling to submit, but in the present case legality as well as the majority principle would be on the side of the workers, for they would constitute the lawful government.

Why did Marx and Engels have so little faith in the willingness of the bourgeoisie to bow to majority will? We have already addressed this question in a different context in chapter 6 but we may call attention here to the two specific examples cited by Marx. His French revolutionary allusion is almost surely to the violent rebellion of reactionary elements — the so-called Vendée — against the authority of the National Convention elected by universal suffrage in September 1792. It would seem safe to speculate that the overwhelmingly royalist Vendée rebels never acknowledged a right of the majority to rule in the first place. But even where democratic principles were generally acknowledged and institutionalized, if really *vital* interests were at stake, defeated minorities have not always bowed to majority will, as in Marx's other example — the American secessionists' refusal to accept the election of Abraham Lincoln in 1860. Marx returned again and again to this insurrection of "300,000 slaveowners" concerned to defend their peculiar institution whatever the cost. Would the American bourgeoisie in general behave any differently when confronted by a workers' majority threatening to socialize their property? Would the British bourgeoisie, however much accustomed to parliamentary government and majority decisions *within* the propertied elite, accept such decisions now that it had lost its "monopoly of the voting power"? Throughout the lifetimes of Marx and Engels the bulk of the propertied classes in Britain and even more on the Continent still identified democracy as mob rule and general spoliation, rather than as universal principles of fair play binding upon themselves. The two men were doubtless pessimistic but not grossly unreasonable in anticipating the likelihood of a pro-slavery rebellion.

Engels seems to have been in a particularly pessimistic mood at the end of *The Origin of the Family* when he explained how the bourgeoisie managed to rule even under democratic conditions. After discussing corruption and indirect financial influences, he proceeded:

And lastly the possessing class rules directly by means of universal suffrage. As long as the oppressed class — in our case, therefore, the proletariat — is not yet ripe for its self-liberation, so long will it in its majority recognize the existing order of society and the only possible one and remain politically the tail of the capitalist class, its extreme left wing. But in the measure in which it matures toward its self-emancipation, in the same measure it constitutes itself as its own party and votes for its own representatives, not those of the capitalists. Universal suffrage is thus the gauge of the maturity of the working class. It cannot and never will be anything more in the modern state; but that is enough. On the day when the thermometer of universal suffrage shows boiling point among the workers, they as well as the capitalists will know where they stand.[33]

Here Engels seemed to foresee no possibility at all that the capitalists would submit peacefully. Universal suffrage was but a thermometer and when it registered boiling point, both sides would understand that a violent showdown was to follow. At such a moment, even before a legal workers' government might be organized, the other side might try to conceal or nullify the election results, dissolve the legislature, illegally alter the constitution, or simply call out the army to suppress the workers' movement. Marx and Engels feared such moves particularly in Germany, as we will see, but similar things had happened elsewhere too, as Marx generalized in his comment on Bismarck's suppression of the legal workers' movement in 1878: "In actuality the government is using *forcible means* to suppress this development because, though finding it hateful, it is unimpeachable *under the law*. That is the indispensable introduction to violent revolutions. It is an old story but remains ever new."[34] For this reason both men counseled the workers to be on their guard: even where the legal path was open it might be slammed shut at the last moment, making violence necessary to enforce the will of the majority and making it advisable for the workers even in democratic countries to be familiar with the use of weapons. Engels linked universal suffrage interestingly with universal military training: "The more workers who are trained in the use of weapons, the better. Universal conscription is the necessary and natural extention of universal suffrage; it enables the electorate to carry out its resolutions arms in hand against any coup that might be attempted."[35] Just as they praised the Communards for not laying down their weapons after their first victory, so Marx and Engels wanted the workers even in democratic countries to stand ready to use arms should that be made necessary by violent or illegal actions of the other side. Such a use of arms might even be required before the workers' movement was ready to rule, required simply for the defense of democratic institutions themselves. During the Boulanger Crisis in France in the late 1880s, when a Bonapartist-style military coup seemed imminent, the pale democrats raised the cry: "The Republic is in danger!" Engels' response was characteristic: "Give each worker a gun and 50 cartridges and the Republic will never be in danger again!"[36]

Engels did not suggest, however, even in the pessimism of *The Origin of the Family*, that the workers in stable democratic countries should boycott universal suffrage because it was only a thermometer, or that they should organize paramilitary forces and launch violent assaults before they became a majority. Indeed, all the passages quoted so far assume the workers' agitation would remain peaceful and legal so long as a legal road to power remained open. Though they were usually reluctant to say so expressly, Marx and Engels seemed quite willing to play by democratic rules of the game so long as the other side did so as well. Here is another example of that tacit understanding discussed in chapter 6: restraint matched by restraint, but readiness to counter violence with violence. On one occasion at least Engels made these assumptions explicit. When the German Social Democrats emerged in 1890 from twelve years of persecution, he advised them to turn to open and legal agitation. He generalized:

> We are not the only ones; all the workers' parties do this in countries where they have a certain measure of legal freedom of movement, and for the simple reason that they find it most effective. All this has as a precondition, however, that the opposing party likewise proceeds legally. . . . Even in the most law-abiding nation of all, England, the first condition for lawfulness on the side of the people is that the other side likewise remain within the bounds of the law; if that does not occur, then according to the English legal tradition rebellion becomes the first duty of the citizen.[37]

The German case was complicated by other factors, as we will see later, but for democratic countries there was no reason, *as far as the workers were concerned*, why the whole changeover to communism could not proceed legally and peacefully.

There was, after all, nothing in the workers' program as conceived by Marx and Engels that required violence against persons; the object was rather to expropriate the *property* of the bourgeoisie. And democratic institutions, as Marx said of the Paris Commune, provided "the rational medium in which that class struggle can run through its different phases in the most rational and humane way." It may be recalled that his vision of a French nation organized in communes had included the prospect of "sporadic slaveholders' insurrections," but, more pertinently for us now, mainly the prospect of "peaceful progress":

> The communal organization once firmly established on a national scale, the catastrophes it might still have to undergo, would be

sporadic slaveholders insurrections, which, while for a moment interrupting the work of peaceful progress, would only accelerate the movement, by putting the sword into the hand of the Social Revolution."[38]

All that was really needed for a rational and humane transition to socialism was the willingness of the bourgeoisie itself to accept the democratic rules of the game. If it did not, if the bourgeoisie broke the tacit understanding, the blame for the resulting violence would rest clearly on its side. As Engels put it in 1886, the new society can come "peacefully if the old has enough intelligence to go to its death without a struggle; forcibly if it resists this necessity."[39]

Marx and Engels even seemed willing that the workers go out of their way to avoid provoking a bourgeois rebellion over the issue most likely to inflame them — socialization of their property. As we observed in chapter 6 the two men rejected any moral or legal claim to compensation for the expropriated bourgeoisie, but Engels nonetheless allowed: "We by no means consider compensation as impermissible in any event; Marx told me (and how many times!) that in his opinion we would get off cheapest if we could buy out the whole lot of them." It would depend, Engels continued, on "the circumstances under which we obtain power, and particularly upon the attitude adopted by these gentry . . . themselves."[40] Again, restraint to match restraint. But it is also characteristic of Marx's unwillingness to offer *public* assurances of his moderation that, however many times he spoke to Engels of buying out the whole lot of them, he never managed to *publish* such sentiments even once in his lifetime.

As final evidence of Marx's private moderation we may turn to a remarkable letter he sent in December 1880 to his new English admirer, H. M. Hyndman. The latter had written to register concern that Marx seemed to endorse violent revolution, while for his own part he hoped that in Great Britain the workers' aims would be attained peacefully. Marx responded:

> If you say that you do not share the views of my party for England, I can only reply that that party considers an English revolution not necessary, but — according to historical precedents — possible. If the unavoidable evolution turns into a revolution, it would not only be the fault of the ruling classes, but also of the working class. Every pacific concession of the former has been wrung from them by "pressure from without." Their action has kept pace with that pressure and if the latter has more and more weakened, if only because the

English working class know not how to wield their power and use their liberties, both of which they possess legally.[41]

Marx first repeated what by then were his and Engels' standard assumptions: that in Britain violent revolution was not necessary or inevitable, because the workers possessed the liberty and power under the law to make all the changes they would require; if a revolution nonetheless occurred — as the precedents of the seventeenth-century bourgeois revolution suggested it might — it would be basically the fault of the ruling classes for not giving in when the time came. But Marx then added a new thought as he chided the British workers of 1880 for their complacency. Unlike their Chartist fathers they were not applying enough "pressure from without" to extract every "pacific concession" they possibly could; they were not using their legal rights to full advantage. Paradoxically, Marx wanted to say, this very passivity might increase the likelihood of eventual violence: if the bourgeoisie grew unaccustomed to yielding concessions and accepting parliamentary defeats in secondary questions, they would be less likely to accept parliamentary defeat when the *primordial* question was put on the agenda. The resulting violence, though still a slaveowners' rebellion, would have to be judged partially the fault of the working class as well. To reduce the likelihood of eventual violence, then, the working class should pressure constantly to extract as many pacific concessions as possible. As we saw in the last section, this was part of Marx and Engels' recommended strategy for the workers of every democratic country during the period before they won their majority.

All this suggests strongly that Marx and Engels were not *looking* for violence, were ready to go out of their way to avoid it, and certainly saw no need for the workers to initiate it in democratic countries. Nonetheless they differed from more tender-minded socialists in that they did not flinch at the prospect, but rather counseled the workers over and over again to rely on their own military potential and to stand ready to resist and suppress any slaveowners' insurrection that might be attempted. As tough-minded democrats they faced up squarely to the central issue of force as the *ultima ratio* of state power. Twentieth-century social democrats characteristically came to trust the willingness of the rich to accept reform legislation even where it injured their interests, and to trust established army and police forces to enforce the authority of left-wing governments even where it was obnoxious to them. The melancholy history of the Weimar Republic provides a number of classic examples of what happened to well-intentioned Social Democrats who ignored the warnings of their old mentors.

The Special Case of Germany

If we now turn at last to Germany, we find a superabundance of source material, particularly in Engels' late essays and in his correspondence with German party leaders. Too often subsequent writers — with the most diverse intentions — have cited this material as evidence of the masters' views on tactics in all democratic countries, or in all capitalist-ruled countries, when in fact Germany was neither of these things (if we remember what the two men had to say about Bonapartism). That country's political structure was indeed so unique, it would be far better not to generalize beyond Germany at all from these tactical writings.[42]

From chapter 2 it may be recalled how Engels found strong similarities between Napoleon's Second Empire and the Reich that Bismarck created to unite Germany in 1871. Germany had moved directly from absolutism to Bonapartism, he declared, and "real governmental authority lies in the hands of a special caste of army officers and state officials." The form of state devised to serve the needs of this caste was "pseudo-constitutionalism, a form which is at once the present-day form of the dissolution of the old absolute monarchy and the form of existence of the Bonapartist monarchy." While the military and civil administration remained quite independent of any direct parliamentary control, "the members of the Reichstag could console themselves for this by the uplifting thought that they had been elected by universal suffrage." The Reichstag was designed essentially to embellish the parasite state with modern-looking decorations.[43]

When the German Social Democratic party (SPD) began to show some strength even in this relatively harmless parliament, Bismarck contrived in 1878 to have it outlawed under an exceptional law. In terms of modern political repression this Anti-Socialist Law was relatively mild: it proscribed the party as an organization, banned its publications, and sanctioned the exile of "professional agitators"; but it nonetheless permitted Social Democratic candidates to stand for election and to speak and vote freely in the Reichstag. The party thrived on this kind of persecution, continuing to grow through twelve years of underground activity until the law was allowed to expire in 1890. In that year the SPD captured 20 percent of the vote, making it now the most popular of the six major German parties. A new party program seemed appropriate, and a first draft of what was to become the Erfurt Program was circulated among party leaders for discussion in the summer of 1891. The political section of this draft contained demands for the most sophisticated democratic techniques in the legislative branch of government — popular initiative, referendum, proportional representation — but remained like the Gotha Program before it strangely silent about the grossly undemocratic features of German executive power. To be sure it was still illegal to demand a republic, but there was not even a call for ministerial responsibility to parliament. The only expansion demanded in the competence of the Reichstag was the right to decide matters of war and peace — an important issue to be sure. Yet one can scarcely escape the impression that the Social Democratic leaders did not want to antagonize the "authorities" who had just restored them to full legality; a few of them were now speaking openly of their hope that Germany would grow gradually and peacefully into socialism.[44]

All this must have rankled Engels a great deal, judging by the fact that he interrupted his vacation to write a long and cogently argued response to the draft that had been sent for his criticism. As has been argued throughout this book, his never-translated "Zur Kritik des sozialdemokratischen Programmentwurfs 1891" constitutes one of the major documents of his political thought and will be used here at the outset to establish his views on the structure of the Bismarckian Reich. Toward the political demands he launched the following opening salvo:

> The political demands of the Draft contained one great fault. What really should be said *is left out.* If all these ten demands were granted we would have various new means for carrying through our principal demand but not the principal demand itself. The Reich Constitution, in the measure of rights assigned to people and their representatives, is plagiarized entirely from the Prussian Constitution of 1850, a constitution which embodies the most extreme reaction in its paragraphs, in which the government possesses all real power and the chambers do not even have the right to withhold taxes; a constitution that the government could interpret in whatever way it chose, as was revealed in the period of the Constitutional Conflict [of 1862–1866). The rights of the Reichstag are exactly the same as those of the Prussian Chamber, and for this reason Liebknecht called this Reichstag the fig leaf of absolutism.

The principal demand Engels would like to have seen included was the demand for a *democratic republic:*

> If one thing is certain, it is that our party and the working class can only come to power under the form of a democratic republic. That is, indeed, the specific form of the dictatorship of the prole-

tariat, as the Great French Revolution [of 1871] has already shown. It is unthinkable that our best people should become ministers under an emperor, like [Johannes] Miquel. Now, it does not appear legally possible to place the demand for a republic directly in the program, although that was permissible even under Louis Philippe in France as it is now in Italy. But the fact that one is not even permitted to put out an openly republican program in Germany shows how colossal the illusion is that a republic could be established there in a comfortable, peaceful manner, and not only a republic but even the communist society.

Nevertheless, one can if need be squeeze by the demand for a republic. What can and should be made, in my view, is the demand for the *concentration of all political power in the hands of the popular representative body.*

Here was Engels' call for ministerial responsibility or some other form of legislative control over the executive. He reaffirmed these democratizing intentions at the lower levels of government when he proposed the following additional demand: "Complete self-administration for the provinces, counties, and communities through officials elected by universal suffrage. Abolition of all local and provincial authorities appointed by the state."[45]

Engels' critique pointed up succinctly just what separated Germany from the genuine constitutional democracies of the West. Social Democrats might indeed elect a majority to the Reichstag, but that would not give them the constitutional authority even to pass legislation (which required the concurrence of the undemocratically chosen upper chamber); much less would it give them the right to appoint their own chancellor, or tamper with the army, or impinge on any of the other prerogatives of the kaiser. Engels' critique expanded on such thoughts as he wrote the lines quoted earlier in this chapter about the possibility of a peaceful revolution in democratic countries like Britain, France, and America. Then he concluded: "But to proclaim such a thing in Germany, where the government is practically all-powerful and the Reichstag and other representative bodies are without real power, to proclaim such a thing moreover when there is no need to do so, is to remove the fig leaf of absolutism and become oneself the screen for its nakedness." "Not many of these things may be placed in the program," he summed up; "I mention them principally to identify . . . the self-deception that wants to lead from such conditions to the communist society in a legal way."[46]

For Engels then it was the sheerest "self-deception" to imagine, as some

Social Democratic parliamentarians now did, that, because the party could agitate freely (more or less) and elect its spokesman to the Reichstag through universal suffrage, therefore a peaceful road to socialism existed. Germany was simply not like the countries to the West. Engels observed mischievously in 1895 that during the previous eighteen months the fifty socialist deputies in the French chamber had helped bring down three ministries and a president: "That shows what a socialist minority can do in a parliament which, like the French or English, is the really supreme power in the country. A similar power our men in Germany can get by a revolution only."[47]

To be sure, if a Social Democrat majority in the Reichstag could not govern, it could at least obstruct. It could reject legislative proposals or refuse to pass the budget. Back in the 1860s the liberals had tried the latter tactic, as Engels noted, during the Prussian constitutional conflict. Bismarck's response had been simply to continue collecting taxes and spending the money unconstitutionally, backing up his illegal actions with the threat of force. A Social Democratic majority in the Reichstag could only produce a similar constitutional stalemate, for no *legal* recourse would be available to either side. Surely it was this situation Engels had foremost in mind when he wrote his famous epigram about universal suffrage being no more than the thermometer of social antagonism — when it registered boiling point in Bismarck's Reich, both sides assuredly would have to look to their extraparliamentary resources.

With this crucial legal context in mind we may turn to the most famous and most misunderstood tactical writings of the late Engels — his 1895 "Preface" to the republication in German of *The Class Struggles in France*. Those who want to argue that Engels died a reformist point to his dismissal here of barricade fighting as out-of-date, along with his lavish praise of legality and the ballot box as the proper road to socialism. Those who want to insist on Engels' revolutionary constancy argue that legality was for him but a tactic, a preliminary to revolution rather than a substitute for it. Both interpretations contain elements of truth; their mutual contradiction is only apparent, and it dissolves as soon as the specific German context of the argument is brought into focus.

Engels began with his well-known panegyric to universal suffrage, declaring that it had indeed been transformed from a means of deception into an instrument of emancipation:

If universal suffrage had offered no other advantage than that it allowed us to count our numbers every three years; that by the regularly established, unexpectedly rapid rise in the number of our votes it increased in equal measure the workers' certainty of victory and the dismay of their opponents, and so became our best means of propaganda; that it accurately informed us concerning our own strength and that of all hostile parties, and thereby provided us with a measure of proportion for our actions second to none, safeguarding us from untimely timidity as much as from untimely foolhardiness — if this had been the only advantage we gained from the suffrage, it would still have been much more than enough. But it did more than this by far. In election agitation it provided us with a means, second to none, of getting in touch with the mass of the people where they still stand aloof from us; of forcing all parties to defend their views and actions against our attacks before all the people; and, further, it provided our representatives in the Reichstag with a platform from which they could speak to their opponents in parliament, and to the masses without, with quite other authority and freedom than in the press or at meetings. . . .

And so it happened that the bourgeoisie and the government came to be much more afraid of the legal than of the illegal action of the workers' party, of the results of elections than those of rebellion.

Next came the famous critique of barricade fighting — to which we will return — with its conclusion that popular insurrections no longer have any real chance against disciplined troops armed with modern weapons. The Social Democrats must not allow themselves to be provoked into hopeless battles, Engels warned. The movement no longer required such violent confrontations anyway:

Its growth proceeds as spontaneously, as steadily, as irresistably, and at the same time as tranquilly as a natural process. All government intervention has proved powerless against it. We can count even today on two and a quarter million voters. If it continues in this fashion, by the end of the century we shall conquer the greater part of the middle stata of society, petty bourgeois and small peasants, and grow into the decisive power in the land, before which all other powers will have to bow, whether they like it or not. To keep this growth going without interruption until it of itself gets beyond the control of the prevailing governmental system, not to fritter away this daily increasing shock force in vanguard skirmishes, but to keep it intact until the decisive day, that is our main task.[48]

So far Engels' remarks seemed indeed to make him out a convert to reformism.

Abruptly, however, he changed pace as he looked forward to the *ultimate* electoral victory:

> The irony of world history turns everything upside down. We, the "revolutionists," the "overthrowers" — we are thriving far better on legal methods than on illegal methods and overthrow. The parties of Order, as they call themselves, are perishing under the legal conditions created by themselves. They cry despairingly . . . legality is the death of us; whereas we, under this legality, get firm muscles and rosy cheeks and look like life eternal. And if *we* are not so crazy as to let ourselves be driven to street fighting in order to please them, then in the end there is nothing left for them to do but themselves break through this fatal legality.[49]

The ultimate electoral victory would lead, as Engels saw it, not to the triumphant formation of a legal Social Democratic government, but to the abandonment of the now stalemated and unworkable constitution by the old regime. A similar abandonment of legality might also happen in democratic countries, of course, if there were a pro-slavery rebellion. But what was a *possibility* in these countries was a virtual certainty in Germany, given its unique constitutional arrangements. The Bismarckian constitution did not require the old government to relinquish power to a socialist majority, and the rigid traditions of German's ruling caste insured it would not do so in any event.

Toward the end of his essay Engels returned to the idea of contract which we have perceived in several of his writings, this time quite explicitly. He addressed the rulers of Germany directly:

> But do not forget that the German empire . . . is a *product of contract;* of the contract, first of the princes with one another and, second, of the princes with the people. If one side breaks the contract, the whole contract falls to the ground; the other side is then also no longer bound. . . . If, therefore, you break the constitution of the Reich, the Social-Democracy is free, and can do as it pleases with regard to you. But it will hardly blurt out to you today what it is going to do then.[50]

German press laws also made it unwise for Engels to blurt out what he had in mind, though he had noted just a few paragraphs earlier that in other countries, by using universal suffrage, "our foreign comrades do not thereby in the least renounce their right of revolution. The right to revolution is, after all, the only *really* 'historical right,' the only right on which all modern states without exception rest." He was even more straightforward in a private letter to one of those foreign comrades, Gerson Trier in Copenhagen: "That the proletariat cannot conquer its political supremacy, the only door to the new society, without a violent revolution — about that we are agreed."[51] Thus, Engels' prognosis for Germany was clear enough: electoral victory would indeed be the signal for revolution and not a substitute for it. Those who interpret the "Preface" as a reformist document mislead us insofar as they imply that Engels denied the inevitability of revolution in Germany. On the other hand, those who interpret it as vindicating a revolutionary stance mislead us if they mean to imply Engels would prefer violence even where a peaceful path existed, or was indifferent to the principle of majority rule.

To make all this clearer, let us now combine other sources with the "Preface" to follow out certain lines of thought. His experiences in 1848–1849 had left Engels with a lifelong respect for real military power. Barricade romanticism never appealed to him in any event, and military progress during this second half of the century, both technological and organizational, convinced him of the enormous advantages modern armies would have over amateur street fighters. Now that the German army had proved itself the mightiest in Europe, it seemed to him particularly foolhardy for the Social Democrats to provoke violence prematurely, or allow themselves to be provoked. Engels was well aware of the more or less constant pressure on the German government from extreme reactionary circles to draw the Social Democrats into some kind of violent action — perhaps by withdrawing universal suffrage — and then to crush the whole movement with massive force. Hence the warnings we have just observed in the "Preface," to beware of "untimely foolhardiness," not to fritter away the party's fortunes in "vanguard skirmishes," not to be so "crazy" as to engage in street fighting, and so on. Warnings such as these can be found dotted throughout Engels' writings and correspondence over the previous decade or more. Behind his tactic of legality lay the conviction that the movement was not yet strong enough to take on the German army, that the army would in fact welcome such a confrontation.[52]

On the other hand, Engels absolutely bristled at any suggestion that the German Social Democrats openly *pledge* themselves to legality, renounce the *right* of revolution. As we have seen, even in democratic countries Engels was reluctant to offer such pledges when the other side never offered any in return; but in Germany, where the legal structure was so grossly skewed against the masses, where reactionaries talked openly of resorting to force themselves — there it would be a despicable sign of weakness and toadying to undertake any such pledge. When the German party leaders received the draft of Engels' 1895 "Preface," they thought it rather too inflammatory. Our enemies will say, Richard Fischer wrote back, "that we refrain from making a revolution today merely because we are not yet strong enough."[53] Engels responded testily:

> I simply cannot believe that you intend to sell yourselves body and soul to absolute legality, legality under all circumstances, legality even regarding laws broken by those who wrote them, in short the policy of offering the left cheek to those who have struck the right one. . . .
>
> I am of the opinion that you will gain nothing if you preach the absolute renunciation of revolt. No one will believe you and there is *no* party in any country that goes so far as to renounce the right to resist illegality with weapons in hand. . . .
>
> You would do better to maintain the standpoint that the obligation of legality is a juristic one, not a moral one . . . ; and that it ceases utterly if those in power break the laws. . . .
>
> Consider your own illegal activities under the Anti-Socialist Law, which they might stick on you again! Legality as long as it suits us, and not legality at any price, not even as rhetoric![54]

Engels once again revealed here his inner conviction that the old regime in Germany would eventually abandon legality itself, abrogating the constitution in some kind of royal coup d'état, or *Staatsstreich*, to use the German expression.

Although the tone of this passage suggests the same defensive rather than offensive resort to violence that Marx and Engels justified in fully democratic countries, one may legitimately question whether Engels in his own mind excluded a first strike. Or more exactly, was he willing to wait for the ultimate electoral victory in Germany, using violence only to impose the majority will, or would he have seized the first favorable opportunity for revolution that came along? The available evidence strongly points to the former alternative. Asked by an interviewer in 1893 whether he expected a socialist government in Germany soon, Engels replied: "Why not? If the growth of our Party continues at its normal rate we shall have a majority between the years 1900 and 1910. And when we do, you may be assured we shall neither be short of ideas nor men to carry them out." Writing privately to the Lafargues he spoke of the need to win votes in the rural districts, "without which we cannot expect to be victorious."[55]

Most interesting of all was his 1892 article entitled "Socialism in Germany." Reviewing the continuing electoral successes of the party, Engels once again predicted violence initiated by the other side. "One fine morning the German bourgeoisie and their government will grow tired of standing with their arms crossed, watching the spring-flood of socialism overflow everything; they will seek refuge in illegality, in acts of violence." Engels' response to this seemed downright chivalrous: "We shall await it. Meanwhile: 'Shoot first, messieurs les bourgeois!'"[56] His historical allusion was to a perhaps apocryphal incident at the Battle of Fontenoy in 1745, where according to the standard French recollection their commander shouted over to the English: "Tirez les premiers, messieurs les anglais!" The standard English recollection has it just the other way around. No matter. In either event gallantry was mixed with a certain amount of guile, for in eighteenth-century line encounters the military advantage lay with the side firing the *return* volley. By the same token there was a mixture of guile in Engels' gallantry, as he revealed in an 1892 letter congratulating Lafargue on the electoral successes of the French party:

> Do you realize now what a splendid weapon you in France have
> had in your hands for forty years in universal suffrage; if only people
> had known how to use it! It's slower and more boring than the call
> to revolution, but it's ten times more sure, and what is even better,
> it indicates with the most perfect accuracy the day when a call to
> armed revolution has to be made; it's even ten to one that universal
> suffrage, intelligently used by the workers, will drive the rulers to
> overthrow legality, that is, put us in the most favorable position
> to make the revolution.[57]

Looking back over forty years Engels was including the Bonapartist period during which, as in Bismarckian Germany, universal suffrage could have been no more than a signal for revolution, but it is noteworthy that even under the Republic he reckoned the odds at ten to one against the rulers' yielding to a socialist majority. It seemed important to Engels, however, that the rulers be the first to abandon legality; that would put the workers in the "most favorable position" for their revolution, presumably by giving them the moral advantage in winning over those elements of the population that might still be uncommitted or straddling the fence. Notice Engels' unspoken — or half-spoken — assumption that the workers should not move until the day that the thermometer of universal suffrage registered boiling point. Though he liked to put the argument in practical rather than moral terms, as he did when speaking against religious persecution, one may well detect a deep-seated respect for the majority principle lying behind the practical argumentation. Once the other side had broken the contract, Engels would feel "free," "no longer bound," as he said in his 1895 "Preface"; but until that time, something held him back. Certainly not legality per se. To what did he feel bound if not to the majority principle?

There do appear to have been two circumstances under which Engels contemplated a different path of development in Germany, where violence would *precede* the winning of a socialist majority. The first might occur if some prior catastrophe — socioeconomic or military — drove the masses spontaneously into a violent upheaval not planned or foreseen by the party. The second might occur if the old regime carried out its *Staatsstreich* ahead of time in anticipation of its eventual electoral defeat. In both cases, if the masses of the population were ready to move, Engels was clearly ready to move with them. Even at the age of sixty-five, he confided to Bebel, "I only hope my old injury will not prevent me from mounting a horse again at the right moment."[58] It is also clear, however, that if the majority of the nation wanted to bring down the old regime but not yet install the Social Democrats, Engels was prepared to wait his turn. The party should not expect to come to power immediately, he repeated in several letters to German Social Democratic leaders during the early 1880s: "The big mistake of the Germans is to imagine that the revolution is a thing to be made overnight. In reality, even under favorable circumstances, it is a process of development of the masses requiring several years." He developed this thought in another letter:

In actuality revolutions begin with the great majority of the people, and also the official parties, rallying *against* the thus isolated government and toppling it. Then, only after those parties that still remain viable have worked themselves — with one another, against one another, after one another — all into the ground, only then the great polarization will come into being that gives us the chance to rule.[59]

Here was the alliance of the majority classes once again, with its same logic of development. In still another letter he made it clear that the most radical among the nonsocialist parties (descendents of the petty bourgeois democrats of the 1848 period) could be expected to rule at first:

> It cannot be expected that at the moment of crisis we shall already have the majority of the electorate and therefore of the nation behind us. The whole bourgeois class and the remnants of the feudal landowning class, a large section of the petty bourgeoisie and also of the rural population, will then mass themselves around the most radical bourgeois party.[60]

In Germany the Progressive party was the logical focal point of such a rallying and would likely be the first party to govern the new republic:

> The first immediate result of the revolution can and *must* be in its form nothing but the *bourgeois* republic. This will be only a short transitional moment here, since happily we have no pure republican bourgeois party. The bourgeois republic, perhaps with the Progressive Party at its head, will serve us at first *for the winning of the great mass of the workers to revolutionary socialism* — that will be accomplished in one or two years — and for the wearing out and self-ruination of all possible middle parties but us. Only then can we take over successfully.[61]

In this projected scenario one sees democratic assumptions abounding, even though it suited Engels' personality to say "when we are strong enough" rather than "when we have majority support." In his mind, as these quotations reveal so well, the two thoughts were one and the same.

It is also interesting to speculate what has become of the dictatorship of the proletariat in this projection. Either the initial provisional government would have to be so labeled, even though dominated by the Progressives — an absurdity — or the eventual Social Democratic government would have to be so labeled, even though presumably it would be elected to office in legal fashion — also an absurdity. Only if the second event signaled a pro-slavery rebellion requiring martial law could one speak at all of a dictatorship of the proletariat. In truth the idea of the dictatorship of the proletariat fitted comfortably only with Strategy I, that classic model of majority proletarian revolution that was sociologically appropriate only for Britain during Marx's lifetime, but which nonetheless dominated both men's minds as the standard or ideal type, of workers' revolution. Engels lived long enough to find a Germany grown sociologically and politically ready for such a revolution and, significantly, used the phrase one last time in its only specific application to Germany. By the early 1890s, Engels was inclined to think the SPD had grown so much, and the bourgeois parties had decayed so much, that "a *pure* bourgeois republic is out of date." He now judged that "in Germany the bourgeois parties are so bankrupt that we shall pass at once from monarchy to the *social* republic."[62] Under such circumstances Strategy II could finally be replaced in Germany by Strategy I, the pure and simple majority proletarian revolution. The masses would rally immediately to the Social Democrats and proclaim a democratic republic. Of such a provisionally established republic Engels could rightly say: "That is the specific form of the dictatorship of the proletariat." The rule of the working-class majority through provisionally established democratic institutions was exactly what Marx and Engels always understood that term to mean, as we saw in volume 1.[63]

Thus, whether the old regime in Germany fell after the thermometer of universal suffrage reached boiling point, or through the more complicated process before that happened, Engels expected that violence would be required to bring it down, almost surely initiated by the old regime itself. There remains to examine what Engels expected of Social Democratic parliamentarians in the period of legal activity before that final conflict. In this area too we find that his views clashed sharply with reformist-minded Social Democrats, for he repeatedly endorsed and defended Bebel and Kautsky's policy of "pure opposition," of extracting concessions whenever possible, but not at the price of any positive collaboration with the regime or with the bourgeois parties. As he explained to a British newspaperman in 1893: "We accept anything which any government may give us, but only as a payment on account, and for which we offer no thanks. We always vote against the Budget, and against any vote for money or men for the Army."[64] This was an allusion to the classic slogan of pre-World War I Social Democracy: "*Diesem System keinen Mann und keinen Groschen!*" (To this system not one man and not one penny!).

In an earlier letter to Bebel, Engels reviewed the implications of pure opposition in greater detail:

The issues on which Social Democratic deputies can step out of pure opposition are very narrowly circumscribed. They are all issues in which the relationship of the worker to the capitalist comes directly into play: factory legislation, normal work day, liability, wage payments in kind, etc. Then, to be sure, improvements in the purely bourgeois sense, that constitute a positive step forward: uniformity of coinage and weights, freedom of movement, extension of personal freedoms, etc. (you won't be troubled with many of these for a while.) In all other economic questions like protective tariffs, nationalization of the railroads, insurance systems, etc., the Social Democratic deputies will always have to maintain the crucial position of *approving nothing that strengthens the power of the government vis-a-vis the people.* (Emphasis added)[65]

From these premises Engels spoke out vigorously against those reformist Social Democratic deputies who voted for protective tariffs, or steamship subsidies, or any nationalization under the existing government, and indeed any measures serving in his judgment to strengthen that government vis-à-vis the people. He likewise opposed those South German reformists who wanted to win rural votes by defending the interests of peasants as proprietors; he was just as eager, to be sure, to win peasant support, but not at the price of defending the doomed small holding: "We can do no greater disservice to the Party as well as to the small peasants than to make promises that even only create the impression that we intend to preserve the small holdings permanently."[66]

No one who reads through Engels' correspondence with German party leaders during the last two decades of his life could possibly imagine that he acquired any sympathy for ideas or tactics that were distinctively reformist. He always expressed faith in the underlying militance of the rank and file and — rather too naïvely — attributed reformism to the influx of bourgeois intellectuals into the Reichstag fraction and the party press. As early as 1879, in a well-known circular letter he wrote jointly with Marx, Engels fired volley after volley of sarcasm at those reformist intellectuals who thought only people like themselves were qualified to lead the movement: "In short: the working class of itself is incapable of its own emancipation. For this purpose it must place itself under the leadership of 'educated and propertied' bourgeois who alone possess the 'time and opportunity' to acquaint themselves with what is good for the workers." "We cannot," the letter concluded, "cooperate with people who say that the workers are too uneducated to emancipate themselves and must first be freed from above by philanthropic bourgeois." Then in November 1894, just a few months before his death, he agreed with Bebel's lament that the party was "going bourgeois." "That is the misfortune of all extreme parties," he philosophized, "when the time approaches for them to become 'possible.'" Fortunately, he added, "there is still time to call a halt."[67]

Turning now to the other side of the socialist spectrum, it must be emphasized in equal measure that Engels was never attracted by those in the SPD who stood to the left of the "centrist" leaders, Bebel and Kautsky. He showed only scorn and derision for the so-called *Jungen*, the radical young intellectuals who challenged the party leadership in 1890. Their university education "does not entitle them to an officer's commission and a claim to an appropriate position in the party," he exclaimed; "in our party everyone must rise from the ranks." The *Jungen* have "much more to learn from the workers than the latter from them."[68] Ultraradical intellectuals thus received the same short shrift as reformist ones. Engels did not live long enough to witness the emergence in 1905 of the new radicalism centered on Rosa Luxemburg's revolutionary activism, but he did express a distinct coolness toward the principal tactical weapon with which Luxemburg hoped to revitalize the movement — the general strike. Such a "political strike must either be immediately victorious — simply through the threat," he wrote, "or it will end it a colossal disgrace, or finally it will lead directly *to barricades*." It was an all-or-nothing weapon, he reasoned, that could only be used when the movement was overwhelmingly strong. "Whenever we are in a position to *try* the universal strike, we shall be able to get what we want for the mere asking for it, without the roundabout way of the universal strike."[69] Luxemburg's argument, that a series of strikes on popular issues was precisely the means to engage the masses and draw them to the colors, Engels probably would have found convincing only for a state already torn asunder by revolutionary turmoil, not for the Germany of his day where the army was looking for precisely such a pretext to crush the movement with overwhelming force.

Perhaps more importantly, given the main trends of twentieth-century "Marxism," Engels saw no point in guerrilla or other paramilitary activities and had no confidence in such means either in Germany or anywhere else. His writings on military subjects, which fill two large volumes, show only the most casual interest in guerrilla warfare. For his generation the classic example of such warfare was to be found in the resistance of Spanish irregulars to Napoleon's rule of that country between 1808 and 1812. The standard lesson drawn from his campaign by military experts was that guerrilla activities could only be successful where they were ancillary to the operations of a regular army (in this case of the British). Engels evidently agreed for he repeated this thought as a general maxim in 1853: "The support of a regular army is now-a-days necessary to the progress of all insurrectionary or irregular warfare against a powerful regular army."[70] In his articles on Napoleonic Spain, Marx had observed the chronic tendency of guerrilla groups to degenerate into praetorian formations serving the ambitions of their commanders rather than the broader needs of the masses.[71] The two men would surely have been dumbfounded to see that "Marxist" movements in the second half of the twentieth century have come to rely *primarily* on the strategy of guerrilla warfare.

How then did Engels imagine that the formidable military power of the modern state *could* be overcome? The strength of the revolutionaries basically would lie in their numbers: "In politics there are only two decisive powers," he had written, "the organized force of the State, the Army, and the unorganized, elemental force of the popular masses."[72] Even so, as his 1895 "Preface" had made clear, unorganized masses, no matter how numerous, had little chance against repeating rifles and explosive shells. "The era of barricades and street fighting has gone for good," he wrote privately to Lafargue; "*if the military fight*, resistance becomes madness."[73] In the preliminary condition lay Engels' hope for a solution to the problem. What if the soldiers refused to fight against the proletarian revolution, just as they had refused to fire upon the populace at crucial moments during the Great French Revolution and during the revolutions of 1848? Engels based this hope not simply on the naïve faith that soldiers would refuse to fire on their countrymen, not even on the more differentiated conviction that workers (as conscript soldiers) would refuse to fire on other workers, but rather on the further calculation that Social Democrats as conscripts would refuse to fire on their party comrades.

Just as the strategy for legal revolution grew out of the extension of democratic institutions in Europe, so this "theory of the vanishing army," as Martin Berger has called it in his perceptive study, grew out of changes in European military systems during the same period of time.[74] The evident superiority of the Prussian army that was demonstrated at Königgrätz and Sedan led the other Continental powers one after another to adopt the Prussian system of universal conscription. Engels saw these developments as positive, partly for reasons having to do with international politics, but mainly because of their domestic implications:

> Competition among the individual states forces them . . . to resort to universal compulsory military service more and more extensively, thus in the long run making the whole people familiar with the use of arms, and therefore enabling them at a given moment to make their will prevail against the war-lords in command. And this moment will arrive as soon as the mass of people — town and country workers and peasants — *will have* a will. At this point the armies of the princes become transformed into the armies of the people; the machine refuses to work, and militarism collapses by the dialectics of its own evolution.[75]

Forced upon the European governments by their fear of each other, the conscription system would ultimately undermine them all — it was one of those delicious ironies of world history that Engels loved to savor.

Since time was working for the proletariat as much in the military sphere as in the political, one can better appreciate Engels' recurring advice of patience and his caution against premature revolt. "With military conditions as they are at present we shall not start our attack so long as there is still an armed force against us," he wrote Bebel in 1884: "We can wait until the armed force itself ceases to be *a force against us*."[76] Social Democratic infiltration of the army — the automatic consequence of universal conscription — was proceeding even more quickly than electoral gains might suggest, as Engels emphasized in 1892:

> The chief strength of German Social Democracy does not rest at all in its voters. One becomes a voter in Germany only at the age of 25, but is already a soldier at 20. And since it is precisely the younger generation that delivers the most recruits to our party, it follows that the German army is more and more infected with socialism. Today we have one soldier in five, in a few years we will have one in three, and about 1900 the army, hitherto the most Prussian element in the country, will be socialist in its majority. This process rolls on as inevitably as a judgment of fate. The government in Berlin sees it coming as clearly as we do, but it is powerless. The army is slipping away from it.[77]

In addition to youth, Engels was particularly encouraged by the spread of Social Democratic ideas to the rural population of Prussia. Here the most reliable regiments of the German army were formed, and when these units likewise became infected, the end would be near. The Reichstag elections of 1890 marked the first significant penetration of the East Elbean rural districts by the party; it signaled "the beginning of the revolution in Germany," according to Engels. "In three years we can have the agricultural workers and then we will have the core regiments of the Prussian army." Boldly he prophesied that "On that day, Prussia will be no more." In one of his last major political writings he urged the party to concentrate its efforts particularly on these rural workers: "It is of vastly greater importance to win the rural proletariat east of the Elbe than the small peasants of Western Germany."[78] Through such a deliberate — though not at all conspiratorial — plan to subvert the army, Engels found a way for the revolution to triumph despite the obsolescence of street fighting.

But would socialist conscripts really defy their officers? Engels appeared to be utterly confident. He must have taken heart in 1891 from reports that in France a detachment of troops at Fourmies had refused to obey an order to fire on May Day demonstrators.[79] When interviewed two years later by a *Figaro* correspondent who expressed skepticism on the point, Engels responded categorically: "On the day when we shall be in the majority, what the French army did by instinct by not firing on the people [in 1789?] will be done by our people in a conscious way."[80] Here again incidently one sees his express assumption of a majority revolution.

As much as the aging Engels insisted that the revolution in Germany would have to be a violent one, it is clear he did not expect intense or protracted violence, a full-scale civil war lasting over many years, and for the simple reason that the old regime would find few soldiers willing to defend it. In the inspired finale to his 1895 "Preface," Engels likened the progress of socialism in the German army to the spread of Christianity through the Roman army of antiquity. When that army had become "overwhelmingly" Christian, it was not surprising to find the Emperor Constantine proclaiming Christianity as the state religion. In a similar way, he implied the resistance of the present-day German emperor would have to collapse as well, once the socialist infection had spread throughout his army. In yet another striking image Engels alluded to "the athletic figure of the German proletariat that Marx foresaw already in 1844, the giant for whom the cramped imperial edifice designed to fit the philistine is even now becoming inadequate and whose mighty stature and broad shoulders are growing until the moment comes when by merely rising from his seat he will shatter the whole structure of the imperial constitution into fragments."[81] Thus the violent revolution, precisely because it would enjoy the support of the mass of the population and therewith the mass of the army, would resemble a giant "merely rising from his seat." This is scarcely the image anyone would have chosen to describe the communist victories of the twentieth century that emerged out of long years of devastating civil and international wars.

If we now put together what we have learned about Engels' views on Germany with what he and Marx said about the Western democracies, we can draw some overall conclusions about the masters' views on legal revolution, Strategy IV, as well as about questions of reform and revolution more generally. It is apparent that neither Marx nor Engels "mellowed" with age on these issues; rather it was external conditions that changed, as various Western countries extended democratic institutions in a way that made "legal revolution" a possibility in their eyes. That possibility did not extend to Germany, even though the establishment of a democratically elected Reichstag there might create such an illusion among the gullible; in Germany a legal electoral victory could only be a signal for violent revolution, not a substitute for it. Indeed, this might well prove to be the case even in the Western democracies, if the workers' victory produced a pro-slavery rebellion on the part of the bourgeoisie. Marx and Engels never supported political violence as an offensive weapon in democratic countries, and were willing to go out of their way to avoid provoking the bourgeoisie to violence. They *desired* a legal and peaceful changeover as much as any reformist; where they differed was in their *estimate of probabilities*, and in their consequent insistence that the workers always stand ready for a forceful showdown when the class struggle reached its climax. The dichotomy here should not be drawn between revolutionaries and democrats, but between tough-minded and tender-minded democrats.

Further, while en route to its majority, Marx and Engels wanted the workers' party to extract all possible concessions but not to enter into any positive collaboration with the old regime or the bourgeois parties that would compromise its "pure opposition." On the day it won a majority — the legal revolution — it must be able to exercise its full and rightful power unencumbered by any vitiating commitments stemming from past compromises. For the reformists, by contrast, the importance of a decisive changeover separating capitalist rule from socialist rule faded and melted away in their gradualist vision of peaceful reform and positive collaboration both before and after the socialist majority. The workers' party might participate in bourgeois coalitions before that day, and bourgeois parties participate thereafter. Thus the day that for Marx and Engels would inaugurate an entirely new world-historical era became for them but another small step, one among many, in the extended process of growing into socialism. What for Marx and Engels was a vision of class conflict played out to a decisive conclusion, possibly but not necessarily under humane rules, became for them a vision of class collaboration and uncontested gradual progress toward a remote goal.

The reformist vision of change was at once democratic, legal, peaceful, and gradual; understandably perhaps they tended to muddle the four elements together. To understand Marx and Engels' position, however, one must keep them all separate: the workers' victory would be the conscious effort and the will of the majority — hence democratic at all events. It *might* be legal, if the other side opened and kept open a legal path to power for the majority. It *might* be peaceful, if the other side submitted to that majority without rebellion. It would be gradual only in the sense of not happening all overnight, but would certainly appear swift and decisive in comparison to the reformist vision.

In their common attachment to democratic values, the reformists might earn higher grades than Marx and Engels on one point only: they characteristically *proclaimed* that attachment without hesitation, which is to say, they bound themselves publicly to the majority principle and all that it implies. Marx and Engels were troubled in this regard by that same moral constipation we observed in the realm of individual rights. Just as the evidence there pointed to an underlying respect for the rights of peaceful opposition which they seemed psychologically unable to express openly and in normative terms, so here too all our evidence points to a respect for the majority principle and the desire to avoid violence which they found it hard to express forthrightly in their public writings. The casual reader of their standard political writings might easily conclude the two men were cynical about democracy, or simply indifferent as to whether the workers came to power peacefully or violently. Such an interpretation, as we can now see, is not really fair to the evidence in its totality — private as well as public, negative as well as positive, deeds as well as words.

As in the case of individual rights, Marx and Engels seemed to have feared that any public assurances binding the movement to respect the majority principle, or other democratic values, would be perceived as weakness and servility. This was certainly Engels' reaction whenever the German Social Democrats were tempted to bind themselves to legality. In that particular case Engels could scarcely be faulted, since the legality to which the German party was asked to pledge itself was grossly stacked against it. Even where the rules of the game were acceptably democratic, one could not ask for an unconditional pledge that would bind the workers even if the other side broke the rules. Yet, without weakening their actual position one iota, Marx and Engels might have declared: Under an acceptably democratic system of laws, we will play by the rules as long as you do, but not a moment longer. And: Though prepared to meet force with force, we will not be the *first* to turn to our weapons. Such assurances need not be regarded as toadying or empty moralizing. To notify one's adversary in advance of the rules one accepts can be a policy consciously adopted to reduce the likelihood of exaggerated or desperate responses. Marx's private willingness to give the bourgeoisie compensation for expropriated property in exchange for peaceable submission might have been an official policy of the movement designed to soften the opposition of that class. Marx and Engels' public threats of brutality to match brutality might have been paired with just as many public assurances of the converse — restraint to match restraint — in an effort to encourage humane behavior from the other side. Without such compensating assurances, a constant stress on the likelihood of violence may ultimately make violence more likely. To anticipate nothing but the worst from one's adversary, just as in an international arms race, may turn out to be a self-fulfilling prophecy.

⟨11⟩

Conclusion:
Democracy Without Professionals

NOWADAYS PEOPLE LABELED as "Marxists" are commonly thought to be more radical than other kinds of socialists, more extreme in the means justified to attain the end. Political assassinations and other acts of terrorism, vanguard parties, guerrilla armies, and one-party dictatorships are thus associated with Marx's name. The original radicalism of Marx and Engels, however, had far more to do with ends than with means.

Let us first review the question of means. It is not really possible to classify the two men either as Social Democrats or Communists in the twentieth-century meaning of those terms, partly because their ideas were formed in the pre-democratic era of European governments. As we have seen, they originally thought of achieving communism by means of violent revolution, to be sure, but violent revolution by a proletarian majority against an entrenched oligarchy of wealth (Strategy I). This program was then modified in the 1848 period to fit the more backward conditions of France and Germany, where the workers were urged to find allies among the peasants and petty bourgeois in an alliance of the majority classes, and to envisage a revolution that would have to pass through several stages before proletarian objectives could be fully achieved (Strategy II). Two decades later, it was still this strategy that Marx and Engels appealed to during their moments of hope that the Paris Commune might expand into a real national revolution. By the mid-seventies they also countenanced the prospect of a mass peasant revolution in Russia, where, because of the surviving traditions of the village community, it seemed at least possible that socialism might be constructed immediately, though Engels always insisted this could only happen with substantial help from a victorious Western proletariat (Strategy III). Finally, in the same period of time Marx and Engels began to allow for the possibility of a legal and

[363]

peaceful transformation in those countries where meaningful democratic institutions had been introduced (Strategy IV).

This last development, however, did not by any means transform Marx and Engels into reformist social democrats. It has been argued here that throughout their lives Marx and Engels were committed to basic democratic values, even if they were reluctant to make proclamations. This commitment they certainly shared with reformist social democrats, along with the view that in democratic countries the workers should organize openly in a mass party, take part in elections, seek to win concessions from the existing order, and avoid violence as an offensive weapon. On the other hand, Marx and Engels were much more pessimistic than the reformists about the willingness of the other side to step down when the time came and bow to the will of a proletarian majority. They repeatedly cautioned the workers even in democratic countries to be on their guard against such a "slaveowners' insurrection," to stand ready to suppress it by relying on their own military potential as a workers' militia. Furthermore, while they approved the winning of "concessions," they opposed any compromising bargains to attain them, any positive collaboration with the existing state or the bourgeois parties — socialist deputies ought to vote against any measure that strengthens the existing order. Finally, Marx and Engels never imagined that the leaders of the workers' movement would simply step into the high offices of state and govern as a professional cadre in much the same manner as their bourgeois predecessors. No social democratic government has achieved the high level of mass participation and the deprofessionalization of leadership functions that Marx and Engels admired so much in the Paris Commune. This last observation leads us toward the question of radical ends, as distinct from means, where original Marxism also needs to be separated sharply from the later social-democratic tradition — a matter we will return to presently.

As regards the twentieth-century Communist tradition, the shared commitments seem fewer, the differences even more profound. Like the Communists, Marx and Engels did not shrink from advocating violence where they thought it justified and necessary. They also seemed to give their blessing to the basic ingredients in the later Bolshevik strategy of skipping stages, of building socialism immediately in Russia with anticipated help from a victorious proletariat in the West. Marx even seemed to allow — very hesitantly and tenuously — that under favorable conditions backward countries might achieve socialism even without help from their Western comrades. But all these possibilities were predicated on the survival of communal institutions and traditions among the peasant masses, a major prerequisite that twentieth-century Communists have either ignored or forgotten. Moreover, Marx and Engels had no use for vanguard parties in any country. If the evidence before 1850 on this point is complicated by the peculiar character of the Communist League, there are no such complications in Marx and Engels' participation in the mass, open, loosely conceived IWA. The International allowed secret sections where necessary to avoid police persecution but otherwise no concessions to the older conspirational and elitist tradition exemplified by Bakunin and later taken up afresh by the Russian Communists. Insofar as such organizational conceptions contain a logic that leads to one-party dictatorship, Marx and Engels must be separated off again, for their praise of the Paris Commune, the only functioning workers' government of their time, contains not a hint of support for such a strategy. That all ideas and factions might peacefully seek support in the workers' state also suggests an underlying respect for individual political rights in Marx and Engels — though they were perversely loathe to acknowledge it — that no present-day Communist regime has established. The two men never believed in the efficacy of what we now call political terrorism. They never advocated political assassinations (though they privately condoned the assassination of Czar Alexander II) and always reacted sharply against indiscriminate bombings. They saw no point in organizing guerrilla armies, for, in their later lives, they expected the military power of the old regime to be undermined by universal conscription. In all these ways they separated themselves from what has become the Communist tradition.

Thus the most radical thing about Marx and Engels does not concern *means* at all — certainly not their advocacy of revolution, since what they advocated was a popular revolution to establish democratic institutions where they did not exist, never a minority revolution to destroy them where they did. The most radical thing about Marx and Engels manifestly concerns *ends:* it was their desire to transcend the division of labor, to create a society of continuous occupational fluidity, a workforce with multiple skills, and — in the political sphere — a democracy without professionals.

The idea is profoundly rooted in Marx's conception of man as an indeterminate being who develops whatever powers lie within him by means of his interactions with the external world, in the first instance, by means of labor. To develop all one's powers to the fullest possible extent becomes thus the categorical imperative in Marx's implicit ethical philosophy — for individuals, and for mankind at large. Communism was for him the answer to the question: How can society be organized so as to insure the fullest development of each and every individual member? And communism would insure this primarily by overcoming the division of labor that confines each of us to a particular livelihood; it would rotate tasks so that individuals would develop multiple skills and talents; ideally all their gifts would mature to full blossom, benefiting society thereby no less than themselves. These ideas were the product of Marx's classical humanist education, in particular, his reinterpretation of the German ideal of *Bildung* (itself a reflection of Renaissance and Greek ideals), democratized and mixed together with some of the insights of the great Utopian socialists.

Marx's initial theory of the state may be set in the same perspective. Mankind cannot attain its destiny so long as one section of society, the enormous majority, is ruled over by another section, a small minority composed of professional administrators and professional soldiers. Such a division of labor inevitably gives the ruling stratum interests to defend that are separate from those of the people they administer. Marx's earliest political passion was a hatred of bureaucracy and it remained with him throughout his life, however ironical this may seem to those who identify him with a bureaucratically administered state socialism. The most hateful forms of state somehow were not the class despotisms but the parasite states – Oriental despotism, European absolutism, and above all Bonapartism. Marx's images for the Bonapartist state – a boa constrictor entoiling the social body, a deadening incubus, a ubiquitous parasite feeding on the vitals of France – betray the depth of his feeling; he wanted to eradicate not merely capitalist bureaucracy but the bureaucratic principle itself from all social institutions. One reason for the stress placed upon the parasite state in the foregoing pages has been to draw its opposite into sharper relief – the opposite of the parasite state is democracy without professionals.

It was such a democracy Marx and Engels perceived in the Paris Commune of 1871, where governmental functions at all levels and in all departments were taken from the hands of a trained caste, and placed into the hands of ordinary people, who were elected to their offices and could be recalled, and who worked in the public view at workmen's wages. In just such fashion would the division of labor be overcome in the eventual worker's state and in the classless society. Under the principles of election and recall for all offices, no higher standard of living for office holders, with the expectation of universal participation and rapid turnover, leadership positions would be taken up for a term and then passed on before anyone could acquire an entrenched interest, and no new governing class could emerge. In this tantalizing vision of a democracy without professionals we must recognize Marx and Engels' real radicalism.

It was not a vision that tantalized their own followers very much. Lenin seemed enthusiastic enough, to be sure, in his *State and Revolution*, about deprofessionalizing state functions, but it was the same Lenin who insisted on a *party* composed of *professional* revolutionaries. Such revolutionaries could scarcely help becoming a professionalized leadership cadre in the later Bolshevik state. Social democratic leaders in Western Europe found themselves becoming professionalized in other ways — not as revolutionaries, but as parliamentarians, party and trade-union officials, newspaper editors, and so forth. By the time their turn came to accept the reins of state power, they had forgotten — if they ever understood — Marx and Engels' vision of a radical participatory democracy. What they provided looked remarkably like the professionalized parliamentary democracy that had gone before. In this sense the presumed political goals of both movements were undercut by the very process they sought to overcome. And perhaps this is more than coincidence. It is arguable that professionalization, especially of leadership functions, is one of the most profound tendencies of modern society generally, so profound that even movements setting out to overcome it find themselves falling victim to it instead. If this is the case, then Marx and Engels' vision may be held quaint but irrelevant, intellectually and morally inspiring, perhaps, but quite beside the point for present-day society.

On the other hand, it is not as if professionalization has *solved* the problems of democratic government. On the contrary, most people would probably find *less* democracy in the result, along with more political corruption and citizen alienation. It is not therefore as if we have no need for alternative ideas. However visionary Marx and Engels' ideal of democracy, we must remember that something like it once existed in the real world, in Periclean Athens, or in smaller units in the New England town meeting. We must likewise remember that visionary ideals, even if never realized, offer useful vantage points from which to examine and criticize existing institutions and search for alternatives. Sometimes they enable us to see the root of the problem. "To be radical is to grasp the root of the matter," Marx had written, "but for man the root is man himself. . . . The criticism of religion ends with the teaching that *man is the highest being for man*, hence with the *categorical imperative to overthrow all relations* in which man is a debased, enslaved, forsaken, despicable being."[1]

NOTES
BIBLIOGRAPHY
INDEX

Notes

SHORT TITLES are used throughout the notes; full citations may be found in the Bibliography. In quotations, bracketed interpolations are by RNH unless marked by the initials of the book's editor or author. Translations modified by RNH are so noted.

Chapter 1. The Origins of the State

1. For general biographies of the two men, see the citations in volume 1, especially the excellent recent work of David McLellan. Other more recent studies include two psychologically oriented works on Marx, of which the first is much the better: Seigel, *Marx's Fate*, and Raddatz, *Karl Marx*. Engels has found a new biographer in Henderson, *The Life of Frederick Engels*; and the current of scholarship that perceives major differences between Engels and his partner has found its most extreme advocate in Levine, *The Tragic Deception*.

2. See volume 1, pp. 59–74, 108–09, 119–20, 124–30.

3. Marx and Engels, *Collected Works*, 5:33. Original German words restored from Marx and Engels, *Werke*, 3:22.

4. *Collected Works*, 5:44–45, 46.

5. Ibid., pp. 46–47.

6. Ibid., p. 47 (and explanatory note "a" on p. 46).

7. Ibid., pp. 33, 34, 90.

8. *Collected Works*, 6:482.

9. Since this work figures prominently as evidence for those who see profound differences between Marx and Engels, it is worth noting that Engels himself mentioned having read the manuscript to Marx, in his preface to the second edition of *Anti-Dühring* (p. 14). Marx not only contributed a chapter to the project but also helped arrange to have his son-in-law, Paul Lafargue, translate portions of it into French for what emerged as the pamphlet, *Socialism: Utopian and Scientific* (see *Werke*, 34:443, 444), for which Marx also wrote an introduction (*Werke*, 19:181–85), though it was unsigned. If Marx disagreed substantially with *Anti-Dühring*, it also seems odd he would send a complimentary copy of it along with some words of praise to Moritz Kaufmann (see *Werke*, 34:346).

10. *Anti-Dühring*, p. 248 (translation modified — RNH; see original German, *Werke*, 20:166).

11. *Anti-Dühring*, pp. 248–49 (translation modified — RNH; a very important "could" was omitted from the italicized portion; see original German, *Werke*, 20:166–67).

12. *Anti-Dühring*, p. 250.

13. Ibid., pp. 252, 205.

14. Ibid., pp. 251, 252.

15. Quotations from "Preface to the First Edition," *Origin of the Family*, p. 71. Lawrence Krader has deciphered and edited *The Ethnological Notebooks of Karl Marx*, to which

he has contributed a long and useful, though overly complicated and frequently opaque introduction.

16. Morgan, *Ancient Society*, pp. 85–86, as quoted in *Origin of the Family*, p. 151.

17. *Origin of the Family*, pp. 151, 149, 148, 150.

18. Ibid., pp. 154–56.

19. Ibid., pp. 158, 159–60; see also Engels' praise of the democratic features of the other gentile societies he examined, pp. 163, 166–69, 184, 188–89, 203–04.

20. The arguments against Engels' position and against evolutionary anthropology in general were classically expressed by Robert H. Lowie in his two books, *The Origin of the State* and *The History of Ethnological Theory*. Morgan has found a recent defender in Terray, *Marxism and "Primitive" Societies*, while Engels has been ably defended by Eleanor Burke Leacock in her introduction to the edition of *Origin of the Family* used here. Among recent writings on the origin of the state, see Krader, *Formation of the State*, and Carneiro, *A Theory of the Origin of the State*. Also see the essays gathered together in Diamond, *Toward a Marxist Anthropology*.

21. *Collected Works*, 6:482.

22. *Ethnological Notebooks*, p. 310; Krader's analysis of Marx's underscorings in Morgan excerpts, pp. 27–28; see Marx's other comments insisting on the democratic character of gentile society, pp. 167, 206, 208.

23. *Origin of the Family*, pp. 160–61. Lucas has stressed Engels' rhapsodizing in contrast to Marx in his "Marx' Studien"; other differences between the two men's ethnological views are perceived by Krader in "The Works of Marx and Engels in Ethnology Compared."

24. *Ethnological Notebooks*, p. 329 (as translated by Krader, p. 39). George Lichtheim has argued fairly persuasively that as Marx grew older he began to emphasize more and more the "positive" side of the primitive community; see *The Concept of Ideology*, pp. 73–76.

25. "The Philosophical Manifesto of the Historical School of Law" (1842), in *Collected Works*, 1:203 (translation modified — RNH; see original German, *Werke*, 1:78).

26. Morgan, *Ancient Society*, p. 562, as quoted in *Origin of the Family*, p. 237.

27. *Origin of the Family*, pp. 181, 228.

28. Ibid., pp. 218–28; slave/citizen ratios from pp. 227n, 230.

29. Ibid., p. 229; also see pp. 179–80, 190–91, 227–28.

30. Ibid., pp. 168, 188, 204, 223; also see pp. 172–73, 211–13.

31. Ibid., pp. 171–81.

32. Ibid., pp. 171, 180.

33. Ibid., pp. 230, 180.

34. Ibid., pp. 180, 230, 191.

35. Ibid., pp. 204–05; also see pp. 223–24.

36. Ibid., p. 230.

37. Ibid., pp. 230, 229. For other instances where Engels pictures the state not apparently but actually standing above society, see *Anti-Dühring*, pp. 248–49; also Marx and Engels, *Selected Works*, 1:438, 2:359. For Marx on the Prussian state, see above, volume 1, pp. 63–66, 125–27.

38. *Origin of the Family*, pp. 230, 229.

39. Ibid., p. 231; also see p. 235.

40. Ibid., p. 192. Karl Wittfogel was to make much of this omission; see discussion below, pp. 28–37.

41. Letter to Conrad Schmidt, October 27, 1890, in Marx and Engels, *Selected Correspondence*, pp. 478, 480.

42. This interpretation of what Engels meant by the "independence" and "apparent independence" of the state would appear to be contradicted by an 1886 remark declaring that the state "makes itself independent vis-à-vis society; and, indeed, the more so, the more it becomes the organ of a particular class, the more it directly enforces the supremacy of that class" (*Ludwig Feuerbach and the End of Classical German Philosophy*, in *Selected Works*, 2:359). Hal Draper is very likely correct in interpreting this curious formulation to mean that the state grows more independent of society as a whole — that is, the masses — as it becomes more dependent upon the possessing class (*Theory of Revolution*, 1:312n). I am unable to follow Draper, however, in holding this to be Engels' usual meaning when speaking of the independence of the state, for Engels more normally described the above condition as an *apparent* independence (concealing actual dependence on the possessing class). If Engels consistently meant independence from the *masses*, he would not have required the word "apparent," since his state by definition was independent of the masses, nothing "seeming" about it. Draper does agree on the main substantive point that for Marx and Engels every state tends to strive for "autonomy," as he prefers to call it (chap. 14).

43. *Ethnological Notebooks*, pp. 213, 210 (as translated by Krader, p. 21).

44. *Collected Works*, 11:186 (original German words from *Werke*, 8:197); see discussion below, pp. 47–63.

45. *Ethnological Notebooks*, pp. 328, 330, 329 (last quotation as translated by Krader, p. 39).

46. *Origin of the Family*, p. 229.

Chapter 2. The Parasite State

1. Letter of June 2, 1853, in Marx, *Colonialism and Modernization*, p. 451. To survey the literature on Oriental despotism, one should probably begin with Wittfogel's classic *Oriental Despotism*; other major studies include Sofri, *Über asiatische Produktionsweise*, and Krader, *The Asiatic Mode of Production*. For some rethinking of the issue by Communist writers of the 1960s, see Tökei, *Sur la mode de production asiatique*, together with the articles printed in a special issue of the Paris journal, *La Pensée*, for April 1964. Shorter pieces of particular merit include Avineri's introduction to *Colonialism and Modernization*, as well as his "Marx and Modernization"; George Lichtheim, "Oriental Despotism," in his *The Concept of Ideology*, pp. 62–93; and chapters 21 and 22 in the first volume of Draper's *Karl Marx's Theory of Revolution*.

2. Letter of June 6, 1853, in *Colonialism and Modernization*, pp. 451–52.

3. (1853), *Collected Works*, 12:127, 128, 131.

4. Ibid., p. 132; "The Future Results of British Rule in India" (1853), ibid., p. 217.

5. "British Rule in India," ibid., p. 132; "Affairs in Holland" (1853), ibid., p. 104.

6. "British Rule in India," ibid., p. 132; also see pp. 217–22.

7. 1859 listing in Marx's preface to *A Contribution to the Critique of Political Economy*, in *Selected Works*, 1:329. These issues are discussed at length in the writings of Avineri and Lichtheim cited above, n. 1.

8. *Pre-Capitalist Economic Formations*, pp. 96, 68, 83 (under this title Hobsbawm published the pertinent sections of the *Grundrisse* well before the full work became available in English; it remains valuable because of Hobsbawm's brilliant introductory essay).

The complete *Grundrisse* is now available in an English translation by Martin Nicolaus. Although it is not often remarked, Engels followed Marx entirely in this historical schema, separating the Oriental path from the Greek and Roman in *Anti-Dühring* (see above, pp. 9–13), and leading the Germans directly into feudalism in chap. 8 of *The Origin of the Family*.

9. *Oriental Despotism*, pp. 401–08. On the tortuous political history of the concept of Oriental despotism, in addition to Wittfogel's highly tendentious account, see Sofri, *Über asiatische Produktionsweise*, pp. 99–127. Also see: Hobsbawm, "Introduction," *Pre-Capitalist Economic Formations*, pp. 60–62; Draper, *Theory of Revolution*, 1:629–33, 657–64; Gandy, *Marx and History*, pp. 22–25.

10. Letter of June 2, 1853, in *Colonialism and Modernization*, p. 450; also see pp. 451, 313–16.

11. "Vorarbeiten zum *Anti-Dühring*" (1876), in *Werke*, 20:590; *Anti-Dühring*, p. 251.

12. P. 791. In one of his 1853 articles Marx also referred to "the Asiatic system making the State the real landlord" (*Collected Works*, 12:215).

13. *Capital*, 3:326; reference to "general slavery" in *Pre-Capitalist Economic Formations*, p. 95. The issues are well discussed in Draper, *Theory of Revolution*, 1:550–53, 562–67, whose improved translation I have followed in the *Capital* quotation — see original German, *Werke*, 25:338.

14. See *Capital*, 3:333.

15. *Capital*, 1:514, n. 2; "Future Results of British Rule," in *Collected Works*, 12:217.

16. 1:358.

17. "Lassalle," in *Collected Works*, 8:464; Wittfogel's chiding in *Oriental Despotism*, pp. 380–82.

18. 3:400 (translation modified — RNH; see original German, *Werke*, 26.3:391).

19. Marx referred to the Egyptian "*Priesterkaste*" in *Capital* (*Werke*, 23:537n) although the word is dropped in the English translation; "Celestial bureaucracy" is from "History of the Opium Trade" (1858), in *Collected Works*, 16:17. Also see *Capital*, 3:790–92; Draper, *Theory of Revolution*, 1:558–71.

20. See above, pp. 10–11.

21. *Pre-Capitalist Economic Formations*, pp. 77–78, 71–72, 89.

22. Ibid., pp. 70–71, 69–70.

23. *Oriental Despotism*, pp. 381, 387. Wittfogel's earlier article, "The Ruling Bureaucracy," makes the same points; cf. Lichtheim's more balanced discussion in "Oriental Despotism," pp. 85–93.

24. Draper has provided the best and only really significant treatment of the subject in chapters 19, 20, and 23 of the first volume of his *Theory of Revolution;* the present account owes much to his insights.

25. *Collected Works*, 5:90, 195; see above, chap. 1.

26. Marx, "Moralising Criticism and Critical Morality" (1847), in *Collected Works*, 6:326; Engels, "The Prussian Constitution" (1847), ibid., pp. 64–65.

27. "Decay of Feudalism and Rise of National States" (1884), in *Peasant War*, pp. 216–17, 218, 219–20 (translation modified — RNH; see original German, *Werke*, 21:398–99. This fragment was intended for inclusion in an expanded new edition of *Peasant War*, a book in which it is not generally recognized that, however much Engels treated the Lutheran Reformation as a social conflict, he also presented the German princes — the architects of budding absolutism — as its ultimate beneficiaries rather than the bourgeoisie or any other social class.

28. *Eighteenth Brumaire* (1852), in *Collected Works*, 11:185. Marx was of course referring to France specifically.

29. Letter of February 20, 1889, in *Werke*, 37:154 (as translated by Draper in *Theory of Revolution*, 1:480).

30. "[The Question of the Abolition of Serfdom in Russia]" (1858), in *Collected Works*, 16:53.

31. *Anti-Dühring*, p. 227; "Moralising Criticism and Critical Morality," in *Collected Works*, 6:333.

32. "The Magyar Struggle," in *Collected Works*, 8:229–30; *Revolution and Counter-Revolution in Germany* (1852), in *Collected Works*, 11:26.

33. *Collected Works*, 13:394–96. For further discussion of this issue, see Draper, *Theory of Revolution*, 1:554–57.

34. "On Social Relations in Russia," in *Selected Works*, 2:53; also see p. 56 and *Anti-Dühring*, p. 251.

35. Letter to Vera Zasulich, March 8, 1881, Second Draft, in *Russian Menace*, p. 222.

36. *Secret Diplomatic History* (1856), p. 125. This obscure writing contains Marx's most extensive general summary of Russian history, in which the villain is the professionalized diplomatic corps.

37. "The Foreign Policy of Russian Czarism" (1890), in *Russian Menace*, p. 47 (translation modified — RNH; see original German, *Werke*, 22:38). Like Marx before him Engels here presented the Russian diplomatic corps as an entirely autonomous force which directed that country's expansionist foreign policy in its own caste interest and not for the sake of any possessing class. On the state's role in creating a bourgeoisie, also see *Werke*, 38:160, 467–68.

38. "Afterword" (1894) to "On Social Relations in Russia," in *Russian Menace*, p. 238.

39. See above, n. 17 and n. 26; "Crown by the grace of God . . ." from "The Trial of the Rhenish District Committee of Democrats" (1849), in *Collected Works*, 8:335.

40. See above, n. 31; "Affairs in Prussia" (1859), in *Collected Works*, 16:159.

41. See above, n. 26; "The State of Germany" (1846), in *Collected Works*, 6:30. In both instances Engels wrote the word "class" in English in these articles for the Chartist press.

42. "Affairs in Prussia," in *Collected Works*, 16:108.

43. For an example of "estate," see Engels, "On Social Relations in Russia," in *Selected Works*, 2:49; for "race," see Engels, *Revolution and Counter-Revolution in Germany*, in *Collected Works*, 11:27; for further examples and Draper's well-informed analysis, see chap. 20 of the first volume of *Theory of Revolution*, especially pp. 504–10.

44. While a great many writers have alluded to Marx's theory of Bonapartism when discussing fascist regimes and other twentieth-century trends, surprisingly few have dealt systematically with Marx's theory itself. The best treatment appears in chaps. 15–18 in the first volume of Draper's *Theory of Revolution*. More disappointing is Rubel, *Marx devant le bonapartisme*. An aspect of the subject is dealt with in Iring Fetscher's interesting "Marxism and Bureaucracy," in his *Marx and Marxism*, pp. 204–27. This same subject is the central theme of Víctor M. Pérez Díaz's perceptive *State, Bureaucracy, and Civil Society*.

45. See above, chap. 1, n. 39.

46. *Collected Works*, 4:123; also see discussion above, volume 1, p. 127.

47. "German Socialism in Verse and Prose" (1847), in *Collected Works*, 6:259; "The Constitutional Question in Germany," ibid., p. 80; also see pp. 19–23.

48. *Collected Works*, 11:104, 185, 186.

49. *Writings on the Paris Commune*, p. 72.

50. An example of the former is Wesolowski, "Marx's Theory of Class Domination," pp. 82–84, 91–97; of the latter, Tucker, "Marx as a Political Theorist," pp.116–17.

51. *Eighteenth Brumaire*, in *Collected Works*, 11:139.

52. Ibid., p. 118.

53. Ibid., p. 159.

54. Ibid., pp. 106, 182, 185, 186, 137.

55. (1850), in *Collected Works*, 10:76.

56. *New York Daily Tribune*, March 12, 1858 (German translation included in *Werke*, 12:400). For other allusions to a possible military coup, see *Werke*, 12:417–19, 505–06, 14:514.

57. *Collected Works*, 11:170, 171, 143; see also pp. 172–73.

58. "A Historic Parallel" (1859), in *Collected Works*, 16:271.

59. *Writings on the Paris Commune*, pp. 198, 149, 72 (the last quotation comes from the published version).

60. "Author's Preface to the Second Edition" (1870), *The Peasant War in Germany*, in *The German Revolutions*, ed. Leonard Kreiger, p. 7. For further evidence that Engels shared Marx's view on these questions, see *Collected Works*, 11:212–15; and below, n. 71.

61. *Collected Works*, 11:195, 194.

62. "The French Crédit Mobilier," *New York Daily Tribune*, July 11, 1856 (German translation, *Werke*, 12:36).

63. "A Historic Parallel," in *Collected Works*, 16:272; also see pp. 94–95. One cannot help wondering if Marx would not have said the same thing about the relationship between the German bourgeoisie and Hitler after his first few years in power. Most Marxist writers have felt obliged to make Hitler into the puppet of the bourgeoisie, however implausible the case, not realizing their master allowed a more sophisticated approach. A refreshing exception, far more in line with Marx's actual views, is T. W. Mason, "The Primacy of Politics."

64. *Eighteenth Brumaire*, in *Collected Works*, 11:186–88.

65. Ibid., p. 191; see above, pp. 28–31.

66. Ibid., pp. 194, 149.

67. Ibid., pp. 150, 149, 182 (translation of last passage modified — RNH; see original German, *Werke*, 8:194).

68. *Collected Works*, 11:195, 197.

69. *Civil War in France*, in *Writings on the Paris Commune*, p. 72.

70. Letter of December 3, 1851, in *Selected Correspondence*, p. 50; also see letters in *Werke*, 27:385, 388–90.

71. *The Prussian Military Question and the German Workers' Party*, in Marx, *Political Writings*, 3:141, 139, 142. See also Engels, *Role of Force*, p. 39.

72. Letter of April 13, 1866, in *Selected Correspondence*, pp. 205–06 (translation modified — RNH; see original German, *Werke*, 31:208).

73. Second Draft of *Civil War*, in *Writings on the Paris Commune*, p. 196; also see p. 38. One must make allowances for Marx's awkward English in the drafts of *Civil War*.

74. *The Housing Question* (1872), in *Selected Works*, 1:548. Also see pp. 582–83; *Role of Force*, pp. 56, 62–63, 96–97; and *Werke*, 18:293–95, for parallel characterizations by Engels.

75. Engels, *Role of Force*, p. 68; Marx, *Critique of the Gotha Program* (1875), in *Selected Works*, 2:31 (translation modified — RNH; see original German, *Werke*, 19:29).

76. *Collected Works*, 11:185–86.

77. See *Werke*, 12:390; *Writings on the Paris Commune*, pp. 149, 196.

78. *Eighteenth Brumaire*, in *Collected Works*, 11:186, 193n.

79. Ibid., p. 139; Burke quoted in "The Turkish War Question" (1853), in *Collected Works*, 12:184; "Affairs in Prussia" (1858), in *Collected Works*, 16:77.

80. *Collected Works*, 11:193.

81. See terminological discussion above, pp. 46–47.

82. *Origin of the Family*, Moscow ed., p. 291.

83. Cf. Draper, *Theory of Revolution*, 1:321–26.

Chapter 3. The Bourgeois Class State

1. Recent scholarship of more than passing interest includes: Draper, *Theory of Revolution*; Maguire, *Marx's Theory of Politics*; Sanderson, *An Interpretation of the Political Ideas of Marx and Engels*; Tucker, *The Marxian Revolutionary Idea*; Miliband, "Marx and the State"; idem., *Marxism and Politics*. Among Communist contributions the most impressive scholarship is to be found in Moore, *The Critique of Capitalist Democracy*; also see Wesolowski, "Marx's Theory of Class Domination"; and *Karl Marx: Begründer der Staats- und Rechtstheorie der Arbeiterklasse*. Specialists may be interested in older classics such as: Kelsen, *Sozialismus und Staat*; Adler, *Die Staatsauffassung des Marxismus*; as well as the underappreciated volume by Rosenberg, *Democracy and Socialism*.

2. *Manifesto of the Communist Party* (1848), in *Collected Works*, 6:486; electoral franchise figures from Palmer and Colton, *History of the Modern World*, pp. 450, 453–54.

3. "Principles of Communism," in *Collected Works*, 6:346 (translation modified — RNH; see original German, *Werke*, 4:368); also see pp. 28–29, 61–63; and above, volume 1, pp. 133–34.

4. Moscow ed., p. 284.

5. See above, volume 1, pp. 136–38, 176–85.

6. *Collected Works*, 6:486, 505; *Anti-Dühring*, p. 388 (also see pp. 386, 389–90); *Origin of the Family*, Moscow ed., p. 235.

7. "Review of Guizot's Book on the English Revolution" (1850), in *Political Writings*, 2:254 (Fernbach's translation is much superior to the one offered in *Collected Works*, 10:254). Although this piece is usually ascribed to Marx, it appeared unsigned when originally published and Engels may have had a hand in it.

8. "Introduction" (1892) to *Socialism: Utopian and Scientific*, in *Selected Works*, 2:97; also see *Collected Works*, 14:51, 53–54.

9. "*The Morning Post* Versus Prussia" (1855), in *Collected Works*, 14:187.

10. "The Elections in England — Tories and Whigs" (1852), in *Collected Works*, 11:327–28, 329.

11. Ibid., pp. 329–30; also see pp. 471–73; *Collected Works*, 14:53–56, 60.

12. Marx, "The Parties and Cliques" (1855), in *Collected Works*, 13:642; Engels, "Introduction," *Selected Works*, 2:102–03.

13. Marx, "Corruption at Elections" (1852), in *Collected Works*, 11:345, 346; also see pp. 333–41; *Collected Works*, 14:194–97, 208–11.

14. "The Chartists," in *Collected Works*, 11:335; also see above, volume 1, pp. 106–12, 116–17, 141, 228–30.

15. Letter to H. M. Hyndman, December 8, 1880, reproduced in the latter's memoirs,

Record of an Adventurous Life, p. 283 (German translation available in *Werke*, 34:482–83). For Marx and Engels' disappointment over the results of the 1867 reform, see *Werke*, 32:207–09; *On Britain*, pp. 503–09.

16. *On Britain*, pp. 518, 520; also see pp. 514–16, 503–09.

17. Letter to Hermann Schlüter, January 1, 1895, ibid., p. 584; also see pp. 33n, 579, 581–82.

18. *Socialism: Utopian and Scientific* (1880), in *Selected Works*, 2:111; also see pp. 96–97.

19. "The Bourgeoisie and the Counter-Revolution" (1848), in *Collected Works*, 8:161; "Moralizing Criticism and Critical Morality" (1847), in *Collected Works*, 6:319 (this last translation modified — RNH; see original German, *Werke*, 4:338).

20. For further comments by Marx on the French Revolution, see *Collected Works*, 4:118–24; 10:251–56. Also see Bruhat, "La révolution française," pp. 125–70; Avineri, *Social and Political Thought*, pp. 185–93.

21. *Eighteenth Brumaire*, in *Collected Works*, 11:127–28, 119–20.

22. *The Class Struggles in France* (1850), in *Collected Works*, 10:50, 48.

23. *Eighteenth Brumaire*, in *Collected Works*, 11:112–13.

24. *Class Struggles*, in *Collected Works*, 10:53, 54.

25. "The June Revolution" (1848), in *Collected Works*, 7:147, 149.

26. *Eighteenth Brumaire*, in *Collected Works*, 11:129; also see pp. 117–19. Two-thirds estimate from *Collected Works*, 10:571; also see pp. 76–77, 90–91, 107–08, 135–59.

27. See above, volume 1, chap. 9, and especially pp. 290–97.

28. "Defeat of the Palmerston Ministry" (1857), in *Colonialism and Modernization*, p. 169. It was mainly Lenin who argued that all class government was essentially dictatorial (see his *Selected Works*, 2:262, 3:74–76, 87–88), but the only source he could find to cite was a single line from "Indifference to Politics" (discussed above in volume 1, pp. 314–15), where Marx spoke of the workers' need to "substitute their revolutionary dictatorship for the dictatorship of the bourgeois class." Because this was a unique and passing reference, it seems more plausible to speculate that Marx was simply carried away by his rhetorical desire to draw parallels; or perhaps that he was thinking of the rule of the capitalists within the factory, which *was* a class dictatorship by his definition. Even here there is no mention of feudal or ancient dictatorship.

29. *Eighteenth Brumaire*, in *Collected Works*, 11:139, 111; see above, pp. 50–54.

30. *Class Struggles*, in *Collected Works*, 10:79.

31. *Writings on the Paris Commune*, pp. 160, 212; cf. pp. 128–29. Even before the Paris Commune, Marx had little faith that the Third Republic would last. "Middle-class republics have become impossible in Europe," he told the IWA general council in February 1871, "it is only a political form to develop the power of the working class" (Institute of Marxism-Leninism, *General Council Minutes*, 1870–1871, p. 130.

32. Engels, *The Prussian Military Question and the German Workers' Party* (1865), in *Political Writings*, 3:144; see below, n. 38.

33. "Antwort an den ehrenwerten Giovanni Bovio" (1892), in *Werke*, 22:280. For uses of "highest," see below, nn. 40, 51; "last," nn. 35, 38.

34. *Selected Works*, 2:30.

35. Ibid., p. 31.

36. Ibid., p. 30; see discussion of the dictatorship of the proletariat above, volume 1, chap. 9, especially pp. 316–19 on the Gotha critique, and pp. 332–34 on the Erfurt critique. Engels' views on prospects in Germany will be treated at length below in chap. 10.

37. Engels to Wilhelm Liebknecht, July 2, 1877, in *Werke*, 34:282; Marx to Friedrich Sorge, September 27, 1877, in *Letters to Americans*, p. 116. See also *Werke*, 19:129–33.

38. Letter of March 24, 1884, in *Werke*, 36:128.

39. Letter of August 27, 1883, ibid., p. 54.

40. Pp. 231–32.

41. "Introduction" (1892) to *Socialism: Utopian and Scientific*, in *Selected Works*, 2:102.

42. Letter of November 12, 1892, in Engels and Lafargues, *Correspondence*, 3:211; letter of March 6, 1894, ibid., pp. 325–26.

43. "Preface" (1882) to *Manifesto of the Communist Party*, in *Selected Works*, 1:23; Engels to Nikolai Franzevich Danielson, October 17, 1893, in ibid., 2:455. Marx and Engels' views on American political forms have not received much scholarly notice. On the other hand we now have several collections of source materials in English, beginning with *Letters to Americans*; also *The Civil War in the United States*, *Marx and Engels on the United States*, and *The Karl Marx Library*, vol. 2, *On America and the Civil War*.

44. "Moralizing Criticism," in *Collected Works*, 6:323; for a sample of subsequent comments, see *Letters to Americans*, pp. 129, 157, 163–64, 225.

45. *Collected Works*, 11:111; see also *Letters to Americans*, p. 44, and especially *Capital*, vol. 1, chap. 38.

46. [On the Slogan of the Abolition of the State and the German "Friends of Anarchy"] (1850), in *Collected Works*, 10:486.

47. Letter of June 3, 1886, in *Letters to Americans*, p. 157.

48. Letter to Friedrich Sorge, December 31, 1892, ibid., p. 243; see also pp. 161, 225; for passage quoted earlier, see above, n. 41.

49. See above, n. 46; *Origin of the Family*, p. 230.

50. See above, volume 1, pp. 33, 69, 76–77, 103.

51. "The London *Times* on the Orléans Princes in America" (1861), in *The Karl Marx Library*, 2:85; "The Civil War in the United States" (1861), ibid., p. 92.

52. Letter of July 1, 1861, ibid., p. 250.

53. *Selected Works*, 2:32.

54. "Zur Kritik des sozialdemokratischen Programmentwurfs 1891," in *Werke*, 22:236, to be discussed below, pp. 344–46; also see *Origin of the Family*, p. 179.

55. Marx to Engels, September 10, 1862, in *Civil War in the United States*, p. 255; Engels to Marx, November 15, 1862, ibid., p. 259.

56. This interview, first published in the *Chicago Tribune* on January 5, 1879, has been reprinted under the title, *An Interview with Karl Marx in 1879*; the passage quoted appears on p. 15. Marx expressed the same idea in an 1871 speech to the London Conference of the IWA — see Freymond, *La Première Internationale*, 2:195.

57. Letter to Friedrich Sorge, December 31, 1892, *Letters to Americans*, p. 244; letter to Sorge, January 6, 1892, ibid., p. 239; "Introduction" (1892) to Marx's "Address on the Question of Free Trade," reprinted in Marx, *Poverty of Philosophy*, p. 185; see also above, n. 40.

58. "Introduction" (1891) to *The Civil War in France*, in *Selected Works*, 1:438–39. For Engels' impressions of his American trip, see *Werke*, 21:466–68.

59. See discussion above, pp. 5–6, 10–11, 22–24, 60–63.

60. "On the Jewish Question," *Writings of the Young Marx*, p. 225 (this translation is still superior to the one offered in *Collected Works*, 3:154); see discussion above, volume 1, pp. 67–74.

61. See above, pp. 50–54.

62. *Pre-Capitalist Economic Formations*, p. 102. On the distinction between "labor" and "labor-power," see *Capital*, vol. 1, chap. 6, and Engels' "Introduction" (1891) to *Wage Labor and Capital*, in *Selected Works*, 1:66–73.

63. *Economic and Philosophic Manuscripts of 1844*, in *Collected Works*, 3:247; also see pp. 238, 250, 272–74; for use of the German terms in the original, see *Werke*, Ergänzungsband 1, pp. 474, 484, 487. Tucker has developed this idea very well in *Marxian Revolutionary Idea*, pp. 79–85; also see Draper, *Theory of Revolution*, 1:270–74.

64. Pp. 200–01; also see pp. 202–08, 319–20 (this modern translation is to be preferred for most purposes over the original translation by Florence Kelley Wischnewetzky which Engels sanctioned and which is reproduced in volume 4 of the *Collected Works*).

65. *Collected Works*, 6:491.

66. *Capital*, 1:330, 332, 334, 356, 424, 435; see discussion of dictatorship above, pp. 76–78, and in volume 1, chap. 9.

67. Ibid., pp. 424, 333.

68. Ibid., p. 176.

69. Ibid., pp. 169, 271; see also *Grundrisse*, pp. 459–71.

70. *Condition of the Working Class*, p. 89.

71. *Collected Works*, 9:198, 203 (incorporating Engels' 1891 changes).

72. P. 464.

73. Ibid., pp. 249, 650, 652.

Chapter 4. The Paris Commune: Revolutionary Strategy

1. The classic debate concerning Marx and Engels' view on the Paris Commune took the form of a pamphlet war between Lenin and Trotsky on the one side and Kautsky on the other. See Lenin, *The State and Revolution* (1917), in his *Selected Works*, 2:238–327, and *The Proletarian Revolution and the Renegade Kautsky* (1918), ibid., 3:65–149; Trotsky, *Terrorism and Communism;* Kautsky, *The Dictatorship of the Proletariat* and *Terrorism and Communism.* The Lenin-Trotsky interpretation reappears in all standard Communist scholarship, as for example in Erik Molnár, *La politique d'alliances du marxisme;* the social-democratic interpretation reappears in scholarly dress in Nicolaievsky and Maenchen-Helfen, *Marx*, and with curious variations in Avineri, *Social and Political Thought.* Wolfe predictably argues that both interpretations can justifiably be drawn from the ambiguous legacy of Marx's contradictory writings, in *Marxism.* An anti-Marxist interpretation appears in Mason, *Paris Commune.* Perhaps the most up-to-date and fair-minded scholarship is to be found in Johnstone's "The Commune and Marx's Conception of the Dictatorship of the Proletariat and the Role of the Party," in *Images of the Commune/Images de la Commune*, ed. James A. Leith, a volume which contains many interesting articles on the Commune and its historiography. That historiography is enormous, of course, but English readers may consult Edwards, *Paris Commune*, an excellent general history with a substantial bibliography to guide them to further literature.

2. *The Class Struggles in France* (1850), in *Collected Works*, 10: 56–57; see discussion above in volume 1, pp. 230–35.

3. *Eighteenth Brumaire*, in *Collected Works*, 11:193n; see also Engels' parallel remarks, 2:358, and *Werke*, 19:132–33. My interpretation owes a good deal to Rosenberg's *Democracy and Socialism*, especially chap. 9; cf. Johnstone, "The Commune and Marx's Conception," pp. 202–04.

4. *First Address of the General Council of the International Working Men's Association on the Franco-Prussian War* (1870), in *Writings on the Paris Commune;* pp. 37, 38.

5. Ibid., p. 36; *Selected Correspondence*, p. 294.

6. Letter to Marx, August 10, 1870, in *Werke*, 33:34; letter to Marx, August 15, 1870, in *Selected Correspondence*, p. 295; also see pp. 294, 296.

7. Letter to Marx, August 20, 1870, in *Werke*, 33:45; see also p. 34, 17:44–47. Marx indicated in a personal way that he expected war but no revolution when he advised his daughter and son-in-law to flee Paris for the safety of Bordeaux (ibid., 33:675, 678).

8. *Writings on the Paris Commune*, p. 48.

9. Letter of September 6, 1870, in *Werke*, 33:54 (translation from Wolfe, *Marxism*, pp. 110–11).

10. Letter to Edward Beesly, September 12, 1870, in *Werke*, 33:143; see also pp. 679–80.

11. Engels to Marx, September 7, 1870, ibid., 33:57; Dupont as quoted in translation by Nicolaievsky and Maenchen-Helfen, *Marx*, p. 312.

12. *Selected Correspondence*, pp. 304–05; letter to Marx, September 7, 1870, *Werke*, 33:58; but cf. Marx's assertion, p. 143.

13. Bakunin's coup described in Carr, *Bakunin*, pp. 417–22; for Marx and Engels' reaction to it, see *Selected Correspondence*, pp. 305–06; *Werke*, 33:656; and Institute of Marxism-Leninism, *General Council Minutes, 1870–1871*, p. 68.

14. Letter of October 19, 1870, in *Selected Correspondence*, pp. 305–06; see also *General Council Minutes, 1870–1871*, p. 349.

15. *General Council Minutes, 1870–1871*, pp. 60, 63, 66, 86, 102, 109, 112; Collins and Abramsky, *Marx and British Labour*, pp. 185–88.

16. Reminiscence of Charles Longuet, as cited in Enzensberger, *Gespräche mit Marx und Engels*, 2:357; Mayer, *Engels*, 2:197, 544–45; Nicolaievsky and Maenchen-Helfen, *Marx*, pp. 317–19.

17. Compare desire to help Gambetta, together with relatively generous comments, (*Werke*, 33:160, 177–78, 180, 182) with excoriation of Trochu (pp. 51, 57, 180–81) and Jules Favre (p. 171).

18. *Civil War*, in *Writings on the Paris Commune*, p. 65.

19. First Draft of *Civil War*, ibid., p.145; see also pp. 25, 191, 195, 219–20. Here and subsequently, the reader must make allowances for Marx's very rough English in the first and second drafts of *Civil War*. Among other awkwardnesses he occasionally anglicizes French and German words in ways that do not exist: in this instance, "hissing" comes from the French "*hisser*" meaning "to hoist."

20. Letter of October 19, 1870, in *Selected Correspondence*, p. 306; see also *General Council Minutes, 1870–1871*, pp. 129, 134.

21. *Werke*, 33:178 (retranslated from German); see also pp. 180–83, 17:257–60.

22. Letter of February 9, 1871, in Rocher, *Lettres de communards*, p. 14.

23. See *General Council Minutes, 1870–1871*, pp. 118–57; quotations from pp. 129, 151; Serraillier's report, pp. 139–45.

24. Letter of September 12–17, 1874, in *Writings on the Paris Commune*, p. 231; for public assertions see p. 207; also Marx and Engels, *On the Paris Commune*, pp. 229–30, 254–55.

25. *General Council Minutes, 1870–1871*, pp. 160–62. The two collections cited in the previous footnote both include all three versions of *Civil War;* the latter adds a larger number of ancillary documents, but the former is rendered more valuable by Hal Draper's

meticulous notes. The same care has gone into Draper's edition of Marx's *Notebook on the Paris Commune: Press Excerpts and Notes.*

26. Edwards, *Paris Commune*, pp. 150–51, 154; G. D. H. Cole, *History of Socialist Thought*, 2:166.

27. *Writings on the Paris Commune*, p. 220 (translation modified — RNH; in most English editions Marx's phrase "mischievous *avorton*" [*Werke*, 33:200] is mistranslated as "mischievous abortion," although the French "*avorton*" means "gnome" or "runt." Marx's intention is confirmed by his use of "mischievous gnome" *in English* in the Second Draft [*Writings on the Paris Commune*, p. 183]). Cf. parallel assessment by Engels, p. 221; all three versions of *Civil War* contain the same thought repeated again, pp. 117, 209, 67.

28. Ibid., p. 221; further enthusiasm, p. 222.

29. Wolfe, *Marxism*, p. 131.

30. *Notebook*, pp. 29–30 (from *Daily News*, March 28, 1871, p. 5, col. 5).

31. *First Draft of Civil War*, in *Writings on the Paris Commune*, p. 115 n. 52; also see pp. 117, 186–87, 59.

32. Jellinek, *Paris Commune*, p. 87; cf. Marx's comment, in *Writings on the Paris Commune*, p. 117.

33. *Notebook*, p. 31 (from *Daily News*, March 30, 1871, p. 5, col. 1). In his First Draft, Marx called it a "monstrous usurpation" (*Writings on the Paris Commune*, p. 118); Engels likewise insisted that the Versailles government was "usurpatory" (*On the Paris Commune*, p. 235). The position of the Commune itself appeared in its *Journal Officiel*, March 21, 1871, p. 3, col. 2, and was transcribed by Marx, *Notebook*, p. 20; see also Rougerie, *Paris libre 1871*, p. 124.

34. First Draft of *Civil War*, in *Writings on the Paris Commune*, p. 117.

35. Marx emphasized these figures in all three versions of *Civil War*, ibid., pp. 132, 206–07, 86–88.

36. Williams, *French Revolution*, pp. 156, 176.

37. *Civil War*, in *Writings on the Paris Commune*, pp. 87–88; Marx followed the development of these repressive actions in the press, *Notebook*, pp. 43, 62.

38. First Draft of *Civil War*, in *Writings on the Paris Commune*, p. 147; Edwards, *Paris Commune*, p. 47.

39. Second Draft of *Civil War*, in *Writings on the Paris Commune*, pp. 208, 188; cf. the other two versions, pp. 62, 147–48; and Engels' account of the same facts, *General Council Minutes, 1870–1871*, pp. 160–61. Excerpts from *Figaro* are in *Notebook*, p. 12.

40. *Notebook*, pp. 14–15 (from *Daily News*, March 20, 1871, p. 3, col. 1), p. 17 (from *La Cloche*, March 21, 1871, p. 1, col. 4), pp. 28, 63–64 (on program), p. 35 (from *Journal Officiel* as quoted by *London Evening Standard*, April 3, 1871, p. 2, col. 5). The Commune's offer, made through the mediation of the American ambassador, Elihu Washburne, was noted by Marx in a later letter (*On the Paris Commune*, p. 258).

41. *Writings on the Paris Commune*, p. 80; see below, pp. 115–19.

42. Letter of July 6, 1869, in *Werke*, 32:336; see also *Collected Works*, 2:358; and above, n. 2.

43. See Marx's comments in the three versions of *Civil War*, in *Writings on the Paris Commune*, pp. 63, 67, 173–74, 177, 192–93, 209; and Engels' comments in *General Council Minutes, 1870–1871*, p. 171. Modern authors agree with this military assessment: see Edwards, *Paris Commune*, pp. 157–58; Mason, *Paris Commune*, pp. 140–44. On Marx and Engels' motives see also Johnstone, "The Commune and Marx's Conception," pp. 210–11.

44. Williams, *French Revolution*, pp. 151–52; Edwards, *Paris Commune*, p. 346; for Marx's account of this repression, see *Civil War*, in *Writings on the Paris Commune*, pp. 85–96.

45. *Revolution and Counter-Revolution in Germany* (1852), in *Collected Works*, 11: 85–86 (quoted more fully above, volume 1, p. 224). Engels' 1885 recollection in *Writings on the Paris Commune*, p. 234.

46. *Notebook*, pp. 17, 34 (Bismarck's words as reported by *La Situation*, March 21, 1871, p. 8, col. 2).

47. Letter of April 17, 1871, in *Selected Correspondence*, p. 311. In Engels' own retrospective judgment of 1886 the Commune appeared as "but a dream," caught as it was between Thiers on the one hand and the Prussians on the other (*Writings on the Paris Commune*, p. 234); for a modern confirmation of Bismarck's readiness to assist, see Edwards, *Paris Commune*, pp. 158–60.

48. The First Draft of *Civil War*, in *Writings on the Paris Commune*, pp. 159–60; see also *General Council Minutes, 1870–1871*, p. 181. For a sample of non-Marxist historians, see Winock and Azéma, *Les communards*, especially pp. 177–80; Williams, *French Revolution*, pp. 130–45; Brogan, *French Nation*, pp. 153–57.

49. Marx noted these developments in his Second Draft of *Civil War*, in *Writings on the Paris Commune*, pp. 206–07; see also *General Council Minutes, 1870–1871*, p. 190; Edwards, *Paris Commune*, pp. 230–32.

50. *Civil War*, in *Writings on the Paris Commune*, pp. 78–80; see also pp. 156–57, 165–66.

51. Ibid., pp. 157–58; on the antagonism, see also *Werke*, 18:61.

52. First Draft of *Civil War*, in *Writings on the Paris Commune*, p. 156; cf. final version of these thoughts, pp. 78–80.

53. Ibid., p. 158; cf. final version, pp. 79–80.

54. *Werke*, 18:630–33; see above, volume 1, pp. 321–22, where this passage is quoted in a fuller context.

55. Ibid.; see above, volume 1, p. 322. The most extensive treatment of peasant and agrarian questions appears in Engels' 1894 essay, "The Peasant Question in France and Germany," in *Selected Works*, 2:381–99; the best analysis of the masters' views on these matters is to be found in Draper, *Theory of Revolution*, 2:317–452; see also works cited above, volume 1, chap. 7, n. 55.

56. First Draft of *Civil War*, in *Writings on the Paris Commune*, p. 158; *Civil War*, ibid., p. 80. Communards' request mentioned above, p. 113.

57. From a letter of Jenny Marx (daughter) to Ludwig Kugelmann, April 18, 1871, in *Archiv für Sozialgeschichte* 2 (1962):242; see also *Werke*, 33:203, 205, 228; and Lafargue's letters to Marx in Rocher, *Lettres de communards*, pp. 13–14, 25.

58. Letter of May 13, 1871, in *On the Paris Commune*, p. 287; see also *Writings on the Paris Commune*, pp. 86–88, 133–35, 206–07.

59. "Introduction" (1895) to *The Class Struggles in France*, in *Selected Works*, 1:117.

60. *Writings on the Paris Commune*, pp. 159–60.

61. *Civil War*, ibid., p. 75; see also pp. 63, 80, 157, 209.

62. "The Berlin *National-Zeitung* to the Primary Electors" (1849), in *Collected Works*, 8:272; see above, volume 1, pp. 217–18, where these words are quoted in a fuller context; also further discussion of these ideas on pp. 184, 300–01.

63. Letter of February 22, 1881, in *Writings on the Paris Commune*, p. 233 (except I have rendered "*Grosstuerei*" as "swagger" rather than "vaunt").

64. *Sozialismus und Sozialpolitik* (Berlin 1887), p. 55, as quoted in translation by Nicolaievsky and Maenchen-Helfen, *Marx*, p. 326.

65. *Notebook*, pp. 64, 65, 69, 72–73, 77; First Draft of *Civil War*, in *Writings on the Paris Commune*, pp. 135–36; Second Draft, ibid., pp. 206–07; *Civil War*, ibid., pp. 86–88.

66. Letter to Marx, March 30, 1871, in *Lettres de communards*, p. 21.

67. See especially his letters to his wife in London, ibid., pp. 17–19, 27–32; also *General Council Minutes, 1870–1871*, pp. 163, 176, 180.

68. Marx's testimony from his letter to Edward Beesly, June 12, 1871, in *On the Paris Commune*, p. 289; Frankel's second letter, in *Lettres de communards*, pp. 38–39.

69. Two letters, April 26 and May 13, 1871, in *On the Paris Commune*, pp. 286–88; cf. Marx's report to Beesly, p. 289. See also Nicolaievsky and Maenchen-Helfen, *Marx*, pp. 328–29; and Avineri, *Social and Political Thought*, p. 246.

70. Letter of May 13, 1871, in *On the Paris Commune*, p. 287.

71. See the First Draft of *Civil War*, in *Writings on the Paris Commune*, pp. 105–06, 170.

72. *On the Paris Commune*, p. 289.

73. "Introduction" (1891) to *The Civil War in France*, in *Writings on the Paris Commune*, p. 30; see also Johnstone, "The Commune and Marx's Conception," p. 206.

74. *The Housing Question* (1872–73), in *Writings on the Paris Commune*, p. 227.

75. "Introduction" to *Class Struggles*, in *Selected Works*, 1:117.

Chapter 5. The Paris Commune: Workers' State

1. *Writings on the Paris Commune*, p. 150; "Indifference to Politics" (1873), in Marx, Engels, and Lenin, *Anarchism and Anarcho-Syndicalism*, p. 95.

2. Letter to August Bebel, March 18–28, 1875, in Marx et al., *Anarchism and Anarcho-Syndicalism*, p. 153.

3. *Writings on the Paris Commune*, pp. 32, 34.

4. *Collected Works*, 11:186, 193n; see above, pp. 60–61.

5. Letter of April 12, 1871, *Writings on the Paris Commune*, p. 221; see also p. 226. In *The Eighteenth Brumaire* Marx had used the verb *"brechen"* in the original German, which he fortified in his letter to Kugelmann as *"zerbrechen,"* meaning "to smash" or "to break to pieces" (compare *Werke*, 8:197 with 33:205).

6. *Writings on the Paris Commune*, pp. 70, 150.

7. Ibid., pp. 70, 73.

8. Ibid., p. 152. Marx had copied down the text of the decree as quoted by *Le Rappel* on March 25, 1871, p. 1, col. 6 (see Marx, *Notebook*, p. 24).

9. *Writings on the Paris Commune*, pp. 147, 82; see also p. 144.

10. Marx et al., *Anarchism and Anarcho-Syndicalism*, pp. 103–04; see also p. 68.

11. *Writings on the Paris Commune*, p. 73.

12. Ibid., p. 153.

13. From the published version of *Civil War*, ibid., pp. 75–76.

14. Ibid., p. 73.

15. Ibid.

16. Ibid., p. 74.

17. Ibid., pp. 72, 63, 73; cf. p. 150.

18. Ibid., p. 74.

19. Ibid., p. 153. Compare Engels' comment four years later on the Gotha Program's

demand for popular referendum: "'legislation by the people,'" he declared, "exists in Switzerland and does more harm than good if it does anything at all. *Administration* by the people, that would be something" (letter to August Bebel, March 18–28, 1875, in *Selected Works*, 2:38).

20. *Critique of the Gotha Program* (1875), in *Selected Works*, 2:29.

21. *Writings on the Paris Commune*, p. 33; see above, p. 90.

22. *Civil War*, ibid., p. 73; "The Crisis and the Counter-Revolution" (1848), in *Collected Works*, 7:430; "The Constitution of the French Republic" (1851), in *Collected Works*, 10:570. Marx and Engels' attitude toward the separation of powers has attracted much more notice in the form of passing comments than in the form of systematic analysis; even Draper's treatment in *Theory of Revolution*, 1:297–302, 314–17, is somewhat disappointing.

23. "Comments on the Latest Prussian Censorship Instruction" (1843), in *Writings of the Young Marx*, p. 91 (this translation is still to be preferred over the one offered in the *Collected Works*, 1:130); "Proceedings of the Sixth Rhine Province Assembly . . . Debates on Freedom of the Press" (1842), in *Collected Works*, 1:166; also see pp. 237–38, 384, 3:41; as well as above, volume 1, pp. 37–39, 65.

24. "The End of the *Criminalistische Zeitung*" (1842), in *Collected Works*, 2:302; also see pp. 136, 141, 307, 359; as well as above, volume 1, p. 103.

25. See above, volume 1, pp. 52–53; Marx, [Draft Plan for a Work on the Modern State] (1844), in *Collected Works*, 4:666; Engels, "The State of Germany" (1846), in *Collected Works*, 6:28 (but compare Engels' curious critique of the English legal system in *Collected Works*, 3:506–12, where he seems to paint himself into the corner of maintaining that *no* conceivable system, not even the jury, can produce fair and impartial judgments).

26. See especially *Collected Works*, 7:201–02, 437, 8:75–80, 197–203, 316–17.

27. "The Agreement Session of July 4 (Second Article)" (1848), in *Collected Works*, 7:205; context described above, volume 1, pp. 291–92.

28. "Affairs in Prussia" (1858), in *Collected Works*, 16:77.

29. "Trouble in Germany" (1859), in *Collected Works*, 16:541, 542.

30. Letter to August Bebel, March 18–28, 1875, in *Selected Works*, 2:38; see pp. 29–31 and 38–39 where Marx and Engels respectively pass over the judicial demand without comment. That demand is reproduced along with the rest of the draft program in *Werke*, 19:548.

31. The draft of the Erfurt Program that Engels had before him has recently been rediscovered and published in Bartel, "Der interne Juni-Entwurf"; Engels passed over the judicial demand in his critique, *Werke*, 22:237.

32. Letter to Laura Lafargue, February 16–17, 1883, in *Werke*, 35:436.

33. See above, n. 15.

34. A convenient review of these arguments may be found in Palmer, *Age of the Democratic Revolution*, 1:479–502.

35. "Agreement Session of July 4," in *Collected Works*, 7:205.

36. "The Trial of the Rhenish District Committee of Democrats [Speech by Karl Marx]" (1849), in *Collected Works*, 8:328–29, 331.

37. "The Counter-Revolution in Berlin" (1848), ibid., p. 15; also see ibid., 7:428–33, and above, volume 1, pp. 292–94, 205–07.

38. This point is made well by Rosenberg in *Democracy and Socialism*, pp. 200–01.

39. "Marx and the *Neue Rheinische Zeitung* (1848–1849)" (1884), in *Selected Works*, 2:302. Despite Engels' recollection here I can find no writing of the 1848 period in which Marx used the phrase, although he certainly described the *malady* often enough (see espe-

cially *Collected Works*, 7:16–19, 49, 8:51–52, 9:135–43, 323–24, 378, 438). Perhaps Engels was thinking of Marx's *Neue Rheinische Zeitung* reference to "the *ideological cretins* of the bourgeoisie, its journalists and suchlike" (*Collected Works*, 8:167). More likely he was remembering *his own* first reference to these assemblies as "parliamentary cretinism" in May 1852 (*Collected Works*, 11:79), which was doubtlessly inspired by Marx's famous use of the phrase in *Eighteenth Brumaire*, to be quoted below.

40. *Eighteenth Brumaire*, in *Collected Works*, 11:139, 161. Marx and Engels also used the phrase to characterize individual parliamentarians who were puffed up with self-importance (see for example *Werke*, 34:399, 413, 36:448).

41. "The English Constitution," in *Collected Works*, 3:495, 494; see above, pp. 70–71.

42. "The Debate on the Address in Berlin" (1849), in *Collected Works*, 9:138.

43. "Affairs in Prussia" (1858), in *Collected Works*, 16:80.

44. *The Prussian Military Question and the German Workers' Party* (1865), in Marx, *Political Writings*, 3:140; see also pp. 124–25, and *Werke*, 31:55.

45. "Trouble in Germany," in *Collected Works*, 16:541.

46. *Collected Works*, 11:185.

47. *Writings on the Paris Commune*, p. 73.

48. "Zur Kritik des sozialdemokratischen Programmentwurfs 1891," in *Werke*, 22:235, 234.

49. *Eighteenth Brumaire*, in *Collected Works*, 11:117.

50. See below, pp. 272–74.

51. For praise of Lincoln, see *Marx and Engels on the United States*, pp. 155–56, 168–71, 193; on abolishing the office, see *Letters to Americans*, pp. 250–51.

52. Jellinek, *Paris Commune*, pp. 179–80.

53. "The Commune and Marx's Conception," p. 215.

54. "Constitution of the French Republic," in *Collected Works*, 10:572.

55. Ibid., p. 570.

56. Letter of June 20, 1866, in *Selected Correspondence*, p. 208; for the argument that Marx was insincere see, for example, Wolfe, *Marxism*, pp. 105–06, 143–47.

57. *Collected Works*, 2:359; cf. Marx's contemporaneous allusions to centralization in 1:182–83, 298–99.

58. "The Civil War in Switzerland," in *Collected Works*, 6:372–73 (translation modified – RNH; see original German, *Werke*, 4:397); also see pp. 78–80, 86–90, 328, and for the *Manifesto* passage, pp. 485–89.

59. *Address of the Central Authority to the League*, in *Collected Works*, 10:285.

60. See above, volume 1, pp. 235–48.

61. For Marx and Engels' views of the 1840s, see *Ireland and the Irish Question*, pp. 33–52, especially pp. 47, 50, and 58; also Bloom, *World of Nations*, pp. 37–39, 81–82; and Davis, *Nationalism and Socialism*, pp. 65–66. Marx and Engels' views on nationality questions generally are treated in Bloom and Davis, along with Cummins, *Marx, Engels and National Movements*, and Wolfe, *Marxism*, chap. 2.

62. Letter of November 2, 1867, in *Ireland and the Irish Question*, p. 143; letter of December 10, 1869, ibid., p. 284; also see p. 148.

63. "Confidential Communication" (1870), ibid., pp. 162–63; also see Marx to Sigfrid Meyer and August Vogt, April 9, 1870, ibid., pp. 292–95 (from which the above "secret of the impotence" phrase is quoted).

64. See above, pp. 47–63.

65. *Collected Works*, 11:185, 193.

66. *Writings on the Paris Commune*, pp. 167–68; for interest in Montesquieu, etc., see pp. 171, 174–75.

67. Ibid., pp. 75, 74.

68. As quoted by Rougerie, *Paris libre 1871*, pp. 153–58. Rougerie argues that the Communards' decentralism was less pronounced than commonly assumed: the compromise April program passed with only one dissenting vote cast by a strict Proudhonist.

69. *Writings on the Paris Commune*, p. 77.

70. Engels, "Introduction" (1891) to *Civil War*, ibid., p. 31. This same idea is suggested more explicitly in Marx and Engels' 1873 polemic against Bakunin's anarchism. If the workers carried out a revolution according to Bakunin's prescription, they argued, the state would first be abolished by a solemn decree and then recreated step by step in real life, first locally and then nationally, as the workers endeavored to carry through their wishes against bourgeois opposition; see *The Alliance of Socialist Democracy and the International Working Men's Association*, in Marx et al., *Anarchism and Anarcho-Syndicalism*, pp. 110–11.

71. "Konspekt von Bakunins Buch *Staatlichkeit und Anarchie*," in *Werke*, 18:634; Johnstone reaches the same conclusions about the softening of Marx's centralism in his "The Commune and Marx's Conception," pp. 213–15.

72. *Collected Works*, 10:285–86n; also see *Werke*, 36:379.

73. Letter of February 4, 1886, in *Werke*, 36:434.

74. "Zur Kritik des sozialdemokratischen Programmentwurfs 1891," in *Werke*, 22:235–36.

75. Ibid., pp. 236, 237.

76. See above, pp. 59–60.

77. Ibid., p. 81; see above, chap. 4, n. 63; cf. Engels' private comment in 1884 that "in *The Civil War* the unconscious tendencies of the Commune were put down to its credit as more or less conscious plans" (ibid., p. 233).

78. Ibid., pp. 76, 81, 153; see also pp. 162, 226. In his 1891 introduction Engels similarly described the principal achievement of the Communards as a "shattering of the former state power and its replacement by a new and truly democratic one" (ibid., p. 33).

79. Ibid., pp. 77–78.

80. Ibid., pp. 150, 152; "On the Jewish Question" (1843), in *Collected Works*, 3:168.

Chapter 6. Individual Rights Versus Tyranny of the Majority

1. The literature dealing with Marx's views on individual rights is surprisingly small. Among Communist classics that touch on the question, see especially Lenin, *Proletarian Revolution* (1918), in *Selected Works*, 3:65–149; Trotsky, *Terrorism and Communism;* and Bukharin and Preobrazhensky, *The ABC of Communism*. For standard anti-Communist treatments, see Stoyanovitch, *Marxisme et droit*, and Pfahlberg and Brunner, "Fundamental Rights," in *Marxism, Communism and Western Society*, 4:55–65. Presenting Marx as a friend of individual rights we find some recent American scholars as well as various East European dissident intellectuals: see Easton, "Marx and Individual Freedom"; Sowell, "Karl Marx and the Freedom of the Individual"; Leonhard, *Three Faces of Marxism*, chap. 1; Schaff, *Marxism and the Human Individual;* Kolakowski, *Toward a Marxist Humanism;* and Petrović, *Marx in the Mid-Twentieth Century*. Those who throw up their hands in despair include Dahl, "Marxism and Free Parties," and Hook, "The Enlightenment and Marxism." On the Marxist idea of freedom generally, the most insightful work is to be

found in O'Rourke, *The Problem of Freedom in Marxist Thought*, which offers some useful distinctions *between* Marx and Engels. Also quite useful are various writings of Fetscher: *Die Freiheit;* "Liberal, Democratic, and Marxist Concepts of Freedom," in his *Marx and Marxism*, pp. 26–39; "Marx's Concretization of the Concept of Freedom"; and "Freedom," in *Marxism, Communism and Western Society*, 4:22–33. Disappointing on the subject, in light of their titles, are Dunayevskaya, *Marxism and Freedom*, and Miller, *Das Problem der Freiheit im Sozialismus.*

2. These writings figure prominently, for example, in the two available collections of free-press writings: Marx and Engels, *Pressefreiheit und Zensur;* and *The Karl Marx Library*, vol. 4, *On Freedom of the Press and Censorship* (1974). Also see analysis of these writings above, volume 1, pp. 31–35, 44–48, 102–04.

3. See above, volume 1, pp. 71–74, 107–09.

4. "On the Jewish Question," in *Collected Works*, 3:161–64. Marx employed this distinction consistently throughout the essay but for one perplexing exception. He wanted to call attention to the irony of the Jacobin regime whose "revolutionary practice is in flagrant contradiction with its theory." Thus the Constitution of 1793 guarantees *"unlimited freedom of the press,"* while Robespierre justifies its complete suppression as soon as, in his judgment, "it endangers public liberty." Marx continued:

> That is to say, therefore: The right of man to liberty [*Menschenrecht der Freiheit*] ceases to be a right as soon as it comes into conflict with *political* life, whereas in theory political life is only the guarantee of human rights, the rights of the individual, and therefore must be abandoned as soon as it comes into contradiction with its *aim*, with these rights of man. But practice is merely the exception, theory is the rule. But even if one were to regard revolutionary practice as the correct presentation of the relationship, there would still remain the puzzle of why the relationship is turned upside-down in the minds of the political emancipators and the aim appears as the means, while the means appears as the aim. (Ibid., p. 165)

Why does freedom of the press appear on this occasion as a right of man rather than a right of citizenship? Does Marx really mean to agree with those who would subordinate it to "political life," to the needs of the community in the sense that Robespierre did? Does he mean to make special allowance for the revolutionary and wartime circumstances of 1793? Nowhere else in any of his writings did Marx treat freedom of the press so casually. All this seems doubly perplexing because Marx's other early comments on the Jacobin dictatorship stressed the futility of efforts to achieve by force and terror a social harmony that could only emerge after the era of private property had passed into history — see the evidence assembled on this point by Shlomo Avineri, *Social and Political Thought*, pp. 185–93.

5. *Collected Works*, 4:115–16; see also pp. 32, 50, 113–15.

6. *Collected Works*, 6:499–500.

7. Ibid., pp. 498, 506.

8. *Collected Works*, 3:504–08 (quotation from p. 505).

9. *Collected Works*, 5:301; also see pp. 304–06.

10. *The Holy Family*, in *Collected Works*, 4:131.

11. *Hegel's Philosophy of Right*, §5, pp. 21–22.

12. *The German Ideology*, in *Collected Works*, 5:78; also see pp. 301–06, 431–32,

438–39. Marx's idea of freedom receives an unusually clear explication in O'Rourke, *The Problem of Freedom in Marxist Thought*, chap. 2.

13. *The German Ideology*, in *Collected Works*, 5:78–79, 80–81.

14. Ibid., pp. 438, 439.

15. See especially Lenin, *Proletarian Revolution*, in *Selected Works*, 3:84–86; and Bukharin and Preobrazhensky, *The ABC of Communism*, pp. 74–77.

16. *Collected Works*, 5:304.

17. Ibid., p. 327; these ideas are developed throughout the entire first section on Feuerbach, pp. 27–96 (see especially pp. 35–37, 53–54). The term "superstructure" comes from Marx's 1859 preface to *A Contribution to the Critique of Political Economy*, in *Selected Works*, 1:329.

18. These questions are forcefully raised in Hook, "The Enlightenment and Marxism," pp. 106–08.

19. "On the Jewish Question," in *Collected Works*, 3:155; see above, volume 1, p. 69.

20. Pp. 133, 159.

21. See for example O'Rourke, *The Problem of Freedom in Marxist Thought*, chap. 2; and especially Dahrendorf, *Die Idee des Gerechten*.

22. *Collected Works*, 10:568–69; cf. *Eighteenth Brumaire* version, ibid., 11:114–15.

23. "Constitution of the French Republic," in *Collected Works*, 10:577–78; also see 16:76–77.

24. "The Communism of the *Rheinischer Beobachter*," ibid., 6:222, 228; also see pp. 75–95, 356–57, 511–12.

25. *The Prussian Military Question and the German Workers' Party*, in Marx, *Political Writings*, 3:139, 143, 144.

26. See above, pp. 91–98.

27. See above, volume 1, pp. 42, 68–69, 96, 99.

28. Marx, "Contribution to the Critique of Hegel's Philosophy of Law: Introduction" (1844), in *Collected Works*, 3:182, 176, 175. For a brief and lucid exposition of Marx and Engels' views on these matters, see Lobkowicz, "Marx's Attitude Toward Religion."

29. *Collected Works*, 3:162.

30. Ibid., p. 156; also see 4:95, 111, 120–21; Avineri, *Social and Political Thought*, pp. 188–91.

31. *Principles of Communism* (October Draft), in *Collected Works*, 6:354; "Draft of a Communist Confession of Faith" (June Draft), ibid., p. 103; German words restored from original version reproduced in Institut für Marxismus-Leninismus, *Der Bund der Kommunisten*, 1:605, 475.

32. *Manifesto of the Communist Party*, in *Collected Works*, 6:504; German words restored from *Werke*, 4:480.

33. *Collected Works*, 6:502; for Marx's remarks on the community of women in the Paris manuscripts, see 3:194–96.

34. Ibid., 7:4.

35. The "Program and Rules of the Alliance," together with Marx's marginal comments, are reproduced in Institute of Marxism-Leninism, *General Council Minutes, 1868–1870*, p. 380.

36. Letter to Carlo Cafiero, July 1, 1871, in Marx et al., *Anarchism and Anarcho-Syndicalism*, p. 48; Marx's remark from his letter to Friedrich Bolte, November 23, 1871, ibid., p. 56.

37. *Writings on the Paris Commune*, p. 73.

38. Ibid., pp. 27–28.

39. *Werke*, 18:531–32.

40. *Selected Works*, 2:33 (translation revised from unexpurgated German version in *Werke*, 19:31).

41. See Benedikt Kautsky, ed., *Engels' Briefwechsel mit Karl Kautsky*, pp. 270–71.

42. Marx, *Interview*, p. 19.

43. *Anti-Dühring*, pp. 437–40 (quotation from p. 440).

44. Letter of January 6, 1892, in Engels and Lafargues, *Correspondence*, 3:154–55.

45. The draft Engels had before him is reprinted in Bartel, "Der interne Juni-Entwurf"; Engels' comment from his "Zur Kritik des sozialdemokratischen Programmentwurfs 1891," in *Werke*, 22:237.

46. As reproduced above, volume 1, p. 321.

47. (1873), in Marx et al., *Anarchism and Anarcho-Syndicalism*, p. 95.

48. "On the Occasion of Karl Marx's Death" (1883), ibid., p. 172.

49. Letter to August Bebel, March 18–28, 1875, in *Selected Works*, 2:39.

50. Tucker, "Marx as a Political Theorist," pp. 119–22.

51. Bartel, "Der interne Juni-Entwurf," p. 301; Gotha draft reproduced in *Werke*, 19:548. Marx and Engels' silence, *Selected Works*, 2:30–32, 38–39; *Werke*, 22:237.

52. The draft program is reproduced in *Werke*, 19:238, 570–71; for comments on disagreements, see 34:475–76, 35:232.

53. *Critique of the Gotha Program*, in *Selected Works*, 2:31; cf. p. 33.

54. As reproduced in Marx and Engels, *Communist Manifesto*, pp. 291–92; see discussion above, volume 1, pp. 147–61.

55. Marx to Engels, November 4, 1864, in *Selected Correspondence*, pp. 161–62; Engels to Marx, November 7, 1864, *Werke*, 31:17.

56. "Provisional Rules of the Association," in *General Council Minutes, 1864–66*, pp. 288–89; cf. later version of preamble where the "rights of man" sentence has been dropped, *Selected Works*, 1:350–51.

57. Bartel, "Der interne Juni-Entwurf," p. 300; Engels, "Zur Kritik des sozialdemokratischen Programmentwurfs 1891," in *Werke*, 22:232; also see *Origin of the Family*, pp. 217, 236.

58. *Collected Works*, 6:505; Engels' draft had specified "rebels against the majority of the people" (ibid., p. 350).

59. Letter to Gerson Trier, December 18, 1889, in *Werke*, 37:328.

60. Letter to Friedrich Sorge, August 9, 1890, ibid., p. 440; letter to Wilhelm Liebknecht, August 10, 1890, ibid., p. 445 ("overt acts" Engels wrote in English).

61. Letter to August Bebel, May 1, 1891, in *Werke*, 38:94; cf. p. 41. Bebel's letter may be found in Bebel, *Briefwechsel mit Engels*, p. 408; this controversy is summarized above in volume 1, pp. 329–30.

62. Letter to Karl Kautsky, February 11, 1891, in *Werke*, 38:35–36; letter to Karl Kautsky, February 3, 1891, ibid., p. 22.

63. Letter to August Bebel, November 19, 1892, ibid., p. 517; also see p. 94.

64. The phrase "magnificent presumption" comes from Wolfe, *Marxism*, p. 202.

65. Letter to Friedrich Sorge, June 10, 1891, in *Letters to Americans*, pp. 234; letter to Florence Kelley Wischnewetzky, December 28, 1886, ibid., p. 166 (translation modified — RNH); letter to Isaak Adolfowitsch Gurwitsch, May 27, 1893, in *Werke*, 39:75; letter to

Conrad Schmidt, August 5, 1890, in *Selected Correspondence*, p. 472. Cf. similar statements, *Letters to Americans*, pp. 163, 168, 263; *Selected Correspondence*, p. 381.

66. As related in Alexei Voden's memoirs and discussed above, volume 1, p. 335.

67. *The Proletarian Revolution*, in *Selected Works*, 3:87, 91.

68. Luxemburg, *The Russian Revolution* (1922), in *Rosa Luxemburg Speaks*, pp. 389–90; see also Kautsky, *The Dictatorship of the Proletariat*; Bernstein, *Sozialismus*.

69. See discussion above, volume 1, pp. 191–227, 291–97.

70. See discussion above, ibid., pp. 247–48.

71. *The Knight of the Noble Consciousness*, in *Collected Works*, 12:504; also see 11:312–16.

72. Marx, *Civil War*, in *Writings on the Paris Commune*, p. 76; Engels, "Introduction," ibid., p. 34.

73. Jellinek, *Paris Commune*, p. 134; also see Mason, *Paris Commune*, p. 135.

74. Program printed in Rougerie, *Paris libre 1871*, p. 154; Marx's summary, *Notebook on the Paris Commune; Press Excerpts and Notes*, pp. 63–64.

75. As quoted by Edwards, *The Communards of Paris, Paris Commune*, p. 92; also see Mason's extended account, *Paris Commune*, pp. 225–33.

76. *Writings on the Paris Commune*, p. 193; also see above, pp. 108–20.

77. Ibid., p. 192; cf. First Draft version, pp. 171–77; and final version, pp. 66–67.

78. Ibid., p. 192.

79. Ibid., p. 175; Marx relied mainly on the *Journal Officiel* of March 22, 1871, as revealed in his notes, *Notebook*, pp. 21, 24–27. For a modern account of this incident, see Edwards, *Paris Commune*, pp. 170–72.

80. *Writings on the Paris Commune*, p. 192.

81. Ibid., pp. 192–93.

82. *Civil War*, ibid., pp. 64, 83; First Draft, ibid., pp. 140–41; see also *General Council Minutes, 1870–71*, p. 182; *Notebook*, p. 51.

83. Williams, *French Revolution*, pp. 130–35; Edwards, *Paris Commune*, pp. 184–85, 210–15, 230; Rougerie, *Paris libre 1871*, pp. 145–46.

84. See discussion by Johnstone, "The Commune and Marx's Conception," pp. 207, 211 (especially n. 51).

85. See above, chap. 4, n. 28.

86. "Introduction," *Writings on the Paris Commune*, pp. 30–31; cf. Marx's very interesting assertion in 1880 that "the majority of the Commune" was not even socialist (ibid., p. 236).

87. See previous discussion of these issues in volume 1, pp. 281–83, and chap. 9, passim.

88. First Draft, *Writings on the Paris Commune*, p. 154.

89. Ibid., p. 162.

90. See above, n. 48.

91. Letter to Ferdinand Domela Nieuwenhuis, February 22, 1881, in *Werke*, 35:160.

92. See above, nn. 47, 48.

93. Mikhail Bakunin, "Programme et objet de l'Organisation Révolutionnaire des Frères Internationaux," as reproduced in Marx and Engels, *L'Alliance de la Démocratie Socialiste et l'Association Internationale des Travailleurs* (1873), in Freymond, *Première Internationale*, 2:471; also see Marx et al., *Anarchism and Anarcho-Syndicalism*, pp. 107, 115.

94. *Writings on the Paris Commune*, p. 30; also see pp. 227, 233; see above, p. 122.

95. Second Draft, ibid., p. 191; *Civil War*, ibid., p. 65.

96. Second Draft, ibid., p. 190; First Draft, ibid., p. 113; Second Draft, ibid., p. 193; cf. final version—"every right of civilized warfare" (p. 68).

97. First Draft, ibid., pp. 113, 130, 115; Marx copied down the provisions of the Law of Hostages in *Notebook*, p. 41.

98. *Civil War*, in *Writings on the Paris Commune*, pp. 68, 94, 95.

99. Ibid., p. 93; Second Draft, ibid., p. 193; cf. similar statements, pp. 68, 113, 131. Also compare Engels' comments on "rules of decency in literary warfare," *Anti-Dühring*, p. 15.

100. *Civil War*, in *Writings on the Paris Commune*, p. 82.

101. Ibid., p. 81; cf. Johnstone's comments in "The Commune and Marx's Conception," p. 211.

102. "Programm der blanquistischen Kommuneflüchtlinge" (1874), in *Werke*, 18:534 (translation adapted from Draper's in *Writings on the Paris Commune*, p. 230).

103. Letter to Marx, September 4, 1870, in *Werke*, 33:53 (translation adapted from *Selected Correspondence*, p. 303, and Wolfe, *Marxism*, p. 166); also see 37:155–56, 317.

104. See above, volume 1, p. 145.

105. *Capital*, 1:9–10.

106. See *On Britain*, p. 542.

107. Engels, "The Peasant Question in France and Germany" (1894), in *Selected Works*, 2:397.

108. The classic advocates of the ambiguous legacy viewpoint are Wolfe, *Marxism*, and Hook, *Marx and the Marxists*; psychological ambivalences are probed by Seigel, *Marx's Fate*.

109. "Kaiserlich Russische Wirkliche Geheime Dynamiträte" (1885), in *Werke*, 21:189–90; see below p. 320; on 1848, see above, volume 1, pp. 198–203.

110. See above, volume 1, pp. 200–01.

111. "From Paris to Berne" (1848), in *Collected Works*, 7:523; on the class alliance strategy as it affected peasants, see above, pp. 115–20, as well as volume 1, pp. 182–83. Also see Draper, *Theory of Revolution*, 2:317–452.

112. *The Class Struggles in France* (1850), in *Collected Works*, 10:137; for other support of universal suffrage in the same writing, see pp. 65, 79, 122.

113. See above, volume 1, pp. 254, 185.

114. See ibid., chap. 9.

115. See above, pp. 126–34.

116. Reproduced in Fromm, *Marx's Concept of Man*, p. 257.

117. Popper, *The Open Society and Its Enemies*, pp. 385–86.

Chapter 7. The Classless Society as a Polity

1. Among the more interesting recent literature on the classless society generally, see: McLellan, "Marx's View of the Unalienated Society"; Fetscher, "Marx, Engels and Future Society"; Draper, "The Death of the State in Marx and Engels"; Tarschys, *Beyond the State*; Maguire, *Marx's Paris Writings*; Bloom, "Withering Away"; Adamiak, "Withering Away"; Merkel, *Marx und Engels*.

2. See the recent writings of Tucker, *Philosophy and Myth in Karl Marx*, chap. 13; Fetscher, "Marx, Engels and Future Society"; Bottomore, "Socialism and the Division of Labor"; Wallimann, *Estrangement: Marx's Conception of Human Nature and the Divi-*

sion of Labor; as well as an interesting anthology of Marx's writings on the subject in Marx and Engels, *Critique de la division du travail*.

3. *Collected Works*, 5:32.

4. *Origin of the Family*, p. 161, translates the word simply as "fall," but compare the original German, *Werke*, 21:97. See above, p. 17.

5. *The German Ideology*, in *Collected Works*, 5:47; see above, pp. 6–9.

6. *Capital*, 1:177, 178, 341, 360.

7. Ibid., p. 645; also see pp. 420–24.

8. Pp. 405, 406.

9. *Capital*, 1:762; also see *Grundrisse*, pp. 162, 325.

10. *The Housing Question* (1872), in *Selected Works*, 1:513.

11. P. 407; also see *Collected Works*, 6:352–54.

12. *Capital*, 1:421, 486–88.

13. *Collected Works*, 5:64, 66; also see *Capital*, 1:352.

14. *Principles of Communism*, in *Collected Works*, 6:351, 354; also see *Collected Works*, 4:252–53.

15. *Selected Works*, 1:568; also see p. 533 and passim.

16. Pp. 412 (where "*grossen Städte*" is rendered as "great towns" — see *Werke*, 20:277), 411; also see *Capital*, 1:505–07.

17. *Collected Works*, 5:44, 33, 46.

18. Pp. 113, 125, 137, 137–38; cf. *Collected Works*, 5:4, 7, 76.

19. *Origin of the Family*, p. 139.

20. *Capital*, 1:489–90.

21. *Principles of Communism*, in *Collected Works*, 6:354; *Origin of the Family*, p. 145.

22. Draper, "Marx and Engels on Women's Liberation."

23. *Collected Works*, 5:44–45; *Capital*, 1:423; see above, pp. 91–98.

24. *Anti-Dühring*, pp. 278, 408.

25. See *Capital*, 1:486.

26. *Collected Works*, 5:394.

27. *Capital*, 1:330–31; also see 3:383.

28. *Contribution to the Critique of Hegel's Philosophy of Law*, in *Collected Works*, 3:51, 50.

29. See above, pp. 129–31.

30. *The German Ideology*, in *Collected Works*, 5:88.

31. See above, nn. 6, 24.

32. Pp. 610–11; also see p. 712.

33. *Capital*, 3:820; also see Marx, *Theories of Surplus-Value*, 3:257; Engels, *Anti-Dühring*, pp. 392–93.

34. P. 712; also see pp. 706–08.

35. *Selected Works*, 2:23.

36. Recent studies concerned with the *Bildung* ideal in Germany include Bruford, *The German Tradition of Self-Cultivation*; Sweet, *Wilhelm von Humboldt*.

37. *The German Ideology*, in *Collected Works*, 5:78, 439; also see *Theories of Surplus-Value*, 2:118.

38. *Collected Works*, 6:506.

39. "Progress of Social Reform on the Continent" (1844), ibid., 3:395, 394.

40. Ibid., 5:47.

41. *Principles of Communism*, ibid., 6:353.

42. "Introduction" (1891) to *Wage Labor and Capital*, in *Selected Works*, 1:73; see above, n. 24.

43. "Nothing human is alien to me," from his daughter's parlor-game questionnaire, reproduced in Fromm, *Marx's Concept of Man*, p. 257 (also see Fromm's comments, pp. 82–83).

44. *Critique of the Gotha Program*, in *Selected Works*, 2:22; also see *Collected Works*, 5:393–95.

45. *Capital*, 1:487, n. 2, 177.

46. An unusually fair-minded treatment of these events may be found in Palmer, *Age of Democratic Revolution*, 2:35–68, 99–131.

47. *Collected Works*, 3:121; see above, volume 1, pp. 74–82.

48. *Werke*, 3:537; see also *Collected Works*, 4:666.

49. "Contribution to Critique of Hegel's Philosophy of Law. Introduction," ibid., 3:186.

50. Ibid., p. 206.

51. Ibid., 5:380 (translation modified — RNH; see original German, *Werke*, 3:364). The German *"politischen Einrichtungen schliesslich beseitigt"* is rendered "ultimately abolishes political institutions" in the Communist-sponsored translation, implying the usual period of proletarian rule before abolishment. *"Schliesslich"* can be translated in either sense, but I submit that my rendering — "at last" after previous revolutions — is more faithful to the context provided by the first half of the sentence and by the previous paragraphs.

52. *Collected Works*, 6:212 (French words restored from original French text, as reproduced in *Pages de Karl Marx*, 2:170).

53. Marx, "Moralising Criticism and Critical Morality" (1847), in *Collected Works*, 6:324; cf. p. 319.

54. Ibid., p. 505.

55. First Draft of *Civil War*, in *Writings on the Paris Commune*, pp. 150, 152; see above, pp. 126–34.

56. Letter to August Bebel, March 18–28, 1875, ibid., p. 231; "Introduction" (1891) to *Civil War*, ibid., pp. 34, 33 (German words restored from *Werke*, 22:199, 198).

57. Marx, *Civil War*, in *Writings on the Paris Commune*, p. 73; see above, pp. 128–29.

58. Engels, "Progress of Social Reform on the Continent" (1843), in *Collected Works*, 3:393, 399; cf. p. 513.

59. Letter from Engels to Theodor Cuno, January 24, 1872, in Marx and Engels, *Selected Correspondence*, pp. 319–20; cf. *Anti-Dühring*, p. 395.

60. Engels, *Origin of the Family*, p. 232; cf. *Selected Works*, 1:577–78.

61. Letter from Engels to Bebel, March 18–28, 1875, in *Selected Works*, 2:39; cf. 1:440; Marx et al., *Anarchism and Anarcho-Syndicalism*, pp. 95, 172.

62. *Collected Works*, 6:505–06 (German words restored from *Werke*, 4:482); cf. Marx et al., *Anarchism and Anarcho-Syndicalism*, p. 74.

63. Letter from Engels to Carlo Cafiero, July 28, 1871, in Del Bo, ed., *Corrispondenza*, p. 35 (German translation in *Werke*, 33:668).

64. As translated above, volume 1, p. 321, 323 (see n. 81).

65. Review of *Le socialisme et l'impôt* by Emile de Girardin, Paris, 1850, in *Collected Works*, 10:333; cf. *Werke*, 27:318.

66. *Collected Works*, 4:249–50.

67. Letter of September 12, 1882, in *Selected Correspondence*, p. 399.

NOTES TO PAGES 240–254   [395]

68. Pp. 388, 389 (German words restored from *Werke*, 20:261, 262).

69. "On the Occasion of Karl Marx's Death" (1883), in Marx et al., *Anarchism and Anarcho-Syndicalism*, p. 172; *Anti-Dühring*, p. 388; see Bloom, "Withering Away," pp. 116–17.

70. P. 248 (translation modified — RNH; see original German, *Werke*, 20:166); see above, pp. 9–11.

71. "Introduction" to *Civil War*, in *Writings on the Paris Commune*, p. 34.

72. "On the Occasion of Karl Marx's Death," in Marx et al., *Anarchism and Anarcho-Syndicalism*, p. 172.

73. See for example the modern translation in *Anti-Dühring*, p. 389; and *Selected Works*, 2:138.

74. See above, nn. 59–62, 64; also "disappears," Marx et al., *Anarchism and Anarcho-Syndicalism*, pp. 74, 103, and *Werke*, 27:318; "dissolves," *Selected Works*, 2:39, and *Anarchism and Anarcho-Syndicalism*, p. 172; "falls asleep," *Werke*, 20:262, 620; "surmounted," *Werke*, 22:418.

75. See Lenin, *Selected Works*, 2:262, 305–06, 309–10; cf. Turetzki, *Die Entwicklung der Anschauungen*, pp. 110–13.

76. *Selected Works*, 2:21, 23 (the long passage omitted within the ellipses is quoted above, n. 35).

77. Ibid., p. 30.

78. See above, volume 1, chap. 9.

79. See above, pp. 77–80.

80. See above, volume 1, p. 327.

81. *Collected Works*, 10:122. Strategy II is introduced above in volume 1, chap. 6, and further elaborated in chap. 7.

82. See above, chap. 6, n. 88.

83. See below, pp. 352–53.

84. *Selected Works*, 2:30 (translation of *"Staatswesen"* changed from "state" to "polity").

85. *Writings on the Paris Commune*, p. 74; also see *Capital*, 3:384.

86. *Collected Works*, 6:505.

87. Engels' paraphrase of Saint-Simon in *Anti-Dühring*, p. 358; also see p. 389; Marx et al., *Anarchism and Anarcho-Syndicalism*, pp. 74, 103.

88. See for example Adamiak, "Withering Away," p. 16; Harris, "Utopian Elements," p. 95.

89. (1874), in *Selected Works*, 1:575, 576, 577.

90. Ibid., pp. 577, 576; letter to Theodor Cuno, January 22, 1872, in Marx et al., *Anarchism and Anarcho-Syndicalism*, p. 70; also see Engels and Lafargues, *Correspondence*, 1:34–35.

91. *Selected Works*, 1:347; orchestra parallel, see above, n. 27.

92. Institute of Marxism-Leninism, *General Council Minutes, 1868–70*, p. 289.

93. *Capital*, 3:440, 387.

94. *Writings on the Paris Commune*, p. 74.

95. As translated above, volume 1, pp. 323–24 (see n. 81).

96. Ibid., pp. 324–25, 323.

97. See for example *Collected Works*, 3:393, 399; *Werke*, 22:418.

98. *The Greek State*, pp. 95, 42, 50, 63, 67, 69–70, 69, 39, 43, 89.

99. *Critique of Hegel's Philosophy of Law*, in *Collected Works*, 3:51; see above, volume 1, pp. 82–84.

100. *Grundrisse,* pp. 487–88, 111; also see pp. 474–76; *Capital,* 1:365, especially n. 3; *Collected Works,* 11:530–31; *Werke,* 30:606.

101. *Origin of the Family,* pp. 181, 179; also see *Collected Works,* 2:61.

102. *Anti-Dühring,* p. 252; *Housing Question,* in *Selected Works,* 1:512; also see *Anti-Dühring,* pp. 390–91.

103. *Grundrisse,* pp. 708, 712, 706.

104. *Principles of Communism,* in *Collected Works,* 6:349; cf. *Grundrisse,* p. 325.

105. *The State and Revolution* (1917), in *Selected Works,* 2:255.

106. See discussion of these issues in Dahl, "Marxism and Free Parties"; Johnstone, "The Commune and Marx's Conception."

107. Letter of January 16, 1863, in *Werke,* 32:20–21; also see 7:468–93, 15:384–88, 22:371–99; Berger, *Engels, Armies, and Revolution,* pp. 142–50.

108. Letter to Otto von Boenigk, August 21, 1890, in *Werke,* 37:447–48.

109. Engels, *Anti-Dühring,* p. 407; Marx, "The Turkish War Question," in *Collected Works,* 12:182–83.

110. See for example Michels, *Political Parties;* Hunt, *German Social Democracy.*

111. Engels, "Introduction" to *Civil War,* in *Writings on the Paris Commune,* p. 33.

112. See for example Fromm, *Marx's Concept of Man,* pp. 42–43; Tucker, *The Marxian Revolutionary Idea,* pp. 37–48.

113. *Economic and Philosophic Manuscripts of 1844,* in *Collected Works,* 3:295; also see p. 280.

114. Engels, *Anti-Dühring,* pp. 478, 477; Marx, *Critique of the Gotha Program* in *Selected Works,* 2:39; also see *Anti-Dühring,* pp. 145–49; *Werke,* 20:579–82.

115. "Progress of Social Reform on the Continent" (1843), in *Collected Works,* 3:394; also see pp. 393, 432.

116. Ibid., 5:535, 537.

117. "Introduction" (1891) to *Wage Labor and Capital,* in *Selected Works,* 1:73.

118. Ibid., 2:22.

119. Pp. 278–79; also see *Werke,* 33:668.

120. *Anti-Dühring,* pp. 477–78.

Chapter 8. The International Working Men's Association

1. The standard history of the IWA is Stekloff, *History of the First International.* More recent accounts include Braunthal, *History of the International;* Drachkovitch, ed., *The Revolutionary Internationals;* and Molnár, *Le déclin de la Première Internationale.* For treatment of IWA activities in individual countries, see Hostetter, *Italian Socialist Movement;* Samuel Bernstein, *The First International in America;* Freymond, ed., *Etudes et documents;* Morgan, *German Social Democrats;* Samuel Bernstein, *The Beginnings of Marxian Socialism in France;* Collins and Abramsky, *Marx and British Labour;* Nettlau, *La Première Internationale en Espagne.*

2. See above, volume 1, pp. 147–75, 259–83.

3. Schroeder, *Geschichte der sozialdemokratischen Parteiorganisation in Deutschland,* pp. 8–9, 60–63.

4. Mayer, *Bismarck und Lassalle,* pp. 59–60.

5. Racowitza, *Autobiography,* pp. 118–19.

6. Marx to Engels, April 9, 1863, in *Selected Correspondence,* p. 146; also see pp. 81, 193; *Werke,* 30:350–51, 369.

7. See above, volume 1, pp. 282–83.

8. Braunthal, *International*, pp. 85–92; Freymond and Molnár, "Rise and Fall of the First International," pp. 3–11.

9. Letter to Engels, November 4, 1864, in *Selected Correspondence*, p. 160; also see Collins and Abramsky, *British Labour Movement*, pp. 30–34.

10. Letter to Marx, November 7, 1864, in *Werke*, 31:17.

11. Letter of October 12, 1864, in Institute of Marxism-Leninism, *General Council Minutes, 1864–1866*, p. 376; also see pp. 35–41; *Selected Correspondence*, pp. 159–63.

12. Letter to Engels, November 4, 1864, in *Selected Correspondence*, p. 162; *General Council Minutes, 1864–1866*, p. 44. On the phrase "truth, morality, and justice," see above, pp. 187–88.

13. Letter of November 4, 1864, in *Selected Correspondence*, p. 161; also see *General Council Minutes, 1864–1866*, p. 171; for details on Mazzini's organization, see Hostetter, *Italian Socialist Movement*, 1:63–65.

14. *Provisional Rules of the Association*, in *General Council Minutes, 1864–1866*, pp. 288–91.

15. Ibid.; see final 1866 version in *General Council Minutes, 1866–1868*, pp. 265–68; also see congress debate in Freymond, *Première Internationale*, 1:38, 39–41.

16. Calculated from data in *General Council Minutes, 1864–1866*, pp. 53, 436, with the aid of the capsule biographies provided by the editors, pp. 440–76.

17. See editors' preface, ibid., pp. 15–16; *General Council Minutes, 1866–1868*, pp. 37, 337, n. 16.

18. *General Council Minutes, 1866–1868*, p. 36; *Werke*, 31:254; Collins and Abramsky, *British Labour Movement*, p. 71.

19. Letter to Engels, September 11, 1867, in *Selected Correspondence*, p. 227; on Engels' skepticism, see *Werke*, 31:17; Collins and Abramsky, *British Labour Movement*, p. 59.

20. I count Dupont, Eccarius, Lafargue, Lessner, Jung, and Marx himself; data from Freymond, *Première Internationale*, 1:133–34; *General Council Minutes, 1866–1868*, pp. 161, 163, 313.

21. For Odger's appearances, see *General Council Minutes, 1866–1868*, pp. 98, 121, 123, 124, 128; Eccarius' election, pp. 133–34.

22. Ibid., p. 161; *Werke*, 31:354; Collins and Abramsky, *British Labour Movement*, p. 131.

23. Letter of September 11, 1867, in *Selected Correspondence*, p. 227; letter of October 10, 1868, in *Werke*, 32:180.

24. Letter of October 13, 1868, in *Political Writings*, 3:156–57; for further comments on this statute and Schweitzer's leadership, see *Werke*, 32:170–71, 177, 179–80, 182.

25. Freymond, *Première Internationale*, 2:129; also see *Werke*, 17:303, 370; Mehring, *Karl Marx*, p. 418.

26. Marx to Engels, October 4, 1867, in *Werke*, 31:354; also see *General Council Minutes, 1866–1868*, p. 166; Collins and Abramsky, *British Labour Movement*, pp. 130–31.

27. Letter to Friedrich Bolte, November 23, 1871, in *Letters to Americans*, pp. 91–92 (translation modified – RNH; see original German, *Werke*, 33:330).

28. See Collins and Abramsky, *British Labour Movement*, pp. 48, 50, 55.

29. Letter of November 4, 1864, in *Selected Correspondence*, p. 163; Bakunin to Marx, February 7, 1865, as quoted by Carr, *Bakunin*, p. 323; also see *Werke*, 31:105, 111, 338.

30. From Bakunin's 1851 *Confession* to the Czar, as quoted by Carr, *Bakunin*, p. 193; also see pp. 168, 191–94, 270–72.

31. Ibid., pp. 323–26, 330–33, 336, 341, 371–72.

32. Ibid., pp. 336, 341–50.

33. Ibid., p. 352.

34. From Bakunin's circular of August 1867, as quoted by Carr, *Bakunin*, p. 352.

35. *General Council Minutes, 1866–1868*, pp. 152–53; also see *Werke*, 31:338.

36. *General Council Minutes, 1868–1870*, pp. 297–98; Freymond, *Première Internationale*, 1:388–89.

37. Letter to Engels, November 7, 1868, in *Werke*, 32:197; Bakunin to Gustav Vogt, in Freymond, *Première Internationale*, 1:449; also see Mehring, *Karl Marx*, pp. 409–10.

38. "Program and Rules of the International Alliance of Socialist Democracy," *General Council Minutes, 1868–1870*, pp. 379–83; request for recognition, p. 53; also see Carr, *Bakunin*, p. 354–62.

39. As recounted by Carr, *Bakunin*, p. 363.

40. *General Council Minutes, 1868–1870*, pp. 53–54; Marx to Engels, December 15, 1868 in *Werke*, 32:234.

41. Letter to Engels, December 18, 1868, in *Werke*, 32:234; letter to Marx, pp. 235–36; for Marx's comments on Bakunin's program and rules, see *General Council Minutes, 1868–1870*, pp. 379–83.

42. Letter of October 30, 1869, in *Werke*, 32:380; also see pp. 351, 587, 593–94.

43. Letter of December 22, 1868, as quoted by Carr, *Bakunin*, p. 365.

44. *General Council Minutes, 1868–1870*, pp. 387–89 (translation modified — RNH; see original French, p. 300).

45. *Werke*, 32:236–37; *General Council Minutes, 1868–1870*, pp. 54, 389.

46. Letter of March 5, 1869, in *Werke*, 32:273–74; also see pp. 276, 279, 674–75; *Werke*, 16:409–10.

47. "The General Council of the International Working Men's Association to the International Alliance of Socialist Democracy," *General Council Minutes, 1868–1870*, pp. 310–11; also see pp. 74–75, 134–35, 431, n. 79.

48. Bakunin's resolution may be found in Freymond, *Première Internationale*, 2:92; Marx's response in *General Council Minutes, 1868–1870*, pp. 322–24; also see pp. 128–33, 137.

49. Freymond, *Première Internationale*, 2:92–96; Marx's reaction, *Werke*, 32:632–33.

50. Freymond, *Première Internationale*, 2:129; Guillaume, *L'Internationale*, 1:206–09; Carr, *Bakunin*, p. 380; for Marx's allegation, see *Werke*, 16:412, 32:672.

51. Circular letter reproduced in *General Council Minutes, 1868–1870*, pp. 399–407; also see pp. 195–96.

52. Letter to Paul and Laura Lafargue, April 19, 1870, in *Werke*, 32:673; also see pp. 641–45, 16:409–20.

53. Letter of October 28, 1869, as quoted by Carr, *Bakunin*, p. 385.

54. Letter of February 19, 1870, in *Werke*, 32:448–49; *General Council Minutes, 1868–1870*, pp. 215–16; also see p. 211; *Werke*, 32:644, 676.

55. *General Council Minutes, 1868–1870*, pp. 224, 226; Mehring, *Karl Marx*, pp. 424–27, 430–32; Carr, *Bakunin*, pp. 375–76, 429–31.

56. Engels to Marx, April 21, 1870, in *Werke*, 32:483–84; *General Council Minutes, 1868–1870*, pp. 412, 256.

57. *General Council Minutes, 1868–1870*, pp. 256, 261, 266–68, 414.

58. The Sonvillier *Circulaire à toutes les fédérations de l'Association internationale des travailleurs* is reproduced in Freymond, *Première Internationale*, 2:261–65; *Fictitious Splits in the International* in *General Council Minutes, 1871–1872*, pp. 356–409.

59. *Circulaire*, in Freymond, *Première Internationale*, 2:262–63.

60. *Fictitious Splits*, in *General Council Minutes, 1871–1872*, p. 391.

61. Freymond, *Première Internationale*, 2:262–63.

62. Thirty-eight co-optations from minutes, *General Council Minutes, 1868–1870*, pp. 168, 169, 172, 177, 202, 211, 214, 226, 237; *General Council Minutes, 1870–1871*, pp. 47, 66, 85, 92, 176, 189, 222, 227, 234, 237, 241, 255, 259, 263, 268, 271; also see pp. 430, 449, 469. Remaining data tabulated from capsule biographies in same volumes, pp. 487–526 and 587–619. There is some minor overlapping because of individuals who fit in more than one category.

63. *Fictitious Splits*, in *General Council Minutes, 1871–1872*, p. 391; also see pp. 339–45.

64. Freymond, *Première Internationale*, 2:263, 265; see above, pp. 281–82.

65. *Fictitious Splits*, in *General Council Minutes, 1871–1872*, pp. 394–97. Marx threatened to suspend the German-Swiss section which came out in favor of the annexation of Alsace-Lorraine—hardly a move for which Bakunin would have reproached him (*General Council Minutes, 1870–1871*, p. 106; *Werke*, 33:170).

66. Freymond, *Première Internationale*, 2:264.

67. *General Council Minutes, 1870–1871*, pp. 38–42, 48, 50; also see *General Council Minutes, 1871–1872*, p. 358; *Werke*, 17:265, 33:27–28, 128–29, 136.

68. *General Council Minutes, 1870–1871*, pp. 244–45; also see p. 259; *General Council Minutes, 1871–1872*, p. 359; *Werke*, 33:255, 260.

69. *General Council Minutes, 1870–1871*, pp. 148–49, 151–52, 245. According to Molnár, Bakunin himself conceded that a public congress was impossible at the time (*Déclin*, p. 46).

70. *General Council Minutes, 1870–1871*, p. 244; *General Council Minutes, 1871–1872*, pp. 359, 371–72; Freymond, *Première Internationale*, 2:209, 241n, 243; *Werke*, 33:365.

71. Freymond, *Première Internationale*, 2:264.

72. On procedures, see *General Council Minutes, 1870–1871*, pp. 269–71, 275–76; *Werke*, 33:304. For the thirteen, compare London delegate list, Freymond, *Première Internationale*, 2:164–65, with general council membership, *General Council Minutes, 1870–1871*, pp. 449–50; also see Molnár, *Déclin*, pp. 52–55.

73. Freymond, *Première Internationale*, 2:264.

74. *Fictitious Splits*, in *General Council Minutes, 1871–1872*, pp. 383–86.

75. Freymond, *Première Internationale*, 2:231; *General Council Minutes, 1871–1872*, pp. 259–60, 418–19.

76. *General Council Minutes, 1870–1871*, pp. 441–42, 449.

77. Ibid., p. 446; Freymond, *Première Internationale*, 2:217–18; also see *General Council Minutes, 1868–1870*, pp. 401–05.

78. *General Council Minutes, 1870–1871*, pp. 297, 440. On the strength of these seemingly modest organizational changes, plus the famous political action resolution, Molnár makes an earnest but quite unconvincing case that at London Marx undertook a "profound transformation" of the IWA, attempting to create a "centralized international party" with a "new form of organization totally different from the old one" (*Déclin*, pp. 101, 137, 93, and passim).

79. Freymond, *Première Internationale*, pp. 206–09; *General Council Minutes, 1870–1871*, p. 448; see above, p. 283.

80. *General Council Minutes, 1870–1871*, p. 441; also see Carr, *Bakunin*, pp. 441–42; and above, p. 285.

81. Freymond, *Première Internationale*, 2:264–65.

82. Letter to Theodor Cuno, January 24, 1872, in *Letters to Americans*, p. 100.

83. See especially Guillaume, *L'Internationale*, 2:319–56.

84. *General Council Minutes, 1871–1872*, pp. 237–38; see also p. 243. On the American imbroglio generally, see Engels' résumé, *Werke*, 18:97–103; and Bernstein, *The First International in America*, chaps. 7–9.

85. *General Council Minutes, 1871–1872*, pp. 241–44, 558, 430–31; Gerth, *The First International: Minutes of the Hague Congress*, p. 209.

86. Gerth, *Hague Congress*, p. 209.

87. The standard English version of this resolution appears in *General Council Minutes, 1871–1872*, p. 263; cf. Gerth, *Hague Congress*, pp. 216–17.

88. Gerth, *Hague Congress*, pp. 209–10, 211–12; also see Guillaume, *L'Internationale*, 2:336–39.

89. Letter to Cesar DePaepe, May 28, 1872, in *Werke*, 33:479; also see pp. 476, 477, 505.

90. *General Council Minutes, 1871–1872*, pp. 221–23, 260–61, 422.

91. Guillaume, *L'Internationale*, 2:321–33.

92. Gerth, *Hague Congress*, pp. 174–77, 179–80, 183, 185–86, 191, 193, 198–99; also see pp. 245–49, 260–68. Sauva was rejected as the delegate for American Section 2 but admitted for Sections 29 and 42; Alerini was rejected for Marseilles but admitted for the Spanish Federation.

93. Letter of July 5, 1872, in *Letters to Americans*, p. 109 (translation modified— RNH; see original German, *Werke*, 33:497); *Werke*, 33:512–13.

94. See Engels' comments, *Werke*, 33:486, 518–20; Hostetter, *Italian Socialist Movement*, pp. 280–87.

95. Letter of June 21, 1872, in *Werke*, 33:491.

96. Guillaume, *L'Internationale*, 2:234; Gerth, *Hague Congress*, pp. 175–77, 182, 186; *Werke*, 33:494, 497, 505.

97. See above, n. 82; also see *General Council Minutes, 1871–1872*, pp. 467–68.

98. "The General Council to all Members of the International Working Men's Association," *General Council Minutes, 1871–1872*, p. 441 (cf. final French version, pp. 463–67); also see pp. 270–72, 316; *Werke*, 33:508, 510, 513–14. The Alliance documents are reproduced in *Werke*, 18:455–71.

99. Gerth, *Hague Congress*, pp. 203–04; committee report, pp. 225–26; also see Guillaume, *L'Internationale*, 2:343–48.

100. Gerth, *Hague Congress*, pp. 225–26; *Werke*, 33:548. See Carr, *Bakunin*, pp. 448–51 for a most perceptive account of this incident.

101. Braunthal, *International*, pp. 188–94; Collins and Abramsky, *British Labour Movement*, pp. 267–82, 300–02; Freymond and Molnár, "Rise and Fall of the First International," pp. 29–35.

Chapter 9. Strategy III: Skipping Stages

1. The best work on this subject is still Krause, *Marx und Engels und das zeitgenössische Russland*; also see Maximilien Rubel's editorial commentary in Marx and Engels, *Russische Kommune*; and Blackstock and Hoselitz's editorial commentary in Marx and Engels, *Russian Menace*. Less useful is Larsson, *Theories of Revolution*.

2. Some standard studies of the Russian revolutionary tradition are Yarmolinsky, *Road to Revolution*; Venturi, *Roots of Revolution*; Malia, *Alexander Herzen and the Birth of Russian Socialism*.

3. See above, volume 1, pp. 176–91, 213–22, 236–48.

4. "Preface" to *A Contribution to the Critique of Political Economy*, p. 21.

5. *Capital*, 1:8–9, 10.

6. Letter of March 18, 1852, in *Werke*, 28:40; also see 32:112.

7. Letter of March 14, 1868, as translated in *Colonialism and Modernization*, pp. 466–67.

8. Letter of November 7, 1868, in *Werke*, 32:197.

9. Letter of October 8, 1858, ibid., 29:360. For Engels' 1851 flight of fancy, see 27:266.

10. "The Emancipation Question" (1858), in *Collected Works*, 16:141, 147; also see Marx's notes on the subject, *Werke*, 19:407–24.

11. See, e.g., *Werke*, 27:226, 29:575.

12. Letter of February 10, 1870, in *Selected Correspondence*, pp. 283, 284. (Flerovsky was the pen name of Vasily Vasilyevich Bervi.)

13. Letter of February 12, 1870, ibid., p. 286.

14. Letter to Laura and Paul Lafargue, March 5, 1870, in *Werke*, 32:659; also see 17:269, 33:140.

15. Letter to Engels, in *Selected Correspondence*, p. 285.

16. Letter of March 24, 1870, ibid., p. 287.

17. Letter of December 12, 1872, in *Werke*, 33:549. (Marx never did provide such a treatment in the manuscripts he left for volumes 2 and 3 of *Capital*.)

18. Letter of February 17, 1870, in *Werke*, 32:650; letter of March 22, 1873, ibid., 33:577. This account of the reasons for Marx's change is based principally on Krause, *Zeitgenössische Russland*; also see McClellan, *Revolutionary Exiles*.

19. As quoted by Engels in "On Social Relations in Russia" (1875), in *Selected Works*, 2:52.

20. Ibid., pp. 46–47.

21. Ibid., p. 54 (translation modified — RNH; see original German, *Werke*, 18:565).

22. See *Russian Menace*, pp. 54, 241; *Werke*, 9:149.

23. "Afterword" (1894) to "On Social Relations in Russia," in *Russian Menace*, pp. 232, 233, 234–35; also see *Selected Correspondence*, pp. 509, 515.

24. Letter to Eduard Bernstein, October 9, 1886, in *Werke*, 36:546; also see p. 559.

25. *Russian Menace*, pp. 217, 218.

26. Ibid., pp. 216, 217 (translation modified — RNH; see original French, *Pages de Karl Marx*, 1:88.

27. Years later Engels asserted that Marx had not sent the letter out of fear it would bring about the journal's suppression (*Werke*, 36:121).

28. Vera Ivanovna Zasulich to Marx, February 16, 1881, in *Russian Menace*, p. 276.

29. The three drafts were reproduced in full in *Werke*, 19:384–406; an attempt to combine what is original in each draft in a single (condensed) whole appears in *Russian Menace*, pp. 219–26.

30. Second Draft, in *Russian Menace*, p. 223; Third Draft, ibid., pp. 220, 221; Second Draft, ibid., p. 224.

31. Third Draft, ibid., pp. 220, 221.

32. Second Draft, ibid., pp. 222–23.

33. Third Draft, ibid., pp. 221–22.

34. First Draft, ibid., p. 226.

35. Engels, see above, n. 23; Marx, Second Draft, in *Russian Menace*, p. 223; Third Draft, ibid., p. 222; Final Version, ibid., p. 279.

36. Engels to Bernstein, October 9, 1886, in *Werke*, 36:546; cf. Engels to Karl Kautsky, February 16, 1884, ibid., 36:109; and *Russian Menace*, p. 238.

37. Final Version, in *Russian Menace*, pp. 278–79.

38. Ibid., p. 228. (Bracketed clause restored from original manuscript; see Blackstock and Hoselitz's notes, ibid., pp. 281–83.)

39. "Introduction" to *Internationales aus dem "Volkstaat"* (1894), in *Russian Menace*, p. 284.

40. Letter of February 24, 1893, in *Selected Correspondence*, p. 509; also see *Werke*, 36:301, 38:196, 304–05, 363–66, 39:149–50.

41. "Afterword" (1894), in *Russian Menace*, pp. 232–33, 238; see above, n. 23.

42. See for example Haimson, *Russian Marxists;* and Ulam, *The Bolsheviks.*

43. *Russian Menace*, pp. 215, 226, 228, 241; *Collected Works*, 16:139–47.

44. "On Social Relations in Russia," in *Selected Works*, 2:56; see also *Werke*, 34:316, 36:120.

45. Letter to August Bebel, September 29, 1891, in *Werke*, 38:160; see also *Russian Menace*, pp. 240–41.

46. Marx, *Interview*, p. 19–20.

47. Letter to Karl Kautsky, February 7, 1882, in *Russian Menace*, p. 119; "The Foreign Policy of Russian Czarism" (1890), ibid., p. 52.

48. Hermann Alexandrovich Lopatin to M. N. Oschanina, September 20, 1883, reprinted in Rubel, *Russische Kommune*, pp. 175–76.

49. Letter of April 23, 1885, in *Selected Correspondence*, pp. 437–38.

50. Letter to Wilhelm Liebknecht, December 28, 1885, in *Werke*, 36:416.

51. Letter to Jenny Longuet, April 11, 1881, ibid., 35:179; also see pp. 174–75, 19:244.

52. "Kaiserlich Russische Wirkliche Geheime Dynamiträte" (1885), ibid., 21:189–90.

53. An extract of this report has been published in English in Marx et al., *Anarchism and Anarcho-Syndicalism*, pp. 105–22; the full text of the original French version may be found in Freymond, *Première Internationale*, 2:383–478; the German version published a year later in 1874 appears in *Werke*, 18:327–471.

54. Mikhail Bakunin, *Aux officiers de l'armée russe* (1872), as quoted by Marx and Engels, *L'Alliance de la Démocratie Socialiste et L'Association Internationale des Travailleurs*, in Freymond, *Première Internationale*, 2:451.

55. Mikhail Bakunin, "Program and Aim of the Revolutionary Organization of International Brothers," as quoted by Marx and Engels, *The Alliance of Socialist Democracy and the International Working Men's Association*, in Marx et al., *Anarchism and Anarcho-Syndicalism*, p. 111.

56. Marx et al., *Anarchism and Anarcho-Syndicalism*, p. 112. *Perinde ac cadaver* ("Be like unto a cadaver") was Ignatius Loyola's demand for unquestioning obedience addressed to new recruits in the Society of Jesus.

57. Mikhail Bakunin, *The Principles of Revolution* and *The Fundamental Principles of the Future Social Order*, as quoted by Marx and Engels, *Alliance*, in Marx et al., *Anarchism and Anarcho-Syndicalism*, pp. 115, 116, 118, and passim.

58. Marx et al., *Anarchism and Anarcho-Syndicalism*, pp. 119–120.

Chapter 10.   Strategy IV: Legal Revolution

1. There is really no systematic treatment of Marx and Engels' views on legal revolution. Perhaps the best researched effort, Moore, *Three Tactics*, is flawed by its uncritical

Leninist assumptions; also see Kramer, *Reform und Revolution*; Wolfe, *Marxism*, chap. 12. Other standard authorities only touch on the subject superficially and in passing.

2. *Collected Works*, 10:122; *Capital*, 1:751; also see Engels, *Anti-Dühring*, p. 255.

3. *Collected Works*, 6:519, 495.

4. *Principles of Communism* (1847), ibid., pp. 349–50.

5. Ibid., p. 356.

6. Letter to Ludwig Kugelmann, February 23, 1865, in *Selected Correspondence*, p. 197; see above, chap. 3, note 14; also *Werke*, 31:84, 110.

7. Speech delivered at a meeting on Poland, January 22, 1867, in Marx and Engels, *Russian Menace*, p. 108.

8. *Capital*, 1:9–10; see above pp. 207–08.

9. *New York World*, July 18, 1871, reprinted in *New Politics* 2 (1962):130. Marx expressed much the same idea in a second interview with the *New York Herald*, but because the reporter garbled his ideas *on other topics*, Marx repudiated the latter interview (see *Werke*, 17:399–400).

10. "Procès-verbaux de la Conférence de Londres de 1871," in Freymond, *Première Internationale*, 2:202.

11. Marx delivered the speech in French, and the fullest and most accurate account seems to be that published in *La Liberté*, September 15, 1872, reprinted in *Pages de Karl Marx*, 2:87. I have translated from this text, using the German version in *Werke*, 18:160, for comparison.

12. Lenin, *The Proletarian Revolution and the Renegade Kautsky* (1919), in *Selected Works*, 3:76–77.

13. See below, n. 31.

14. *Civil War*, in *Writings on the Paris Commune*, p. 74; for Marx and Engels' views on the importance of universal suffrage in *real* parliaments, see above, volume 1, p. 229; volume 2, pp. 76–79.

15. See *Werke*, 19:132–33.

16. See above, chap. 9, n. 46.

17. As reproduced in the French original in *Pages de Karl Marx*, 2:90; cf. Engels' reference to this phrase in *Selected Works*, 1:119.

18. "Zur Kritik des sozialdemokratischen Programmentwurfs 1891," in *Werke*, 22:234; presented in fuller context below, pp. 344–46.

19. Letter to Paul Lafargue, March 6, 1894, in Engels and Lafargues, *Correspondence*, 3:325–26; see above, pp. 81–85.

20. "Preface" (1887), American edition of *The Condition of the Working Class in England*, in *Marx and Engels on the United States*, pp. 284–85; for parallel remarks on Britain, see Marx and Engels, *Letters to Americans*, p. 185, and above, pp. 70–72; on France, see *Letters to Americans*, pp. 124–25, 155.

21. Letter of November 29, 1886, in *Letters to Americans*, pp. 162–63.

22. Ibid., p. 167; cf. parallel thoughts on the Social Democratic Federation in Britain, in Engels and Lafargues, *Correspondence*, 3:58, 338, 397.

23. See above, chap. 9, n. 52; also see Marx and Engels, *Ireland and the Irish Question*, pp. 149, 336.

24. Letter to Eduard Bernstein, May 22, 1886, in *Marx and Engels on the United States*, p. 306; letter to Laura Lafargue, May 23, 1886, ibid; see also p. 309.

25. Letter to Laura Lafargue, February 9, 1886, Engels and Lafargues, *Correspondence*, 1:333–35.

26. See Engels' summary of these activities, *Werke*, 22:76–79.

27. Letter to Paul Lafargue, February 25, 1893, Engels and Lafargues, *Correspondence*, 3:244.

28. Letter to Paul Lafargue, March 6, 1894, ibid., p. 326.

29. Among those who have found him a reformist are: Lichtheim, *Marxism*, p. 265; Wolfe, *Marxism*, pp. 219–25; Levine, *The Tragic Deception*, passim.

30. *New York World* interview, p. 133.

31. "[Konspekt der Reichstagsdebatte über das Sozialistengesetz]," in *Werke*, 34:498–99 (translation adapted from Moore, *Three Tactics*, p. 48).

32. *Capital*, 1:6.

33. *Origin of the Family*, p. 232; other examples of pessimism, *Werke*, 37:326; Engels and Lafargues, *Correspondence*, 3:211; but cf. optimism of Erfurt Program critique, above, n. 18.

34. "[Konspekt]," in *Werke*, 34:499.

35. *The Prussian Military Question and the German Workers' Party* (1865), in Marx, *Political Writings*, 3:133.

36. Letter to Paul Lafargue, February 16, 1886, in Engels and Lafargues, *Correspondence*, 1:339; also see 2:65.

37. "[Abschiedsbrief an die Leser des *Sozialdemokrat*]," in *Werke*, 22:78–79.

38. First Draft of *Civil War*, in *Writings on the Paris Commune*, p. 154.

39. *Ludwig Feuerbach and the End of Classical German Philosophy* (1888), in *Selected Works*, 2:327.

40. "The Peasant Question in France and Germany" (1894), ibid., p. 397.

41. Letter to H. M. Hyndman, December 8, 1880, reproduced in latter's memoirs, *Record of an Adventurous Life*, p. 260 (German translation in *Werke*, 34:482–83); Hyndman's own letter reproduced in Tsuzuki, *H. M. Hyndman and British Socialism*, pp. 33–34.

42. The best recent literature on prewar Social Democratic policies includes Steinberg, *Sozialismus und deutsche Sozialdemokratie*; idem., "Revolution und Legalität"; Lehnert, *Reform und Revolution*; and more briefly Kramer, *Reform und Revolution*; and Steenson, "*Not One Man! Not One Penny!*"

43. See above, pp. 56–59.

44. For the June Draft used by Engels see Bartel, "Der interne Juni-Entwurf."

45. *Werke*, 22:233–35, 237; on local self-administration, see above, pp. 147–59; and on this issue of "dictatorship of the proletariat," see above, volume 1, pp. 332–34.

46. *Werke*, 22:234, 236.

47. Letter to Laura Lafargue, January 19, 1895, in Engels and Lafargues, *Correspondence*, 3:361–62.

48. *Selected Works*, 1:119–20, 124–25.

49. Ibid., p. 125.

50. Ibid., p. 126.

51. Ibid., p. 124; letter of December 18, 1889, in *Werke*, 37:326.

52. For a few examples, see *Werke*, 22:6, 10, 37:14, 362, 365–66, 368, 39:413.

53. As reproduced in Steinberg, "Revolution und Legalität," p. 181.

54. Letter to Richard Fischer, March 8, 1895, in *Werke*, 39:424–26; also see 21:200–02, 36:238–41.

55. Interview with the *Daily Chronicle* (London), July 1, 1893, reproduced in Engels

and Lafargues, *Correspondence*, 3:400; letter of June 20, 1893, ibid., p. 263; also see *Werke*, 38:64–65.

56. *Werke*, 22:251; also see pp. 6, 10.

57. Letter of November 12, 1892, in Engels and Lafargues, *Correspondence*, 3:211.

58. Letter of November 17, 1885, in *Werke*, 36:391.

59. Letter to Eduard Bernstein, August 27, 1883, ibid., 36:55; letter to August Bebel, October 28, 1882, ibid., 35:381–82.

60. Letter to Bebel, December 11, 1884, in *Selected Correspondence*, p. 433; also see *Werke*, 36:240, 38:179–80.

61. Letter to Bernstein, August 27, 1883, in *Werke*, 36:54–55.

62. Letter to Franz Mehring, July 14, 1893, ibid., 39:99; letter to Paul Lafargue, June 27, 1893, in Engels and Lafargues, *Correspondence*, 3:272.

63. See discussion above, volume 1, chap. 9; volume 2, chap. 3, chap. 5.

64. Interview with the *Daily Chronicle* (London), July 1, 1893, in Engels and Lafargues, *Correspondence*, 3:397.

65. Letter of November 24, 1879, in *Werke*, 34:423–24.

66. "The Peasant Question in France and Germany" (1894), in *Selected Works*, 2: 395; Engels' running critique of Social Democratic parliamentary activity is well covered in Lidtke, *The Outlawed Party*.

67. Letter to Bebel, Wilhelm Liebknecht, Wilhelm Bracke, and Others, Middle of September, 1879, in *Selected Correspondence*, pp. 371, 377; letter to Paul Lafargue, November 22, 1894, in Engels and Lafargues, *Correspondence*, 3:344.

68. "[Antwort an die Redaktion der *Sächsischen Arbeiter-Zeitung*]" (1890), in *Werke*, 22:70; also see pp. 66–69, 80–85.

69. Letter to Karl Kautsky, November 3, 1893, ibid., 39:161; letter to Laura Lafargue, May 10, 1890, Engels and Lafargues, *Correspondence*, 2:376.

70. "The Holy War," in *Collected Works*, 12:432–33; see Berger, *Engels, Armies, and Revolution*.

71. *Collected Works*, 13:422–23.

72. *Role of Force*, p. 62.

73. Letter to Paul Lafargue, November 3, 1892, in Engels and Lafargues, *Correspondence*, 3:208.

74. On this subject see Berger, *Engels, Armies, and Revolution*, chap. 9; also Höhn, *Die Armee als Erziehungsschule der Nation;* Wette, *Kriegstheorien deutscher Sozialisten*.

75. *Anti-Dühring*, p. 236; also see *Werke*, 22:285.

76. Letter of November 18, 1884, in *Selected Correspondence*, p. 429; also see *Werke*, 36:255.

77. "Der Sozialismus in Deutschland," in *Werke*, 22:251; also see *Selected Correspondence*, p. 434.

78. Letter to Paul Lafargue, March 7, 1890, in Engels and Lafargues, *Correspondence*, 2:366–67; letter to Liebknecht, March 9, 1890, in *Werke*, 37:365; "The Peasant Question in France and Germany," (1894), in *Selected Works*, 2:398–99; also see *Werke*, 22:48n, 37:365.

79. Engels and Lafargues, *Correspondence*, 3:65.

80. Interview with *Le Figaro* (Paris), May 13, 1893, reproduced ibid., 3:393.

81. "Introduction" to *The Class Struggles in France*, in *Selected Works*, 1:126–27; "On the History of the Communist League" (1885), ibid., 2:323.

Chapter 11. Conclusion: Democracy Without Professionals

1. "Contribution to Critique of Hegel's Philosophy of Law. Introduction," in *Collected Works*, 3:182.

Bibliography

Writings of Marx and Engels

INCLUDED BELOW are the editions of Marx and Engels' writings that have been used in the foregoing book. Since the publication of volume 1, a definitive English-language edition, the *Collected Works*, has begun to appear. Seventeen of the anticipated fifty volumes are available at this writing, which include all the masters' works up to 1860 (except for correspondence), and I have used this collection for all pre-1860 citations. For writings after that date and for correspondence I have used English-language versions where available, scattered in the various editions and collections indicated. For the rest there remains the *Werke* published in East Germany, still the most complete set available. The most comprehensive bibliography of Marx's writings (including most of Engels') can be found in Maximilien Rubel, *Bibliographies des oeuvres de Karl Marx* (Paris: Rivière, 1956), together with its *Supplément* published in 1960.

Engels, Friedrich. *Anti-Dühring*. Moscow: Foreign Languages, 1954.

————. *The Condition of the Working Class in England*. Translated and edited by W. O. Henderson and W. H. Chaloner. Stanford: Stanford, 1968.

————. *The Origin of the Family, Private Property and the State*. Edited by Eleanor Burke Leacock. New York: International, 1972.

————. *The Origin of the Family, Private Property and the State*. 6th ed. Moscow: Foreign Languages, n.d. Cited as Moscow ed.

————. *The Peasant War in Germany*. Moscow: Foreign Languages, 1956.

————. *The Peasant War in Germany*. In *The German Revolutions*. Edited by Leonard Kreiger. Chicago: Chicago, 1967.

————. *The Role of Force in History*. Translated by Jack Cohen and edited by Ernst Wangermann. New York: International, 1968.

Marx, Karl. *Capital: A Critique of Political Economy*. 3 vols. Moscow: Progress, 1965–66.

————. *A Contribution to the Critique of Political Economy*. New York: International, 1970.

————. *The Ethnological Notebooks of Karl Marx*. 2nd ed. Edited by Lawrence Krader. Assen: Van Gorcum, 1974.

————. *Grundrisse: Foundations of the Critique of Political Economy*. Translated by Martin Nicolaus. New York: Vintage, 1973.

————. *An Interview with Karl Marx in 1879*. Edited by Thomas W. Porter. New York: AIMS, 1972.

————. *The Karl Marx Library*. 7 vols. Translated and edited by Saul K. Padover. New York: McGraw-Hill, 1971–77.

————. *Karl Marx on Colonialism and Modernization*. Edited by Shlomo Avineri. Garden City, N.Y.: Doubleday Anchor, 1969.

————. *Notebook on the Paris Commune: Press Excerpts and Notes*. Edited by Hal Draper. Berkeley: Independent Socialist Press, 1971.

[407]

————. *Pages de Karl Marx: Pour une éthique socialiste*. 2 vols. Edited by Maximilien Rubel. Paris: Payot, 1970.

————. *Political Writings*. 3 vols. Edited by David Fernbach. New York: Random House Vintage, 1974.

————. *The Poverty of Philosophy*. New York: International, n.d.

————. *Pre-Capitalist Economic Formations*. Translated by Jack Cohen and edited by Eric J. Hobsbawm. New York: International, 1964.

————. *Secret Diplomatic History of the Eighteenth Century*. Edited by Lester Hutchinson. New York: International, 1969.

————. *Theories of Surplus-Value*. 3 vols. Moscow: Progress, 1971.

————. *Writings of the Young Marx on Philosophy and Society*. Translated and edited by Loyd D. Easton and Kurt H. Guddat. Garden City, N.Y.: Doubleday, 1967.

Marx, Karl, and Engels, Friedrich. *On Britain*. 2nd ed. Moscow: Foreign Languages, 1962.

————. *The Civil War in the United States*. 3rd ed. New York: International, 1961.

————. *Collected Works*. 17 volumes to date. New York: International, 1975–.

————. *The Communist Manifesto*. Edited by D. Ryazanoff. New York: International, 1930.

————. *Critique de la division du travail*. Edited by André Gorz. Paris: Editions du Seuil, 1973.

————. *Ireland and the Irish Question: A Collection of Writings by Karl Marx and Friedrich Engels*. Edited by R. Dixon. New York: International, 1972.

————. *Letters to Americans, 1848–1895*. Translated by Leonard E. Mins. New York: International, 1953.

————. *Marx and Engels on the United States*. Moscow: Progress, 1979.

————. *On the Paris Commune*. Moscow: Progress, 1971.

————.*Pressefreiheit und Zensur*. Edited by Iring Fetscher. Frankfurt a/M: Europäische Verlagsanstalt, 1969.

————. *The Russian Menace to Europe*. Edited by Paul W. Blackstock and Bert F. Hoselitz. Glencoe: Free Press, 1952.

————. *Die russische Kommune: Kritik eines Mythos*. Edited by Maximilien Rubel. Munich: Hanser, 1972.

————. *Selected Correspondence: 1846–1895*. Translated by Dona Torr. New York: International, 1942.

————. *Selected Works*. 2 vols. Moscow: Foreign Languages, 1951. Cited as *Selected Works*.

————. *Werke*. 39 vols. Berlin: Dietz, 1956–68.

————. *Writings on the Paris Commune*. Edited by Hal Draper. New York: Monthly Review, 1971.

Marx, Karl; Engels, Friedrich; and Lenin, V. I. *Anarchism and Anarcho-Syndicalism*. New York: International, 1972.

Other Primary Sources

Andréas, Bert. "Briefe und Dokumente der Familie Marx aus den Jahren 1862–1873." *Archiv für Sozialgeschichte* 2 (1962): 167–293.

Bartel, Horst."Der interne Juni-Entwurf zum Erfurter Programm." *International Review of Social History* 12 (1967): 299–302.

Bebel, August. *Briefwechsel mit Friedrich Engels*. Edited by Werner Blumenberg. The Hague: Mouton, 1965.

Del Bo, Giuseppe, ed. *La corrispondenza di Marx e Engels con italiani, 1848–1895*. Milan: Feltrinelli, 1964.

Engels, Friedrich; Lafargue, Paul; and Lafargue, Laura. *Correspondence*. 3 vols. Translated by Yvonne Kapp. Moscow: Foreign Languages, 1959.

Enzensberger, Hans Magnus, ed. *Gespräche mit Marx und Engels*. 2 vols. Frankfurt a/M: Insel, 1973.

Freymond, Jacques, ed. *La Première Internationale: Recueil de documents*. 2 vols. Geneva: Droz, 1962.

Gerth, Hans, ed. *The First International: Minutes of the Hague Congress*. . . . Madison: Wisconsin, 1958.

Guillaume, James. *L'Internationale: Documents et souvenirs*. 4 vols. 1905. Reprint. New York: Franklin, 1969.

Hegel, Georg Wilhelm Friedrich. *Hegel's Philosophy of Right*. Translated and edited by T. M. Knox. Oxford: Clarendon, 1962.

Hirsch, Helmut, ed. *Eduard Bernsteins Briefwechsel mit Friedrich Engels*. Assen: Van Gorcum, 1970.

Hyndman, H. M. *Record of an Adventurous Life*. London: Macmillan, 1911.

Institute of Marxism-Leninism (Moscow). *Documents of the First International: The General Council . . . Minutes*. 5 vols. Moscow: Progress, 1964. Cited as *General Council Minutes* with appropriate date.

Institut für Marxismus-Leninismus (Berlin). *Der Bund der Kommunisten: Dokumente und Materialen*. Vol. 1: *1836–1849*. Berlin: Dietz, 1970.

Kautsky, Benedikt, ed. *Friedrich Engels' Briefwechsel mit Karl Kautsky*. Vienna: Danubia, 1955.

Liebknecht, Wilhelm. *Briefwechsel mit Karl Marx und Friedrich Engels*. Edited by Georg Eckert. The Hague: Mouton, 1963.

Lissagardy, Prosper Olivier. *History of the Commune of 1871*. Translated by Eleanor Marx Aveling. New York: Monthly Review, 1967.

Morgan, Lewis Henry. *Ancient Society*. 1877. Reprint. New York: World, 1963.

Rocher, Jules, ed. *Lettres de communards . . . à Marx, Engels et autres*. Paris: Bureau d'Editions, 1934.

Steinberg, Hans Josef. "Revolution und Legalität: Ein unveröffentlicher Brief Friedrich Engels an Richard Fischer." *International Review of Social History* 12 (1964): 177–89.

Secondary Literature

For the sake of handy reference, the following list is arranged in simple alphabetical order. Readers interested in a particular *topic* may consult the notes to the foregoing text at the point where the topic is first seriously introduced. There I have tried to comment on, or at least list, the more significant literature on each particular topic dealt with in the work.

Adamiak, Richard. "The Withering Away of the State: A Reconsideration." *Journal of Politics* 32 (1970): 3–18.

Adler, Max. *Die Staatsauffassung des Marxismus*. Vienna: Volksbuchhandlung, 1922.

Adler, Mortimer J. *The Idea of Freedom*. Garden City, N.Y.: Doubleday, 1958.

Althusser, Louis. *For Marx*. Translated by Ben Brewster. New York: Pantheon, 1969.

Ansart, Pierre. *Marx et l'anarchisme*. Paris: Presses Universitaires, 1969.

Aptheker, Herbert, ed. *Marxism and Democracy: A Symposium*. New York: Humanities, 1965.

Ash, William F. *Marxism and Moral Concepts*. New York: Monthly Review, 1964.

Avineri, Shlomo. "Marx and Modernization." *Review of Politics* 31 (1969): 172–88.

———. *The Social and Political Thought of Karl Marx*. Cambridge: Cambridge, 1968.

Avineri, Shlomo, ed. *Marx's Socialism*. New York: Lieber-Atherton, 1973.

Axelos, Kostas. *Alienation, Praxis, and Technē in the Thought of Karl Marx*. Translated by Ronald Bruzina. Austin: Texas, 1976.

Berger, Martin. *Engels, Armies, and Revolution: The Revolutionary Tactics of Classical Marxism*. Hamden: Archon, 1977.

Berlin, Isaiah. *Karl Marx: His Life and Environment*. 3rd ed. New York: Oxford, 1963.

Bernstein, Eduard. *Der Sozialismus einst und jetzt*. Stuttgart: Dietz, 1922.

Bernstein, Samuel. *The First International in America*. New York: Kelley, 1962.

———. *The Beginnings of Marxian Socialism in France*. Revised edition. New York: Russell and Russell, 1965.

Bloom, Solomon F. "The Withering Away of the State." *Journal of the History of Ideas* 7 (1946): 113–21.

———. *The World of Nations: A Study of the National Implications in the Work of Karl Marx*. 1941. Reprint. New York: AIMS, 1967.

Blumenberg, Werner. *Portrait of Marx: An Illustrated Biography*. Translated by Douglas Scott. New York: Herder and Herder, 1972.

Bottomore, T. B. "Socialism and the Division of Labor." In *The Concept of Socialism*, edited by Bhiku C. Parekh, pp. 154–66. New York: Holmes and Meier, 1975.

Bottomore, T. B., ed. *Karl Marx*. New York: Prentice-Hall, 1973.

Braunthal, Julius. *History of the International*. 2 vols. New York: Praeger, 1967.

Brogan, Denis W. *The French Nation from Napoleon to Pétain, 1814–1940*. New York: Harper, 1963.

Bruford, W. H. *The German Tradition of Self-Cultivation: Bildung from Humboldt to Thomas Mann*. New York: Cambridge, 1975.

Bruhat, Jean. "La révolution française et la formation de la pensée de Marx." In *La pensée socialiste devant la Révolution française*, edited by the Société des Etudes Robespierristes, pp. 125–70. Paris: Clavreuil, 1966.

Bukharin, Nikolai, and Preobrazhensky, E. *The ABC of Communism*. 1922. Reprint. Ann Arbor: Michigan, 1966.

Bünger, Siegfried. *Friedrich Engels und die britische sozialistische Bewegung, 1881–1895*. Berlin: Rütten & Loening, 1962.

Carneiro, Robert L. *A Theory of the Origin of the State*. Menlo Park, Cal.: Institute for Humane Studies, 1970.

Carr, E. H. *Michael Bakunin*. 1937. Reprint. New York: Vintage, 1961. Centre d'Etudes et de Recherches Marxistes (Paris). *Sur la "mode de production asiatique."* Paris: Editions Sociales, 1969.

Chang, Sherman. *The Marxian Theory of the State*. Philadelphia: Spencer, 1931.

Cohen, G. A. *Karl Marx's Theory of History: A Defence*. Princeton: Princeton, 1978.

Cohen, Marshall. *Marx, Justice and History*. Princeton: Princeton, 1980.

Cole, G. D. H. *A History of Socialist Thought*. 5 vols. in 7. New York: St. Martin's, 1953–60.

Collins, Henry, and Abramsky, Chimen. *Karl Marx and the British Labour Movement*. London: Macmillan, 1965.

Cummins, I. *Marx, Engels and National Movements*. New York: St. Martin's, 1980.

Curtis, Michael, ed. *Marxism*. New York: Atherton, 1970.

Dahl, Robert A. *After the Revolution: Authority in a Good Society*. New Haven: Yale, 1970.
———. "Marxism and Free Parties." *Journal of Politics* 10 (1948): 787–813.
Dahrendorf, Ralf. *Die Idee des Gerechten im Denken von Karl Marx*. Hannover: Verlag für Literatur und Zeitgeschichte, 1971.
Davis, Horace B. *Nationalism and Socialism: Marxist and Labor Theories of Nationalism to 1917*. New York: Monthly Review, 1967.
Del Bo, Giuseppe, ed. *La Commune di Parigi*. Milan: Feltrinelli, 1957.
Diamond, Stanley, ed. *Toward a Marxist Anthropology: Problems and Perspectives*. The Hague: Mouton, 1979.
Drachkovitch, Milorad M., ed. *The Revolutionary Internationals, 1864–1943*. Stanford: Stanford, 1966.
Draper, Hal. "The Principle of Self-Emancipation in Marx and Engels." In *The Socialist Register 1971*, edited by Ralph Miliband and John Saville, pp. 81–109. London: Merlin, 1971.
———. "The Death of the State in Marx and Engels." In *The Socialist Register 1970*, edited by Ralph Miliband and John Saville, pp. 281–307. New York: Monthly Review, 1970.
———. "Marx and Engels on Women's Liberation." In *Female Liberation, History, and Current Politics*, edited by Roberta Salper, pp, 83–107. New York: Knopf, 1972.
———. *Karl Marx's Theory of Revolution*. 2 vols. to date. New York: Monthly Review, 1977–.
———. *The Two Souls of Socialism*. New York: Independent Socialist Clubs, 1966.
Dunayevskaya, Raya. *Marxism and Freedom . . . from 1776 until Today*. New York: Bookman, 1958.
Easton, Loyd D. "Marx and Individual Freedom." *The Philosophical Forum* 12 (1981): 193–213.
Edwards, Stewart. *The Paris Commune 1871*. London: Eyre & Spottiswoode, 1971.
Edwards, Stewart, ed. *The Communards of Paris, 1871*. Ithaca, N.Y.: Cornell, 1973.
Ehrenberg, Victor. *The Greek State*. 2nd ed. London: Methuen, 1969.
Evans, Michael. *Karl Marx*. Bloomington: Indiana, 1975.
Fetscher, Iring. *Marx and Marxism*. Translated by John Hargraves. New York: Herder and Herder, 1971.
———. "Freedom." In *Marxism, Communism and Western Society: A Comparative Encyclopedia*. 9 vols. New York: Herder and Herder, 1976.
———. *Die Freiheit im Lichte des Marxismus-Leninismus*. 3rd ed. Bonn: Bouvier, 1962.
———. "Marx, Engels and Future Society." *Survey* 38 (1961): 103–10.
———. "Marx's Concretization of the Concept of Freedom." In *Socialist Humanism*, edited by Erich Fromm, pp. 260–71. Garden City, N.Y.: Doubleday, 1965.
Freymond, Jacques, ed. *Etudes et documents sur la Première Internationale en Suisse*. Geneva: Droz, 1964.
Freymond, Jacques, and Molnár, Miklós. "The Rise and Fall of the First International." In *The Revolutionary Internationals, 1864–1943*, ed. Milorad M. Drachkovitch, pp. 3–35. Stanford: Stanford, 1966.
———. *Marx's Concept of Man*. New York: Ungar, 1961.
Gandy, D. Ross. *Marx and History: From Primitive Society to the Communist Future*. Austin: Texas, 1979.
Garaudy, Roger, *Karl Marx: The Evolution of His Thought*. New York: International, 1967.
Gould, Carol C. *Marx's Social Ontology: Individuality and Community in Marx's Theory of Social Reality*. Cambridge: MIT, 1978.

Haimson, Leopold H. *The Russian Marxists and the Origins of Bolshevism*. New York: Collier, 1965.

Harrington, Michael. *Socialism*. New York: Saturday Review, 1972.

Harris, Abram L. "Utopian Elements in Marx's Thought." *Ethics* 60 (1950): 79–99.

Henderson, W. O. *The Life of Frederick Engels*. 2 vols. London: Cass, 1976.

Herrmann, Ursula. *Der Kampf von Karl Marx um eine revolutionäre Gewerkschaftspolitik in der I. Internationale 1864 bis 1868*. Berlin: Tribüne, 1968.

Höhn, Reinhard. *Die Armee als Erziehungsschule der Nation*. Bad Harzburg: Verlag für Wissenschaft und Technik, 1953.

Hook, Sidney. *Marx and the Marxists: The Ambiguous Legacy*. Princeton: Van Nostrand, 1955.

———. "The Enlightenment and Marxism." *Journal of the History of Ideas* 29 (1968): 93–108.

Hostetter, Richard. *The Italian Socialist Movement*. Vol. 1, *Origins, 1850–1882*. Princeton: Van Nostrand, 1958.

Hunt, Richard N. *German Social Democracy, 1918–1933*. New Haven: Yale, 1964.

Institute of Marxism-Leninism (Berlin). *Ex Libris Karl Marx und Friedrich Engels: Schicksal und Verzeichnis einer Bibliothek*. Edited by Bruno Kaiser. Berlin: Dietz, 1967.

Jellinek, Frank. *The Paris Commune of 1871*. 1937. Reprint. New York: Grosset & Dunlop, 1965.

Johnstone, Monty. "The Commune and Marx's Conception of the Dictatorship of the Proletariat and the Role of the Party." In *Images of the Commune/Images de la commune*, edited by James A. Leith, pp. 201–24. Montreal: McGill-Queens, 1978.

Kamenka, Eugene. *The Ethical Foundations of Marxism*. New York: Praeger, 1962.

———. *Marxism and Ethics*. New York: St. Martin's, 1969.

Kamenka, Eugene, ed. *Paradigm for Revolution?: The Paris Commune, 1871–1971*. Canberra: Australian National University, 1972.

Karl Marx: Begründer der Staats-/und Rechtstheorie der Arbeiterklasse. Berlin: Staatsverlag, 1968.

Karl Marx: Chronik seines Lebens in Einzeldaten. Edited by Marx-Engels-Lenin Institute. Moscow: Marx-Engels, 1934.

Kautsky, Karl. *The Dictatorship of the Proletariat*. Translated by H. J. Stenning. 1919. Reprint. Ann Arbor: Michigan, 1964.

———. *Terrorism and Communism*. London: National Labour, 1920.

Kelsen, Hans. *Sozialismus und Staat: Eine Untersuchung der politischen Theorie des Marxismus*. 1920. Reprint. Vienna: Volksbuchhandlung, 1965.

Kolakowski, Leszek. *Toward a Marxist Humanism*. New York: Grove, 1968.

Krader, Lawrence. *The Asiatic Mode of Production: Sources, Development and Critique in the Writings of Karl Marx*. Assen: Van Gorcum, 1971.

———. *Formation of the State*. Englewood Cliffs: Prentice-Hall, 1968.

———. "The Works of Marx and Engels in Ethnology Compared." *International Review of Social History* 18 (1973): 223–75.

Kramer, Dieter. *Reform und Revolution bei Marx und Engels*. Cologne: Pahl-Rugenstein, 1871.

Krause, Helmut. *Marx und Engels und das zeitgenössische Russland*. Giesen: W. Schmitz, 1958.

Landauer, Carl. *European Socialism*. 2 vols. Berkeley: California, 1959.

Larsson, Reidar. *Theories of Revolution: From Marx to the First Russian Revolution*. Stockholm: Almqvist & Wiksell, 1970.

Lehnert, Detlef. *Reform und Revolution in den Strategiediskussionen der klassischen Sozialdemokratie.* Bonn: Verlag Neue Gesellschaft, 1977.

Leith, James A., ed. *Images of the Commune/Images de la commune.* Montreal: McGill-Queens, 1978.

Lenin, V. I. *Selected Works.* 3 vols. Moscow: Progress, 1975.

Leonhard, Wolfgang. *Three Faces of Marxism.* Translated by Ewald Osers. New York: Holt, Rinehart, and Winston, 1970.

Levine, Norman. *The Tragic Deception: Marx Contra Engels.* Santa Barbara: Clio, 1975.

Lewis, John. *The Marxism of Marx.* London: Lawrence & Wishart, 1972.

Lichtheim, George. *The Concept of Ideology and Other Essays.* New York: Vintage, 1967.

_____. *Marxism: An Historical and Critical Study.* New York: Praeger, 1961.

_____. *A Short History of Socialism.* New York: Praeger, 1970.

Lidtke, Vernon L. *The Outlawed Party: Social Democracy in Germany, 1878–1890.* Princeton: Princeton, 1966.

Lobkowicz, Nicholas. "Marx's Attitude Toward Religion." In *Marx and the Western World*, edited by idem, pp. 303–35. Notre Dame: Notre Dame, 1967.

Lowie, Robert H. *The History of Ethnological Theory.* New York: Farrar and Rinehart, 1939.

_____. *The Origin of the State.* New York: Harcourt, 1929.

Lucas, Erhard. "Marx' Studien zur Frühgeschichte und Ethnologie, 1880–1882, Nach unveröffentlichten Exzerpten." *Saeculum* 15 (1964): 327–43.

Lucas, J. R. *Democracy and Participation.* Harmondsworth: Penguin, 1976.

Luxemburg, Rosa. *Rosa Luxemburg Speaks.* Edited by Mary-Alice Waters. New York: Pathfinder, 1970.

McClellan, Woodford. *Revolutionary Exiles: The Russians and the First International and the Paris Commune.* London: Cass, 1979.

McLellan, David. *Karl Marx: His Life and Thought.* New York: Harper and Row, 1973.

_____. "Marx's View of the Unalienated Society." *Review of Politics* 31 (1969): 459–65.

McMurtry, John, *The Structure of Marx's World-View.* Princeton: Princeton, 1977.

Maguire, John M. *Marx's Paris Writings: An Analysis.* Dublin: Gill and Macmillan, 1972.

_____. *Marx's Theory of Politics.* Cambridge: Cambridge, 1978.

Malia, Martin. *Alexander Herzen and the Birth of Russian Socialism.* New York: Grosset & Dunlop, 1965.

Márkus, György. *Marxism and Anthropology: The Concept of "Human Essence" in the Philosophy of Marx.* Assen: Van Gorcum, 1978.

Mason, Edward S. *The Paris Commune.* New York: Macmillan, 1930.

Mason, T. W. "The Primacy of Politics: Politics and Economics in National Socialist Germany." In *Nazism and the Third Reich*, ed. Henry A. Turner, Jr., pp. 175–200. New York: Quadrangle, 1972.

Masters, Anthony. *Bakunin: The Father of Anarchism.* London: Sidgwick & Jackson, 1974.

Mayer, Gustav. *Bismarck und Lassalle: Ihr Briefwechsel und ihre Bespräche.* Berlin: Dietz, 1928.

_____. *Friedrich Engels: Eine Biographie.* 2 vols. The Hague: Nijhoff, 1934.

Mayo, Henry B. *Democracy and Marxism.* New York: Oxford, 1955.

Mehring, Franz. *Karl Marx: The Story of His Life.* Translated by Edward Fitzgerald. 1935. Reprint. Ann Arbor: Michigan, 1962.

Merkel, Renate. *Marx und Engels über Sozialismus und Kommunismus.* Berlin: Dietz, 1974.

Meyer, Alfred G. *Marxism: The Unity of Theory and Practice.* 2nd ed. Cambridge: Harvard, 1970.

Michels, Robert. *Political Parties: A Sociological Study of the Oligarchical Tendencies of Modern Democracy.* New York: Collier, 1962.

Miliband, Ralph. *Marxism and Politics.* Oxford: Oxford, 1977.

———. "Marx and the State." In *The Socialist Register 1965,* edited by Ralph Miliband and John Saville, pp. 278–96. New York: Monthly Review, 1965.

Miller, Suzanne. *Das Problem der Freiheit im Sozialismus.* Frankfurt a/M: Europäischer Verlagsanstalt, 1964.

Molnár, Erik. *La politique d'alliances du marxisme (1848–1889).* Budapest: Akadémiai Kiadó, 1967.

Molnár, Miklós. *Le déclin de la Première Internationale: La Conférence de Londres de 1871.* Geneva: Droz, 1963.

———. *Karl Marx. Friedrich Engels et la politique internationale.* Paris: Gallimard, 1975.

Moore, Stanley W. *The Critique of Capitalist Democracy.* New York: Paine-Whitman, 1957.

———. *Three Tactics: The Background in Marx.* New York: Monthly Review, 1963.

Morgan, Roger. *The German Social Democrats and the First International, 1864–1872.* London: Cambridge, 1965.

Nettlau, Max. *La Première Internationale en Espagne, 1868–1888.* Dordrecht: Reidel, 1969.

Nicolaievsky, Boris, and Maenchen-Helfen, Otto. *Karl Marx: Man and Fighter.* Translated by Gwenda David and Eric Mosbacher. Philadelphia: Lippincott, 1936.

Ollman, Bertell. *Alienation: Marx's Conception of Man in Capitalist Society.* Cambridge: Cambridge, 1972.

O'Rourke, James. *The Problem of Freedom in Marxist Thought.* Dordrecht: Reidel, 1974.

Palmer, R. R. *The Age of the Democratic Revolution.* 2 vols. Princeton: Princeton, 1959–64.

Palmer, R. R., and Colton, Joel. *A History of the Modern World.* 5th ed. New York: Knopf, 1978.

Pateman, Carole. *Participation and Democratic Theory.* Cambridge: Cambridge, 1970.

Pérez Díaz, Víctor M. *State, Bureaucracy, and Civil Society: A Critical Discussion of the Political Theory of Karl Marx.* London: Macmillan, 1978.

Petrović, Gajo. *Marx in the Mid-Twentieth Century.* Garden City, N.Y.: Doubleday, 1967.

Pfahlberg, Bernhard, and Brunner, Georg. "Fundamental Rights." In *Marxism, Communism and Western Society: A Comparative Encyclopedia.* 9 vols. New York: Herder and Herder, 1976.

Plamenatz, John. *German Marxism and Russian Communism.* London: Longmans, Green, 1954.

———. *Karl Marx's Philosophy of Man.* Oxford: Clarendon, 1975.

Popper, Karl P. *The Open Society and Its Enemies.* Princeton: Princeton, 1950.

Pranger, Robert J. "Marx and Political Theory." *Review of Politics* 30 (1968): 191–208.

Racowitza, Princess Helene von. *Autobiography.* Translated by Cecil Mar. New York: Macmillan, 1910.

Raddatz, Fritz J. *Karl Marx: A Political Biography.* Translated by Richard Barry. Boston: Little, Brown, 1978.

Radjavi, Kazem. *La dictature du prolétariat et le dépérissement de l'état de Marx à Lenine.* Paris: Editions Antropos, 1975.

Rosenberg, Arthur. *Democracy and Socialism.* Translated by George Rosen. London: Bell, 1939.

Rougerie, Jacques, *Paris libre 1871.* Paris: Seuil, 1971.

Rubel, Maximilien. "Le concept de démocratie chez Marx." *Le contrat social* 6 (1962): 214–20. Modified version in English in *New Politics* 1, no. 2 (Winter 1962): 78–90.

_____. *Karl Marx devant le bonapartisme*. Paris: Mouton, 1960.

_____. *Karl Marx: Essai de biographie intellectuelle*. Paris: Rivière, 1957.

_____. *Marx – Chronik: Daten zu Leben und Werk*. Munich: Hanser, 1968.

_____. *Marx Critique du Marxisme*. Paris: Payot, 1974.

Rubel, Maximilien, and Monale, Margret. *Marx Without Myth: Chronology of His Life and Times*. Oxford: Blackwell, 1975.

Sanderson, John. *An Interpretation of the Political Ideas of Marx and Engels*. London: Longmans, 1969.

_____. "Marx and Engels on the State." *Western Political Quarterly* 16 (1963): 946–55.

Schaff, Adam. *Marxism and the Human Individual*. Translated by Olgierd Wojtasiewicz. New York: McGraw-Hill, 1970.

Schroeder, Wilhelm. *Geschichte der sozialdemokratischen Parteiorganisation in Deutschland*. Dresden: Kaden, 1912.

Seigel, Jerrold E. *Marx's Fate: The Shape of a Life*. Princeton: Princeton, 1978.

Seliger, Martin. *The Marxist Conception of Ideology: A Critical Essay*. New York: Cambridge, 1977.

Shaw, William H. *Marx's Theory of History*. Stanford: Stanford, 1978.

Skrzypczak, Henryk. *Marx Engels Revolution*. Berlin: Colloquium, 1968.

Sofri, Gianni. *Über asiatische Produktionsweise*. Frankfurt a/M: Europäischer Verlagsanstalt, 1972.

Sowell, Thomas. "Karl Marx and the Freedom of the Individual." *Ethics* 73 (1963): 119–25.

Steenson, Gary P. *"Not One Man! Not One Penny!": German Social Democracy, 1863–1914*. Pittsburgh: Pittsburgh, 1981.

Steinberg, Hans-Josef. *Sozialismus und deutsche Sozialdemokratie: Zur Ideologie der Partei vor dem I. Weltkrieg*. Hannover: Verlag für Literatur und Zeitgeschichte, 1967.

Stekloff, G. M. *History of the First International*. London: Lawrence, 1928.

Stoyanovitch, K. *Marxisme et droit*. Paris: Pichon, 1964.

Sweet, Paul R. *Wilhelm von Humboldt: A Biography*. Vol. 1. Columbus: Ohio State, 1977.

Tarschys, Daniel. *Beyond the State: The Future Polity of Classical and Soviet Marxism*. Udderalla: Läromedelsförlagen, 1972.

Terray, Emmanuel, *Marxism and "Primitive" Societies*. Translated by Mary Klopper. New York: Monthly Review, 1972.

Thomas, Paul. *Karl Marx and the Anarchists*. London: Routledge & Kegan Paul, 1980.

Tökei, Ferenc. *Sur la mode de production asiatique*. Budapest: Akadémiai Kiadó, 1966.

Tsuzuki, Chushichi. *H. M. Hyndman and British Socialism*. Oxford: Oxford, 1961.

Trotsky, Leon. *Terrorism and Communism*. 1920. Reprint. Ann Arbor: Michigan, 1961.

Tucker, Robert C. "Marx as a Political Theorist." In *Marx and the Western World*, ed. Nicholas Lobkowicz, pp. 103–31. Notre Dame: Notre Dame, 1967.

_____. *The Marxian Revolutionary Idea*. New York: Norton, 1969.

_____. *Philosophy and Myth in Karl Marx*. Cambridge: Cambridge, 1961.

Turetzki, W. A. *Die Entwicklung der Anschauungen von Marx und Engels über den Staat*. Berlin: Deutscher Zentralverlag, 1956.

Ulam, Adam B. *The Bolsheviks*. New York: Collier, 1965.

_____. *The Unfinished Revolution: An Essay on the Sources of Influence of Marxism and Communism*. New York: Random House, 1960.

Venturi, Franco. *Roots of Revolution*. Translated by Francis Haskell. New York: Grosset & Dunlop, 1960.

Wallimann, Isider. *Estrangement: Marx's Concept of Human Nature and the Division of Labor*. Westport: Greenwood, 1981.

Walton, Paul, and Hall, Stuart, eds. *Situating Marx: Evaluations and Departures.* London: Human Context Books, 1972.

Wesolowski, Wlodzimierz. "Marx's Theory of Class Domination: An Attempt at Systematization." In *Marx and the Western World,* edited by Nicholas Lobkowicz, pp. 53–97. Notre Dame: Notre Dame, 1967.

Wette, Wolfram. *Kriegstheorien deutscher Sozialisten.* Stuttgart: Kohl-Kammer, 1971.

Williams, Roger L. *The French Revolution of 1870–1871.* New York: Norton, 1969.

Winock, M., and Azéma, J. P. *Les communards.* Paris: Seuil, 1964.

Wittfogel, Karl A. *Oriental Despotism: A Comparative Study of Total Power.* New Haven: Yale, 1957.

———. "The Ruling Bureaucracy of Oriental Despotism: A Phenomenon That Paralyzed Marx." *Review of Politics* 15 (1953): 350–59.

Wolfe, Bertram D. *Marxism: One Hundred Years in the Life of a Doctrine.* New York: Dial, 1965.

Yarmolinsky, Avrahm. *Road to Revolution.* New York: Collier, 1962.

Index